RIDING THE IRON ROOSTER

By the same author

Fiction

Waldo
Fong and the Indians
Murder in Mount Holly
Girls at Play
Jungle Lovers
Sinning with Annie
Saint Jack
The Black House
The Family Arsenal
The Consul's File
Picture Palace
A Christmas Card
London Snow
World's End
The Mosquito Coast
The London Embassy
Doctor Slaughter

Criticism

V. S. Naipaul

Non-fiction

The Great Railway Bazaar
The Old Patagonian Express
The Kingdom By the Sea
Sailing Through China
Sunrise with Seamonsters
The Imperial Way

Drama

The White-Man's Burden

RIDING THE IRON ROOSTER

BY TRAIN THROUGH CHINA

by

PAUL THEROUX

Hamish Hamilton
London

HAMISH HAMILTON LTD

Published by the Penguin Group
27 Wrights Lane, London W8 5TZ, England
Viking Penguin Inc., 40 West 23rd Street, New York, New York 10010, USA
Penguin Books Australia Ltd, Ringwood, Victoria, Australia
Penguin Books Canada Ltd, 2801 John Street, Markham, Ontario, Canada L3R 1B4
Penguin Books (NZ) Ltd, 182–190 Wairau Road, Auckland 10, New Zealand

Penguin Books Ltd, Registered Offices: Harmondsworth, Middlesex, England

First published in Great Britain 1988 by Hamish Hamilton Ltd

1 3 5 7 9 10 8 6 4 2

British Library Cataloguing in Publication Data

Theroux, Paul, *1941–*
Riding the iron rooster.
1. China. Description & travel – Personal
observations 2. Tibet. Description &
travel – Personal observations
I. Title
915.1′0458

ISBN 0-241-12547-2

Filmset in Linotron Times by
Rowland Phototypesetting Ltd,
Bury St Edmunds, Suffolk
Printed in Great Britain by
Richard Clay Ltd, Bungay, Suffolk

To Anne

‘A peasant must stand a long time on a hillside with his mouth open before a roast duck flies in.’

– Chinese proverb

‘The movements which work revolutions in the world are born out of the dreams and visions in a peasant’s heart on a hillside.’

– James Joyce, *Ulysses*

Contents

Note

At the beginning of my time in China, $1 was worth about 3 *yuan*; this changed to about 4 *yuan* during my visit. Sterling equivalents given in the text are based on an approximate rate of $1.60 to £1.

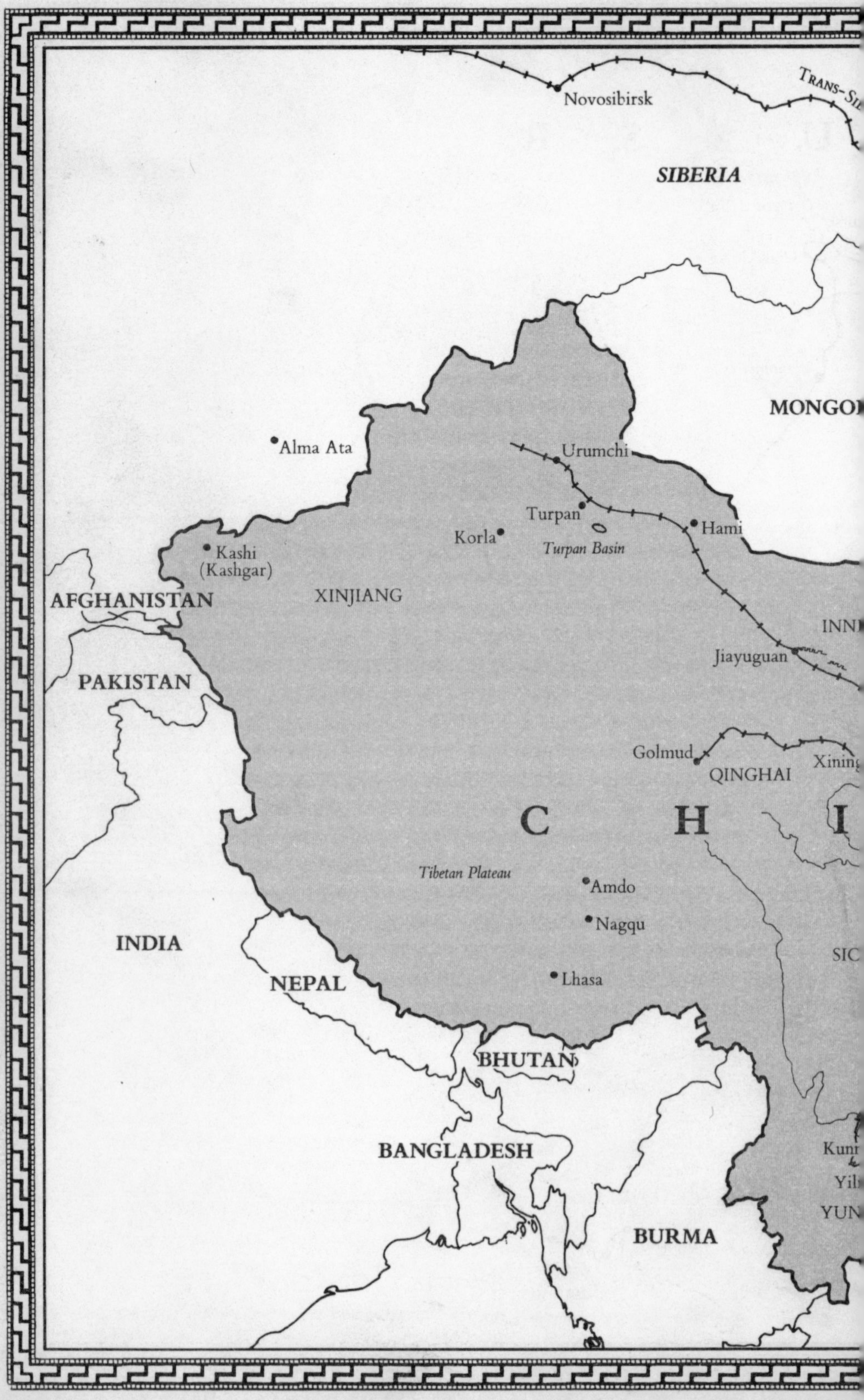

Novosibirsk
TRANS-SI
SIBERIA
MONGO
Alma Ata
Urumchi
Turpan
Hami
Korla
Turpan Basin
Kashi
(Kashgar)
XINJIANG
AFGHANISTAN
INN
Jiayuguan
PAKISTAN
Golmud
Xining
QINGHAI
C
H
I
Tibetan Plateau
Amdo
Nagqu
INDIA
SIC
Lhasa
NEPAL
BHUTAN
BANGLADESH
Kun
Yil
YUN
BURMA

U. S. S. R.
Ozero Baykal
Irkutsk
Ulan Ude
Ulaanbaatar
Heilong Jiang (Amur) River
Khabarovsk
Manzhouli
HEILONGJIANG
Langxiang
Harbin
MANCHURIA
JILIN
Changchun
Vladivostok
Erlian
Shenyang
Fushun
LIAONING
NORTH KOREA
GREAT WALL
Baotou
Hohhot
Darong
Peking
Qinhuangdao
Dalian
Tianjin
Bo Hai
SOUTH KOREA
Huang (Yellow) River
Tangyuan
Yantai
SHANXI
Jinan
Qingdao
JAPAN
SHANDONG
A
Zhengzhou
YELLOW SEA
Xian
SHAANXI
Nanjing
Changzhou
Hefei
Shanghai
EAST CHINA SEA
Wuhan
Hangzhou
Chang Jiang (Yangtze) River
Jinhua
ZHEJIANG
Shaoshan
Changsha
Zhuzhou
HUNAN
FUJIAN
Taipei
Guilin
Xiamen
Quemoy
GUANGXI
GUANGDONG
TAIWAN
Guangzhou (Canton)
HONG KONG
SOUTH CHINA SEA

1

The Train to Mongolia

The bigness of China makes you wonder. It is more like a whole world than a mere country. 'All beneath the sky' (*Tianxia*) was one Chinese expression for their empire, and another was 'All between the four seas' (*Sihai*). These days people go there to shop, or because they have a free week and the price of a plane ticket. I decided to go because I had a free year. And the Chinese proverb *We can always fool a foreigner* I took to be a personal challenge. To get to China without leaving the ground was my first objective. And then I wanted to stay for a while – in China, on the ground, going all over the place.

The railway was the answer. It was the best way of travelling to Peking from London, where I happened to be. Every modern account of Chinese travel I had read seemed weakened by jet lag – an unhappy combination of fatigue and insomnia. 'We were very tired there' is a common remark by travellers to China, the gasping sightseers and bargain-hunters. This desire to sit down could be maddening in a country where everyone else was full of beans. Wasn't that the whole point of the Chinese – that they were always on the go? Even after 5,000 years of continuous civilization they were still at it. And one of the lessons of Chinese history is that they never know when to stop.

I had seen China in the winter of 1980. It looked bleak and exhausted, all baggy blue suits and unconvincing slogans on red banners. If you said, 'Surely these people ought to be wearing something more than cloth slippers in this snow and ice,' you were told how lucky they were and that they used to go barefoot. The whole country was dark brown from the soot and dust. There were few trees. I went bird-watching but saw only crows and sparrows and the sort of grubby pigeons that look like flying rats. The rarer birds the Chinese stuffed into their mouths.

The Chinese, then, would point through the drizzle, where a factory was coughing up smoke at the end of a muddy lane; where bent-over people were dragging wooden carts loaded with pig-iron. And they would say, 'This was once all prostitutes and bad elements and gambling and bright lights and dance-halls.' You were supposed to be glad this sinful frivolity was gone, and fascinated by the factories; but I just sighed. I saw young women destroying themselves in mills, smashing their pretty fingers on wooden looms, or blinding themselves doing finicky 'forbidden stitch' embroidery. People whispered when they mentioned Mao's name. Stricken and overworked, they said, 'Owing to the success of the Great Proletarian Cultural Revolution –' And they served me bowel-shattering meals.

Americans came back from China saying, 'Acupuncture! No flies! No tipping! They give you your used razor blades back! They work like dogs! They eat cats! They're so frisky!' And Americans even praised Chairman Mao, unaware that many Chinese were privately sick of him.

But that was the past, my brother Gene said, and he told me that I was a fool not to go now. China had become a different place, and it was changing from day to day. He knew what he was talking about: he had travelled to China 109 times since 1972, as a lawyer – one of the new *taipans*. I planned to go in the spring this time. The word was that it was a new season in every other sense, too. I kept telling myself: New people, new scenes – fresh air, and the pleasure of anonymity. There were two ways of doing it: the way of the English poet, Philip Larkin, who said, 'I wouldn't mind seeing China if I could come back the same day'; and total immersion.

My idea was to take a train in London, go to Paris, keep going, head for Germany and Poland, maybe stop in Moscow, take the Trans-Siberian, get off in Irkutsk, take the Trans-Mongolian, and spend May Day in Ulaanbaatar. Essentially the way to China was the train to Mongolia. It was travelling slowly across Asia's wide forehead and then down into one of its eyes, Peking.

Going to Mongolia that way ought to be relaxing, I thought. And ought to give me a feeling of accomplishment. I would read a little and make notes and eat regular meals and look out of the window. I pictured myself in a sleeping-compartment reading *Elmer Gantry* and hearing the hoot of the train whistle echoing on the steppes and thinking: Pretty soon I'll be there – as I drew the blanket up to my chin. And then one day I would snap up the blind and see a yak standing in an immensity of brown sand and I would know it was the Gobi Desert. A day or so later, the landscape would be green and people would be standing knee-deep in rice fields, wearing lampshade hats, all of that, and I would step off the train into China.

It was not that simple. It never is, and so an explanation is necessary – this book. It was my good fortune to be wrong; being mistaken is the essence of the traveller's tale. What I had thought of as the simplest form of getting there – eight trains from London to the Chinese border – turned out to be odd and unexpected. Sometimes it seemed like real travel, full of those peculiar discoveries and satisfactions. But more often it was as if I had lost my footing in London and had fallen down a long flight of stairs, perhaps one of those endless staircases designed by a surrealist painter, and down I went, bump-bump-bump, and across the landing, and down again, bump-bump-bump, until I had fallen half-way around the world.

I was not alone – perhaps that was why. I joined a tour in London – twenty-odd people, old and young. I thought: I'll be invisible, just slip into this crowd of people – and off we'd go, smiling and chatting quietly as the sleet hit the windows. I had not had much experience of tours. I did not know the most elementary things –

that the English go on tours to save money, and elderly couples like the Cathcarts would say, 'We had ever such a nice time going overland to India last year, and in Eye-ran we'd make cups of tea in the back of the bus.' I did not know that English youths went to places like the Bratsk Hydroelectric Dam on package tours in order to get drunk on cheap vodka, and that eastern Europe was uproarious with nurses from Birmingham.

Americans took these tours to meet other people, and showed me snapshots from other trips.

'The ones in the straw hat are the Watermules, from San Diego. Lovely couple. We still get Christmas cards from them. That was the Galapagos trip. They're grandparents now. That's their son, Ricky. He's very big in semiconductors.'

Americans also went on these tours to shop. Shopping seemed to be the whole point of their travel. I honestly had not known that. It seemed as good a reason as anything else, and much better than going to Russia to get drunk. And there were Australians, but wherever you see Australians in the world they always seem to be on their way home.

The other thing about tours I had not known was their utter lack of privacy. It was all swapping names and information, almost from the first moment, and if you forgot their names they reminded you. It was mostly couples – the Cathcarts, the Scoonses, Cyril and Bug Winkle, the Westbetters, the Wittricks, the Gurneys; and the single people, who all seemed a little sad and uncertain and too eager, Wilma Perrick, Morris Least and his friend Kicker, an old Californian who called himself Blind Bob, a smiling cockney called Ashley Relph and a man known only as Morthole. There was Miss Wilkie, who stood no nonsense; she was from Morningside in Edinburgh. There was the leader, Mr Knowles. He was Chris. I was Paul. They preferred first names, and never asked me my surname.

In London Ashley Relph said he was dead keen to get to Hong Kong, and blinked, and whispered, 'I hear you can get a life-sized latex model of your dick somewhere in Hong Kong. One of these Chinese places. Costs about a fiver.'

Morris Least was from Arizona, travelling with his old army buddy, a loud-voiced man who urged us to call him Kicker. Kicker had been in the war. He had a metal plate in his skull. Morris and Kicker had matching jackets and shoes. They wore the same sort of crushproof hat. The two American veterans were in their late sixties, and although they were bad-tempered, they agreed on everything. It seemed to me that these two men had entered into a profound sort of marriage.

Kicker said, 'I've never been to Europe before. Amazing, huh? Like I was in the Marines for twenty-two years and never saw Europe. I was in China, though. Back in forty-six. Chingdow.'

He had crooked teeth – a cruel smile. I asked him what he wanted to do most in Europe.

'See the *Mona Lisa*,' he said. 'And try the beer.'

'I hear China's clean as a whistle,' Rick Westbetter said.

Miss Wilkie said, 'I've heard it's filthy.'

Hoping to please her, Rick said, 'But London's clean!'

'London's a shambles,' Miss Wilkie said, and reminded him that she came from Edinburgh.

'London looks clean to us,' Rick said, taking his wife's hand. Her name was Millie. She was sixty-three and wore track shoes. They were one of those oldish hand-holding couples who leave you never quite sure whether they're being happy or defiant.

'Of course it looks clean to you,' Miss Wilkie said. 'Americans have lower standards than we do.'

Bella Scoons said in her west Australian whine, 'How far are you going, Miss Wilkie?'

'Hong Kong,' the old lady said.

Then everyone thought: Ten thousand miles and six weeks of this. Good lord.

At least I did.

The Scoonses were from Perth – the other side of Australia. Bella always measured distances by comparing them to the trip to Kalgoorlie. The distance from London to Paris was to Kalgoorlie and back. The trip to Berlin was 'To Kalgoorlie, and back, and back again to Kalgoorlie.' Moscow was seven trips to Kalgoorlie. And once I heard her mumbling, working out the distance to Irkutsk, in Siberia, and I heard her finish, 'And back to Kalgoorlie.'

Riding the Iron Rooster

When we set off from Victoria Station that rainy Saturday in April, Bella said to her husband Jack, 'It's less than to Kalgoorlie.' She was referring to the distance to Folkestone.

We had eaten breakfast at the Grosvenor Hotel. The Americans sat together, and the Australians were at another table; the British were at two tables, and three old men were silently eating alone. At a solitary table there was a couple in hiking gear – knapsacks and sling bags and cameras. I was eating my breakfast thinking: Is this a mistake? One of the old men was staring at me. It made me very uneasy, the way he was gaping, but then I noticed that his glasses were very thick, and that perhaps he was not staring at me, but only looking out of his glasses the way people look out of windows on rainy days.

When we got on the train I sat next to him. He said, 'This trip is kind of a big thing for me. My oculist told me I'm going blind and if there was anything I wanted to do before I went blind I should do it this year. So I'm going to China and, boy, am I going to keep my eyes open. I figure, hey, it's my last chance and, hey, I'm going to enjoy it.'

Then he told me his nickname was Blind Bob and that he was from Barstow in California. When I looked around this train I realized that I was one of a large group and that I did not know any of these people. All I had to go on were their faces. But faces say a great deal. Theirs certainly did. The sight made me very apprehensive.

They stared out of the train windows at the houses, and the houses returned the stares. One of the disconcerting aspects of a railway journey is that the houses near the line seem to have their backs turned to the traveller – you see rear entrances, and drains, and kitchens, and laundry. But these are more telling than porticoes and lawns. The depressing thing about the London suburbs is not that they look seedy, but rather that they also look eternal. It is a relief to look inside those houses and see lives being lived – the man redecorating the bathroom, the woman feeding the cat, the girl combing her hair upstairs, the boy fiddling with his radio, the old lady with her nose in the *Express*. It is wrong to pass by in a train and not wish them well. They are unaware that they are being scrutinized. It is one of the paradoxes of railway lines that the passengers can see the people in the houses, but those people cannot see anything of the train passengers.

We were ferried across the Channel. Morris and Kicker reminisced about D-Day and the Normandy landings and how the American troops got the worst of it.

The water was leaden-looking and it slopped against the ferry. The wind from the north-east was cold. It blew hard across the quay when we landed, and we shuffled through Customs to have our passports examined. Our luggage was searched.

At Boulogne, the people in the tour amused each other by calling out, 'All aboard! All aboard!' and I discovered myself next to an English woman who was fat and entirely bald and wore mittens and said she was planning to emigrate to New Zealand. Her name was Wilma Perrick and she was about thirty-two. She said she had just lost her job. She seemed very sad and I was on the point of sympathizing with her baldness when she leaned over and said, 'What are you writing?'

When the Paris train started, the man known as Morthole said, 'You were probably wondering what I was doing in the trainyard on those tracks.'

No one had been wondering. No one had seen him. Anyway, who was Morthole talking to?

'I was collecting rocks,' he said. 'I collect rocks from every country. Listen, in a lot of places it's illegal – the South Pole, for example. I've got some rocks from the South Pole. They could put me in gaol for that. I've got them from everywhere. Canada. Ohio. London. Each one is the size of a golf ball. I've got hundreds. I'm a kind of geologist, I guess.'

In *Elmer Gantry* I read:

> Set in between the larger boulders (of the fireplace) were pebbles, pink and brown and earth-colored, which the good bishop had picked up all over the world. This pebble, the bishop would chirp, guiding you about the room, was from the shore of the Jordan; this was a fragment of the Great Wall of China . . .

The east wind that had blown coldly across the Channel that morning had brought a dusting of snow to Picardy. Snow in April!

It lay in a thin covering on hillsides, like long torn bedsheets, the earth showing through in black streaks. It made the ordinary-looking landscape seem dramatic, the way New Jersey looks in bad weather, made houses and fences emphatic, and brought a sort of cubism to villages that would otherwise have been unmemorable. Each place became a little frozen portrait in black and white.

It seemed to me that railway lines like this needed a little variation. It was almost as if these hills and villages had been seen by so many people passing by that they had been worn away from being looked at. One of the attractions of China to me was that it had been closed to outsiders for such a long time that even the most hackneyed sight of a pagoda would seem fresh, and in distant Xinjiang a traveller might feel like Marco Polo, because no foreigner had been there for years. But this part of heavily travelled France had been rubbed away by the eyes of sightseers and railway passengers: most landscapes near busy railway lines had that same look of simplification, as if in a matter of time they would disappear from being looked at so much.

The people on the tour were still getting acquainted with each other. They asked me questions, too. Where was I from? What did I do? Was I married? Did I have children? Why was I taking this trip? What was that book in my lap? What were my plans in Paris? First time in China?

I was Paul, I was unemployed, I was evasive, and – how does Baudelaire put it? – 'The real travellers are those who leave for the sake of leaving' and something about not knowing why but always saying *Allons!* An appropriate sentiment here in the environs of Amiens.

What I wanted to reply to these questions was something I heard a man say to an inquisitive woman at a dinner party in London.

'Please don't ask,' he said softly. 'I don't have anything interesting to tell you. I've made a terrible mess of my life.'

What kept me from saying that was that it was a sad memory, because about six months later that man killed himself. It seemed unlucky, and unkind to his memory, to repeat it.

The sad man called Blind Bob fumbled with the flap of his valise – his eyesight was terrible, his nose was against the hasp – and brought out two rolls of toilet paper.

People asked him what it was for – surely not Europe?

'For China,' he said.

I decided not to say that Professor Needham had proved that the Chinese invented toilet paper. In the fourteenth century they were making perfumed toilet paper for the imperial family (it was three inches square), and everyone else used any paper they could lay their hands on. But some Chinese knew where to draw the line. In the sixth century a scholar, Yen Chih-T'ui, wrote:

> Paper on which there are quotations or commentaries from the *Five Classics* or the names of sages, I dare not use for toilet purposes.

Ashley Relph said, 'He's taking bog-roll to China!'

Mr Cathcart said, 'I think they've heard of loo paper in China.'

'Sure, they've heard of it. Lots of people have heard of it. But do they have any, is the question. I'll bet they don't have any on the Trans-Siberian, and how much do you think they'll have in Mongolia, huh?'

No one was laughing at Blind Bob now. The thought of crossing Asia without toilet paper made everyone thoughtful; there was a sort of hum of reflection in the carriage after he had spoken.

We came to Paris and were met by a bus and brought to a hotel. This was in the fourteenth *arrondissement* near the end of the Metro line, in a district that was indistinguishable from the outskirts of Chicago, or South Boston. It was mainly post-war blocks of flats that had once been light stucco and were now grey. There were too many of them, and they were too close together, and people said: 'Is this Paris? Is this France? Where's the Eiffel Tower?' The centre of Paris is a masterpiece of preservation, but the suburbs such as this one are simple and awful. The brutal pavements and high windows of Saint-Jacques seemed designed to encourage suicide.

Then I was told ('funnily enough') that Samuel Beckett lived in one of those blocks of flats and indeed had been in it for years. That was where he wrote his stories and plays about the sheer pointlessness and utter misery of human existence. I thought: *No wonder!* I was told that he often came over to our hotel, the Hotel Saint-

Jacques, to have a morning coffee. The hotel was a newish, spick and span place that resembled the lonely hotels that are found just outside American airports, where people stay because there is nowhere else. Beckett came here for pleasure? I walked the streets, I lurked in the coffee shop, I prayed for him to appear; but, nothing. It was a lesson, though. When people read 'Samuel Beckett lives in exile in Paris', they did not know that it meant a poky little flat on the fifth floor of number thirty-two – a tall grey building in which residents waited for Godot by watching television. And it was seventeen stops on the Metro from the centre of Paris, the Left Bank, the museums.

We went to the Jeu de Paume, the museum still then devoted to the Impressionists. I wandered behind the group, listening and looking at pictures.

In a room full of Sisleys, Richard Cathcart said, 'I don't like any of these.'

We passed Monet's series of Rouen Cathedral, bluish and purply and rose-tinted.

'Now I would not mind having something like them in my home,' Mrs Wittrick said, and the Gurneys agreed and said they'd like to cart them back to Tasmania, except that they'd probably be arrested!

Of Rousseau's *La Guerre: La Chevauchée de la Discorde*, Rick Westbetter said, 'Hey, I like these. These are good. These are more like American pictures.'

A child staggering behind his parents in the Van Gogh room said, 'But *why* was he mad?'

A little crowd formed around a Monet of Venice.

Bud Wittrick was saying, 'That's the Grand Canal. That's St Mark's. That's where the Bridge of Sighs is – down that canal. And see, that's the hotel we stayed at. Of course it wasn't a hotel in those days. That's where we walked, and there's where we had the spaghetti, that's where I bought the postcards.'

It rained, it snowed, and the snow silenced both pedestrians and traffic. Early one morning we left for Berlin.

It was a wet black morning in Paris, the street-sweepers and milkmen doing their solitary rounds by the light of street-lamps, and just as dawn broke over the eaves and chimney pots we plodded out of the Gare de l'Est. I thought we had left the suburbs behind in the rue Saint-Jacques, but there were more, and they were deeper and grimmer. The people in the group, with their faces at the windows of the train, were shocked and disillusioned. It wasn't gay Paree, it wasn't even Cleveland. The Americans looked very closely. We were unused to this. We put up suburbs too quickly and cheaply for them to wear well. We expected them to decline and collapse and be replaced; they weren't built to last, and they look temporary because they are temporary. But French suburbs – villas, terraced houses and blocks of flats – are solid and fairly ugly and their most horrific aspect is that they look as though they will last for ever. It had been the same in outer London: how could houses so old look so awful?

'That was a battlefield,' Morris said, as we crossed into Belgium. He had been telling war stories since we crossed the Channel. 'Some buddies of mine died there.'

He was smirking at the bare trees, the young poplars standing like switches and whips, the dark sludge and stained froth in the black canals.

I was still reading Sinclair Lewis and scribbling notes on the flyleaf.

'Making notes?' Mrs Wittrick asked.

I denied it.

'Keeping a diary?'

I said no.

I hated being observed. One of the pleasures of travel is being anonymous. I had not realized how everyone was conspicuous in a group, and the person who kept to himself was a threat. I decided to make notes on those big blank postcards that look like filing cards.

Wilma, the bald girl, said, 'I haven't seen anyone use those postcards for years.'

And then I regretted that I told her I was sending them back home, because it gave her the excuse to ask me where I was from.

'I do a little teaching,' I said to Wilma.

As far as I could tell there were no readers in the group, no one likely to buttonhole me after lunch about American fiction, or be threatened by my scrutiny. I liked being a teacher. I liked the way they looked at me and thought: Poor guy, doesn't seem to have a lot to say, might as well leave him alone.

It was extremely hard for me to appear to be a quiet, modest, incurious person. These people seemed to be illiterate, which was a virtue, because they didn't know me. But neither could they be trusted with the slightest piece of information. Not long after I told Wilma I happened to be living in London, Richard Cathcart came up to me and said, 'I hear you live in London –'

At Namur, Bud Wittrick confided to me that Belgium was a hell of a lot uglier than America, and when I agreed that it did look hideous, he said, 'You said it, Paul!'

When had I told him my name?

The only empty seat in the dining-car at lunch was next to Wilma. It seemed as though everyone was avoiding her, but when I sat with her everyone avoided me. She told me she had been fired from her job, selling toys somewhere in London. She complained that the New Zealanders had made a hoo-hah about her emigrating, but that she was going there just the same, probably for good. She said she liked a challenge.

I made a note of the fact that we had just stopped at Liège. I had an idea that I could look it up later and write:

> We passed Liège, famous for its lace-making and its sausages, birthplace of Georges Simenon . . .

Wilma said, 'You're always writing.'

'No, I'm not,' I said, too quickly, and I thought: Stop looking at me!

I dozed after lunch and was awakened by Morris saying, 'Hey, Kicker, it's Aachen!' And both men stood in the aisle, blocking the traffic.

It was obvious that the Germans on the train were very irritated by these two loud Americans, and would probably have been very glad to throw them off. It was unlikely that the Germans were able to follow the loud twanging monologue, in which Morris revealed that he had been in the three-week battle for Aachen, during the war. This monkey was a liberator! It seemed poetic justice that he had returned to bore the pants off everyone within earshot.

At Cologne I noticed that there were four new people on the tour. They were French – three women and a man. They stayed together. They spoke to no one except themselves for almost the whole trip. They quarrelled a great deal, but no one knew why. About one month later, in southern Mongolia, I saw one of these French women standing alone on a railway platform. We had just eaten a disgusting meal of cold potatoes and mutton fat.

I smiled and said in a companionable way, 'Isn't the food dreadful?'

'When I am travelling I don't notice the food,' this woman said. 'But of course when I am in Paris I am very particular about what I eat and demand only the best.'

That was all she ever said to me.

Even here in Germany I could tell that the French members of the tour were not extroverts. But that was fine. I was also keeping to myself and it was agreeable not to be pestered with questions.

It was near the end of a long day. We passed Wuppertal, piled against a hillside – full of steep ugly tenements. There were slag-heaps at Unna, and farther on, at Hamm and Gütersloh, it seemed as though the Germans had succeeded in miniaturizing Indiana and putting it down here. The rain blackened Bielefeld and I prayed for night to fall and simplify this landscape with darkness. Prosperity had disfigured Germany, and the whole country looked blighted with industrial civilization. Under the brown sky of Munsterland there were factories called Droop & Rein and Endler & Kumpf which seemed like doom-laden names. The peculiar dreariness about this part of Germany was the absence of trees. The Germans identified with forests, but acid rain had killed half of them and the other half they had chopped down; the trees had been replaced with factory chimneys.

Earlier in the day, the people in the group were talking like patients in a hospital. The travel had frightened and tired them. They dozed and when they woke asked each other questions. How did you sleep? How was the meal? What time is dinner? They began to describe the progress of their bowels. They reported on how they felt, and whether they were tired or hungry.

I watched closely for meaningful changes – women who begin to screech, men who stop shaving, or anyone who puts on a track suit.

At Helmstedt we crossed the border into East Germany. The train passed between the pair of barbed wire fences, a passageway about as wide as a turnpike. Every few hundred yards there was a watch-tower, and bright lights, and the silhouettes of soldiers standing sentry-duty.

Beyond the border it was a landscape of snow and mud – the spring mess in the slender trees of the post-war woods. What cities I could see seemed far drearier than any I had seen in West Germany, but the countryside was noticeably wilder and more wooded, with huddled farms and poorly lit roads. There were not many people visible, but when I saw one here he really did look like a peasant.

We arrived at Zoo Station ('Hold on to your handbags, this place is full of drug addicts') in the dark. In the twinkling lights and the traffic Berlin seemed romantic and lively to some members of the group – they regarded it as the last frontier of civilization. After this was Poland, then Russia, then Mongolia. Berlin was gaiety and sex, bookshops and fatsoes. It looked richer than America.

But Berlin seemed to me a monstrosity and not much fun. It is such an odd specimen, such a special example of metropolitan schizophrenia, that its conceits and hypocrisies are fascinating. But it is also a fool's paradise, and it is hard to think of anyone living there for any length of time and remaining sane. It is an ancient city, and it was itself for 700 years; but under the Nazis it cracked, it stopped being a city and became a symbol, and then an idea, and after the war it was rethought and the idea reduced to an absurdity. It is still a bad idea and it is growing worse. Any sensible person has to find it a monumental illustration of stupidity, petulance and stubbornness. It would be laughable if it were not so pathetic, for as Nathanael West said, nothing is sadder than the truly monstrous.

Helmut Frielinghaus, a Düsseldorfer, was himself a visitor to Berlin. He said to me, 'Do you want to see the most interesting place in Berlin?'

I said yes.

He took me to the Ke De We, a huge department store that is

known by its initials rather than its full name, Kaufhaus des Westens. What he wanted to show me were the floors devoted to food, and in particular the stalls and shops that retailed expensive and pretty delicacies.

'This is the new thing,' Helmut said. 'The food culture. People are obsessional about it. You see? Two hundred kinds of cheese, forty kinds of coffee, twenty-eight sizes of sausage, and also food for vegetarians, food for health cranks, a whole shop selling fish eggs.'

They were food boutiques, selling snobbish food, rare and indigestible items, all prettily arranged and beautifully wrapped. Pastries, fruit juice, ninety kinds of bread, a whole wall of tea caddies, every possible shape of pasta. At first glance it was not food at all, but specialist merchandise set out like expensive clothes. If there was such a thing as designer food, this was it. Perfect penile asparagus, each spear labelled, £12.50 a pound.

I developed a horror-interest in the meat section, where stall upon stall was laden with cuts of meat – gleaming red flesh that had been trimmed with great care: legs, shoulders, feet, rumps and elbows, a whole rack of tongues, a case of hearts, a brisket with a paper cap, pigs' heads wearing ruffled collars. Most of the meat was decorated in this way – a sort of dramatic presentation, so that the last thing you thought of was slaughter or butchery.

There were more browsers than shoppers, which was the weirdest thing of all – people gaping at food, and salivating, and moving on ('Look at those fish cheeks, Wolfgang!'), and the effect of this scrutiny and obvious hunger was of the food being used to tempt and titillate, and so it all seemed to me – and the meat especially – the most modern kind of pornography.

'Good, no?' Helmut said. 'If you see that, you understand Berlin.'

We were leaving the Ke De We when we saw a stop-press edition of a German paper saying that American planes had bombed Libya. This was in retaliation for the bombing supposedly by Libyan terrorists of a dance-hall here in Berlin. The news had travelled fast. Already, young Germans had started to gather near the Europa Centre for a demonstration, and police vans – about thirty of them – were parked just off the Kurfürstendamm. Policemen were unloading steel barricades and stacking them by the roadside.

Helmut said, 'We have only recently discovered how different we are from the Americans.'

He spoke with slight bitterness. I decided not to remind him of Germany's uniquely horrible history.

'I think we bombed Libya because we have been dying to bomb someone in the Middle East ever since the hostage crisis,' I said. 'The Iranians humiliated us more than any other country has done in recent years. We still haven't got over it. I don't think the average American makes much distinction between Iran and Libya. They're seen as dangerous and worthless fanatics, so why should we waste our time being subtle about them?'

'That's the way Americans think about us,' Helmut said.

'Not really.'

If he mentions the war, I thought, I'm going to say *You started it*. But he didn't. He said he found Berlin very strange and provincial; it was mostly old people and had high unemployment. He said he couldn't wait to go back to Düsseldorf.

I spent the rest of the day shopping for provisions. I bought mint tea, sherry, chocolates and antibiotics. Tomorrow we would be in Warsaw, where such things might not be available.

The demonstration began in the early evening when about 8,000 youths chanting anti-American slogans marched towards the American cultural centre called Amerikahaus, behind the Kurfürstendamm. The rumour was that they planned to set it on fire. But the police, with riot shields and tear-gas, massed in front of it and behind the high steel barricades. The demonstration became unruly, and turned into something approaching a riot. Rioters threw stones and broke the windows of American cars, and chased tourists and anyone who looked like an American.

I missed the riot. I was at the Deutsche Oper on Bismarckstrasse seeing *Don Giovanni*. I had gone on the spur of the moment when, back at the hotel, I heard the members of the group arguing about the bombing of Libya, and Kicker saying: 'Them fucken Arabs have been asking for that.' Do I want to listen to this? I asked myself. Mozart seemed preferable.

I went alone and found it pleasant to have an empty seat next to me, an entire arm-rest to lean on, and to enjoy this excellent production. But after the intermission the seat was taken by a young woman, and several times in the darkness, while Don Giovanni was gasconading or Donna Anna was singing, this woman was staring at my head.

'Do I know you?' she asked, when the opera ended.

I said no.

'I have this feeling I do. What is it?'

I sensed what it was, but I didn't say anything. Until then I had been proud of the fact that no one on the tour had the slightest idea that I was a writer – and of travel books about train trips, too. I thought it would inhibit them, or else, and just as bad, provoke them to importune me ('Boy, have I got a story for you'). Some of the members of the group I had told I was in publishing, and others I had told I was a teacher. I hardly ever entered a conversation. I listened, I smiled, I made notes. When Kicker was being outrageous I blinked and shuffled away. I was the man who got up from lunch before it was over and people started talking about themselves. I was the man who was constantly drifting away – the man with no last name. I was the man with the book that you didn't want to interrupt. I was the quiet, dim, dull fellow in the old mackintosh, standing and whistling tunelessly on the platform. I agreed with everything you said. You hardly knew me – in fact, it was only when you saw me on the train that you remembered I was on the trip, and even then I was unobtrusive and faintly barmy-looking, just harmlessly scribbling.

'I've seen you on television,' the woman said. 'Haven't I?'

'Probably,' I said, and told her my name.

'Amazing,' she said. 'My sister won't believe this – she's read all your books.'

Her name was Rachel Tickler, and I found it a relief to tell her I was on my way to Mongolia, and then China – yes, to do some writing – and that I had just come from London. What was that about the States? Oh, yes, I did spend part of the year on the Cape – yes, it's a wonderful place. A far cry from this trip, which was involving me in note-taking. I told her everything, I bought her some tea and we sat up late so that I could be confessional. There was no risk. Unlike the members of the tour, Rachel Tickler was a perfect stranger.

It did me a lot of good to tell her these things, because I had been so secretive on the tour it was like being invisible. It certainly wasn't much fun to be the dim, dull fellow in the mackintosh, keeping out of every conversation. Keeping quiet gave me chest pains. I longed to lecture them about the Middle East, and if they gave me half a chance on the subject of travel I could seize their wrists like the Ancient Mariner and a tale unfold.

Rachel herself was in Berlin working on lawsuits connected with asbestos hazards, one of the current growth areas in lawsuits. A lawyer from New York, she was attending a conference of insurance companies – reading papers and evaluating information.

Having told her everything, I went to bed strengthened in my resolve. In one sense we were like an adulterous couple – or more accurately it was like a one-night stand. It was tender and I was eager to be candid, and she was a good listener. At five o'clock the next morning I joined the group and it was like being back with a lot of distant relatives.

We had taken the train to East Berlin, and changed, and were now on the Warsaw train, making a slow trip to the Polish border. Police, customs officials, soldiers – it was impossible to tell them apart – got on, examined passports, demanded to see money and scribbled receipts. Theirs was a mysterious business. They all wore old terrifying shoes.

Poland from the train looked altogether senile – exhausted fields, decaying blocks of flats, broken roads, and great dusty factories. It had the appearance of an elderly country – it is visibly doddering – but it has the most humane and polite people I have ever met, thoroughly gentle and civilized, which is probably the reason theirs is a history of being overrun and occupied.

In my compartment was a little group travelling together – mother, daughter, grandson. They were from Katowice and being with the daughter reminded me that young Polish women are madly attractive, with clear skin and large limpid eyes and lovely hair.

'Don't go to Mongolia,' Ewa said. 'Come to Katowice and I will show you interesting things.'

The mother rolled her eyes and said, 'She's crazy – pay no attention to her.'

Woityek the little boy was solemn-faced and sat without making a sound. A Polish man offered Woityek an apple, which the little boy took but didn't eat. That was another thing. The Poles seemed to me to be very kind and courteous to each other; the Germans were less so; the Russians not at all.

Ewa said, 'We have relations in Chicago, in New Jersey, in Los Angeles, too. If it weren't for them we'd probably starve. They send us money. I'd like to go there – the States. Or maybe to Paris. I could learn French.'

Ewa was twenty-eight and had been divorced for two years. She worked in a bank in the foreign exchange section. I told her I wanted to withdraw some money I had in a bank in Warsaw, the Bank Handlowy. She gave me precise instructions, the address, the telephone numbers. She said it would be easy.

When this family took out their lunch they offered me some sandwiches and fruit, and so I broke out one of my bottles of Amontillado and we drank it together.

'Mongolia's so far away,' Ewa said. And then it sounded as though she were saying to Woityek, 'He's going all the way to Mongolia on the train!'

'They came here once, you know – the Mongols.'

The battle of Liegnitz (1241), about eighty miles south of here; we had just stopped at Zbaszyń. The Mongols annihilated a combined army of Germans and Poles.

'Everyone came here,' Ewa said. 'That's why Poland is such a mess.'

Out the window, on the station platform, two fat white workmen slathered brown paint on an iron bench. The paint dripped and ran, and when they painted the feet of the bench they slopped paint on the platform. Some Poles watched disapprovingly but said nothing. They wore snapbrim hats and carried plastic briefcases. Most Poles seemed overweight; they talked constantly about food and food shortages – but that wasn't odd. Food is a frequent topic with fatties. They wore old clothes, and had sour bready breath, and lived in pockmarked houses.

Ewa and her mother and child got out at Poznań to catch the train for Katowice, but gave me their address.

'Send us a postcard from Mongolia –'

We were delayed in Konin. That was convenient. I could write without my arm being jogged. I wrote:

> In brown April, in Poland, it looks as though spring will never come – bare trees, dead grass like rags, cold winds, rubbly earth, flats plastered with wet washing, furrowed fields with nothing sprouting, a man ploughing with one skinny horse, men shovelling dust, muddy creeks and ditches, a plastic bag jammed on a stick to scare birds; such monotony . . . But this is the view in April, when things in Poland look so bleak that even the ducks seem to be drowning, and the chickens are frantic. In a month or so, things will be different: spring will come, the whole country will be in bloom. Yet it still seems an awful fate to be a Pole.

It seemed to me, as we set off again, that the only really interesting buildings were the churches – the only ones with curves, at any rate. The rest were all right angles and had flat roofs.

The landscape brightened in the environs of Sochazew – patches of woods, better houses, birch groves; but the struggle continued – people labouring everywhere, doing clumsy jobs, shovelling, breaking rocks, chopping wood. All the work looked very hard, and Poland seemed like a glimpse of the past.

Catholicism is obvious, not only in the churches, and the rosaries people wear around their necks, and the way they bless themselves before the train starts; but also in the statuary. There was a statue of the Virgin Mary forty feet high, on an eight-foot pedestal, on the forecourt of the railway station at Szymann. That was something I had never seen in Italy or Spain, or even in Ireland, which claimed the Blessed Virgin as the Queen of Ireland. There were more Virgin Marys on pedestals in bean fields, and in the distance, beyond the man ploughing, was always a Virgin Mary.

They served a devotional purpose, and it was possible they were useful in scaring birds, but I felt there was yet another motive in their ubiquity. They were the classic Lady of Fatima statues, and what the commissars didn't know – but something every Catholic learns early – is that the message Mary gave to the three little children at Fatima in Portugal, in July 1917, was that if they prayed very hard Russia was going to be converted from atheistic communism to Catholicism. 'And now we will pray for the conversion of Russia,' priests announced throughout the fifties, all over America.

That was what this statue represents to most Catholics and probably to all Poles: the Mother of God at her most political.

I had finished *Elmer Gantry* and given it five stars, and now I was reading Balzac's *Old Goriot*. A Polish proverb was quoted in that book: *Hitch five oxen to your cart* – meaning take precautions, so that nothing can go wrong. But reading this in Poland seemed very odd. There were no oxen at all, and the carts were rickety things. I spent an entire day travelling slowly through western Poland, almost 300 miles, from the East German border to Warsaw. I did not see any mechanized farming at all and not a single tractor. Instead, I saw the picturesque hopelessness of the farmer gently whipping his horse as the poor beast struggled with an old ploughshare.

'It doesn't look too bad,' Ellen Wittrick said, raising her eyes to Warsaw for the first time. The late afternoon sun had gilded the façades of the narrow buildings on Jerozolomskie and given that whole block the look of Harrods.

'Get me out of here,' Millie Westbetter whispered to Rick, who replied, 'Take it easy, honey. We'll be back on the train tomorrow.'

And then I gave them all the slip and plunged into Warsaw. Two men, one after the other, asked me to change money, at five times the official rate; that was outside the hotel. I crossed the street and while I was looking at a big clumsy chess set carved from purple wood a man approached me with the same question. I was pursued by another man, and all the way down Marszalkowska was asked the same money-changing question and quoted rates of exchange.

'Aren't you afraid of the police?' I said.

'The police change money, too,' he said.

The merchandise in the shops looked substandard – the clothes, the radios, the pots and pans; even the food looked unappetizing, the fresh food somewhat wilted and dusty, the canned food dented and with faded labels. And in every shop my arm was tugged and the same whispered question, 'Change money?' Poverty can make people look bowed down and beaten, but just as often it can make them shameless, fearless, predatory and dangerous. I found all these apparent law-breakers rather worrying, but when I mentioned it to one man he said, 'Don't worry – it's a double morality. Everyone does it.'

This look of bankruptcy in Warsaw was also a facial expression: stricken, demoralized, lonely and a bit desperate, a look of suffering on some, cynicism on others. It is surprising that people so victimized can have such dignity and can also be so polite and friendly. It is a good thing, too, because that courtliness takes the curse off their other side – the hunger that makes them food-bores, the poverty that makes them seem grasping, the deprivation that has made them appear materialistic, and the economic policies that have turned them into religious nuts.

The bar of my hotel, the Forum, was crowded and smoky, so I wandered around, dropped into the Habana night-club and watched people jitterbugging. As I watched, a voice whispered in my ear, 'Change money? Seven *zlotys* for one dollar.'

'What would I do with all those *zlotys*?' I said, and turned.

A plump girl in a black dress was smiling at me. Perspiration had given a stickiness to her orange make-up and there were little sooty flecks on her eyelashes.

'You can buy Polish vodka, you can buy curios. Poland is famous for amber. You can buy. Or stamps. You are staying at a hotel?'

'Yes, I am.'

'I can visit you in your room. We make love. Fifty dollars.'

'What about this amber?'

'*Bursztyn*,' she said, explaining that it was the Polish word. 'It is lovely. It comes from under the sea.'

'My problem is that I have *zlotys* but not many dollars.'

'I prefer dollars,' she said. 'We need dollars. In Poland it is impossible to do anything without dollars.'

'Where do you get the dollars?'

'From you,' she said.

'Not tonight.'

I left, looked at the gloomy shop windows, marvelled at the wide empty streets, and went back to the Forum.

My challenge the next day was first to withdraw some Polish *zlotys* from Bank Handlowy – royalties that I could not take out of Poland; and then to spend them all before the train left. The bank opened at 9.30, the train was going two hours later. I estimated that I would have about an hour and a half to spend whatever amount I withdrew. In New York it would not have been difficult. But this was Warsaw.

I knew only my account number. The bank was in a modern building, a steel and glass tower, the top of which was wreathed in fog. It was a rainy day, and it seemed to me that I was on an absurd errand. But it would have been more foolish to leave my Polish money where it was and not try to withdraw some. I had vowed that I would never give it to Lech Walesa, the leader of the Solidarity movement, because he had once publicly boasted that he had never read a book in his life. The last thing that man deserved were my book royalties.

I entered the bank. The entire ground floor was an open-plan office – hundreds of employees tapping on computers, calculators, typewriters, or else pushing stacks of tattered money around. Just looking at the enormity of the operation made me feel I didn't have a chance.

At the marble counter I explained to the woman that I had an external account and wanted to make a withdrawal.

'Please write your account number.'

I did so on a scrap of paper.

'Passport, please.'

I handed it over.

Without hesitating, and without leaving the counter, the woman stretched out her arm and fished a small wooden box, like an old cigar box, from beneath the marble slab. She glanced at my account number and plucked another scrap of paper out of the small box.

'How much do you want to withdraw?'

'How much have I got?'

'You have 260,000 *zlotys*.'

'I'll have 100,000.'

That meant $600, or around £375, at the official rate.

The woman passed the scrap of paper she had initialled to the clerk, who called me over and counted out the money. The whole operation had taken less than five minutes.

My pockets were now bulging with Polish money.

'You could buy half a car,' Gregory the taxi driver said, when I told him my problem. 'You could buy 100,000 kilos of ham.'

Gregory spoke perfect South Jersey English – he had worked for an Ocean City trucking company for two years. But then he had returned to Warsaw. He explained, 'Warsaw is miserable, yes, but Warsaw is my city. My father was born here, my grandfather was born here, and so . . . and so . . .' He shrugged. 'You like this song?'

A bouncy little ditty crackled from his car radio. I said yes, it was melodious.

'I sing it for you.'

I thought: Forget it.

Cry, little woman, cry!
Go ahead and cry!
Cry, little woman, cry!

'Good, eh?'

'Wonderful,' I said. 'Maybe I could buy an antique with my money.'

'The shops open at 11.30,' he said. 'You'll miss your train.'

'What about amber – *bursztyn*?'

'Very nice. We go to old city.'

But the jewellery shops didn't open until 10.30. While we lurked in the old Warsaw – cobblestone streets, medieval buildings, the ramparts of a fort – Gregory told me he wasn't a member of Solidarity. 'I don't need a party. My wife is my party. My kid – my family. That's my party.'

A man accosted me and asked if I was interested in buying a very rare stamp of the German occupation. He showed me a head of

Hitler with a Kraków postmark, and another, a Polish stamp depicting saints or angels, overprinted with swastikas.

'How many stamps have you got?'

From under his jacket he produced a stamp album – about twenty pages. He riffled through: more Hitlers, more angels, more overprinting and interesting postmarks; about 400 stamps.

'I'll give you 10,000 *zlotys* for it.'

Without a word he handed over the album and took the money.

We passed a butcher shop. I said, 'I could get some sausages.'

'You need one of these.' Gregory showed me his meat ration book. He was allowed 2.5 kilograms of meat a month. That was his May book – with some coupons missing. He had used up his April book, though today was only the 16th of April. 'Not much meat in Poland. We have to sell it – for dollars. I've seen more Polish ham in Ocean City than I've seen in Poland.'

'Why not become a vegetarian?'

'No, no,' he said, showing me his sharp carnivore's teeth. 'And you know, Poles hate everything except cow meat and pig meat. They don't eat lamb, they don't eat chicken.'

I said that surely there were some vegetarians in Poland.

He only knew one, he said – an old lady, whose doctor had forbidden her to eat meat. It seemed to me characteristic of Polish conservatism that they should be unwavering in their eating habits, and would spend all morning queuing in front of a butcher shop (Warsaw was full of such queues) instead of developing a taste for quiche or ratatouille. It occurred to me that people who refused to change their diet were not only stubborn and self-defeating but probably very superstitious as well.

When the jewellery shops opened I bought some amber, and on the way back to the hotel half a dozen bottles of Polish champagne, some yellow caviare, pickled mushrooms and sardines. I paid Gregory, and tipped him for helping me. I still had 20,000 *zlotys* left and nothing to buy with them.

It was then that I remembered Ewa and Woityek, from the train. 'Send us a postcard from Mongolia,' Ewa had said, and scribbled her address. I put the remainder of the *zlotys* into an envelope and a note saying 'This is for Woityek' and sent it to them.

It was a wet day in Warsaw, rain completing the picture of utter misery; and rain was sweeping against the train as we set off for Moscow.

I had a crate of Polish provisions and decided to have a party in my compartment before we got to Brest Litovsk. I had invited Ashley, Morthole, Chris and the less inquisitive members of the group.

We drank most of the champagne before we got to the Soviet border. Ashley was drunk and put his face against mine and said, 'I've got a bet with Morthole that you're with the State Department.'

'You lose,' I said.

At the border, the train was searched by customs officials. One of my champagne bottles blew its cork while the customs woman was in my compartment, but she didn't blink. She was looking for guns, books, money, jewellery. 'No guns,' I said, and showed her what I had.

In the mean time the wheels of all the railway cars were changed – the wheel assemblies unhitched and wide-gauge ones attached.

'They took two of our guys!' It was Morris Least, yelling. He complained to the tour leader. 'The Russians just marched them away.' Morris was breathless and frightened. And yet he had been expecting this.

'I'm keeping my head down,' Kicker said.

They had taken Bud Wittrick for questioning. He had apparently been flaunting a copy of *The Economist*. Was that a crime? And Rick Westbetter had been cleaning the windows of his compartment with a squeegee he had brought from Maryland. He had to be a spy – why else would he want clean windows?

Just before we set off for Moscow, Wittrick and Westbetter were returned to us, and over dinner they told stories of their captivity and interrogation.

I drank the last of my Polish champagne and read more of *Old Goriot*, and then went to sleep. We passed through Minsk and Smolensk in the night. I woke to snow on the fields and ice in the ditches beside the tracks. The dwellings were wooden huts and bungalows, and the bumpy roads showed wheel-tracks through the mud-splashed ice-crust.

'That's what Ohio looked like, when I was growing up,' Rick Westbetter said. 'That's the nineteen-thirties.'

'No sightseeing for me,' I told the tour leader, when we arrived in Moscow. I decided to walk in the city, for in a few days we would be on the Trans-Siberian Express and unable to walk. In any case, the sights in Moscow were limited: the Kremlin Museum was closed, many of the churches were shut, because of restoration work, and what my fellow tourists were faced with was nothing more than a long bus ride around the city. I went to the Intourist Hotel and bought tickets for *The Nutcracker* at the Bolshoi and a modern ballet at the Stanislavski Theatre. When I remarked that it seemed easy to get tickets the clerk said, 'Because you have dollars.'

I walked to St Basil's, and to the Metropole Hotel, where I had stayed in 1968 – it was now a sort of monument – and I strolled through the GUM store, looking at the merchandise.

While I was staring at some very inferior-looking alarm clocks, I realized that the woman on my right and the one on my left were sidling nearer to me.

'Is nice clock? You like clock?'

I said, 'Alarm clocks wake you up. That's why I hate them.'

'Is funny,' the woman on my right said. She was dark, in her early twenties. 'You want to change roubles?'

The surprising thing to me was that one of these young women was pushing a little boy in a pram, and the other had a bag of what looked like old laundry. They were pretty women, but obviously preoccupied with domestic chores – airing the baby, doing the wash. I invited them to the ballet – I had bought pairs of tickets. They said no, they had to cook dinner for their husbands and do the housework, but what about changing some money? The rate was seventy-two cents to the rouble: they offered me ten times that.

'What would I do with all those roubles?'

'So many things.'

The dark one was Olga, the blonde Natasha – a ballet dancer, she said. Olga spoke Italian; Natasha spoke only Russian, and had a dancer's slimness and pallor and china-blue eyes with a Slavic slant and an expressive Russian mouth.

I said I was walking – I needed the exercise.

'We will go with you!'

That was why, about ten minutes later, I came to be walking with a Russian woman on each arm, and carrying Natasha's laundry – Olga pushing little Boris in his pram – down Karl Marx Prospekt. Olga was chatting to me in Italian and Natasha laughing.

'You seem to be doing all right for yourself, Paul!'

It was a group of people from the tour, heading back to the bus. I was delighted that they saw me – what would they make of it?

We stopped at a café and had a hot chocolate and they said they wanted to see me again – 'We can talk!' They made a fuss about the time, probably because they were deceiving their husbands, but we agreed on a time when they would call me.

That evening I went to the circus and was reminded of how much I hate circuses, especially communist ones. Everyone says: 'Rumanians are wonderful acrobats! Bulgarians are brilliant jugglers! You haven't lived until you've seen a Russian on a tightrope – and a Chinese performer can balance a whole set of crockery on a chopstick he's holding in his teeth!' Why is this so? Why all the flying humans, and people tumbling like ferrets, and doing amazing things with stools?

This Moscow Circus had bears that walked and danced – the big hairy things slavering and pirouetting; and dogs that balanced on one leg; and seals that gleamed and manipulated balls with their flippers. All the animals looked human in their frightened way – walking stiffly and unnaturally on their hind legs, and giving pleading glances to their trainers, as if they were going to be kicked or electrocuted if they did the wrong dance-step.

It all made me very uneasy; it seemed to me funless and frantic. Was I taking it too seriously by thinking that it was the most vulgar expression of peasant entertainment? It was what poor people did to get copecks thrown at them in the bazaars and market-squares. It was open-air amusement and it made me think of serfs and slaves and gypsies: men leaping like dogs, dogs goose-stepping like men. And virtually all the interest in the women performers was inspired by their scanty costumes – so shocking in the puritan society of political commissars.

It is hard to imagine a well-educated and fair-minded society producing circus performers, or any sensitive person training a bear to dance. Circuses may flourish in some prosperous countries, but the artists, so-called, come from elsewhere. The Ringling Brothers were Wisconsin farmboys – very poor – who liberated themselves by learning to juggle and tumble. Rudolf Ringling could balance a plough on his chin. Today, Ringling Brothers and Barnum and Bailey Circus gets most of its stars from either Eastern Europe or China.

The simplest explanation is that most people like a spectacle – music, tumbling, noise, sex, patriotism and cheap thrills. They enjoy watching chimps riding bikes or one of the more popular acts that Ringling Brothers presents: twenty-five black people playing basketball on unicycles. There is another side to this. 'The desire to turn men into animals was the principal motive for the development of slavery,' Elias Canetti wrote in his chapter 'Transformation' in *Crowds and Power*. 'It is as difficult to overestimate its strength as that of its opposite desire: to turn animals into men . . . popular amusements like the public exhibition of performing animals.' That was true of the Moscow Circus. Nothing was more revealing of Soviet thought than a Russian lion-tamer, and the process that lay behind that big brown bear's clumsy jig or the lobster-quadrille said a great deal about the political system.

I also thought: What a stupid man I am to be sitting alone at a circus in Moscow. I could not imagine why I wasn't doing something vastly more enjoyable, like sailing off East Sandwich. And then I remembered that I was on my way to Mongolia and China.

There was a message waiting for me when I got back to the Hotel Ukraine: 'Olga will call tomorrow at 12.' She called on the stroke of noon the next day to say she would call again at 2.00. At 2.00 she said she would meet me at 3.30. These phone calls had the effect of making our meeting seem necessary and inevitable. It was only when I was waiting on the hotel steps that it occurred to me that I had no idea why I was seeing them at all.

Natasha walked by but did not greet me. She was wearing old clothes and carrying a shopping-basket. She winked at me; I followed her to a taxi, in which Olga was already sitting and smoking. When I got in, Olga gave the driver an order and he drove off. After that they intermittently quarrelled over whether this was the right direction or the quickest way.

After twenty minutes of this – we were now deep in the high-rise Moscow suburbs – I said, 'Where are we going?'

'Not far.'

There were people raking leaves and picking up litter from the streets. I had never seen so many street-sweepers. I asked what was going on.

Olga said that this was the one day in the year when people worked for nothing – tidying up the city. The day was called *subodnik* and this work was given free to honour Lenin – his birthday was two days away.

'Don't you think you should be out there with a shovel, Olga?'

'I am too busy,' she said, and her laugh said: *Not on your life!*

'Are we going to a house?'

Olga gave more directions to the driver. He turned right, entered a side-street and then cut down a dirt road and cursed. That bad road connected one housing estate with another. He kept driving on these back roads among tall bare blocks of flats and then he stopped the car and babbled angrily.

'We can walk the rest of the way,' Olga said. 'You can pay him.'

The driver snatched my roubles and drove off as we walked towards a sixteen-storey building, through children playing and their parents sweeping the pavements in a good *subodnik* spirit.

No one took any notice of me. I was merely a man in a raincoat following two women down a muddy pavement, past walls that had been scribbled on, past broken windows and through a smashed door to a hallway where three prams were parked, and some of the floor tiles were missing. It could have been a housing estate in south London or the Bronx. The lift had been vandalized but it still worked. It was varnished wood, with initials scratched on to it. We took it to the top floor.

'Excuse me,' Olga said. 'I couldn't get my friend on the phone. I must talk to her first.'

But by now I had imagined that we had come to a place where I was going to be threatened and probably robbed. There were three huge Muscovites behind the door. They would seize me and empty my pockets, and then blindfold me and drop me somewhere in Moscow. They didn't go in for kidnapping. I asked myself whether I was worried, and answered: Kind of.

I was somewhat reassured when I saw a surprised and sluttish-looking woman answer the door. Her hair was tangled, she wore a bathrobe. It was late afternoon – she had just woken up. She whispered a little to Olga and then she let us in.

Her name was Tatyana and she was annoyed at having been disturbed – she had been watching television in bed. I asked to use the toilet, and made a quick assessment of the flat. It was large – four big rooms and a central hall with bookshelves. All the curtains were drawn. It smelled of vegetables and hair-spray and that unmistakable odour that permeates places in which there are late-sleepers – the smell of bedclothes and bodies and feety aromas.

'You want tea?'

I said yes, and we all sat in the small kitchen. Tatyana brushed her hair and put on make-up as she boiled the kettle and made tea.

There were magazines on the table: two oldish copies of *Vogue*, and last month's *Tatler* and *Harper's Bazaar*. Seeing them in that place gave me what I was sure would be a lasting hatred for those magazines.

'My friend from Italy brings them for me,' Tatyana said.

'She has many foreign friends,' Olga said. 'That is why I wanted you to meet her. Because you are our foreign friend. You want to change roubles?'

I said no – there was nothing I wanted to buy.

'We can find something for you,' Olga said, 'and you can give us US dollars.'

'What are you going to find?'

'You like Natasha. Natasha likes you. Why don't you make love to her?'

I stood up and went to the window. The three women stared at me, and when I looked at Natasha she smiled demurely and batted her eyelashes. Beside her was her shopping-basket with a box of detergent, some fresh spinach wrapped in newspaper, some cans of food, a pack of plastic clothes-pegs and a box of disposable nappies.

'Here?' I said. 'Now?'

They all smiled at me. Out of the window people were sweeping the pavements, and raking leaves, and shovelling up piles of rubbish – a little unselfish demonstration of civic pride for Lenin's birthday.

'How much will it cost me to make love to Natasha?'

'It will cost 170 US dollars.'

'That's rather a precise figure,' I said. 'How did you arrive at that price?'

'That's how much a cassette recorder costs at the Berioska shop.'

'I'll think about it.'

'You have to decide now,' Olga said sternly. 'Do you have a credit card?'

'You take credit cards?'

'No, the Berioska shop can.'

'That's an awful lot of money, Olga.'

'Hah!' Tatyana jeered. 'My boyfriends give me radios, tape recorders, cassettes, clothes – thousands of dollars. And you're arguing about a few hundred dollars.'

'Listen, I'm not boasting – believe me. But if I like someone I don't usually buy her before we go to bed. In America we do it for fun.'

Olga said, 'If we don't have dollars we can't buy radios at the Berioska. It closes at six o'clock. What's wrong?'

'I don't like being hurried.'

'All this talk! You could have finished by now!'

I hated this and had a strong desire to get away from the nagging. It was hot in the kitchen, the tea was bitter, all those people raking leaves sixteen floors down depressed me.

I said, 'Why don't we go to the Berioska shop first?'

Tatyana dressed and we found a taxi. It was a twenty-minute ride and well after 5.00 by the time we arrived. But for me it was simply a way of saving face – and saving money. I had been disgusted with myself back there in the flat.

Before we went into the shop the three women started bickering. Olga said that it was all my fault for not making love to Natasha when I should have. Tatyana had to meet her daughter at school, Natasha was due home because she was going to the Black Sea tomorrow with her husband and small child – and was counting on having a cassette recorder; and Olga herself had to be home to cook dinner. '*Vremya*,' Natasha said, '*vremya*.' Time, time.

I had never seen such expensive electronic equipment – over-priced radios and tape decks, a Sony Walkman for $300.

'Natasha wants one of those.'

Olga was pointing to a $200 cassette machine.

'That's a ridiculous price.'

'It's a good cassette. Japanese.'

I was looking at Natasha and thinking how thoroughly out of touch these people were with market forces.

'*Vremya*,' Natasha said urgently.

'These are nice.' I began trying on the fur hats. 'Wouldn't you like one of these?'

Olga said, 'You must buy something now. Then we go.'

And I imagined it – the cassette recorder in a Berioska bag, and the dash to Tatyana's, and the fumble upstairs with Natasha panting '*Vremya, vremya*,' and then off I'd go, saying to myself: You've just been screwed.

I said, 'Tatyana, your daughter's waiting at school. Olga, your husband's going to want his dinner on time. And Natasha, you're very nice, but if you don't go home and pack you'll never make it to the Black Sea with your husband.'

'What are you doing?'

'I have an appointment,' I said, and left, as the Berioska shop was closing.

I went to the Bolshoi, and I noticed at the cloakroom and the buffet and the bar Russian women gave me frank looks. It was not lust or romance, merely curiosity because they had spotted a man who probably had hard currency. It was not the sort of look women usually offered. It was an unambiguous lingering gaze, a half-smile that said: *Maybe we can work something out*.

Moscow had a chastening effect on the tour group. They became very quiet and rather wary. They seemed actually afraid – something I had not expected. Was it the glowering soldiers and police? Or perhaps the repeated security checks, and having to show your hotel ID card before you were allowed into the lobby? Or was it the big bare buildings and wide streets? Ashley said he felt very small in Moscow.

Kicker winked and told me that in his three days in Moscow he did not leave the hotel. He said he was afraid of being picked up and never heard of again.

'Why would they do that?'

'I was a Marine,' he said. 'They kill you for things like that in Russia. Let's get out of here. That's what I say.'

It was a dark rainy afternoon when we set off from Yaroslav Station on the Trans-Siberian. The people in the group were nervous and chatty – glad to be going but apprehensive about what it would be like. Some had never spent a night on a train. They were faced with four nights to Irkutsk, living in close quarters – Americans in one compartment, British in another, Australians in a third, the nameless French foursome together. From the moment I was assigned to my compartment I knew it would be a splendid trip: I was alone. I had my Polish provisions, and chocolate and champagne that I had bought in Moscow. I had books, and my short-wave radio. I was looking forward to four days of bliss.

It is an unusual feeling in the Soviet Union, because they do not cater to the individual – they hardly seem to notice that the solitary traveller exists. If a person enters a Russian restaurant it takes ages for him to be served; but the group of thirty-five drunken Finns chanting '*Suomi! Suomi!*' ('Finland! Finland!') are fussed over and fed and are back on their tour bus in less than an hour. The Soviets prefer to feed large groups of people; they like herding them and lecturing them and counting them and sending them on their way. The individual is often dangerous and always a nuisance. Why bother with him when it is so much easier to bully a whole mob of tourists? The solitary traveller is despised and feared, and if he manages to triumph over the bureaucracy he will find it twice as expensive as travelling with a group. Soviet society does not recognize the individual. The answer is simple: travel with a group and, when it suits you, drop out.

Travelling on my own I would never have had a sleeping-compartment to myself. But two whole coaches had been allotted to this tour, and as the tour only filled one and a half coaches, some of us lucked out and were on our own.

That was why, rolling towards Kirov that first day, I was very happy – reading, drinking, listening to the news on the BBC, and writing down the odd episode with Olga and Natasha. It seemed to me like a sort of rest-cure – idleness, and undemanding scenery, and they woke you for meals. And because we were in a group we were served before anyone else.

The experience of the Trans-Siberian Express is both monotony and monkish beauty: all day outside the loud hurrying train it is birch trees and undulant hills, and after the utter blackness of night on that line, you see more birch trees and more undulant hills; and all that day too, until it seems more like wallpaper than a landscape – the kind of wallpaper that is so simple and repetitious that you look at the seams rather than the design.

There is no more austere sight in nature than birch trees set among small snow-covered hills, a study in black and white that is made starker by the crows and their nests, the fat black birds in the branches or looking deranged, flapping in the white sky.

We went through Perm, and passed the East–West marker at 1100 miles; and then to Sverdlovsk. The dwellings diminish and change from concrete towers in cities, to brick flats on the outskirts, and then to houses made of planks, that grow rougher until huts made of split logs appear, and these are replaced in the hinterland by plain log cabins with turf jammed between the chinks. In fifty or a hundred miles you see the entire history of Russian architecture.

Over lunch I was sitting with Blind Bob, Wilma and Morthole. Morthole brought us up to date on his rock collection: one from Berlin that had been thrown by a rioter, a chunk from Warsaw, a pebble from Moscow. He was planning to snatch something interesting at the twelve-minute stop in Omsk.

'These houses are horrible,' Wilma said. She was wearing a wool hat over her baldness.

Morthole hadn't shaved and was looking whiskery. It always seemed ominous to me when a man stopped shaving on such a trip.

I remarked that they didn't seem to paint many of their houses out here – usually it was just the trim. In the poorer villages there was no paint at all. The log cabins and shacks just blackened in the rain and sun, and there was the proof out of the window: a whole settlement of black chubby huts.

Wilma said, 'I'd like to read something about it.'

Blind Bob said, 'Did you read that book by Paul Theroux, about taking this train?'

'No,' Wilma said, and addressed me, 'Did you?'

Flattening my face against the window, I said, 'Look at those birches! Isn't it amazing that you never see a fat one? They're all slender. Why do you suppose –'

'I read it,' Morthole said, across the table. 'The Gurneys have one of his books, I don't know which one. I saw Malcolm reading it in his compartment.'

I made a mental note to avoid the Gurneys, but even so – sitting here – I felt like a hypocrite. But what was I to do? I hated being an object of attention. I had paid for my ticket, and so I had a right to my privacy. I hadn't deceived anyone; I had merely been economical with the truth. The alternative could be irksome – not just the conversations about writing books and 'You should get yourself a word-processor,' but what I feared would be the duties of an unpaid guide. I had been on this train before; therefore, I ought to know whether that thermos-bottle thing was a church steeple, and the name of that river, and if you could buy film in Irkutsk.

It was easy for me to keep to myself. I had my own compartment – plenty of space, plenty of provisions, the grapes, cookies, chocolates and tea that made being on the Trans-Siberian like a luxurious form of convalescence. It was a surprise to me that my little radio worked inside the train. At certain times of day I got the BBC news, and at other times Radio Australia or the Voice of America. I listened to the Top Twenty, and the report of a Shakespeare Festival in China, and the fall-out from the bombing of Libya. From the samovar at the end of the sleeping-car I got hot water for tea. And I divided the day into three parts and set myself tasks to perform: reading and writing.

That night a full moon was shining in the cloudless sky, and beneath it water was lying everywhere – the melted snow flooding the birches. At midnight the moon shone from above and below this water and made the earth a glittering mirror, on which leafless trees trembled, looking frail.

Every day is the same on the Trans-Siberian: that is one of its reassuring aspects. In itself it is not interesting, which is why it is such a pleasure to be a passenger and so maddening to write about it. There is nothing to write about. This train is an occasion, not a subject. It is more like an ocean-liner than any other train I know – the solid steady travel, the sameness of the view. But in the thirteen years since I had last been on it, it had changed in many ways, and most of those changes were improvements. I assumed Gorbachev's cost-efficient approach to Soviet life was behind this. He had publicly criticized the uncaring attitude of Soviet workers: the old grizzled *provodniks* on the sleeping-car were gone, and in their place was a young couple who occupied one small compartment and worked in shifts. Gorbachev had denounced the drunkenness that was common in the country – and the Trans-Siberian reflected this: a trip on it was no longer a binge. There were a few drunks on the train, but none dared to enter the dining-car, and no alcohol was sold. The carriages were cleaner, and the officials fairly good-natured, and the passengers more prosperous-looking. Still, at the longer stops, when I was strolling down the station platform I was buttonholed by Russians who asked: 'Want to sell your shoes? Want to sell your jeans? Want to sell your T-shirt?' Perhaps it was only my imagination, but it seemed to me that there was something fundamentally wrong with a country whose citizens asked to buy your underwear.

Each day I moved my watch back one hour: Irkutsk is five hours ahead of Moscow. Losing an hour a day did not cause jet lag. Just after I awoke on the third day I looked out and saw a huge lake to the south: Lake Chany (Ozero Chany). Very soon we stopped at Barabinsk, which was cold – below freezing. Zhenia the sleeping-car attendant squinted at the sky and hugged himself and muttered, '*Sneg*.' Morthole drew my attention to the fact that some of the birches on the Barabinsk steppe were as fat as beer barrels – thicker than any birch I had ever seen. These older birches had black burst-open bark on their trunks.

We came to Novosibirsk, on the river Ob. It is strange that this Siberian city should be so large, though not stranger than Chicago – and like Chicago it is a city the railway put on the map. Much odder than this was the sight of so many seagulls on the river – black-headed gulls, laughing gulls diving among the ice floes, over 1,000 miles from the sea. The Ob itself at 3,461 miles long is the fourth longest river in the world – longer than the Yangtze.

Once, Malcolm Gurney quoted with approval this know-it-all traveller, Theroux, who had done the trip some years ago. Everyone at the table listened with interest and apparent agreement. It seemed as though I was the only person who didn't agree with the wild generalization, and so I excused myself and left.

But I wanted to reveal myself and tell them that this train was much better than the one I had taken in 1973. It was more orderly, and cleaner, and seemingly more tolerant. What I remembered was that the dining-car had run out of decent food after a few days, and we had lived on eggs and watery soup and stale bread; and I had a very clear memory of the thin soup sloshing in the steel soup bowls as the train jolted around long curves.

Clouds were massing and building towards the dazzling white moon, just before I turned in. It had grown cold. In the immensity of the Siberian forest, amid the blue pools of snow and spiky trees, there were wolves and wild dogs – farther on I saw their skins being stretched on frames. It seemed to me hateful that they should make wolves into hats. When the moon was lost in the cloud-cover a blackness overwhelmed the view. I awoke at Taishet the next morning to driving snow.

It was spring snow – sudden, heavy and deep. The whole landscape was buried in it, with only a few brown muddy creeks showing through – no water, just a creek-shape of chocolate ice cream straggling through the snow. The strange silence and isolation that snow brings to a place was intensified here in Siberia – or technically Eastern Siberia, as it said in Russian on the sign at the little wooden station at Uk. It snowed all day, and at times, as the train rolled through it, the snow was so thick that everything was white – the sky, the earth: nothing but a blankness with a few faint tracings of trees.

I had Rick Westbetter's word that the wooden townships looked like small towns in the Midwest in the nineteen-twenties – one-storey wooden houses with steeply pitched roofs; and outside town a couple of filthy factories whose smoke was the same browny-grey as the clouds, and all around an expanse of prairie – in this case the great Gromboolian Plain of the steppes. Those places a few hours out of Zima all looked like Gopher Prairie. I was now reading *Main*

Street and marvelling at the similarity: the boom town in the middle of nowhere.

The snowstorm lessened in the afternoon, and later as we approached Angarsk what looked like a blizzard was the wind whipping the snow from the ground; it had stopped falling. Where the ground had been scoured by the wind, the soil was light brown and dry, the sort of frozen ground you can stub your toe against. It was not until I saw a falcon roosting on a bare tree that I realized that there was little sign of life here – just bare ground and drifted snow under an iron-dark sky. The train raced along, and I looked for more. I thought I saw magpies and crows but it might have been a trick of the light.

We were almost at Irkutsk, after four and a half days of the Trans-Siberian's crossing the vastness of the steppes. The astonishing thing is not that it took so long to get there, but that for anyone who chooses to go on to Vladivostok, there are four more days of it, and they are much the same. It was like crossing an ocean.

It was nine o'clock at night, but we did not stay in the city. We were directed to a bus and driven to a hotel forty miles away on the shore of Lake Baikal. The Wittricks called it Lake Bacall, like the actress.

The lake was frozen solid, with great shoved-up ice slabs at the shore, because of the pressure. Baikal is the largest lake in the world – it contains one-fifth of the earth's fresh water, and the Russians suggest that there are monsters in it as well as fat seals and numerous varieties of fish. The ice is six feet thick, they boasted. You can walk the length of it – over 400 miles. Or take a sleigh across to Babushkin, which they do to save time in winter. They had amazing things here in Baikal. Natural wonders! Over at Bashaiyarischka they had fur farms – they raised ermine and lynx and mink, and made them into hats. They trapped sable – the little devils wouldn't breed in captivity, but there were plenty of them around and they fetched $1,000 a pelt. They had coral in the lake, they boasted. And just down the shore at Listvyanka they had a church. There was a priest in the church – a real one.

They never boasted about the hotels. In Moscow it had been a vast and dusty place, with straw mattresses and a shrivelled floor, ragged carpets, blankets blackened with cigarette burns, and stinking bathrooms – leaky pipes, cracked cisterns. 'The bogs are tragic,' Richard Cathcart said. I thought that was about right. The hotel at Baikal was marble and mausoleum-like, and it was clean. But I had to be shown three rooms until I found one with hot water, and in the last there was no toilet seat, and none of them had curtains on the windows. The babushkas dusted and mopped, but apart from that there was no maintenance – not only in the larger sense of the drains working or the water running, but in details: knobs were missing from the drawers, and latches from the windows – which didn't open in any case; the locks jammed, the lamps were either dead or bristling with bare wires. Repairs were carried out with bits of sticky tape and pieces of string. It is true that every traveller has to expect to put up with discomfort, but there were huge areas of Soviet life that seemed to me not simply uncomfortable but downright dangerous.

The members of the group were not happy here: it was too cold, the hotel was a wreck, the food was dreadful, and why didn't these Siberians smile?

Honeymooners came to the hotel – some stayed, some merely stood in front and had their pictures taken, some roistered there. On my second night the room next to mine was occupied by a pair of newly weds playing Russian rock-and-roll on a cassette machine until, at 2.00 in the morning, I banged on their door and told him to shut up. The groom appeared – drunken and drooling and a foot taller than me, but when he saw I was a foreigner he decided not to attack me. Behind him in the room, a young woman encouraged him. In defiance, they turned the music even louder for about ten minutes, and then they switched it off.

It was a custom for just-married couples to drive to where the Angara river flowed from the lake – it was all eider ducks and ice floes – and these newly weds parked by the shore, opened a bottle of champagne and toasted each other, while the driver took their picture. The bride wore a rented dress of white lace, and the groom a dark suit with a wide red ribbon worn as a sash. In the course of one walk in this direction I saw four couples do this – have a ceremonial drink, then pose for a picture. The shore was littered with champagne bottles.

I found this very depressing. Was it the ritual, or was it the fact that the Soviet divorce rate was so high that everything related to marriage there looked like a charade? It might have been nothing more than the cold: Baikal was freezing, and the lake looked like a plain of snow and ice in Antarctica. Well, after all it was winter in Siberia.

There were any number of people eager to explain why Irkutsk was the capital of Siberia, an education centre, an Asiatic crossroads; but I thought Rick Westbetter had it just about right when he said, 'Grand Rapids used to look like this, when I was a kid. Look, outdoor privies. We haven't seen those since the twenties.' I told him that I had been reading Sinclair Lewis and that these Siberian cities and towns looked like tired versions of Zenith and Gopher Prairie: not only the wooden houses with porches, but the main street and the old cars and the trolleys, and the wide-fronted department stores that looked as though they should be called The Bon-Ton Store. If there was a difference it was that the class system was probably more rigid in Siberia, and the local version of George F. Babbitt would be a party hack rather than a real-estate man.

An Estonian rock group called 'Radar' was playing in Irkutsk, a freezing wind blew across the river, the toilet seat in my room had been cut from a flat and splintery piece of plywood. How had these people sent rockets to Mars?

Young men and fox-faced women lurked on the promenade and importuned what foreigners they could find.

'Want to sell –'

They wanted to buy blue jeans, T-shirts, track shoes, sport shoes, watches, sweaters, sweat shirts, lighters. They paid in roubles – or else I could have Annushka for an hour. Did I have a radio? And what about a pen?

That night, listening to my little short-wave radio, I heard the news on the BBC World Service. It was the usual headmistress's voice, but the message seemed portentous.

Swedish officials say they have detected high radioactive levels in the atmosphere, and they link these with other reports that Finland, Denmark and Norway have also detected much higher concentrations of radioactivity than usual. At first, it had been thought that the radioactive material had leaked from a Swedish plant near Uppsala, north of Stockholm. But officials from different parts of Sweden say they think the leak has come from the east, in other words from a nuclear power station in the Soviet Union. Easterly winds have been blowing over Scandinavia for several days. According to one report, radiation levels are up to six times above normal level in Finland, and half as much again as normal in Norway.

This was the first inkling of the disaster at Chernobyl nuclear power station, near Kiev. It had happened two days before, when I was in the Soviet Union – in Baikal, cursing the Soviets for never bothering to fix leaky pipes.

In the morning we left Irkutsk for Mongolia. The people in the group complained that the train was three hours late, but that didn't seem bad – after all, it had come from Moscow, which was almost 4,000 miles away. It was the direct Moscow-to-Mongolia train, following the route of the Trans-Siberian as far as Ulan-Ude and then becoming the Trans-Mongolian Express when it turned south from there. It takes in the most rugged and beautiful part of Siberia, the mountainous region south of Lake Baikal called Buryatskaya, inhabited by the nomadic Buryats. The train skirts the lake, passing the ice-fishermen at Slyudyanka and keeping to the shore, to Babushkin and beyond. To the south-west there is a tremendous mountain range, the Khrebet Khamar Daban, very snowy, and with great peaks, one behind the other, like the Rockies and rising to 15,000 and 16,000 feet. These mountains constitute the frontier and it is necessary to travel around them in the flat valley of the Selenga river in order to enter Mongolia.

The last time I was here I did not see anything. I was going west, and the westbound trains round Baikal at night. So this was all new to me: icy mountains in brilliant sunshine. The sleeping-car had a punished and dusty look; written on its side in Cyrillic were the words *Mongolian Railways*, and there was the Mongolian state seal – a fur-hatted horseman galloping. When we stopped, scores of flat-faced Mongolians in blue track suits jumped out of the train and began running on the spot there on the platform. It was the prize-winning Mongolian wrestling team, on their way back from a successful series of matches in Moscow. One of the wrestlers told me that the horseman on the emblem was the liberator of Mongolia, Suhe Baator. The name means 'Suhe the Hero'.

On Russian trains there are loudspeakers in all the coaches, sometimes broadcasting music, sometimes news or comment. The drone is always in the background, and the Russians appear not to notice it. It has a practical value, giving information about the next stop and how long the train will be there. In the past the volume could not be regulated – the knobs were removed from the volume control, and so it droned day and night. One of the improvements on Soviet trains has been the replacement of the volume control knob. On Mongolian trains these knobs are missing and the traveller is subjected to an ear-bashing in the Mongolian language.

'Isn't there anything they can do about it?' Miss Wilkie said pleadingly.

'I'd like to take an axe to that thing,' Kicker said.

They petitioned the Mongolian attendant, a tough-looking woman, who waved them away – a don't-bother-me gesture.

'Maybe she doesn't have the knob,' I said. 'In which case, you're in luck. Because if you turn it off we won't be able to turn it back on.'

A duck-like voice ranted from the loudspeaker.

'It's driving us nuts,' the Westbetters said.

I made myself very popular with the group by showing them how to shut it off. I wrapped a rubber band around the metal stump and this rubber offered enough of a grip to turn the thing off. The beauty of it was that I could then take the rubber band away, and so it stayed off.

We crossed the Selenga, and it looked as though the wilderness went on for ever. Mountain streams coursed out of the forest, and chunks of ice as big as cars floated on the river. The earth was brown and dusty, and though it was very cold there were tiny buds on the trees. The Soviet city of Ulan-Ude lay in the wide flat valley, and it sprawled – low wooden houses, and tall electric poles, and a marshalling yard full of freight cars loaded with tree-trunks. It was a region of lumberjacks and trappers, though no one of this description boarded the train. In fact, from what I could see, the train carried a great number of young Soviet soldiers.

Leaving the Trans-Siberian route, and heading south, the train climbed the bare brown hills and in the brown valley below was the river clogged with muddy ice, and the hideous city smoking on its banks. Just a few miles south of Ulan-Ude the land is arid and desert-like, the *gobi* that is more or less changeless as far as China: big bushes rather than trees, and rough grasslands beaten by sand, and a few settlements, but even those few are sorry places. In many empty places, watching the train go by, was a man in a brown fur hat and padded jacket, smoking a cigarette. He was motionless and solitary, almost emblematic. How had he got there?

The great dune-shaped hills were covered with dust and yellow grass. There were no trees. Black goats browsed near some isolated cabins, and horses were tethered. The people did not show themselves. It seemed to me that almost nothing is known of these settlements – no foreigner is allowed in them; they produce no writing; they are mute. They were places of utter simplicity, too – their water came from holes in the ground, their heat from the firewood stacked against the cabin. It was a desolate part of the Soviet Union. It was as though we had already entered Mongolia. Outside the larger settlement were graveyards, each grave surrounded by a rectangle of fence, to prevent – what? Probably wolves from digging up the corpses.

At midnight we reached the Mongolian border, and spent several hours on each side going through formalities. The Russians and the Mongolians were equally rude. They searched luggage, they took beds apart and lifted the floorboards of the sleeping-car.

'English books? English magazines?'

I showed them what I had, but they were not interested. Their great search was for pornography, I was told, which they considered vastly more dangerous than political propaganda. The Mongolians in particular felt pornography was evil.

Perhaps accustomed to outsiders not speaking their language, the Mongolians went about their business silently, hardly gesturing, only occasionally muttering – but when they muttered they did so in Russian.

That was why I almost jumped out of my skin when the fierce attendant barked at me early the next morning. I had locked my compartment, but she had a master key. She knocked and an instant later whipped the door open and went *'Woof-woof!'* She made me understand that she was saying 'Get up' in her language. She wanted the bedding. But we hadn't been able to go to sleep until 2.00 in the morning – that was the hour we had left the frontier. It was now 7.00. We were due in Ulaanbaatar ('Red Hero') at 9.30. I rolled over and went back to sleep.

Then this Mongolian attendant did an amazing thing – the sort of trick that clever adults attempt at children's parties. She re-entered the compartment, barked softly, and seized the edges of my bedding in both hands. And in one swift manoeuvre (*'Woof!'*) she jerked my bedding off me – sheets and blankets – leaving me shivering, and she hurried away on bandy legs. Mongolian men and women alike had boyish faces.

We were travelling on long straight tracks through the enormous expanse of grassland, among bulgy hills and smooth slopes. In sheltered and shadowy places there were crescent patches of snow. There was the occasional horseman, bundled up against the wind, making his way in the emptiness – no roads, no tracks, nothing but the circular tents known as yurts (the Mongols themselves call these *ghurrs*). It was an extraordinary landscape – pale yellow, under a blue sky – extraordinary because it was not a desert, but rather the largest pasture imaginable: here and there a herd of horses, here and there a camel, or a man, or a tent. It was inhabited, but with a sparseness that was impressive.

The Mongols reached the eastern limits of China. They rode to Afghanistan. They rode to Poland. They sacked Moscow, Warsaw and Vienna. They had stirrups – they introduced stirrups to Europe (and in that made jousting possible and perhaps started the Age of Chivalry). They rode for years, in all seasons. When the Russians retired from their campaigns for the winter the Mongols kept riding and recruiting in the snow. They devised an ingenious tactic for their winter raids: they waited for rivers to freeze and then they rode on the ice. In this way they could go anywhere and they surprised their enemies. They were tough and patient and by the year 1280 they had conquered half the world.

But they were not fearless, and looking at these great open spaces you could almost imagine what it was that spooked them. They had a dread of thunder and lightning. It was so easy to be struck by lightning here! When an electric storm started they made for their tents and burrowed into layers of black felt. If there were strangers among them they sent these people outside, considering them unlucky. They would not eat an animal that had been struck by lightning – they wouldn't go near it. Anything that would conduct lightning they avoided – even between storms; and one of their aims in life, along with plundering and marauding and pillaging, was propitiating lightning.

As I was watching this wilderness of low hills, the city of Ulaanbaatar materialized in the distance, and a road hove into view, and dusty buses and trucks. My first impression of the city was that it was a military garrison; and that impression stayed with me. Every block of flats looked like a barracks, every car-park like a motor pool, every street in the city looked as though it had been designed for a parade. Most of the vehicles were in fact Soviet army vehicles. Buildings were fenced in, with barbed wire on the especially important ones. A cynic might have said that the city resembled a prison, but if so the Mongolians were very cheery prisoners – it was a youthful, well-fed, well-dressed population. They had red cheeks, and wore mittens and boots; in this brown country they favoured bright colours – it was not unusual to see an old man with a red hat and a purple frock-coat and blue trousers stuck into his multicoloured boots. But that way of dressing meant that the Russians were more conspicuous, even when they weren't soldiers. I say the city looked like a garrison, but it was clearly not a Mongolian one – it was Russian, and there was little to distinguish it from any other military garrison I had seen in Central Asia. We had been passing such big dull places all the way from Irkutsk: barracks, radar dishes, unclimbable fences, batteries, ammo dumps, and surely those mounds that looked like tumuli were missile silos?

The hotel was bare and smelled of mutton fat. That was the smell of Ulaanbaatar. Mutton was in the air. If there had been a menu it would have been on the menu. It was served at every meal: mutton and potatoes – but gristly mutton and cold potatoes. The Mongolians had a way of making food inedible or disgusting, and they could transform even the most inoffensive meal into garbage, by serving it cold, or sprinkling it with black carrots, or garnishing it with a goat's ear. I made a point of visiting food shops, just to see what was available. I found fat black sausages, shrivelled potatoes and turnips, black carrots, trays of grated cabbage, basins of yellow goats' ears, chunks of rancid mutton and chicken feet. The most appetizing thing I saw turned out to be a large bin of brown unwrapped laundry soap.

The shops sold Vietnamese pens (Iridium brand), North Korean teddy bears and toys, Russian radios. A Russian television set that was the size of a clothes-cupboard, with an eighteen-inch screen, cost 4,400 *tugriks* ($1,500 or about £900 at the official rate of exchange, roughly a Mongolian's annual income). They made their own shoes, and they made lovely boots and saddles. They made holsters. They sold wolf pelts, and mink coats, and ermine, squirrel, sable and rabbit by the pelt. Their lambskin coats were cheap. I bought a sheepskin waistcoat for the cold. Ten dollars; and stamped in the skin, *Made in Mongolia*.

'Are you a hunter?' a Mongolian asked me on the street.

It seemed an odd question, but in fact most foreigners who stay in Mongolia – as opposed to those who are just passing through – are hunters. They take light planes to the Altay Mountains in the west of the country and ambush bears and blow wolves' brains out and do handsome bucks to death.

I asked this man about the food – those goats' ears, that mutton. He said his favourite food was candy. Ulaanbaatar I subsequently discovered was full of candy shops. It was nothing fancy, it was hard candy, boiled sweets, which they sucked probably because the air was so dry.

Almost no rain at all falls on Ulaanbaatar and Mongolia itself gets only a few inches a year. The skies are eternally blue, and the ground hard and dusty. These people in boots and breeches, dressed for the desert, seemed unlikely residents of barracks. Half the population of Mongolia lived in Ulaanbaatar but they could hardly be classified as urban – 35 per cent of the city dwellers still lived in tents.

The members of the tour had become travel-weary – tired and grumpy and on each other's nerves. They did not complain out loud; they muttered their regrets. The Americans couldn't understand why there was so little to buy; the Australians hated the food – 'Prison food,' the Gurneys said; the French quarrelled among themselves; the English people said 'Mustn't grumble'; and Miss Wilkie said, 'I think I'm going mental.'

I merely listened.

The BBC news sounded like Orson Welles's version of *The War of the Worlds*. After the initial report that high radiation had been detected in Finland and Denmark, more reports were broadcast of radiation in Germany and Switzerland. And then came the news a day later of a nuclear reactor on fire near Kiev. The disaster occurred on a Friday. Saturday was confusion. Sunday the news was still muddled and alarmist. I listened to a summary – this was on the Monday – of the British Sunday newspapers. They spoke of as many as 4,000 people dead, of the mass evacuation of Kiev, of casualties in the tens of thousands and the fire out of control. These suppositions were modified on subsequent days, but it was clear something terrible had happened.

All this time travellers were arriving from Irkutsk. I asked the Russians what they knew of Chernobyl. They knew nothing, they said I was listening to propaganda, and a week later, when everyone in the west knew about the disaster, a Russian just arrived in Mongolia said that the news on Soviet television was that a nuclear power plant was being moved from Kiev.

I found it depressing that no one in Mongolia should know anything of Chernobyl, especially when they themselves had the same sort of nuclear power plants. It was bad enough that they had been colonized and occupied by the Soviets, but it was much worse that this paternalism was taken so literally that they were treated like children and not told anything. They were in the dark. And their conception of communism was very old-fashioned – typified by the thirty-foot bronze statue on the main street, of Joseph Stalin.

I joined the tour to the Mongolian State Museum and saw

dinosaurs which looked like none I had ever seen before – with beaks and horns and claws, and huge simple monsters suggested by an eight-foot bone: 'That is its pelvis.'

In a room filled with stringed instruments, the Mongolian guide said, 'This we call *morin huur.* Its name comes from a very ancient story, about a man who had a wonderful horse. He loved the horse very much. He rode the horse all over Mongolia. He loved the horse more than his family! He treated the horse as you would a loved one or a family. But eventually the horse died. The man was very, very sad. He was so sad he cut the horse to pieces and took out its bones and carved them into a sort of shape like a violin. The horse's tail he made into strings, and he made a bow as well, from bones and from the horse's hair. And he spent the rest of his life playing this violin and thinking of his horse. That is the meaning of *morin huur* – violin of the horse.'

An air of palpable isolation hung over Mongolia. Half the population lived in Ulaanbaatar – the easier to regiment them – and so that meant the countryside was practically empty: it was wilderness, wolves and bears, dinosaur bones and scattered nomads. Ninety per cent of the Mongolians outside Ulaanbaatar lived in tents, and the terrain was so barren – so like the landscape of New Mexico and Arizona – that East European countries made cowboy movies in Mongolia. The Yugoslavs had recently finished shooting *Apache* – a political cowboy movie, about exploitation.

On May Day, the entire population of Ulaanbaatar turned out for the parade – not to watch it but to join it. It was a Mongolian custom for everyone to be in the parade. The only spectators were tourists – some Finns and us: Kicker, Bud, Morris, Miss Wilkie, Wilma, Morthole, Ashley, the Gurneys, and all the rest. I stood behind Blind Bob.

'Who are those people with the flags?'

They were the round-shouldered wrestlers from the train, but this time wearing their medals. There was something simian in their posture and in the way they walked. It seemed so sad that Blind Bob's last visions on earth should be the messy thaw in Poland, the dreariness of Russia, Siberian hotels and Mongolian wrestlers. Stepping off the pavement for a closer look he tripped and fell.

'I'm all right!' he cried, rubbing his knee. 'No harm done! My own darn fault!'

There were thirty people marching in a row, and a row passed me every two seconds. The parade lasted one hour and fifteen minutes. That was 67,500 Mongolians. They carried flags and banners; they dipped these when they passed the Lenin-like mausoleum of their leader from the nineteen-twenties, Suhe Baator, the Red Hero.

There were no soldiers, no uniforms, no weapons at all – how inconvenient it would have been for the Soviets if the Mongolians had an army. The faces on their banners were Marx, Engels, Lenin, Suhe Baator and Gorbachev. There were large banners bearing the likeness of (so I was told) Chairman Batmunkh, of the Mongolian Revolutionary People's Party and head of the Great People's Assembly.

Over a loudspeaker, a man howled, 'May the Mongolian Revolutionary People's Party prosper!'

The parading people cheered and repeated this slogan.

Children marched by, beating drums, wearing fur hats and singing.

May the sun shine in the sky for ever
May the sky be blue for ever
May my mother live for ever
May the world be peaceful for ever.

A big pictorial banner was paraded past, showing Lenin and Suhe Baator in 1921. Suhe had a big bony skull and wore a traditional dress-like gown. Lenin wore his train-conductor's cap. The title of the banner was UNFORGETTABLE MEETING.

There was another portrait, of the Mongolian cosmonaut, Gurragchaa, who in 1981 went into space in a Soviet rocket and produced a detailed study of Mongolian topography.

WARSAW PACT FOR PEACE, one banner said; and another: WE ARE FOLLOWERS OF THE MONGOLIAN REVOLUTIONARY PEOPLE'S PARTY.

'What does that one say?'

The guide translated the banner: CONGRATULATIONS TO WORKERS IN CAPITALIST COUNTRIES.

'That's us,' Rick Westbetter said.

That was the end of the parade.

At Mongolia's only working monastery the next day, listening to the monks in the watch-towers blowing conch-shells, as a summons to other monks to pray, I reflected on this country. Once there were 2,000 monasteries, all Buddhists of the Yellow Sect. Now there was only this wooden wreck of a place behind a block of flats. Once, Mongol armies had conquered the world. Now there was no army. Mongols had been Chinese emperors – the Manchus were a Mongol dynasty. That had ended. Once these people had lived on the plains and in the mountains. Now they lived in two-room flats in this lifeless and stark city. They were in every sense a subject race, and in this – one of the largest and emptiest countries on earth – they lived cheek by jowl. They lived out of the world, almost totally cut-off. It had not made them angry. It had kept them innocent in many ways. There was something very sweet about the Mongolians.

Perhaps that was the whole point about Mongolia: that after a Soviet-inspired revolution in which everything was destroyed and swept away – religion, the old economy, the army, the social order – the country was so changed that it could not function without Soviet help. The Mongolians had been reduced to a state of infancy. All their old habits and institutions were gone. The Soviets stepped into this vacuum: they brought Soviet buildings and urban structures, Soviet railways and roads, Soviet schools, and the Soviet ideology displaced Buddhism. The Mongolian script was abolished and the Russian Cyrillic alphabet introduced. The old Mongolian hatred of the Chinese was whipped up, and the Mongolians gladly accepted forts and garrisons and Soviet missile installations. A simple town is practically unknown in Mongolia; every settlement of any size is a military establishment: Russian soldiers cursing their luck in having been posted there.

All this Soviet authority, meddling, advice and financial aid had a profound effect: it turned the Mongolians into children. It is hard to imagine a more dependent and helpless people. And they are dependent on the Soviet Union in a sort of frantic way, because they cannot be dependent on anyone else. They have no other friends in the world, no family ties. The very country that turned them into orphans, adopted them and – since one of the grimmer features of the country is the permanence of the Soviet presence – won't let them grow up.

All Mongolian aggression is turned against the Chinese. The rockets and tanks and cannons are directed at the Chinese border, and the Chinese are portrayed as torturers and imperialists (the Chinese reply by calling Mongolia an example of 'rampant and reactionary hegemonism'). In its military and political guise this aggression takes the form of Russian divisions patrolling the edges of the Chinese provinces of Xinjiang and Inner Mongolia. Its simpler form is stone-throwing.

There was one Chinese sleeping-car on the train I took from Ulaanbaatar to the border, and moments after we left the station an enthusiastic Mongolian standing by the track flung a stone and broke a window. The Chinese – who can be nags and bores about the sanctity of state property – stopped the train, made a scene and demanded immediate restitution. They would not proceed unless the Mongolians swore that they would hand over a window. The Mongolians promised.

Morthole was outside the train when I went to look at the broken window. But he wasn't looking at the window.

'I'm trying to find that stone for my collection,' he said.

He found one, but a policeman told him to put it back on the ground.

Then we left the dead centre of Mongolia and headed south. The train climbed the brown hills outside the city, and after folding itself double on a series of hairpin bends it rolled into the grasslands – the grass and the whole landscape had the look of a fine sheepskin pelt, carefully clipped fleece, the same colour, a yellow that was whitish and then golden. It was the texture of the grass, it was the wind and sun. This seemingly barren *gobi* was full of live creatures – I saw grey cranes, herds of wild camels, eagles, hawks, buzzards, and brown, long-bodied, gopher-like animals that were probably marmots. But no yaks. Every time I looked out of the window I saw something, and when there was not a wild animal there was a Mongol – one of those middle-of-nowhere horsemen, heading into the wind.

It was clear and sunny. Every day is clear and sunny in the *gobi* every sunset is spectacular – the sun softening and sliding down in a red mass and soaking into the ground – and every night is cold.

That night, at dinner, we were served Chinese food.

'Tomorrow we'll be in China,' Miss Wilkie said.

'And there I'll have to leave you, I'm afraid,' I said.

'Whoever you are,' Ashley said. 'Those French dicks call you "lom mistair".'

'That's me.'

I looked around the dining-car at sedate tables. After three weeks of steady travel the mood in this group had changed: it was slightly more irritable but less rambunctious. People knew exactly who to avoid, and which subjects were unwelcome in conversation, and who was crazy and who was safe. But also they kept pretty much to themselves: French, American, Australian, English; and the ones left out – Wilma because of her baldness, Blind Bob because he couldn't see, Morthole because of his obsession with rocks, Miss Wilkie because of her sharp tongue – made up a foursome.

I listened to my short-wave radio and learned that many of the earlier scare-stories about Chernobyl had been wrong. But it was very bad, and still dangerous; the fire had not yet been extinguished.

I slept fitfully, because of the cold, and just as I dropped into a slumber there was a knock at the door and the Mongolian attendant demanded my bedding. When I hesitated, she employed the grip-and-snatch technique, removing everything from the bed except me, in one pull.

We were just outside the Mongolian border post at Dzamïn Üüd. It was the perfection of a frontier: sandy desert, blowing dust, nothing growing, a desolate wreck of a town looking absolutely on the edge. The railway station looked like the plaster version of a German town hall. But there were no formalities. I waited, watched birds, and four hours passed; the sun climbed to noon. So much of travel is waiting or delay.

The small blue thing in the desert was a Chinese engine. It

chugged up the line and rammed us and was coupled, and then it took us across the border, in bright sunshine, from Mongolia into China.

2

The Inner Mongolian Express to Datong: Train Number 24

Whenever I heard the Chinese word for railway I thought my name was being mentioned. *Tielu* ('iron road') sounds something like a Chinese person attempting the French pronunciation of Theroux. The word never failed to turn my head. What were they saying about me?

The word for train is *huoche*, 'fire wagon'. This one took us across the border to Erlian. I was aiming to go through the Chinese province of Inner Mongolia. Xanadu is in Inner Mongolia, but Kublai Khan's stately pleasure dome exists only as a few acres of broken mud walls. Inner Mongolia is an immensity of grass, and is such a quiet place that the arrival of the train makes Mongolians stare.

Erlian is only a few miles from the border town of Dzamïn Üüd in Outer Mongolia, but the places were very different. Dzamïn Üüd was a wreck of a town set on glaring sand, and was so lacking in events that when a camel went by everyone watched it. But Erlian was a tidy town of brick buildings and flower beds. New saplings lined the streets. The post office was open, the telegraph office worked, the shirt factory was in operation, and the hotel welcomed us. It was not an elegant place, but it was orderly. A work-gang was painting an iron fence green.

'Look, Rick. They're smiling. They're waving!'

'Hi there!'

'It's been ages since anyone smiled. The Russians never smiled. I'm going to get a picture of that.'

The travellers on the train were completely won over by the smiles. But were they smiling? It seemed to me that this work-gang of Mongolian painters were simply dazzled by the sun, though they might well have been smiling in recognition at our exact match of the Chinese slang for foreigners: 'big noses' (*da bidze*).

It was a very hot day in May, and the whole town shimmered in the heat. Christmas decorations (holly, tinsel and strings of tiny lights) had been put up in the station and in the hotel. The train was shunted into the shed to have its wheels changed. But it was not just the wheels – the whole undercarriage was unbolted and replaced, Chinese-style, by hoisting the train, looping it with cables and pulling it apart until ninety tons of cast iron were swinging back and forth.

The arrival of a train was something of an occasion. There were only two trains a day, but they tended to carry some foreigners – people with money to spend or hard currency to exchange. These passengers were either leaving China or just arriving – in any case, a little unsteady and anxious. The Chinese, seeing an opportunity, offered them food and souvenirs. No Chinese destination is complete without a restaurant, and the Chinese do not consider that they have visited a place until they have eaten there. So Erlian had a hotel with a big dining-room, and eight-dish meals were served to the train passengers, who ate gratefully and with a sense of relief: China was tidier than they had imagined, and if the rest of it was no worse than this they might even end up liking it.

Bud Wittrick said, 'Aw, it's great. They're friendly, they're warm –'

He meant that the Chinese knew how to scuttle around and pour tea. They knew how to be polite, but that did not keep them from staring at our big noses and our huge flapping feet. This fascination – or perhaps horror – was mistaken for affection; and every grimace was interpreted as a Chinese smile.

The Westbetters waved at three passing Chinese. The Chinese fluttered their fingers in imitation.

'They're waving back at us!'

Which was worse – hearing right-wing tourists curse the Russians, or hearing them gush about the Chinese? No one cared about the rotten political systems, but only whether the people smiled at them or not. In a simple and clumsy way the Chinese knew how to manipulate these visitors, but it was so obvious that it was like children making friends with other children.

I walked around for three and a half hours, waiting for the train to return with new wheels.

A plane went overhead, flying west in the clear sky. With glasses of Krug champagne in their hands, the First Class passengers were studying the menu: *parfait* of pheasant and goose-liver, smoked salmon mousse and fresh squid salad, and a *frisée* salad with smoked duck julienne, followed by turbot with prawns and apples, roast rack of lamb, or crab leg and prawn ragout, and someone was saying, 'How is the quail breast today?'

Down here in Inner Mongolia, an old man squatted holding a bowl against his nose and flicking rice grains into his mouth with chopsticks.

If any of the passengers in the plane looked down, they saw nothing more than a light brown land, yellower where the grass was. It was practically all empty space, but I did not know then that empty space is the rarest landscape in China.

We set off again, to cross the plains, and it was a long hot afternoon, with only the merest glimpse of people or animals. I saw camels grazing, and herds of horses, and sparrow-hawks. At the railway stations with Mongolian names – Qagan Teg and Gurban Obo – the buildings were frugally built but freshly painted, with tiled roofs and flared eaves. Chinese travellers were lined up in an orderly way on prearranged spots as the train pulled in, but when the train stopped the people broke ranks and began fighting for the doors. They were dressed differently from the way I had remembered: fewer blue suits, more colour and sun-hats, sun-glasses and bright sweaters, some women in skirts. All of this was new to me, and I wanted to see more; I was glad that I had come. Towards dusk there were hills in the distance, the limit of the province of Inner Mongolia and the beginning of Shanxi.

That provincial border is marked by a section of the Great Wall. We clattered along the Wall for a while and then, in darkness, passed through it. The Wall is broken and sloping and piled up here – a muddy-looking heap of brown bricks and rubble. We had arrived at the big brown city of Datong.

The Chinese guide said, 'We were going to put you up at the Datong Guesthouse, but it is not very clean these days. Now, only Chinese people stay there.'

We were taken to the locomotive works, which was one of those Chinese factories that is so self-contained it is like a city. It was formerly a commune; it had schools, and a hospital, and stores, and a wall around it. It had a hotel, the Datong Locomotive Works Hotel, and that was where we stayed.

After all those weeks of getting there, China seemed shabby and busy and orderly, with great crowds of people, and glaring lights, and the sharp smell of burning coal. It seemed odd for a place seemingly so battered and depleted to have such a buzz. And it was dark and dusty, so that being in Datong was like being in an old movie, in black and white. Chinese clothes were part of the same effect – low hemlines and white blouses and sensible shoes, and men in pin-striped suits and most of them wearing hats. Chinese-made cars were like the black limousines in old gangster movies. And the street-lights were high, on fluted iron lamp-posts, and they weren't very bright. The skyline was all factory chimneys – no sign of the Great Wall. The smoky air and flickering lights made it seem like an old movie, too. But that was Datong.

I fell asleep reading and woke late. The tourists had gone and I was on my own from now on. When I went downstairs breakfast was over, and waiters and waitresses were clearing the table – about ten of them picking up plates. One was eating the left-overs. He was wolfing the bread and hard-boiled eggs that no one had touched. He stopped chewing while I looked around, and then I pretended to be busy and he resumed, stuffing himself and carrying plates and cups. He moved in a rapid scavenging way.

A morning walk which I took intending to see the famous Nine Dragon Screen involved me in detours and then I was fooled and lost. I was deceived by the simple city map into thinking the distances were not so great. But I was much more content looking at half-obliterated slogans which had once said LONG LIVE THE THOUGHTS OF MAO ZEDONG! Large and small, they were everywhere, and there were too many to rub out. But it was clear from the way they had been vandalized – because the Chinese don't vandalize anything ('Love public property' is one of the Five Loves) – that people frankly hated these painted mottoes from the Cultural Revolution.

There were people working by the roadside – tinsmiths, carpenters, people drying beans and washing clothes and processing rags and sorting spinach. And repairing vehicles: it is the commonest sight on a Chinese road, people pumping tyres, or fiddling with engines, or welding an axle; the bus jacked up and the mechanic's legs sticking out from under it.

The yellow smog in Datong was a combination of desert dust and fog and industrial smoke. It is a coal-burning city – one of the largest open-pit mines in China is just outside the city limits. The fog was thick and sulphurous in the early morning, and it made the buildings look ghostly and ancient and the people wraith-like. But the buildings weren't old and the people were well fed and fairly friendly.

The biggest difference between this first Chinese city and all the others that I had seen since West Berlin was that the shops were full of food and goods, and the market was piled high with fruit and vegetables. I kept thinking of the empty shelves and the dented cans in Warsaw, Moscow, Irkutsk and Ulaanbaatar; the women in black shawls carrying string bags and pleading to buy a peck of wrinkled potatoes or six inches of withered sausage. In Moscow I had seen long queues of people – thirty or more to a queue – trying to buy tomatoes from hawkers on the street, because the tomatoes had just arrived, overripe and soft, from the Caucasus; and they were scarce. After all that, China seemed a land of plenty.

The Chinese are the last people in the world still manufacturing spittoons, chamber-pots, treadle sewing-machines, bed-warmers, claw-hammers, 'quill' pens (steel nibs, dunk-and-write), wooden yokes for oxen, iron ploughs, sit-up-and-beg bicycles, and steam engines.

They still make grandfather clocks – the chain-driven mechanical kind that go *tick-tock!* and *bong!* Is this interesting? I think it is, because the Chinese invented the world's first mechanical clock in the late Tang Dynasty. Like many other Chinese inventions, it was forgotten about; they lost the idea, and the clock was reintroduced to China from Europe. The Chinese were the first to make cast iron, and soon after invented the iron plough. Chinese metallurgists were the first to make steel ('great iron'). The Chinese invented the crossbow in the fourth century BC and were still using it in 1895. They were the first to notice that all snowflakes have six sides. They invented the umbrella, the seismograph, phosphorescent paint, the spinning wheel, sliding calipers, porcelain, the magic lantern (or zoetrope), and the stink bomb (one recipe called for fifteen pounds of human shit, as well as arsenic, wolfsbane and Cantharides beetles). They invented the chain pump in the first century AD and are still using it. They made the first kite, 2,000 years before one was flown in Europe. They invented movable type and devised the first printed book – the Buddhist text, the *Diamond Sutra*, in the year AD 868. They had printing presses in the eleventh century, and there is clear evidence that Gutenberg got his technology from the Portuguese who in turn had learned it from the Chinese. They constructed the first suspension bridge and the first bridge with a segmented arch (this first one, built in 610, is still in use). They invented playing-cards, fishing-reels and whisky.

In the year 1192, a Chinese man jumped from a minaret in Guangzhou using a parachute, but the Chinese had been experimenting with parachutes since the second century BC. The Emperor Gao Yang (reigned 550–9) tested 'man-flying kites' – an early form of hang-glider – by throwing condemned prisoners from a tall tower, clinging to bamboo contraptions; one flew for two miles before crash-landing. The Chinese were the first sailors in the world to use rudders; westerners relied on steering-oars until they borrowed the rudder from the Chinese in about 1100. Every schoolboy knows that the Chinese invented paper money, fireworks and lacquer. They were also the first people in the world to use wallpaper (French missionaries brought the wallpaper idea to

Europe from China in the fifteenth century). They went mad with paper. An excavation in Turfan yielded a paper hat, a paper belt, and a paper shoe, from the fifth century AD. I have already mentioned toilet paper. They also made paper curtains and military armour made of paper – its pleats made it impervious to arrows. Paper was not manufactured until the twelfth century in Europe, about 1,500 years after its invention in China. They made the first wheelbarrows, and some of the best Chinese wheelbarrow designs have yet to be used in the west. There is much more. When Professor Needham's *Science and Civilization in China* is complete it will run to twenty-five volumes.

It was the Chinese who came up with the first design of the steam engine in about AD 600. And the Datong Locomotive Works is the last factory in the world that still manufactures steam locomotives. China makes big black choo-choo trains, and not only that – none of the factory is automated. Everything is hand-made, hammered out of iron, from the huge boilers to the little brass whistles. China had always imported its steam locomotives – first from Britain, then from Germany, Japan and Russia. In the late nineteen-fifties, with Soviet help, the Chinese built this factory in Datong, and the first locomotive was produced in 1959. There are now 9,000 workers, turning out three or four engines a month, of what is essentially a nineteenth-century vehicle, with a few refinements. Like the spittoons, the sewing-machines, the washboards, the yokes and the ploughs, these steam engines are built to last. They are the primary means of power in Chinese railways at the moment, and although there is an official plan to phase them out by the year 2000, the Datong Locomotive Works will remain in business. All over the world, sentimental steam railway enthusiasts are using Chinese steam engines, and in some countries – like Thailand and Pakistan – most trains are hauled by Datong engines. There is nothing Chinese about them, though. They are the same gasping locomotives I saw shunting in Medford, Massachusetts, in 1948, when I stood by the tracks and wished I was on board.

The Datong factory was like a vast blacksmith's shop, the sort of noisy, filthy and dangerous factory that existed in the United States in the nineteen-twenties. Because none of it is automated, it is indestructible; if a bomb dropped on it today they could be back at work tomorrow. It is essentially just a complex of sheds, but one that covers a square mile. Men squat in fireboxes, hunched over blowtorches; they crawl in and out of boilers, slam bolts with hammers, drag axles and manoeuvre giant wheels overhead using pulleys. You have to look at the locomotive works very hard to see that it is an assembly line and not pandemonium. And you have to step carefully: there are gaping holes in the floor, and sharp edges, and hot metal; few of the workers wear hard hats or boots. Mostly it is cloth caps and slippers – thousands of frail but nimble workers scampering among hunks of smoking iron to the tune of 'The Anvil Chorus'.

These workers earn 100 *yuan* a month, basic pay – about £25 – but there are bonus and incentive schemes for high productivity.

Mr Tan, a worker who was showing me around, said, 'Workers in higher positions earn more.'

'I thought everyone earned the same.'

'Not any more. The basic pay might be the same, but one of the reforms in China is the bonuses. They vary according to your position, and the kind of work you do, and also to where you live and what prices are like.'

This sliding pay scale was more or less heretical, but it was the way the Chinese economy now operated. I asked Mr Tan if this reform of the pay structure had been successful.

He was very open with me. He shrugged and said, 'Datong is behind in many ways – say, with regard to pay and conditions. This is an out-of-the-way place. There are many things that can be improved here. Other parts of China are much better off, particularly in the south.'

As we talked, donkey carts carried heavy iron fittings through the factory, the donkeys sniffing the fires of the forges and looking miserable but resigned.

Mr Tan gave me more statistics. At best statistics are misleading, but Chinese ones are like hackneyed adjectives – a million of this, two million of that – and ultimately meaningless and improbable.

'Eighty-six blocks of flats,' he said, but so what? The flats are dark and dingy, in bad repair, with coal piles stacked against the kitchen door, and cracked walls, and painted-out slogans, and two beds in every room. The rarest room in China is the one that does not contain a bed.

'This hospital has 130 rooms,' he said. But the hospital is not a pretty place: it is draughty, and not particularly clean, and it is very noisy.

The oddest feature of the Datong Locomotive Works is the portrait of Chairman Mao in the visitors' room. There are very few portraits of Mao on view in China, though another grand Chinese statistic is that there were 70 million Mao portraits hanging at the time of his death in 1976. Deng Xiaoping regards all portraits as feudal and instituted a no-portrait policy in 1981 at a party congress that summed up the mistakes of the Cultural Revolution.

'What did you do with your Mao portraits?' I asked Mr Tan.

'Threw them away.'

'Why didn't you keep them with your souvenirs?'

'Because I didn't want to remember.'

The slogans on the banners in the factory were not political. Many were about safety, and others about working together. One said WORKERS SHOULD GO ALL OUT FOR THE THREE GREATEST GOALS. I asked what these goals were and was told: timing production, so that no work was wasted; keeping the right mental attitude; and increasing productivity. Their virtue was their vagueness. In the past – the recent past – factory slogans had been concerned with Mao-worship and smashing imperialists and their running dogs.

It seemed to me that as this was a machine shop, any machine could be made here. The same technology that produced these boilers and pipes could produce military tanks and cannons.

'That's true,' Mr Tan said. 'But we already have a factory that makes tanks in Datong.'

I did not know whether his telling me this military secret was deliberate candour or simple innocence, but whatever it was I liked him for it; and I asked him more questions.

Mr Tan was about thirty, but looked older. The Chinese look young until their mid twenties and then they begin to look very haggard and beaten. A certain serenity returns to their features when they are in their sixties, and they go on growing more graceful and dignified and become not old but ageless. Mr Tan had been through the Cultural Revolution, and had been a Red Guard in Datong.

'But I was a follower, not a leader.'

'Of course.'

'I'm glad it's over. When Mao died, it ended, but then we had a few more years of uncertainty,' he said. And then glancing around the great clanging factory, he added, 'But there are people on the Central Committee who would like to take over from Deng and run things their way.'

'Is that bad?'

'Yes, because they would set themselves up as dictators.'

'Do people write about this in the newspapers?'

'The papers don't write about democracy. Even the very word "democracy" is regarded as bad. If you say it you're in trouble.'

'How do you know that?'

He smiled and said, 'I used to write for the *Datong Daily*. But they changed my articles and turned them into propaganda. It wasn't what I had written, so I stopped being a reporter.'

'How could you stop, just like that?'

'They stopped me, I mean. I was criticized and given a different job to do with less money. But I don't care. What is the point of writing stories if they are changed when they are published?'

We talked about the rich and the poor – people who stayed in good hotels and people who lived in caves (Shanxi and Gansu provinces were full of cave-dwellers). Mr Tan said there was a big gap, but that you would not necessarily be respected merely because you had money.

'These Chinese people who have money we call "second-hand sellers".' He meant hustlers, pedlars, junk dealers. 'They don't read or go to museums or temples. They have money, that's all.'

I taught Mr Tan the word 'philistine'.

I went to the Yungang Caves outside Datong, where travellers used to draw chalk circles on the beautiful frescoes and Chinese workmen would hack them off the wall and wrap them up; and where another lively business was the beheading of Buddhas. Even so, there are plenty of Buddhas left – and several in the larger caves are as tall as a three-storey building. But there is something predictable about Chinese sightseeing and even the best – which these Buddhist caves were – have been renovated and repainted until all the art is lost. What travellers had begun to destroy by snatching and plundering, the Red Guards finished in the Cultural Revolution, and the only reason the Red Guards were not totally successful in wiping out the sculptures in the Yungang Caves was that there were too many of them. So they survived but they were not quite the same afterward.

The same was true of the Hanging Temple, the 'mid-air monastery', an odd structure built during the northern Wei Dynasty. Its steep stairs and balconies were built against the vertical side of a ravine at Hengshan about forty miles south of Datong. The Chinese flock to it; tourists are encouraged to visit. But it too had been wrecked by Red Guards, and it too had been rebuilt, and a great deal had been lost in the restoration. It looked garish and clumsy and patched.

Sightseeing is one of the more doubtful aspects of travel, and in China it is one of the least rewarding things a traveller can do – primarily a distraction and seldom even an amusement. It has all the boredom and ritual of a pilgrimage and none of the spiritual benefits.

Much more interesting to me on this visit to the Hanging Temple was the Valley of the Lings, a great dry gorge in which most of the Lings lived in caves. They had hollowed out parts of the steep walls where there were ledges, and scooped out passageways, and chopped windows into them. There were mud huts on the floor of the valley, but the rest were terraces of cave dwellings and crudely cut doors and windows in the reddish rock. It looked very strange and primitive, but walking around the place I could see that life was going on as normal – they tended vegetable gardens, they fished, they did their laundry and cooked and aired their mattresses and ran a few shops and had a school and a brickworks. And they were in a dramatic cleft in the mountains and must have known how lucky they were to have this space and this good air.

One of the weirder Chinese statistics is that 35 million Chinese people still live in caves. There is no government programme to remove these troglodytes, and put them into tenements, but there is a scheme to give them better caves. The *China Daily* (19 May 1986) described how a far-sighted architect, Ren Zhenying, had designed 'an improved cave' by making the caverns larger and added bigger windows and doors and ventilators. One model cave had forty-two rooms, and a number of three-bedroom apartments. He was quoted as saying, 'It stays cool in summer and warm in winter, and saves energy and land that could be used for farming.'

It seemed to me a kind of lateral thinking. Why rehouse or resettle these cave-dwellers? The logical solution was to improve their caves. That was very Chinese.

It was a bit like the steam locomotive – the brand-new antiques that they turned out year after year. It was not a bad design – it just looked old-fashioned. In a coal-producing country they were very economical.

If this was a time-warp it was a very reassuring one. My hotel bedroom had a spittoon and a chamber-pot. The armchairs had slip-covers and antimacassars, and the varnished desk was covered by an embroidered cloth, and it held a water jug, a propped-up calendar and a vase of plastic flowers. In the drawer was a small bottle of ink, and a pen-holder with a steel nib. None of it could be called modern but most of it was unbreakable.

It seems comic and perhaps absurd to most westerners; but it is not a joke – not in a society where they fish in rivers using nets designed 2,000 years ago. China has suffered more cataclysms than any other country on earth. And yet it endures and even prospers. I began to think that long after the computers had exploded and the satellites burned out and all the jumbo jets crashed and we had woken from the hi-tech dream, China would be chugging along with choo-choo trains, and ploughing the ancient terraces, and living contentedly in caves, and dunking quill pens in bottles of ink, and writing its history.

3

Night Train Number 90 to Peking

Never mind that their uniforms don't fit, that their caps slip sideways and their toes stick out of their sandals; what most Chinese officials illustrate is how bad-tempered and unbending Chinese bureaucracy is. They are in great contrast to the average person who doesn't wear a uniform, who is fairly flexible and who will probably be willing to make a deal. Such hustlers are found in the Free Market – as the new bazaars are called – and not on China Railways.

The glowering and barking woman at the gate in Datong Station at midnight was exactly like Cerberus. Three minutes before the Lanzhou train pulled out she slammed the entry gate and padlocked it, leaving a group of soldiers and many other latecomers clinging to the bars, and making them miss their train. As a further indignity she switched off the overhead lights of the ticket barrier and left us all in the dark. She would not let me through until the Peking train pulled in. And then she slammed the gate again and made more latecomers watch while I boarded. It is not merely unbending; there is often a lot of sadism in bureaucracy.

It was almost midnight. I found my berth in the sleeping-car and, ignoring the other occupants (was one a woman?), went to bed. At

5.30 in the morning, Chinese bureaucracy rose up again and flung the door open, switched on the lights and demanded the blankets and sheets. I turned over, trying to return to my dream – tacking in a light breeze across Lewis Bay. The sleeping-car attendant in a white pastrycook's hat and apron dug her fingers into my hip and yelled at me to get up.

'The train doesn't arrive until 7.15!'

'Get up and give me the bedding!'

'Let me sleep!'

A young man sitting on the berth opposite said to me, 'They want you to get out of bed. They are folding the sheets.'

'What's the hurry? We won't arrive for almost two hours. I want to sleep.'

The sleeping-car attendant took hold of the blankets and I knew she was going to do the Mongolian trick of snapping the bedding off me in one stroke.

My Chinese was functional and unsubtle. I said to the young man, 'Do me a favour. Translate this, If they're so eager to do a good job, tell them to go clean the toilet. It was so disgusting last night I couldn't use it. The floor's dirty. The windows are dirty. There's no hot water in the thermos jug. What's so important about the blankets?'

He shook his head. He wouldn't translate. He knew – and so did I – that if the blankets and sheets were folded the sleeping-car attendants could go straight home as soon as we arrived in Peking Central Station. They were not paid overtime for folding laundry.

Shhllooopp: she whipped the bedding off me and left me shivering in my blue pyjamas in the pre-dawn darkness.

'I couldn't tell them,' the young man said. 'They wouldn't listen.'

He meant they would lose face. After all, they were only doing their job. His name was Mr Peng. He was reading *Huckleberry Finn* to improve his English. I always softened to people I saw reading books, but I told him that one would not do much for his English. He was twenty-seven, a native of Datong. He was married. His wife was a secretary. He said she was a simple girl – that was what had attracted him to her. They had no children. 'We are only allowed to have one, so we're waiting a little while.'

*

Dawn came up on Peking. It was immediately apparent that this sprawling and countrified capital was turning into a vertical city. It was thick with tall cranes, the heavy twenty-storey variety that are shaped like an upside-down L. I counted sixty of them before we reached Peking Central Station. They were building new blocks of flats, towers, hotels, office buildings. There were overpasses and new tunnels and most of the roads looked recent. The traffic choked some of these streets. The city was bigger, noisier, brighter, more prosperous – it amazed me, because I had seen it in thinner times. And of course I was thinking also of the Russian gloom and Mongolian deprivation and Polish anger; the self-denial and rapacity, the food shortages, the banged-up cars. Peking was being transformed, as if someone had simply sent out a decree saying, 'Build this city.' In a way, that was exactly what had happened. This new mood – this boom – was less than five years old. In Chinese history that is no more than an eye-blink, but it was clear that the city was rising.

That was my first impression – of newness: new taxis, new buildings, clean streets, bright clothes, billboards. It was not a city that looked lived in, but rather one for visitors – tourists and businessmen. There were nine new hotels going up, and more restaurants and department stores. No new theatres, or parks. The new schools specialized in languages and offered courses in tourism; and one of the larger new schools did nothing but train taxi drivers. Some cinemas had reopened but there were no new orchestras. Peking had stopped being an imperial city and had begun to be a tourist attraction. The most disturbing sign of its transformation was that it was full of foreign bankers and accountants.

It is probably true to say that any nation that is passionate about putting up new buildings is equally passionate about pulling old ones down. For 1,000 years or more Peking was surrounded by a high and elaborate wall, with vast pillars and gates, that had made the city into a fortress. In 1963, to make room for some hideous tenements, the wall was knocked down. Its absence has not been particularly lamented. The traditional Chinese compounds they call 'yards' (*siheyuan*), with the wall, the circular moon gate and screen behind it, and the rambling house – these made up the residential sections of Peking. They too are mostly gone – again sacrificed to the tower blocks. The little inns and guesthouses are going or gone, and huge hotels have taken their place – the Holiday Inn and the Sheraton Great Wall are but two of about thirty high-priced hotels. The part of Peking that has not changed at all is the Forbidden City, for even the Chinese know that if they were to pull that down there would be no reason for anyone to visit Peking. And any sentiment the Chinese may have about Tian An Men Square is contradicted by the Kentucky Fried Chicken outlet they have recently installed in the south-west corner, not far from the Mao Zedong Memorial Hall.

That Chinese history is layer upon layer, the present half-obliterating the past, is dramatically evident in the big-character slogans of Chairman Mao's thoughts that have been painted over with Toyota ads or turned into billboards for toothpaste and watches. Just beneath the new car or the computer or the brand name it is often possible to read ALL REACTIONARIES ARE PAPER TIGERS! or WE SHOULD SUPPORT WHATEVER THE ENEMY OPPOSES! There are far too many of these and they are far too boldly inscribed for anyone to do anything but repaint them – and there is usually a reminding remnant that is legible. They are possibly the reason that there are so many billboards and printed slogans of a commercial nature in Peking – it is not that these billboards are in themselves valuable but they are useful in covering up the Mao-worship in six-foot Chinese characters that were known as 'Highest Instruction' (*zuigao zhishi*) – the phrase pertains only to Mao.

I asked Mr Peng why they crossed them out.

'They were just political.'

'Is that bad?'

'They weren't practical.'

But in 1985 a victory celebration after a football game turned into a xenophobic riot in which foreigners were attacked and car windows broken. And the focus for some of the violence was billboards advertising Japanese goods. Subsequently, some of the billboards were quietly removed or modified. On a previous occasion another football victory (China beat Bulgaria) caused a crowd of several thousand Chinese fans to gather late one night in front of the Peking Hotel and chant, 'We beat you! We beat you!'

Then only foreigners stayed in that hotel, which was why it was the focus of the mob's gloating. But now the phrase 'foreign friends' is on everyone's lips.

A nineteenth-century Chinese verse by the poet Yen-shi Chiu-T'u goes:

> Last year we called him the Foreign Devil,
> Now we call him 'Mr Foreigner, sir'.
> We weep over the departed but
> Smile when a new wife takes her place.
> Ah, the affairs of the world are like the turning of a wheel.

Because of a prior arrangement, and because foreign travellers are assigned to hotels, I was at the Yan Xiang Hotel, paying 160 *yuan* (£35) a night. Mr Peng was in what he called a Chinese hotel – it didn't have a name, it had a number – for which he paid three *yuan* (66 pence) a night. This was not unusual. There are Chinese prices and foreigners' prices, a double standard that ranges from restaurants and shops to entrance fees in museums and exhibitions; on buses, in taxis, planes and trains. On the average a foreigner is required to pay three or four times more than a Chinese person. An American of Chinese extraction, who has lived in Boston since birth and speaks no Mandarin, is not classified as a foreigner: overseas Chinese are another category. Businessmen and official visitors are yet another class, with certain privileges.

It is impossible to come across these complicated class distinctions and not feel that in time they will create the kind of conflicts that led to the Cultural Revolution. Mr Peng said, 'Maybe' – because the average wage (100 *yuan* a month) was still too low, bonuses too irregular, and for the first time in its history, the People's Republic was experiencing inflation.

'But I hope it won't happen,' Mr Peng said. 'I think revolution is destructive.'

'If there hadn't been a revolution in China your life would have been rather different.'

'Maybe better; maybe worse,' he said.

I said, 'But can't you say that you've lived through an interesting period of history?'

'Just a little bit of it. Chinese history is enormous. The Cultural Revolution was hardly anything.'

In *The House of Exile*, Nora Waln writes:

I asked what war this was. Shun-ko's husband answered, 'It is not a war. It is just a period. When you are adequately educated in Chinese history you will comprehend. We have these intervals of unrest, sixty to a hundred years in length, between dynasties, throughout the forty-six centuries of our history.

Mr Peng had not been a Red Guard. He was twenty-six, which meant that he was in his early teens during the Cultural Revolution. But he had resisted joining the unit. It had not made him popular.

'To show that I loved Chairman Mao I had to engage in the demonstrations. But my heart wasn't in it. It was regarded as wonderful to wear an armband that showed you were a Red Guard. And the best thing was to be the leader of your Red Guard unit.'

'Who was the leader at your school?'

'A boy called Wei Dong – he gave himself the name, because it's a way of saying "Defender of Mao Zedong". He was a very important boy. He knew all the slogans. He made us say them. It was a strange time. The whole country was in a state of revolution.'

'What happened to Wei Dong?'

'I see him now and then. He is completely changed. He is a teacher. He has children. He's an ordinary worker. That's the worst thing to be – it's so hard. He has very little money and no respect. No more speeches or slogans. No one blames him for what happened, but no one is interested in him either.'

'Don't you think anything was achieved in the Cultural Revolution?'

'No – and a lot was lost. We wasted time. Mao was muddled. His brain was tired. Zhou Enlai could have saved us from it, but he let Mao lead. We really trusted Zhou, and that was why the Qingming Festival in 1976 was a real event. Thousands of people showed up to mourn him. It was spontaneous. But we didn't know what to do. Tian An Men Square was full of people feeling very confused.'

'When did you stop feeling confused?'

'When Deng took over and did away with portraits and opened China's doors,' Mr Peng said.

'Maybe this is just one of those short periods in Chinese history.'

'I hope it's a long period,' Mr Peng said.

Bette Bao Lord, the wife of the American ambassador to China, is a great deal better known than her husband both in America (where her novel *Spring Moon* was a bestseller) and in China (where the book is being filmed). The name Winston Lord seemed so patrician that it was more that of a character in a certain kind of women's fiction; but not Bette Bao Lord's. Her novel was rightly praised as an accurate portrayal of a family caught in the cross-winds of Chinese history. It was set in a period that Mrs Lord observed first-hand. It seemed wonderfully symmetrical that having been born in China and educated and raised in the United States, she had recently returned to China as the ambassador's wife.

With less than a day's notice from me she arranged a lunch party for sixteen people. When I met her this seemed less surprising. She did not strike me as a person to whom anyone had ever said no.

She was slim and had the severe good looks of a Chinese beauty – skin like pale velvet and a lacquered elegance that fashion magazines call devastating. She had the alert and yet contented air of someone who has had everything she has ever wanted, and probably been given it lavishly rather than having had to demand it. Her jet-black hair was yanked back tightly into a knot and stabbed with a stiletto. She wore a stylish white jacket and skirt, a striped blouse and cruel shoes, and large white coral earrings were snapped against the sides of her head like earphones designed by Fabergé. She was so eager to put me at my ease I immediately became tense.

In the steamy May heat of Peking, Mrs Lord was uncommonly energetic. This was her way. Her gusto was a kind of confidence, and she could be hearty in two languages. She was brisk, she laughed loudly and deep in her throat, and she had the very un-Chinese habit of poking my arm, or rapping my knee, or hitting my shoulder, to get my attention or make a point. These would have been exhausting qualities in another person, but in Mrs Lord they were stimulating. I liked being poked in the arm by this glamorous woman.

Once, tapping me, she said (speaking of the importance of planning), 'It's like choosing the right husband or wife – '

I thought this was odd, because I had never regarded marriage as a conscious choice. It was something else: you fell in love and that was it, for better or worse. But she seemed very rational – that was certainly Chinese of her – and I guessed that she had spent her life making the right choices.

She told me she felt very lucky. I imagined that many women must hate her, since she was what most people want to be – a ravishing over-achiever, a little empress in her own right. She told me she was forty-seven. She looked about thirty-five and – because some Chinese faces are unalterable even by time – would probably look that way for a long while.

We talked about publishing. Her career has been blessed – two books, both huge successes. She had been in Peking only six months, and had planned to write a new novel. But running the embassy household, doing menus, dealing with servants and guests and family, had turned her into a sort of Victorian house-mother. To give herself a sense of order she said she was keeping a diary – probably for publication.

'I find myself sitting next to Deng Xiaoping, or being introduced to a visiting head of state, and I think, "I must write this down!" Don't you think that's important?'

'Yes, but people mainly read diaries to discover trivial things and indiscretions. My advice would be: put everything down, don't edit or censor it, and be as indiscreet as possible.'

'Is that what you do?' she said, swiftly crossing her legs and wrapping herself into a querying posture.

'I only keep a diary when I travel,' I said. I did not say that I think diaries are death to writing fiction – trying to remember all that stuff.

'Because travelling is so interesting?'

'No. Because travel writing is a minor form of autobiography.'

And then a woman entered without knocking to say that the guests had arrived.

'They're all party members!' Mrs Lord said confidentially. She was pleased with herself, and who wouldn't be? Out of one billion people, only 44 million are members of the Chinese Communist Party – 4.4 per cent.

These guests were writers and scholars. Most of them had been abroad and nearly all of them spoke English perfectly. Nor were they daunted by the western menu – the soup first, and then the prawns and meatloaf – or the knives and forks. Indeed, one of them told me that not long ago Hu Yaobang the party secretary had advocated knives and forks. Chopsticks were insanitary, Mr Hu maintained, and the Chinese habit of taking food from common dishes was a factor in the spread of germs. Mr Hu frequently made mischievous remarks of this kind. He had also said that Marxism was outdated and that the Han Chinese should perhaps vacate Tibet.

I asked the woman next to me whether she agreed with Mr Hu about chopsticks or anything else.

'I'd like to keep an open mind,' she said. Her accent was extraordinary – not just English, but upper-class English, the intonation of a well-bred headmistress. She sounded like the head of Cheltenham Ladies College and she seemed the sort of woman the English praise by calling her 'a bluestocking'. I was not surprised to hear that she taught at Peking University or that her chief subject was Henry James.

She said she was exasperated by the bad translations of James into Chinese.

'When Caspar Goodwood says to Isabel "Just wait!" they translate it as "Wait a minute" – as if he's going to pop right back, you see. It's very trying, but what can one do?'

I asked her whether the government interfered with her teaching – after all, until recently foreign novels had been regarded as a poisonous bourgeois influence ('sugar-coated bullets').

'The government leaves us alone and lets us get on with the job. It was quite different during the Cultural Revolution,' she said, daintily separating her butterfly prawn from its tail. 'There were loudspeakers on the campus and they were on all the time.'

'Did you hate it?'

'At first, yes. And then I was bored by it. That was the worst of the Cultural Revolution. The boredom. One would wake to the loudspeakers. They would be saying very loudly, "Never forget class struggle." One would brush one's teeth and on the toothbrush was the slogan NEVER FORGET CLASS STRUGGLE. On the wash-basin it said NEVER FORGET CLASS STRUGGLE. Wherever one looked there were slogans. Most people hated them – it was really very insulting. I was thoroughly bored.'

All this in her soft and rather fatigued English accent; and then she spoke up again.

'But there was very little that one could do.'

Xiao Qian, listening quietly to this woman, was a man in his seventies who had spent the years 1939 to 1945 in Britain. Because of the war he had not been able to sail home; but he pointed out that because he had spent those war years in Britain he had seen the British at their best. He was wearing what looked like an old school tie. I asked him whether this was so. He said yes, it was the tie of King's College, Cambridge, where he had read English.

'I don't think of China as being a tie-wearing society,' I said, and I told him a story about a Frenchman I had once met. Had all the violence and turmoil in the sixties changed his way of thinking? I had asked. 'Yes,' he said, '*I no longer wear a cravat.*'

Mr Xiao said, 'People have started wearing them. And of course a tie is often necessary if you travel abroad.'

He had recently been to Singapore, he said.

'I used to teach there,' I said.

'It is an economic miracle,' he said, and smiled, adding, 'and a cultural desert. They have nothing but money. Their temples are like toys to us. They are nothing – they are not even real. Their Prime Minister, Lee Kwan Yew, is an Oriental posing as a westerner. But he is not all bad. For example, he has a Confucian idea of the family in politics. In Singapore, if you take an old person into your household you get a reduction in taxes. There is something Confucian in that. It's a good idea.'

'My students were bullied by the government of Singapore,' I said. 'If they studied English or political science they weren't given scholarships. The government only gave money to students who did economics or business studies – money-making subjects, it was thought. And some of the students at the University of Singapore were informers. Oddly enough, they were looking for

Maoists and reporting on anyone sympathetic to the People's Republic.'

'Now they are quite keen to do business with us,' Mr Xiao said. 'But it is a very severe government. They always watching and listening. People in Singapore are afraid.'

It seemed very odd to hear a comrade in the People's Republic tut-tutting about authoritarianism and fear.

I said, 'But is it so different here in China?'

'Even during our worst times,' he said, 'even during the Cultural Revolution, we did not have these – what do you call these machines that listen to your voice?'

'Bugging devices?'

'Exactly. No listening devices. But in Singapore, before anyone opens his mouth, he feels with his hands under the table to see whether there is a device that is listening.'

He was not drinking, but others were, and downing glasses of wine they grew red-faced and a bit breathless.

A young man next to Mr Xiao asked me what I was doing in China.

'Just travelling around, taking trains,' I said.

'Are you writing a report?'

'Not at all,' I said, and I told him my motto: *Grin like a dog and wander aimlessly*.

He said that was precisely what he enjoyed doing. In fact, somewhat in the manner of Studs Terkel, he was cycling around the country tape-recording people's reminiscences. He was about to publish the transcripts in book form under the title *Chinese Profiles*. He wondered whether there was anything I wished to ask him about the Chinese railways – he said he was an expert. His name was Sang Ye.

I told him that I was particularly looking forward to taking the train from Peking to Urumchi – the longest railway journey in China: four and a half days of mountains and desert.

'They call that train "The Iron Rooster",' he said.

He explained that Iron Rooster (*Tie Gongji*) implied stinginess, because 'a stingy person does not give away even a feather – nor does an iron rooster'. It also meant useless and was part of a larger proverb which included a porcelain crane, a glass rat, and a glazed cat (*ciqi her, boli haozi, liuli mao*). The list didn't include a white elephant but that was what it meant. There was also a bit of word-play with Iron Rooster, because it included a pun on 'engineering' and 'engine'.

But the stingy reference was its real meaning, because until recently this accident-plagued line was run by the Xinjiang government. Technically, Xinjiang is a vast reservation of Uighur people – romantic desert folk with a Mongolian culture quite distinct from the Han Chinese. And this remote railway ministry in the autonomous region would neither surrender control of the railway nor would they maintain it. This was more than I wanted to know about the Iron Rooster, but the name made me more than ever eager to climb aboard.

When lunch was over Mrs Lord invited me to say something. The formal progress of a Chinese banquet depends on little speeches: a word of welcome from the host, followed by something grateful from the guest – that is at the beginning; and afterwards, more formal pleasantries, some toasts, and a very abrupt end. No one lingers, no one sits around and shoots the bull. All the Chinese banquets I attended concluded in a vanishing act.

I made my little speech. I said my thanks and sat down. But Mrs Lord needled me. Hadn't I been to China before? And shouldn't I say something to compare that visit with this?

So I stood up again and I said frankly that even six years ago people had been very reluctant to talk about the Cultural Revolution. It was worse than bad manners: it was unlucky, it marked you, it was a political gesture, it wasn't done. And when they had referred to it they had spoken of it in euphemisms, like the British referring to the Second World War as 'the recent unpleasantness'. But these days people talked about those ten frenzied years, and they had stopped calling it simply the Cultural Revolution but usually prefixed it with the phrase 'so-called' (*suowei*) or renamed it the Ten Years' Turmoil. Surely it was a good thing that people talked about it in a critical way?

'Is that all you've noticed?' Mrs Lord said, encouraging me to continue.

I said that the tourists and business people seemed to constitute a new class and that such privileged and bourgeois people might be demoralizing to the much poorer Chinese.

'We have never taken foreigners seriously,' one of the guests said. He was a man at the end of the table. 'The most-quoted proverb these days is *We can always fool a foreigner*.'

'I think that's a very dangerous proverb,' I said.

Mrs Lord said, 'Why "dangerous"?'

'Because it's not true.'

Mrs Lord said, 'The Chinese don't know what goes on in the hotels – they don't go in.'

'We're not allowed in,' the bluestocking said. 'But no one actually stops you. I went into a big hotel a few months ago. There was a bowling alley and a disco and a bookshop. But I didn't have any Foreign Exchange Certificates, so I couldn't buy anything.'

Someone said, 'I think that the regulation forbidding Chinese from going into tourist hotels is going to change very soon.'

Mrs Lord said, 'My friends talk about this privilege thing. Of course it's a problem. My Chinese friends tend to be pessimistic, but I'm an optimist. I think things will go on improving. And I want to help. I feel I owe it to this country. I've had everything.'

I said, 'Oddly enough, I was affected by the Cultural Revolution. It was the sixties upheaval, and I was in Africa when China was seeking influence there. I read the Thoughts of Mao and the *Peking Review*. I felt like a revolutionary.'

'I had one of those Thoughts of Mao books,' a man said. 'I put it away. I don't know where it is. I suppose I've lost it. You don't actually mean you read it?'

To prove my point, I recited, 'A revolution is not a dinner party' from the *Little Red Book*; and another that I often thought of in my travelling through China: 'Investigation may be likened to the long months of pregnancy, and solving a problem to the day of birth. To investigate a problem is, indeed, to solve it.'

A sigh of exasperation went up.

'He set us back thirty years,' someone said.

'If you go to the inner part of Peking University you'll see a statue of Mao,' one of the scholars said. 'But there aren't many around. And on the base where they once said LONG LIVE THE THOUGHTS OF MAO ZEDONG there is nothing but his name.'

It was not for me to tell them they were out of touch with the thinking of the Central Committee, which had recently met (September, 1986) and passed a resolution which reaffirmed 'the Four Guiding Principles: keeping to the socialist road; upholding the people's democratic dictatorship; upholding the leadership of the Communist Party; and upholding Marxism-Leninism and Mao Zedong Thought'.

But these people at the lunch were part of a class that has always existed in China – the scholar gentry. They were special and a little suspect and set apart. They were important but no emperor had ever really felt easy with them, and Mao had actually tried to cut them down to size and even humiliate them by sending them into the countryside during the Cultural Revolution. It was a philosophy encapsulated in the remark: 'If you think you're so smart you can start shovelling that pig-shit into the wheelbarrow.' And at night these rusticated intellectuals studied the works of Marx and Lenin. It had all worked like a harsh form of aversion therapy, which was why the mood in China was so different now.

'Most of the people in this room would much rather have their child be an underpaid scholar than a rich merchant,' Mrs Lord said. 'That's a fact.'

I felt it would be rude to mention that the choice wasn't exactly that – between being a merchant or an intellectual; not in a country where 900 million people were peasant farmers.

It was obvious that the sixteen card-carrying intellectuals at Mrs Lord's were not typical, and they were westernized enough to like drinking coffee – one of the rarest drinks in China is coffee – and to linger after the meal to talk a little more.

Professor Dong Luoshan had recently translated Orwell's *1984* – he had actually translated it in the year 1984, which seemed wonderfully appropriate. He had also translated Kurt Vonnegut and Saul Bellow into Chinese, but it was Orwell I wanted to talk about.

He said, 'I think it is a very gloomy novel.'

'Did it seem familiar to you?'

'You are speaking of the recent past in China,' he said, with a wink. 'But I tell you the Cultural Revolution was worse. It was much worse.'

'Why don't more people write about it then?'

'We are still trying to understand it, and it is a very painful subject.'

There is a special category of writing about the Cultural Revolution, known as 'wound literature' (*shang-hen wenxue*), so 'painful' was an appropriate word. A popular Chinese writer, Feng Jicai, writes almost exclusively about the Cultural Revolution. But the best book I had read, *The Execution of Mayor Yin*, by Chen Jo-hsi (1977), had not appeared in China.

'Reading *1984* might get people thinking about it,' I said.

Professor Dong inclined his head in a cautioning way and said, 'But most people cannot read it. It is a restricted book – it is *neican* –'

'Restricted' means placing it on a sort of index of books reserved for the exclusive use of people who were sober and trustworthy readers. The average person couldn't read a book that was *neican*, and there was another phrase, *neibu*, for the things they couldn't talk about to foreigners – or at least weren't supposed to. But I seldom found the Chinese cagey; they talked about everything, and usually in a very candid way.

Professor Dong was still talking about *1984* and how only intellectuals could read it. 'It is necessary to have special permission to read such books.'

He said that bookshops and libraries all had an 'inner reference' section. You needed an approved 'passbook' to get in and read this reckless and inflammatory stuff. But he said that in practice most people could read the books because they could be loaned from person to person once they were bought. It was the Chinese intellectuals themselves who limited the circulation of such books. The stiff-necked scholar gentry were not in the habit of loaning the books to slobs, who might get the wrong idea.

The funny thing was that, after all this explanation, I walked into a public library eight months later in the south China port of Xiamen and found a copy of Professor Dong's translation of *1984*. I asked the librarian whether it was freely circulated and she said, 'Yes, of course. Is it any good?'

The really strange and dangerous books, Professor Dong said, were the erotic classics – books like *Jin Ping Mei*, a sort of semi-sexy title meaning *Plum in a Golden Vase*. This particular one was written in the Ming Dynasty – say the fourteenth century – and translations have been available to westerners for a hundred years or more. Clement Egerton's version, done in the thirties, is regarded as one of the best. It concerns the life of a young decadent merchant and his various sexual encounters.

'Do you actually think that book is harmful?'

'Not to me,' Professor Dong said, in the blinkered and superior way that makes Chinese intellectuals the butt of Chinese jokes and the object of a certain amount of party hostility. And he went on, 'To the ordinary reader it is very harmful. You see, Chinese is not explicit. It is full of innuendo. *Jin Ping Mei* is like that. It does not say exactly what is happening, so you imagine all sorts of things. I think it should be restricted.'

I asked Professor Dong what he was doing at the moment, and he said that he had recently compiled a handbook of English phrases the average Chinese would not find in an English dictionary. He gave as examples 'Walter Mittyism' and 'Archie Bunker mentality'.

He asked what I was doing. I said I had just finished a novel set in the near future.

'No one writes about the future in China. We hardly think about it. There is a little science fiction, but nothing about the future.'

'Doesn't anyone think, as Orwell did, that you can comment on the present by writing about the future?'

He said, 'We have a saying, "Use the past to criticize the present." That is a Chinese preoccupation. There was a mayor in Peking who wrote a play about an obscure figure during the Ming period. People were very shocked. "You are criticizing Mao!" they said. That mayor was removed very soon after. And he disappeared.'

'Had he been criticizing Mao?'

'Of course – yes!'

About half the guests left, but the ones that stayed behind wanted to talk about religion. I said it was not my favourite subject but I would try to answer their questions. Were people in America religious? Why was there a sense of religion in Steinbeck and

Faulkner and not in any present-day writers? They were familiar with many British and American authors, but their way of mentioning book titles suggested to me that they might have read them in translation: Dickens's *A Story about Two Places* and *Difficult Years*, Hawthorne's *The Red Letter*, Steinbeck's *Angry Grapes*, and so forth. I recommended Sinclair Lewis, having just read him on the train. And I asked them about their own writing.

'We are sick of politics,' one of the young writers said. 'Our writers have been dealing only with politics. People think of Chinese writers as obsessed with it. But that is changing. We want to write about other things. But we need to find an audience.'

I said I didn't think they would have any difficulty finding an audience, because politics and politicians were so boring. 'If you write about something else you'll have many readers.'

'But we have to please the first reader,' another man said, and stuck a finger in the air.

'He means the political censor,' someone said.

It seemed to me that there was a certain hypocrisy in believing in censorship for the lower orders but not for intellectuals, but I didn't want to intimidate them by questioning their logic. I told them that Henry Miller had been banned in England and America until the nineteen-sixties, and the *Lady Chatterley* trial was in 1960. So much for the enlightenment in the west.

'We are improving,' one of the scholars said. 'We have just published a series of volumes on the economics of Keynes.'

I said that perhaps John Maynard Keynes to them was like D. H. Lawrence for us, and I tried to imagine what forbidden, dark, brooding supply-side economics might be like.

I was sobered up just before I left Mrs Lord's when a young man approached me and said he heard that I was interested in Chinese railways.

'There is a certain railway line that you should see,' he said. 'It is called "Death Road". During the Cultural Revolution people used to kill themselves on this section of track. One person a day, and sometimes more, jumped in front of the train. In those days the buildings in Peking weren't very tall – you couldn't kill yourself by jumping out of the window of a bungalow. So they chose the train, because they were too poor to buy poison.'

Also, if you were killed by a train China Railways was obliged to bury you, free of charge.

'A few years ago, we used to see the tourists and say, "Americans are so old",' a man told me in Peking. And it was true: only old people went to China then, because it was very expensive and took time, and being a wealthy retiree helped if you wanted to go. But nowadays everyone went. There were tycoons, budget travellers, freeloaders, cyclists, tourists, archaeologists and prospective students of kung fu. In Peking every one of them visited the Great Wall, the Forbidden City, the Summer Palace, the Temple of Heaven and the Friendship Store. I had seen these sights on my previous trip. Very interesting, I thought; very big, too. But I had come to China to find things that were unspectacular.

I went to Death Road. It was immediately clear why it had been chosen for suicides: it was a curve in the line hidden by a footbridge, with a dusty culvert on either side. It was possible to see where people jumped and where they fell. Apart from that it seemed an ordinary place, just a section of track, but in its ordinariness lay all of its horror.

Then I decided to go to the big foreign language bookshop on Wangfujing Street to see if Professor Dong's book of English phrases was available. It was not, but I was given *A Dictionary of New and Difficult English Words*. In the *B*s I found *balled*, *ball-up*, *ballsy*, *ballahoo* (sic) and *banged*, and under *shit* the expression I *feel shitty in my body* – a newly minted American colloquialism. But most of the words were chemical compounds – *methyloxylate, sulphur dioxide*, and their Chinese equivalents.

An elderly Chinese man was perusing a copy.

'It is not much use to me,' he said, 'because I usually translate music theory and this is very scientific. You probably don't know many of these words.'

'Some of them look familiar,' I said.

His name was Zhang Mei. He was a musician, adept at several instruments including the piano; a composer, a conductor, and lately a music teacher. He also sang, he said – he was a baritone. As well as Chinese music he played and sang Schubert ('very sad'), Verdi and Handel ('my personal favourite'). He also liked Stephen

Foster. He said that Foster was one of the most popular composers in China.

'When I hear "Beautiful Dreamer" I feel like weeping,' I said.

'I prefer Handel,' Mr Zhang said.

He was small and frail and rather bent over, but when I said I was going for a walk he offered to come with me. He looked older than his years – he was seventy-five – but he walked nimbly. He said he had just seen his son off at Peking Central Station – the son was taking the train to Paris, to study singing, but he was not stopping on the way. I said, 'It's a nine-day trip,' but Mr Zhang said, 'He has a berth – he can sleep – he's very lucky.'

I asked him whether the government disapproved of western music. He said no, not these days. Later I found out that there were official directives about such matters; for example, on 7 March 1977 the party sent forth a decree lifting a ban on the playing of Beethoven's music.

Mr Zhang had never studied music. He said, 'I am self-taught. I was in the New Fourth Army against the Japanese. I led the chorus, forty men. That was to rouse the troops. Also I wrote music and composed songs.'

I asked him for an example.

'In the town of Huangzhou in Jiangsu Province we won an important battle. I commemorated it by writing "Baking The Cakes".'

He explained that it was a patriotic song based on people baking a particular kind of cake, called *shao bing*. They served them when the soldiers went off to battle and they welcomed the soldiers back with more cakes.

I said, 'Didn't you write songs about the Japanese as evil little fiends?'

'Oh, yes,' Mr Zhang said. 'In the songs we called them all sorts of names. Ghosts. Robbers. Rapists. Because they were robbing and raping. If you say "rapist" most people will know immediately that you're talking about a Japanese, even now.'

'Were they ghosts?'

He laughed. 'Ghosts are *guizi*. They are cruel. Well, not exactly cruel. They are abominable.'

I liked him. I asked him whether he was hungry. He said yes, but he also said he had very bad digestion. Nevertheless, we went to a restaurant and he ordered an enormous amount of food. It cost 33 *yuan* and we ate very little of it. He paid for it in ordinary Chinese money (*Renminbi*) and then I gave him the equivalent in Foreign Exchange Certificates, which were like hard currency. It was quite a transaction but it occurred to me that my changing this money was the whole point of his ordering this expensive meal.

He said he had chosen the restaurant because it was Cantonese, and so was he. While we were eating he overheard four Cantonese men speaking about their bill – their meal had come to 35 *yuan*.

'They must be merchants to have paid so much for their meal,' he said. He asked them if this was so, but they told him they worked in a nearby government office.

'Times are changing,' he said. As a veteran he had various pensions and subsidies that came to 271 *yuan* a month. He said he felt fairly well-off.

I asked him what he thought of so many Japanese tourists visiting China after they had caused so much misery for the Chinese by occupying the country and fighting so tenaciously.

'We have forgotten all that. It is better to forget. Anyway, Chairman Mao said, "Most foreigners are good – only a few are bad."'

'I wonder what Chairman Mao would say if he saw what was taking place in Peking right now.'

Mr Zhang said, 'He would be interested. Certainly surprised.'

'He might not like it.'

'He would have to like it. The facts would teach him. He could not deny it.'

He said what most people had told me, that Mao in old age was senile. After 1957, Mao was not the same. He kept making mistakes and was easily misled by Lin Biao (China's Trotsky) and the Gang of Four.

'People worshipped him. It was very bad. He did not encourage it but he tolerated it.'

I asked Mr Zhang whether he was optimistic about the changes in China.

'Yes,' he said. 'Things are much better. We should have more money to spend, but if we tighten our belts for a few years I think we'll see some results.'

'Don't you think there could be a change for the worse when Deng dies?'

'No. He has already chosen his successors.'

'So you don't see any problems?'

'Overpopulation is a problem. Traffic is a problem – already we have too many cars. We have to manage that. But we are doing well in many areas, like agriculture.'

He said he liked what was happening to China. Chinese history was long, but it had distinct phases. This was a very tiny part of it and it might be years before we could assess it. That reminded me of Mao's reply when someone had asked him about the French Revolution – what did he think of it? 'It is too early to say,' Mao said.

Mr Zhang then told me some of his war stories, as we strolled down Wangfujing. He had been a translator for General Chen-yi who, in April 1946, had a top-level meeting with an American general whose name he could not remember. Liu Shaoqi (later chairman of the People's Republic and much later tortured to death by Red Guards) was also present at this meeting.

'The American general gave a carton of Camel cigarettes to General Chen-yi, and some chocolates to Liu Shaoqi, and a box of rations to me.

'"We are in Shandong," General Chen-yi said. "We have many fruit trees here. You have my permission to encourage Americans to open a fruit-canning factory here." But they didn't accept the invitation.

'Then I gave them all a shock. I shook hands with the American general. The American translator did not dare to shake hands with General Chen-yi. Afterwards these Americans, who were members of UNRRA [United Nations Relief and Rehabilitation Administration] said to me, "You're very progressive, comrade."

'"All men are equal," I said.'

He was a nice man, and before we parted he said, 'The food at that restaurant wasn't very good, but I like this conversation. When you come back to Peking come to my house and have some real Chinese food.'

*

From the train Peking had looked impressive: a city on the rise, cranes everywhere, and workmen scrambling across girders, and the thump of pile-drivers going *Zhong-guo! Zhong-guo!*

But when I went a little closer and walked around them, these new tenements looked very shaky. Some were made as if with a large-scale version of children's blocks, or put together out of three-room modules – a sort of gigantic building-puzzle kit. And it was clear why these prefab methods were being used. When a structure was put up from scratch, brick by brick, the windows were wonky and the doors weren't square and there were bulges in the walls, and the whole thing had a hand-made look that the kinder architects call 'the vernacular style'.

'No one knows how long they'll last,' an American in Peking told me. 'They might turn out to be like those Hong Kong buildings that were put up with spit and sawdust and fell down about a year later.'

'Why do you think that?' I asked.

'Because most of them are being put up by people from Hong Kong.'

Certainly the development called the Hua Guofeng Wall is beginning to crack. It is a hideous stretch of flats and tower blocks that was put up as a prestige project by Mr Hua before he was politically out-manoeuvred by Mr Deng. The buildings are not only mismatched and cracked and stained, but also – only seven years old – have begun to fall down.

I nosed around a tall block of flats and fell into conversation with Mr Zheng Douwan on the ninth floor. He said that everything was fine at the moment, but he was tentative and I knew there was more to say.

'Is it always fine?' I asked.

'Not in the summer,' he said. 'The water-table is so low in Peking that the pressure is bad. We can only get water as high as the fifth floor. This is a fifteen-storey building, so the people on the upper ten floors have to get water in buckets.'

Droughts and water shortages are greatly feared in Peking, he told me: for the past six years the rainfall had been way below average and the outlook this year was not good. (In the event, very little rain fell, though buildings continued to rise.)

Mr Zheng said, 'From the bath point of view it's like England in the thirties. There is no hot water in any of these flats. If you want a bath you heat a kettle and pour it into a tin bathtub. It is very inconvenient, but I don't complain because that is how everyone lives.'

But not tourists, not high party officials, and not the new classes of people with money – taxi drivers and some traders. In 1980 there were three taxi companies in Peking; now there are 230, with 14,000 taxis. All are controlled by the government or by official agencies, but the drivers do well out of it because the people who take taxis are generally foreigners and they pay in Foreign Exchange Certificates.

The Free Market (*ziyou shichang*) allows anyone to do business and keep the profits. This was one of Deng's reforms, and it is the reason why factory workers are often very cross – and why they demand high bonuses and complain about inflation. The street traders in the Free Market can quite easily earn five times a factory worker's salary, and after an informal survey of the hawkers and traders in various Peking markets I figured their monthly earnings to be between 500 and 700 *yuan* – enough to buy the Big Three.

One market woman told me, 'What people used to want were a bicycle, a radio and a gas stove. Now the Big Three are a refrigerator, a cassette machine and a colour television.'

Some of the markets are operated by retired factory workers who simply want a friendly place to go during the day. They say things like 'I've always been interested by old beads and pots,' and they have the flea-market mentality that is familiar to anyone from Cape Cod. They love talking about the bits of peculiar junk they've accumulated and, being pensioners, are not really doing this for a living. These traders are not to be confused with the people who have been doing business in the same place for years – the specialists in birds, or fish, or herbs. In most Chinese cities, the Bird Market is a specific location and may have been unchanged for hundreds of years.

Flea market seemed to me an appropriate comparison, since that was how most people pronounced it. I saw an opium pipe on one little stall. It was about eighteen inches long, with a silver bowl and a jade mouthpiece.

'That's a genuine old piece. Forty *yuan* and worth every bit of it. Take it away.'

'I'll give you twenty,' I said.

'Listen, if you weren't with this Chinese man I would have written "120" on a piece of paper and said "Take it or leave it".'

'All right, twenty-five.'

He pretended he hadn't heard me. He said, 'The interesting thing about this pipe is its mouthpiece. See how strong it is?' He banged it against the table-top. 'A man would ride his horse with this hanging by his side. If he saw a thief, or if someone attacked him, he would bop him on the head with it. See, use it like a club – bop! bop!'

'Thirty.'

'The bowl is real silver. This is a hundred years old. I've been collecting these pipes my whole life. I worked in a shoe factory. I'm retired! I don't have to sell you this pipe, but you're a foreigner and I want to do you a favour.'

'Thirty is my highest offer.'

'This is an antique, comrade. It's a collector's item. It's a pipe. It's a weapon. Take it.'

'OK, thirty-five.'

'Fine. It's yours. Shall I wrap it up? Here' – he said, taking out an old copy of *The People's Daily*, and folding the pipe into it – 'serves two functions. Wrapping paper and afterwards you can read it.'

I had stopped at that Free Market on my way to the bath-house. Because of what Mr Zheng had told me about the inconvenience of bathing I had enquired and found out that Peking was full of public bath-houses – about thirty of them, subsidized by the government. They are one of the cheapest outings in China: for 60 *fen* (10 pence) a person is admitted and given a piece of soap, a towel and a bed; and he is allowed to stay all day, washing himself in the steamy public pool and resting.

The one I found was called Xing Hua Yuan. It was open from 8.30 in the morning until 8.00 at night. Many people who use it are travellers who have just arrived in Peking after a long journey and want to look presentable for their friends and relatives – and of course who don't want to impose on them for a bath.

The beds were in little cubicles, and men wrapped in towels were resting or walking around talking. It was like a Roman bath – social, with the scalded Chinese, pinkish in the heat, sloshing themselves and yelling at each other in a friendly way. It was also possible to get a private room, for about double the ordinary rate.

I was thinking how Roman and Victorian the bath-house looked (there was a women's bath-house next door), how useful for travellers and bathless residents, how like a club it was and how congenial, when a homosexual Chinese man set me straight.

'Most people go there to take a bath,' he said. 'But it is also a good place to go if you want to meet a boy and do things with him.'

'What sort of things?'

He didn't flinch. He said, 'One day I was in Xing Hua Yuan and saw two men in a private room, and one had the other one's cock in his mouth. That sort of thing.'

A few days later I was walking down the street, and a young Chinese girl approached me and said hallo. She fell into step next to me and before we had gone thirty yards she slipped her arm into mine and off we went, like a pair of old-fashioned lovers.

She was leading the way. I liked not having the slightest idea of what was going to happen next.

At first I thought she might be lame, because she had caught hold of me and held on tightly. But she was walking very briskly. 'Where are we going?' I asked.

She smiled beguilingly and led me on. When we passed the Friendship Store she steered me in, and at the door she began to hug me. She was still hugging in a sort of newly wed's embrace as we looked at chairs ('These look comfortable') and crockery ('Don't you think they have anything cheaper?'). This seemed very pleasant. I had no idea what I would say if I met someone I knew, but it hardly mattered.

I said, 'What is your honourable surname?'

'Ma,' she said, and giggled. There are so many different *Ma*'s in Chinese that a nineteen-word tongue-twister has been made from them.

We looked at the tea section. They had no peppermint tea – indeed, had never heard of it.

'I have never tasted it,' Miss Ma said.

Or perhaps Mrs Ma, because a moment later she let go of me and ran ahead and embraced a young Chinese man. He was not surprised to see her. I assumed they had arranged to meet. The trouble was that, being an ordinary comrade, she felt she would have been stopped from entering this store unless she was in the company of a foreigner.

What disturbed me was that her affection towards me had seemed unforced. In a split second I was forgotten: she didn't look back.

I had been on my way to meet a Chinese teacher named Chen. When I told him what had happened he said, 'The security guards can be very harsh with us sometimes.'

Still, that didn't bother the importuning money-changers who lurked near the tourist hang-outs pestering foreigners to change hard currency into local currency, offering about 20 per cent more than the official rate. They sidled up and said, 'Shansh marnie?'

I said to Chen that I did not understand why so many years of the Cultural Revolution hadn't made people more socially and politically aware. A few years ago it was 'Serve the people,' and now it was 'Change money?'

Chen said that it was because of the Cultural Revolution that people had started a free-for-all, because that political convulsion had discredited politicians.

He said, 'The so-called Cultural Revolution was wonderful in teaching us never to follow blindly. Now we will never trust what politicians say.'

Chen and I were drinking tea at a stall. He held up his white cup.

He said, 'If Mao said, "This is black," we would all agree and say, "Very black." Now we'd never do that. A spokesman in the government said recently "The Japanese are our friends." Everyone laughed. The Japanese – let's be frank – are no one's friends.'

I asked him whether he felt humiliated by the memory of the Cultural Revolution.

'That's the word – humiliated. So many of the Red Guards who went to the countryside got married there, gave up being intellectuals, and became farmers. Now they can't come back – and they want to. It would be a loss of face to come back.'

'Were you a Red Guard?'

'Yes,' he said promptly. 'School three days, learning from a peasant farmer the other three days, and reading the Thoughts of Mao on our day off. We harvested and planted rice. It's a good thing I was young, because I didn't take it very seriously. I treated it like a game. But it was no game.'

He went on to say that he was surprised by how liberated the young people were these days in Peking. They criticized the party. They talked about democracy and free speech. He said, 'I'm amazed by some of the things they say.'

'In the past,' he said, 'the intellectuals and the scholars were discredited. No one really wanted to go to school, and only the secure party officials advanced. You had a choice of being a worker or a peasant.'

'What do people want now?'

'Now that we are no longer judged by our political consciousness people have begun to be fanatical about education. That's the biggest single change in this country.'

'But these former Red Guards and the refugees from the Cultural Revolution – surely they're out of school.'

'No,' Chen said. 'There's a whole army of night-school students.'

I wanted to leave for Shanghai and then to rattle around China on trains as the mood took me. But, inspired by Chen, before I set off I decided to offer my services as a night-school teacher, just to see whether what Chen had said was true. I took classes at the Peking Sun Yatsen Spare-Time School, which was housed in a big, gloomy high school in central Peking. My subject was English, which was the most popular subject in the school; but the students – there were 3,000 of them – also studied business methods, typing, accounting and computer science. One of the computer teachers was from the United States, but I didn't meet him.

I felt a sort of giddy depression at the sight of so many students toiling in the semi-darkness of this haunted-looking building. The light was poor, the chalk squeaked, the desks creaked, the textbooks were greasy and frayed, and the dictionaries were crumbling. The youngest student was eight, the oldest seventy-four. All of them worked during the day, if not at a salary-paying job then at an impromptu stall at the Free Market, boosting cassette tapes, or toys, or clothes that were sent up from Canton, where they had been made cheaply – there was a 30 per cent mark-up on clothes, but even so they were very cheap.

I taught from a book called *Modern American English*.

'You're lucky to have me. I'm a modern American and I speak English,' I said. They thought this was incredibly funny.

I was filling in for their regular teacher, Miss Bao, whose mother was being treated for hypertension at the Peking Capital Hospital near the duck restaurant (thus its name 'The Sick Duck').

It took us three days to deal with the lesson about health care.

'The cost of health care in the United States is truly staggering,' the text ran.

'Excuse me,' Miss Lin said, 'what is "glaucoma"?'

'Excuse me,' Mr Zhao said, 'what is "Blue Cross"?'

'Excuse me,' Mr Li said, 'but some weeks ago your president ordered the bombing of Libya. Did you agree with that?'

I said no, and explained why. And then I asked them whether they agreed with everything their government did. They said no, and giggled nervously, but didn't elaborate.

Each night the students gathered in the twilight, and then they sat sleepily in the hot dusty classrooms for two hours; and they went home in the dark.

When I finished my stint I made a farewell speech.

'People always tell you that night school is a good thing,' I said. 'But they are the same people who go home after a day's work, and eat, and snooze, and listen to the radio. You students are doing one of the hardest things in the world – studying at night, when you're tired. It's hard to remember things when you're tired. And everyone else is resting. Doing this and also doing a job is like having two jobs.'

This struck a responsive chord. They nodded and urged me to continue.

'You may get discouraged and wonder why it's so hard for you to study at night school,' I said. 'Believe me, it's hard for everyone. It takes courage to do it. I am very proud of you, and you should be proud. If you weren't tough you wouldn't be here. I wish you all the very best of luck.'

They applauded softly and, because we had overstayed the time, they were shooed into the night by the caretaker who wanted to lock the place. On the page the night-school folk might seem a little dim and wraith-like, eagerly waiting to become substantial in daylight, but with no vice or peccadillo to give them colour. What can one do except to say that they are worthy and that they are doing all they can to find their way through the Chinese mob? It is always difficult for a writer to make virtuous people interesting.

4

The Shanghai Express

But even though that's true – that it is difficult to make virtuous people interesting – it is also true that it is fairly easy to make vicious people memorable, and sometimes fascinating. It was not just those folks in the flesh – the short buttocky young man and his androgynous bride on the Shanghai Express, but all those hustlers at Peking Station, pestering travellers to use their hotels or their taxis or to eat at their restaurants. It is not enough that the Chinese have relaxed the ban on commercial advertising; they are not content with putting up a billboard or a sign. They tend to the personal touch – buttonholing Chinese tourists, badgering yokels who have just arrived from distant Gansu, yelling into megaphones, wagging banners in their faces, and installing screaming jingles and advertisements on the loudspeakers in the trains themselves. And to complete my study of Chinese vices, I had chosen as reading material the erotic novel that had been whispered about in Peking, *Jin Ping Mei*, also known as *The Golden Lotus*. It had been banned in China since the Ming Dynasty, and it seemed there was no higher recommendation than that. From its earliest pages it was a ruthless novel, and it was also graphically sexual. The perfect book for the Shanghai Express – or maybe for a whole trip through China, since it was about 2,000 pages long.

This little fat fellow and his skinny wife slept in the berth just above my head. He filled the space and she curled about him like a wood shaving. She was just as thin and delicate and she was the colour of newly planed wood. They chattered and smooched. He was from Singapore, she was from Hong Kong; he was a wise-guy, one of the new breed of humourless computer people, who plug themselves into their machines and begin to resemble their mainframe – his big bum looked like part of a console. And she was always fluttering and giggling; she was dizzy, didn't know anything, couldn't cook, didn't even speak English in spite of having grown up in a British colony – didn't speak Mandarin – but what did it matter, as long as fatso paid the bills and bought trinkets for her. His name was Ding and he was always pushing his chubby face into her.

The fourth person – just across from me, on the other side of the folding table and the hot-water jug – was an old woman, about seventy-odd, whose luggage consisted of a small plastic shopping-bag, a basket of apples and a jam-jar half-full of soggy tea-leaves. She unscrewed the lid, filled it with hot water from the jug and then blew and slurped in a dainty way.

In the upper berth, the Chinese man was murmuring to his snickering bride.

This situation reminded me of a vicious thrilling story I had once planned to write, about a very near-sighted old terror who always sat nagging about damnation while her conniving daughter and her boyfriend made love across the room in a chair, the girl on his lap, like a melon on a knife – and all the while the old woman believed she was making a terrific impression.

Indeed, Ding in the upper berth reminded me even more strongly of the book I was reading, the *Jin Ping Mei*. Where was the innuendo and subtlety I had been told about? This was one of the most sexually explicit novels I'd ever come across. I had just finished an episode in which the central character, Hsi-mên, reclining with one of his many women, throws plums between her parted legs, and the third plum comes to rest against her vulva. He chafes her with it and presses it into her vagina, until she has an orgasm; and then he eats that plum.

'Want some candy?' asked the fat man in the upper berth, and offered me some Chinese chocolate.

It was almost midnight: he was also guzzling milk, and he had not stopped tickling his very thin wife. They seemed to me amazingly active for that time of night and I wondered whether they were honeymooners.

I took some candy to be friendly, but the old woman refused. She looked tearful, but she wasn't unhappy. There is a certain Chinese face that looks grief-stricken – swollen eyes and a sad compressed mouth. Sometimes I saw a man and I imagined that he had just been sobbing. But no, it was just that face – maybe he was from Guangdong. The old woman had that look. She lay down and went to sleep, and now asleep – pale and motionless – it was as though she were either dead or dying.

The young woman swung across the ceiling into her own berth, and her fat little husband went after her. She laughed and dived into the berth above me. Was this going to go on all night? They were dressed in the skin-tight clothes that the Chinese had begun to wear, perhaps as a reaction against the baggy suits that had been forced upon them for the past thirty-five years.

'You can keep the light on,' he said. 'We're all right.'

But I was falling asleep over my book. I finished a chapter, marvelling at its rowdiness, and then switched off the compartment light.

There was a thud: the man hoisting himself into his wife's berth.

I was awakened in the night by sounds that reached me from the upper berth. They began like the rustle of curtains, and then a sudden tumbling motion – the thrashing of a body in a bed – and then sucking and swallowing noises, as of someone working on a piece of candy. There was a whisper. It was so low I could not say whether it was the man or the pretty woman – the word 'No . . . no . . . no . . . no,' repeated in a breathless yes-like way, '*Bu . . . bu . . . bu . . . bu.*'

It went on for a long while, sometimes very slowly, as the passing stations flashed through the parted curtains. The sounds aroused me, and then when I was wide-awake they made me completely objective. I felt like a ghost, which is the usual condition of a writer. I was hollow and insubstantial, hovering between the old woman and the lovers.

At dawn we left Shandong Province, which was the setting of the steamy Chinese novel I was reading. It was a happy blend of sex, wisdom and fine writing. Here is the first glimpse the priapic Hsi-mên has of the discontented housewife (and soon to be his mistress), Golden Lotus:

> Her hair was black as a raven's plumage; her eyebrows mobile as the kingfisher and as curved as the new moon. Her almond eyes were clear and cool, and her cherry lips most inviting . . . Her face had the delicate roundness of a silver bowl. As for her body, it was as light as a flower, and her fingers as slender as the tender shoots of a young onion. Her waist was as narrow as the willow, and her white belly yielding and plump. Her feet were small and tapering; her breasts soft and luscious. One other thing there was, black-fringed, grasping, dainty and fresh, but the name of that I may not tell . . . it had all the fragrance and tenderness of fresh-made pastry, the softness and appearance of a new-made pie.

Those tiny feet are interesting. In another chapter, Hsi-mên is beguiled by the sight of another woman's bound feet – the so-called 'lily-feet'.

> Old woman Hsueh found an opportunity to lift Mistress Meng's skirt slightly, displaying her exquisite feet, three inches long and no wider than a thumb . . .

I mention this because after we left Shandong and crossed the Grand Canal (*Da Yunhe*) we came to the city of Xuzhou (formerly Tongshan) and I saw an old woman with small stumpy feet on the platform, and she was walking painfully on these deformities that had once been thought to be so ravishing.

It was at Xuzhou in the yellow light of early morning that I saw the first real greenery since leaving London over a month before – fields of ripening rice, and young trees in leaf by the roadside, and large blowing poplars. It was the flat plain of eastern China, once a conglomeration of communes and now a region of smallholdings – an immensity of vegetables, cabbage as far as the eye could see, with big black pigs balanced neatly on their trotters in the foreground. I saw puddles and streams, and farmers ploughing with tractors or bullocks, and people carrying heavy loads with a yoke-stick and a pair of baskets; white swimming ducks and fluttering geese, a small girl in a blue tunic sitting astride a buffalo, and field-workers sleeping off their breakfast against an embankment like drunken peasants in a Flemish painting. And there was a dark sow so heavily pregnant that her udders grazed the dusty earth of the farmyard as she plodded.

Some rice was already being harvested. China is proud – as well it should be – of the fact that it not only feeds itself but for the first time in its history it now exports more grain than it imports (generally speaking it sells rice and buys wheat). This activity is dramatized by the fact that for the past few years field-workers have begun to wear bright clothes – and so they are highly visible as they hoe and harvest. From time to time, however, the rigid thing you take to be a scarecrow turns out to be a comrade either leaning on his shovel or practising *wushu* or *tai-chi* with his arms stuck out.

A few hours later the train pulled into Bengbu, a railway junction in the middle of Anhui Province. Our train was needed there for a little while, because a movie scene was being shot on Bengbu Station – a young man and woman seeing someone off on our train, probably an irritating relative. A great crowd had gathered to watch the action, and the film crew and the railway police struggled to shift the mob out of the shot. There was no rough stuff. Everyone – even the police – was interested in the movie. There was no pushing, no anger; and I was impressed by the good humour. But unless they had a brilliant editor, I was sure the result would show the two actors waving goodbye and being watched by 2,000 goggling Chinese.

In any event there was only one take. When the Shanghai Express pulled out of Bengbu that was the end of the shot.

Then we were in the green fields again. I was sure that the main difference between this visit and my previous one (six years earlier I had sailed down the Yangtze) was that last time I had come in the middle of winter, when everything had been bleak. Then, a Chinese landscape seemed to me to be composed of rain, smoke, fog; and collapsing houses on a muddy road; and people with their hands shoved into their sleeves; and all those fat-faced pictures of Mao on the wall. And whenever I asked someone a question the answer was always either 'Maybe' or 'You think so?'

Spring and half a dozen years seemed to have made a significant difference. Because China is so intensively agricultural, spring is splendid all over the country. It is impossible to see crops being planted, and weeded, and harvested, and not feel optimistic. The country was greener, leafier, visibly cheerier and more hopeful. It was not an illusion, this new cycle of Cathay. If people seemed a little impatient it was perhaps because they knew well that in Chinese terms a cycle lasts sixty years. Lynn Pan began her book about recent events in China by describing what a cycle means in Chinese terms, and then she became specific: 'In June 1981 the Chinese Communist Party, founded at a secret meeting in Shanghai in 1921, completed its first cycle of sixty and began on its next.' It was also in June 1981 that Deng Xiaoping was made Number One (apart from being head of the Politburo he has no real title) and opened China's doors – and then the west hurried in. Only a few years had passed, but the result was obvious. Nothing is more conspicuous than something that has been westernized.

The passengers mobbed the corridors and hogged the windows just after 11.00, and when I asked what was up they said we would be crossing the Yangtze river soon. But they didn't call it that – the word 'Yangtze' hardly exists in Chinese – they called it *Chang Jiang*, the Long River. Crossing it is an event, because it is China's equator, the north–south divide. The Chinese on the north are different from the Chinese on the south. In the north, the Chinese say, they are imperious, quarrelsome, rather aloof, political, proud noodle-eaters; and across the river they are talkative, friendly, complacent, dark, sloppy, commercial-minded and materialistic rice-eaters.

The river is wide, sluggish and brown at this point – the city of Nanjing. The bridge over the river is a famous landmark, because half-way through its construction the Russians pulled out, believing the Chinese could not possibly finish it themselves; but they did, and it remains one of the few modern engineering feats in China that is actually pleasing to the eye. Beneath its leaping spans were the Yangtze boats – like a whole history of Chinese river-boats, every style and size, from the sampans and dugouts to the junks and river-steamers – these last belong to the East Is Red fleet that sails the 1,500 miles from Chongqing to Shanghai.

I went on reading the *Jin Ping Mei*, marvelling at its blend of manners, delicacy and smut. What a shame it was still banned in China after five centuries. Truly, if the Chinese were allowed to read it, I felt, they would discover a great deal about themselves. I did not believe they would be morally undermined by this stuff, and yet it would be a real thrill as well as a revelation.

The proof that it was pornography was its feeble pretence of being a morality tale. After well over 1,000 pages of sexual acrobatics – and detailed descriptions of aphrodisiacs, potions, pills, silver clasps, love rings and harnesses – the story ends with the main character, Hsi-mên Ch'ing, literally screwing himself to death with the passionate Golden Lotus.

He arrives home too drunk to perform. Golden Lotus is disappointed:

> She played delicately with his weapon, but it was as limp as cotton wool and had not the slightest spirit. She tossed about on the bed, consumed with passionate desire, almost beside herself. She squeezed his prick, moved it up and down, put down her head and sucked. It was in vain. This made her wild beyond description.

She wakes him and gives him a strong aphrodisiac: three pills. 'She was afraid that anything less would have no effect.' Although he falls asleep again, his penis is erect, and so she mounts him.

> Her body seemed to melt away with delight . . . she moved up and down about two hundred times. At first it was difficult because it was dry but soon the love juices flowed and moistened her cunt. Hsi-mên Ch'ing let her do everything she wished, but himself was perfectly inert. She could bear it no longer . . . She twisted herself towards his penis which was completely inside

her cunt, only his two balls staying outside. She stroked his penis with her hand, and it was wonderfully good. The juices flowed and in a short time she had used up five napkins. Even then Hsi-mên kept on, although the tip of his prick was swollen and hotter than a live coal. It was so tight that he asked the woman to take off the ribbon, but his penis remained stiff and he told her to suck. She bent over and with her red lips moved the head of his prick to and fro, and sucked. Suddenly white semen poured out, like living silver, which she took in her mouth and could not swallow fast enough. At first it was just semen, soon it became blood which flowed without stopping. Hsi-mên Ch'ing had fainted and his limbs were stiff outstretched.

Golden Lotus was frightened. She hastily gave him some red dates. Blood followed semen, and the blood was followed by freezing air. Golden Lotus was terrified. She threw her arms around him and cried, 'Darling, how do you feel?'

Readers, there is a limit to our energy, but none to our desires. A man who sets no bounds to his passion cannot live more than a short time . . .

This book is a sort of phantom in China. Everyone knows of it; no one has seen it. I don't think there would be a counter-revolution if it were published. Banning it has made it notorious. It was only when *Lady Chatterley* was published freely that people realized what a silly and unreadable book it is. Anyway, *Jin Ping Mei* was better railway reading than *Red Star Heroes* or *We Fight Best When We March Our Hardest*.

Outside Danyang, but in the middle of nowhere, a tractor rolled down a steep road and collided with the train. We came to a screeching halt ('Where are we?' 'Is this a station?' 'No, it's an accident – I think someone's killed') and there was a flurry of activity. No one dared to get off the train for fear of being left behind. A railway official plugged a portable phone into a track-side socket and described in detail what had happened. We all listened carefully.

'He says it's a broken tractor. He says we should call the police. He says no one is hurt. He says it was the farmer's fault. He says we can't go until the responsibility is decided.'

The smashed tractor lay near the train, beside the tracks. A crowd gathered – all of them field-workers, rather sullenly watching the more prosperous travellers at the train windows. A railway crew appeared with walkie-talkies and notebooks, and a long discussion ensued over the nub of every Chinese problem: who is to blame? That was always another way of saying: who is paying for this mistake? A man was hurt and yet after twenty minutes of argument the matter was determined to be too trivial to hold up this train – the fastest long-distance train in China, no stops except to take on fuel, from Peking to Shanghai. The peasants were guilty of allowing one of their tractors to ram the train – and as for the injured man, it was his own fault. We started on our way once again.

The fat young man, Ding, chased his thin wife into her berth and thrashed her with a pair of trousers. She sank her teeth into his ankle and bit him, and he howled. They were playing. The old woman snored in a soft punctured way, and her son came in and gazed on her, didn't wake her, just smiled as she snored.

In order to get Ding to stop horsing around I asked him what he was doing in China.

'I come here every six months,' he said. 'I do business.'

He was a mechanical engineer. He had been educated in Toronto. He made rather an issue about his having come back from Canada. It was a sacrifice – 'Lee Kwan Yew ruined the Singapore economy. There's 8 per cent unemployment. I could have stayed in Canada and made a lot of money.'

I said I thought it was interesting that the little prosperous island of Singapore had started to fail just as China was mightily rising – and the overseas Chinese were starting again to see China as a homeland.

'This is a useless place,' Ding said, jerking his thumb out the train window. It was soon clear what he was pointing at. 'China,' he said, 'it spends too much money on hi-tech that it can't use. They have 28,000 computers that they can't use. Only 10 per cent are functioning. They buy things just to have them, so they can look good, and then they let them gather dust.'

'You're saying that they have a kind of primitive pride that makes them irrational about spending,' I said. 'But it seems to me that the Chinese are very frugal – that they don't invest and spend enough. They are always sort of cheating themselves and muddling through and making a virtue of not complaining.'

'Sure, they work hard – especially the farmers,' Ding said. 'And they can feed themselves. That's a good thing.'

'So what's the problem?'

Ding glanced around and seeing the old woman asleep he said confidentially that the problem was in their heads.

Tapping his head he said, 'They're backward. They're peasants. They're ignorant. They go crazy. They're not like us.'

'Who's "us"?' I asked.

Ding laughed. Did he mean me? He didn't reply. He took his wife on his lap and tickled her until her shirt-tail came loose. Her stomach was the pale floury colour of a steamed bun and her small breasts hardly dented her bra. I found this tormenting.

Pretty soon the old woman's son came in and woke her. We were arriving in Shanghai.

Shanghai is an old brown riverside city with the look of Brooklyn, and the Chinese – who are comforted by crowds – like it for its mobs and its street-life. It has a reputation for city-slickers and stylishness. Most of China's successful fashion designers work in Shanghai, and if you utter the words *Yifu Sheng Luolang* the Shanghainese will know you are speaking the name of Yves Saint-Laurent. When I arrived in the city, there was an editor of the French magazine *Elle* prowling the streets looking for material for an article on China called 'The Fashion Revolution'. According to the Chinese man who accompanied her – whom I later met – this French woman was mightily impressed by the dress sense of the Shanghai women. She stopped them and took their picture and asked where they got their clothes. The majority said that they got them in the Free Market in the back-streets or that they made the clothes themselves at home, basing them on pictures they saw in western magazines. Even in the days of the Cultural Revolution, the women workers showed up at their factories with bright sweaters and frilly blouses under their blue baggy suits; it was customary to meet in the women's washroom and compare the hidden sweaters before they started work.

Because it is a cosmopolitan city and has seen more foreigners – both invaders and friendly visitors – than any other Chinese city, it is a polyglot place. It is at once the most politically dogmatic ('Oppose book worship', 'Political work is the life-blood of all economic work': Mao) and the most bourgeois. When changes came to China they appeared first in Shanghai; and when there is conflict in China it is loudest and most violent in Shanghai. The sense of life is strong in Shanghai, and even a city-hater like myself can detect Shanghai's spirit and appreciate Shanghai's atmosphere. It is not crass like Canton, but it is abrasive – and in the hot months stifling, crowded, noisy, and smelly.

It seemed to me noisy most of all, with the big-city, all-night howl which is the soundtrack of New York (honks, sirens, garbage trucks, shouts, death-rattles). Peking was rising and would soon be a city of tall buildings, but Shanghai had been built on mud and was growing sideways and spreading into the swamps of Zhejiang. All day the pile-drivers hammered steel into this soft soil to fortify it, and one was right outside my window – a cruel and dominating noise that determined the rhythm of my life. *Zhong-guo! Zhong-guo!* It affected the way I breathed and walked and ate: I moved my feet and lifted my spoon to *Zhong-guo! Zhong-guo!* It orchestrated my talking, too, it made me write in bursts, and when I brushed my teeth I discovered I did it to the pounding of this pile-driver, the bang and its half-echo, *Zhong-guo!* It began at 7.00 in the morning and was still hammering at 8.00 at night, and in Shanghai it was inescapable, because nearly every neighbourhood had its own anvil clang of *Zhong-guo!*

I walked the back-streets in order to keep away from the traffic and the crowds. And I realized that it would be dishonest to complain too much about noise, the pile-drivers and the frantic energy, because on my first visit to Shanghai I felt it was dreary and moribund and demoralized. Why was it that they never knew when to stop? Even the back-streets were crowded, with improvised stalls and households that served as shopfronts and markets set up in the gutters, and people mending shoes and bicycles and doing carpentry on the pavement.

Towards the Bund – Shanghai's riverbank promenade – I saw a spire behind a wall and found a way to enter. It was St Joseph's

Church, and the man I took to be the caretaker, because he was so shabbily dressed in a ragged jacket and slippers, was the pastor, a Catholic priest. He was both pious and watchful, soft-spoken and alert – it is the demeanour of a Chinese Christian who has been put through more hoops than he cares to remember. The church had been wrecked during the Cultural Revolution, daubed with slogans, and turned into a depot for machinery, and the churchyard had been a car park.

'*Sacramentum*,' the priest said, pointing at the flickering candle, and he smiled with satisfaction: the consecrated host was in the tabernacle.

I asked him why this was so. Was there a service today?

No, he said, and brought me to the back of the church where there was a coffin with a white paper cross stuck to it. He said there was a funeral tomorrow.

'I take it you're busy – lots of people coming to church.'

'Oh yes. And there are five churches in Shanghai. They are always full on Sundays.'

He invited me to attend Mass, and out of politeness I said I might; but I knew I wouldn't. I had no business there: I was a heretic. And I was often annoyed by westerners who, although they never went to church at home, would get the church-going bug in China, as an assertion of their difference or perhaps a reproach to the Chinese – as if religious freedom was the test of China's tolerance. Well, it was one test, of course, but it was exasperating to see the test administered by an American unbeliever. So I didn't go to church in China, but sometimes when I saw a bird in the grass I dropped to my knees and marvelled as it twitched there.

A few days later, on one of my walks I came to People's Park and as it was a Sunday I decided to verify something that I had heard in Peking. It was said that in Beihei Park there, and in People's Park here in Shanghai, there was an area reserved for anyone who wanted to speak English. This proved to be a fact. They called it the English Corner, half an acre of Chinese gabbing in English under the trees. Originally it started when a few old men who still spoke pre-revolutionary English (having gone to mission schools) met on Sundays in the park to talk so that their English wouldn't get rusty. And then they found themselves the object of attention, and they were consulted in a respectful way by Chinese youths who wanted to learn English. What began as a casual one-hour interval in 1979 had become by 1986 a full-day Sunday institution. The Chinese can be very ritualistic in these matters; no one decreed the formation of the English Corner. It just happened, and it has evolved very formally. English is the unofficial language of the new China.

There were about 200 Chinese in People's Park, and the way they stood and the sound of their English made them seem like geese. Some were practising or looking for friends, but many of them I discovered to be seeking advice about English-speaking jobs or applications to English-language universities. English speakers in Shanghai comprised a sort of subculture, as in no other Chinese city.

I met Leroy, who was twenty-four and who had learned to speak English in People's Park. He had been at it for five years.

'When I first came here in 1981 a man said to me, "What is your name?" I couldn't tell him my name. I couldn't say anything in English. I was very frustrated. I decided to learn. I bought some books and I came along every Sunday.'

He spoke English well, but a question still nagged: what about his name? How long had he been Leroy?

It was a simple explanation. As soon as his English improved, this young man Li Ren started to call himself Leroy. He said that English names had been regarded as bourgeois during the Mao era, but with the proliferation of English they had come back. There was usually an obvious choice. A girl called Zhen-li might call herself Jenny, Zhu-lan would become Julian, and Chen would probably decide upon John. Leroy had a friend Li Bing who chose the name Bingley, and made himself sound like a Tory Member of Parliament. A student at Fudan University changed his name to Rambo, and over the next few months I met several Zeldas and a Ringo. I could not resist the conclusion that for these Chinese youths this was a way of distancing themselves from a culture which until recently had been intensely chauvinistic. It was also one in the eye for the Cultural Revolution if you went around calling yourself Bill and wearing a funny hat and sun-glasses. Such people frequented the English Corner.

Leroy earned 80 *yuan* a month as an engineer in a textile factory – he was a college graduate – but his aim was to be hired as a trainee-anything at the new Sheraton Hotel, the Hua Ting, on the outskirts of Shanghai. There were thirty-one hotels in Shanghai but the Sheraton Hua Ting was regarded as the choicest.

'What are your chances of being hired?'

'I have already been offered a job. I was one of twenty people chosen from 400 applicants. But you know in China we cannot just quit our job. We have to get permission to resign or to change jobs. I could earn 250 *yuan* a month at the Sheraton, but my boss won't release me.'

'That's terrible. Isn't there anything you can do about it?'

'Well, he says he has a daughter-in-law who needs a job. He knows my father is a foreman. If my father can find that woman a job, then my boss will release me. If not, I have to stay.'

It was because of this problem that he had come today to the English Corner – to see some of his friends and ask their advice. So it was a sort of Agony Corner too.

He had the nervous attentiveness of a person who is self-taught and still learning. He said he was interested in Africa.

I wondered how up-to-date he was on Africa and so asked him the new name of the Republic of Upper Volta.

'Burkina Faso,' he said.

'What's the capital?'

'Ouagadougou.'

'Very good!'

He said he had a lot of catching up to do, because he had spent so much time during the Cultural Revolution doing useless things. I asked him to be specific.

'School was suspended most of the time. But sometimes there were classes. We would go to school and criticize this one. Then we would criticize that one. We criticized Confucius. We criticized Laozi. We criticized the teacher. If a teacher was bad we called them bourgeois and made them write confessions. Then we went home. It was a waste of time. But I didn't take it seriously.'

I tried to picture a schoolroom full of red-hatted little beasts and brats menacing their teacher. It was very easy to imagine. And of course 'criticize' in Chinese is a euphemism for many things. A woman on the English Department at Fudan University walked with a cane as a result of criticism by Red Guards – she was kicked and beaten, for advocating the reading of the bourgeois feudalist, William Shakespeare. But times had changed. This same woman had just been a faculty adviser on a student production of *Much Ado About Nothing* at the Shanghai Shakespeare Festival in the spring of 1986.

The advantage for a Chinese person in learning English is that he can circumvent a great deal of official obstruction. Many books that are banned in Chinese are available in English. Leroy said that he had read *1984* and *Animal Farm*. I expressed surprise, because Professor Dong had told me Orwell was *neican*, for internal circulation. But Leroy didn't know this – didn't even know there were Chinese translations, because the translations were banned.

'What do you think of *1984*?' I asked.

'It is like China today. Like certain parts. Like Tibet. And it is like Shanghai sometimes.'

I said I thought the book was about fear and uncertainty, but when I pressed him for examples he became evasive, and not wishing to interrogate him I let the matter drop. He knew about the erotic classic, *Jin Ping Mei*, but did not know it was available to scholars or indeed that the book was circulated. For him, the book was part of the oral tradition, a lot of raunchy stories that people whispered to each other.

I asked him what changes in Shanghai had made the greatest impression on him. He said the difference in the way people dressed was the most obvious one, but that people's attitudes had also greatly altered – in thinking for themselves and in their expectations. He said I should see the Free Market and especially the sort of money-making work that people now did at home, such as tailoring, mending pots, fixing washtubs. And giving lessons: English lessons, music lessons, or dress-making lessons. For 20 *yuan* you could be taught to sew by an established tailor – that was the going rate for about two months of twice-weekly lessons. There had never been any reason to learn to make clothes before, because everyone wore the same clothes, which were made – the one blue cotton suit – in a factory.

'But the biggest difference is that we can all get jobs now. In the past if you didn't have a job you stayed at home. The government gave you nothing, and you had to take money from your parents. Now everyone can find something to do. There is plenty of work.'

I wished him well in pursuit of the job at the Sheraton, and I continued walking to test what he had said about people working at home. It seemed to be true that most people were toiling away at something or other to earn extra money – sewing, making pots, mending shoes, fixing umbrellas, selling home-made clothes. This sort of freelancing was unheard of until about 1980. And the Free Market was also brisk, with small traders hawking vegetables, eggs, pet food, clocks, old watches, used eye-glasses and birds they had snared.

A bloody revenge movie was showing in Shanghai. It was called *Mister Legless* and the hero of the title was shown on a poster in a wheelchair blowing the head off the man who had maimed him. Chinese were milling around and fighting for tickets, which they said were very scarce. All movies were popular and violent ones the most popular of all – *Rambo* had recently been shown to packed houses all over China.

An old man with a red armband was denouncing someone on the pavement, and when I enquired I discovered this man to be part of the Anti-Spitting Brigade – there was a widespread campaign against spitting going on. I approved of that, but Chinese spitting is not half as bad as Chinese throat-clearing: the hoick that can be heard for fifty yards and that sounds like the suction on a monsoon drain. After that, the spitting itself is rather an anticlimax.

Back at the English Corner in the park – which had a festive club-like atmosphere – I met Doctor Qin, who told me he was a psychiatrist.

I said I had been under the impression that there were no psychiatrists in China – certainly no universities had departments of psychology. And were there mental hospitals?

'Five years ago psychiatry was permitted – that was when I began studying,' Doctor Qin said. 'Before then there was no mental care. If someone had symptoms and was referred he was treated with acupuncture.'

'Can you treat depression and schizophrenia with acupuncture?'

'No. And yet there were many cases. We see them all the time at the Shanghai Medical Centre, where I practise. We have a famous medical system now, and there are eminent Chinese psychiatrists. They are old men who studied in Germany and the United States.'

'How do you treat your patients?'

'We use drugs – medicine – and we talk to them. There are not many violent cases, but we have many depressives. That seems to be a Chinese problem. And about 70 per cent of our patients are schizophrenics. Doctors in factories refer people to us, and we treat them.'

I asked him whether he got many cases of paranoia.

'Not many. It is very rare in China. I only know of three such cases at the clinic.'

'In the United States a paranoid person often thinks he's George Washington, and in other places paranoiacs say they're Hitler or Napoleon. Who does a Chinese paranoiac with a delusion of grandeur claim to be?'

'The emperor. Chairman Mao. Or God.'

As I was talking to Doctor Qin a man approached me and said, 'You speak German?'

'*Ja wohl*,' I said, and babbled a little to please him. He spoke German very well and said that he had learned it as a messenger in the German consulate in Shanghai in the nineteen-thirties.

A little crowd had gathered around us. 'Speak English!' some-one said, and another bewildered Chinese said, 'What language are you speaking – is that French?' Soon there were about twenty people listening to this man speaking German.

'If you want to stay here you must speak English,' an officious Chinese man said, and took hold of the old man.

To calm matters, I asked the man his name. He said he was Mr Zeng and he asked me to guess his age. I said, 'About seventy.'

'I was born in 1906,' Mr Zeng said. 'I remember my father saying, "The Emperor is on the throne." He also told me about the old woman behind him' – the dowager empress – 'that evil old woman.'

'How do you manage to stay so young-looking, Mr Zeng?'

'It is easy. My father said, "Never smoke opium," and I never did. At that time, everyone smoked it and they became very unhealthy. But I was strong – strong lungs.' He puffed out his chest and then exhaled. 'And I had another good reason. If I smoked opium my father would have beaten me on the backside.'

I said, 'You've lived through almost the whole of the twentieth century. What was the best period you've seen?'

'The best was just after Liberation. That was wonderful. Everyone was happy. There was peace.'

'Is that the reason – because there was peace?'

'Not only that. I had two daughters. Before Liberation, girls were regarded as worthless – everyone wanted sons. But after Liberation I didn't have to worry, and my daughters didn't have to be ashamed of it any more. Shall I tell you about my wife?'

'Please do,' I said. Mr Zeng had an impish and old-fashioned way of speaking, and the crowd of Chinese listeners leaned forward to catch what he said.

'About a year after I was born my parents decided that I was to marry a certain girl from the village. When I was twenty-three I finally married her. She was the most wonderful wife a man could have – the best cook. She made noodles. She made fishballs. She made the best dumplings. I can still taste those delicious dumplings.' He licked his lips and the watching Chinese laughed. He was aware that he was the centre of attention, but he did not lose his poise. 'She was my best friend! Shall I show you her picture?'

I said I would like to see it, and Mr Zeng reached down and fossicked in his plastic bag – he had a bottle of Chinese rice wine and a pile of cookies; a comb; some pills; a blackened banana and a smudged newspaper. The crowd of onlookers pushed their heads forward as he searched for the picture.

There were loud gasps and hisses of disgust as Mr Zeng brought out the picture. He flourished it – it was a corpse in a coffin, a small pale head among some ruffles of satin; some wilted flowers; an incense burner; the withered face of the dead woman.

'She was a good wife,' Mr Zeng said proudly, and he smiled at the picture, and when he showed it around the Chinese made faces and began to leave.

This business about girls being equal was disputed by other people I met in Shanghai, and it is obvious that Chinese society is dominated by males. With a one-child policy – and severe penalties for people who have more than one – the preference is for a boy.

There was no shortage of whisperers who told of the large number of girl infants who were drowned like unwanted kittens, or strangled at birth, and infanticide was said to be very common. But these atrocities are difficult to substantiate. It is much more likely that determining the sex of the foetus before birth has led to a dramatic rise in abortions – I was unsuccessful in gettting abortion statistics, but the figures are very high; any woman can get an abortion at any time – it is regarded as a patriotic duty. I would bet that more female foetuses are aborted than male ones, and when I put this supposition to Chinese in Shanghai they said it was likely.

Sang Ye, the co-author of *Chinese Profiles*, had told me in Peking that when I got to Shanghai I must definitely visit the industrial suburb of Min Hong, about fifteen miles outside the city.

'It will be a revelation to you as a traveller,' he said. 'In Min Hong the peasants from very rural areas have been turned into factory workers. They are people who are used to living in huts and now they live in high-rise apartments. The problem is with their habits. They are not used to flushing toilets. They keep their chickens and ducks in their rooms with them.'

He painted a picture of Dogpatch in a tower block: stinking toilets, livestock in the corridors, pitchforks propped against the walls, pigs wandering up and down stairs.

'And they have not abandoned other peasant customs,' he said. 'Every night before dinner it is usual for a villager to stroll around to see what his relatives are going to eat. But this is hard to do in a block of flats. That's why the lift man goes out of his mind every day as people get into the lift and go from floor to floor checking on their relatives.'

He finished by saying, 'Min Hong is an interesting mess, and no tourist ever goes there.'

That was all I needed to encourage me: I could already see the pigs and chickens, and those unspeakable toilets. I went out to Min Hong one day. I was disappointed by the blocks of flats. None of them was higher than six storeys and, as it is a law in China that only blocks of flats higher than six storeys need lifts, the lift story was erroneous. And it is a big nondescript township – about 30,000 people: a power-plant, factories, shops, a little market. Where were the pigs and ducks?

I prowled around the fairly ordinary lanes behind the houses and saw nothing remarkable. There were cyclists and pedestrians, people going to and from their jobs, to and from school, shoppers, old men gasping on stairs, people thinking: What is this foreigner looking at?

A man I met said that there was a joint-venture in progress making toys – 'matchbox cars'. Not very interesting. A cosmetics factory. I tried not to yawn. Pepsi Cola was thinking of opening a bottling plant.

I said, 'I've heard the flats are unusual.'

He seemed bewildered but he said that if I wanted to look at one I could look at his.

That was typical Chinese hospitality. Very early in my trip I had found they were unfailingly friendly and unsuspicious. This was particularly so in outlying areas: they were eager to talk, proud of their family, curious to know my reaction to the changes in China, and they were fairly open. And they hadn't the slightest idea who I was.

'Go right in,' the man said.

It was a two-roomed flat, smelling of vegetables. There was also a big hallway, a bathroom and a kitchen. Five adults and two children lived here. These people, originally from up the line at Wuxi, had come here in 1959 when Min Hong was established.

They worked locally – all five had jobs, two men, three women. There were two beds in each room, and chests of drawers, and chairs, a table and a television. It was very neat; and there were potted plants on the window sills. There were no books.

When I remarked on the television they turned it on and got a cowboy movie – Gregory Peck and Olivia De Havilland, speaking Chinese. We watched it for a while, and they gave me tea and we talked about Min Hong.

'I was told that some people here in Min Hong keep chickens and ducks.'

'No, we have no chickens or ducks.'

One of the women said, 'But you ride horses in America.'

'Just for fun,' I said.

They didn't quite believe this. They had the idea that there were cowboys all over America, and I secretly felt that they had pigs and ducks in Min Hong.

'So you don't get on your horse.'

That was a joke. The expression *ma shang* ('get on your horse') meant 'quickly' or 'hurry'.

'I have to get on my horse now,' I said.

So I left Min Hong. It was dull but it was decent: Sang Ye had been wrong. But why was squalor regarded as more interesting than order?

There was a stylish, youthful-looking man named Wang whom I met one day in Shanghai. It turned out that we were both born in the same year – the Year of the Snake (but Wang used the Chinese euphemism for snake, 'little dragon'). He was so friendly and full of stories that I saw him often, usually for lunch at the Jin Jiang Hotel. He was a sensitive soul, but had a sense of irony, too, and said he had never been happier than when he was walking the streets of San Francisco on his one trip to America – he hinted that he was eager to emigrate to the United States, but he never became a bore on the subject and did not ask me for help. He was unusual, even in Shanghai, for his clothes – a canary-yellow French jacket and pale blue slacks, a gold watch, a chain around his neck, and expensive sun-glasses.

'I like bright clothes,' he said.

'Could you wear them during the Cultural Revolution?'

He laughed and said, 'What a mess that was!'

'Were you criticized?'

'I was under arrest. That's when I started smoking. I discovered that if you smoked it gave you time to think. They had me in a room – the Red Guards. They said, "You called Mao's wife, Jiang Qing, a crazy lady." She was a crazy lady! But I just lit a cigarette and puffed on it so that I could think of something to say.'

'What did you say?'

'The wrong thing! They made me write essays. Self-criticism!'

'Describe the essays.'

'They gave me subjects. "Why I Like Charles Dickens", "Why I Like Shakespeare".'

'I thought you were supposed to say why you didn't like them.'

'They wouldn't believe that,' he said. 'They called me a reactionary. Therefore, I had to say why I liked them. It was awful. Six pages every night, after work-unit, and then they said, "This is dog-shit – write six more pages".'

'What work did you do?'

'Played the violin in the Red Orchestra. Always the same tunes. "The East Is Red", "Long Live The Thoughts Of Mao", "Sailing The Seas Depends On The Helmsman", all that stuff. They made me play in the rain. I said, "I can't – the violin will fall apart." They don't know that a violin is glued together. I played in the rain. It fell apart. They gave me another one and ordered me to play under the trees during the Four Pests Campaign – to keep sparrows from landing in the branches.'

The other three pests were mosquitoes, flies and rats.

'That's absurd,' I said.

'We painted Huai Hai Lu – that's more absurd,' Wang said.

'How can you paint a street?' I asked – the street he named was one of the main thoroughfares of Shanghai.

'We painted it red, out of respect for Chairman Mao,' Wang said. 'Isn't that stupid?'

'How much of the street did you paint?'

'Three and a half miles,' Wang said, and laughed remembering something else. 'But there were stupider things. When we went to the work-unit we always did the *qing an* [salute] to Mao's portrait on the gateway. We'd hold up the Red Book, say "Long Live Chairman Mao" and salute him. Same thing when we went home. People would make things in Mao's honour, like a knitted Mao emblem, or a red star in needlepoint, and put it in the special Respect Room at the unit – it was painted red. That was for Mao. If they wanted to prove they were very loyal they would wear the Mao badge by pinning it to their skin.'

'That must have impressed the Red Guards,' I said.

'It wasn't just the Red Guards – everyone blames them, but everyone was in it. That's why people are so embarrassed at the moment, because they realize they were just as stupid about Chairman Mao as everyone else. I know a banker who was given the job of fly-catcher. He had to kill flies and save their little bodies in a matchbox. Every afternoon someone would come and count the dead flies and say, "117 – not good enough. You must have 125 tomorrow." And more the day after, you see? The government said there was going to be a war. "The enemy is coming – be prepared."'

'Which enemy?'

'The imperialists – Russia, India, the United States. It didn't matter which one. They were going to kill us,' Wang said, and rolled his eyes. 'So we had to make bricks for the war effort. Ninety bricks a month for each person. But my parents were old, so I had to make their bricks. I used to come home from the unit, write my essay "Why I Like Western Music", and make bricks – I had to deliver 270 a month. And they were always asking me about my hole.'

'Your hole?'

'The *Shen wa dong* – Dig Deep Holes edict. That was for the war, too. Everyone had to have a hole, in case of war. Every so often the Red Guards would knock on your door and say, "Where is your hole?"'

He said there were bomb shelters all over Shanghai, which had been built on Mao's orders ('for the coming war'), and of course they had never been used. I asked him to show me one. We found this subterranean vault – it was just like a derelict subway station – on 1157 Nanjing Road and it had been turned into an ice-cream parlour. The fascinating thing to me was that it was now obviously a place where young folks went to kiss their girlfriends. It was full of Chinese youths locked in the half-nelson they regard as an amorous embrace. The irony was not merely that these kids were making out and feeling each other up in a place that had been built by frantic and paranoid Red Guards in the nineteen-sixties, but also that it was now called the Dong Chang Coffee Shop and owned and operated by the government.

I was talking to Wang one day about my trip through the Soviet Union when I mentioned how the scarcity of consumer goods there meant they were always pestering foreigners for blue jeans, T-shirts, track shoes, and so forth.

'That never happens in China,' I said.

'No,' Wang said. 'But that reminds me. About three years ago there was a Russian ballet dancer at the hotel in Shanghai. I went to see the ballet – fabulous! And this dancer was very handsome. I recognized him, and he smiled at me. Then he pointed to my track shoes and pointed to himself. He wanted them, I understood that. They were expensive shoes – Nike, cost me fifty *yuan*. But I don't care much about money. We measured feet, side by side. Exact fit. I don't speak a word of Russian, but I could tell he really wanted those shoes.'

'Did you sell them to him?'

'I gave them to him,' Wang said, and frowned at the triviality of it. 'I felt sorry for someone who just wanted a pair of shoes. It seemed sad to me that he couldn't get them in his own country. I took them off and walked to my office barefoot! He was really happy! I thought: He'll go back to Russia. He'll always remember this. He'll say, "Once I was in China. I met a Chinese man and asked him for his shoes, and he gave them to me!"'

A moment later he said, 'You can get anything you want in China. Food, clothes, shoes, bicycles, motor bikes, TVs, radios, antiques. If you want girls, you can find girls.' And then in a wide-eyed way, 'Or boys – if you want boys.'

'Or fashion shows.'

'They have fashion shows on television almost every week,' Wang said. 'Shanghai is famous for them.'

I asked him what the old people made of these developments – hookers and high fashion in a country where just a few years ago foreign decadence was condemned and everyone wore baggy blue suits.

'The old people love life in China now,' Wang said. 'They are really excited by it. Very few people object. They had felt very repressed before.'

A few days later I had an occasion to test that reaction. I was invited to the house of a former civil servant, recently retired – the Chinese use the French term *cadre* to describe these officials. This man, Ning Bailuo, was sixty-seven and a passionate Maoist. He'd had no formal education; he had risen through the ranks of the New Fourth Army, from 1940 to 1949, mainly organizing political programmes and collecting food and money for the troops, first in their fight against the Japanese and then against the forces of

Chiang Kai-shek. One of his earliest memories was of missing the ferry late one night to cross the Huangpu in Shanghai and a Japanese soldier beating him with a stick for being out too late. He soon joined an anti-Japanese organization and later the army.

'Don't your experiences make you hate the Japanese?'

'No,' he said, 'it is only the generals we hate.'

Chinese blaming is always reserved for high-ups: underlings are always innocent. That was how they had been able to cope with the monstrous guilt in the aftermath of the Cultural Revolution. The entire horror-show, the whole ten years of it, in every city and town in China, from Mongolia to Tibet, had been the work of four skinny demons: the Gang of Four. No Red Guard was ever held personally responsible for any act of terror – there were no trials, and I never heard any recrimination other than loud clucking.

Comrade Ning – as I thought of him – was thin and bony, with a Bogart face and long creases on his cheeks, and the same Bogart slurring of speech as his tongue snagged against his teeth. It was easy to see that he was a hardliner, the tough and puritanical official who had known the privations of the nineteen-thirties, and all the phases that had led to this present boom. He still wore blue. He seemed to me the perfect person to ask about developments.

Although he was personally rather ascetic-looking, his flat was very large by Chinese standards – four spacious rooms, as well as a kitchen and a foyer. In accordance with Chinese practice there were beds in every room. Comrade Ning shared this flat with his wife, his unmarried daughter, his son, his son's wife and two grandchildren.

His wife gave me a bowl of sweet lumps made of puffed rice. 'You'll like them. They're Mongolian.'

They tasted exactly like the concoction you see described on the back of cereal boxes in the States: *Tastee 'n' Fun-licious Dessert Idea That Will Have Those Kids Asking for More!!!* They were sticky and crunchy.

Picking fragments out of my teeth, I said that if he had been in the New Fourth Army he must have come across the song, 'Baking The Cakes'.

'My wife and I can sing that song,' Comrade Ning said.

I told them I had met the man who had composed it – Zhang Mei, in Peking – and how we had talked about the patriotic songs in which the Japanese had been referred to as ghosts, rapists, robbers, devils and so forth.

'I have nothing personal against the Japanese,' Comrade Ning said, 'and I have no objection to their doing business in China. But there is a militaristic element in Japanese society – that is something we have to be very careful of. Apart from that, the Chinese and Japanese have a great deal in common.'

I said that when I had been in China six years before it had seemed very different, but that there had been a sort of equality in poverty. I said, 'Doesn't it worry you that some people are getting rich – and a few people very rich?'

'You know about the water-melon tycoon?'

Wang had told me the story. A penniless peasant who knew the Chinese fondness for eating water-melon seeds started a small business which grew and grew. He hired workers, he bought land, he made millions; and then he bullied his workers, the government taxed him heavily, and recently he had renounced all his millions. He returned to his peasant life. A moral fable in the form of a play was written about him and staged with government approval. It was called *The March of a Foolish Man*.

'He was a fool,' Comrade Ning said. 'But there is nothing wrong with being rich. Our aim is for everyone to be rich.'

'But surely wealth will produce a privileged class that will undermine the socialist state.'

'In China, privilege is not bought with money,' Comrade Ning said. 'Power comes from the political sphere, not the financial sphere.'

'What about cases of corruption – back-handers?' I said. The Chinese term is *hou men* – 'back-door' business.

'Of course, there are such cases. The danger is when people have an excessive regard for money.' Up went Comrade Ning's skinny finger. 'Man should manipulate money – money should not manipulate man.'

We talked about corruption. There was a current example – a Chinese businessman who had been taking bribes and embezzling from the government was found guilty in a Shanghai court. His woman accomplice was given a long sentence, but he was executed – the Chinese way: a bullet in the back of the neck.

'He had Hong Kong connections,' Comrade Ning said, as if this sordid fact explained everything.

'Do you think the death penalty might be regarded as a little severe in a case of stealing?'

Comrade Ning laughed at me for this. His teeth were yellow, and so were his long fingernails. 'There is a certain amount of money that makes this case serious. If anyone steals this amount he has to be killed.'

'So you believe in the death penalty?'

'It is a Chinese custom,' Comrade Ning said. 'If you kill someone you pay with your life. That is simple. And his was the same sort of serious crime.'

That leap in logic was characteristic of Chinese thinking, and *laodong gaizao* – Rehabilitation through Labour – had declined in popularity. I specifically wanted to know what Comrade Ning thought about capital punishment since, along with Deng's reforms, in the three years between 1983 and 1986, 10,000 people were executed in China – and not only murderers, but also rapists, arsonists, swindlers and thieves. On 30 August 1983, there was a public execution in Peking of thirty convicted criminals. It was staged in a sports stadium, which held a cheering crowd of 60,000 people. Soon after, the list of capital crimes was widened to include pimps, spies, armed robbers, embezzlers and organizers of secret societies. It is easy to calculate the number of Chinese who receive the final solution (their hands are tied, they are forced to kneel before witnesses, and they are dispatched with one bullet to the occiput, where the neck joins the skull). Their photographs were always displayed in whatever town they lived in – often at the railway station or outside the post office. In the rogues' gallery tacked to these bulletin boards, a red mark appeared beside the criminals who had been executed.

I said, 'Personally I don't believe in the death penalty.'

'Why not?' Comrade Ning asked.

'Because it's savage and it doesn't work.'

'What would you have done with those terrorists who bombed the dance-hall in Berlin a few weeks ago?'

'Not condemned them to death, if that's what you mean,' I said. 'Anyway, don't you make a distinction between political violence and criminal violence? Let's suppose these men, whoever they are, were Palestinians. That's an army of liberation, isn't it?'

'We would regard what they did in Berlin as terrorism,' Comrade Ning said. 'That is a crime. Armed struggle,' he went on, using the Maoist term for people's war, 'is another matter. That is legitimate.'

He could not be budged from wishing to execute every pimp and hooligan, along with every strangler and arsonist. He maintained that such drastic action kept the crime rate down. It was Maoism at its most anti-Confucian. Confucius abhorred capital punishment and had always been regarded by Maoists as a dangerous softie for his humane views (as in *Analects* XII, 19). But even a relatively open-minded man like Deng Xiaoping has revealed himself to be an energetic hangman, clinging to the Chinese belief in the efficacy of 'killing a chicken to scare the monkeys'. In a pep talk to the five-man standing committee of the Politburo (reprinted in a book of his talks and speeches entitled *Fundamental Issues in Present-Day China*) Deng said, 'As a matter of fact, execution is the one indispensable means of education.'

Returning to the subject of money, Comrade Ning said that he did not think there were financial problems in this new, go-ahead, money-making economy. The government would control the workforce, protect the workers, tax the people getting rich and in general supervise all businesses. He said it seemed to him much more serious that prices were rising, in some cases to double-digit inflation – he used that English term in his Chinese sentence. But salaries were also rising. His wife knew a draughtswoman in her native town of Wuxi who earned 300 *yuan* a month. That was regarded as a high salary, but most of it came from bonuses, because she was productive.

'So, Comrade Ning, you're an optimist.'

'Of course!'

'No dangerous tendencies that you can see?'

'Yes, there are some. But we are trying to deal with them. The government has instituted a programme called "Spiritual

Civilization". Look at the posters and slogans. You'll see a big-character poster near Suzhou Creek –'

The 'Spiritual Civilization' programme was a direct response to various types of anti-social behaviour that emerged after the relaxation of restrictions – the Open Door policy. It was started in 1985 and as Chinese dogma is always expressed in clusters it was made up of 'the Five Talks' and 'the Four Beauties'.

The Five Talks were concerned with communication. They were: politeness; civil behaviour; morality; attention to social relations; and attention to the hygiene of one's surroundings. This was all to combat a slob-factor that had become very obnoxious; and the slobs that weren't changed by the Five Talks might be altered by considering the Four Beauties. These were beautiful language, beautiful behaviour, beautiful heart, and beautiful environment.

As a programme and prescription it seemed rather twee, but it was a great deal better than the brutishness that was called for in 'Smashing the Four Olds' (burning churches, turning monasteries into shoe factories, and so forth), or observing the Eight Antis – persecuting intellectuals, burning books, and making teachers wear dunce caps and having them recite, 'I am a cow demon,' all day in front of a mocking classroom.

It was Comrade Ning who explained the Spiritual Civilization programme to me. I liked him, and I was impressed by him. He knew what the world news was and he was hospitable to a total stranger. His tolerance was of course a willing suspension of disbelief – at heart he clung to Mao's Thoughts – but he was without greed or envy, and he didn't have the slightest trace of vanity. He wasn't a bully either, and I respected him for arguing with me.

But afterwards, I heard that his wife had been rather cross with him. She had been listening the whole time.

She said to him, 'If we have any criticisms or doubts about the current policies we should keep them to ourselves and not talk to foreigners about them.'

There is a Chinese conundrum. If a place has a reputation for being beautiful, the Chinese flock to it, and its beauty is disfigured by the crowd. If a train is very fast, like the Shanghai Express from Peking, everyone tries to take it, and it is impossible to get a seat. The same is true for restaurants: the good ones are jammed. And hotels: reservations are unthinkable. And the worst of it is that you are sometimes laughed at for ever believing that you had a chance: the Chinese can be extremely rude in turning you away – the Chinese elbow is very sharp.

This conundrum is constant in Shanghai. For example, Shanghai is known to be a city of pavements – wonderful for pedestrians, an excellent city for perambulating. Therefore, everyone walks; and the mobs are impenetrable.

None the less, if you push – as the Chinese do – it is possible to walk around Shanghai. Long ago, the Chinese overcame the natural human horror of being touched. The crowd reduces your progress to a shuffle, but it seemed to me that anything was preferable to a Shanghai bus.

Following Comrade Ning's suggestion I walked to Suzhou Creek and looked at the Spiritual Civilization sign (CLING TO THE FOUR BEAUTIES). Then I walked farther, to the docks, a tangled, greasy, busy place of warehouses and the storerooms that Chinese call godowns, and little indoor factories of tinsmiths and lock-makers and box-assemblers and rope-twisters. I came to the Shanghai Seamen's Club, a venerable building with teak-wood panelling and Art Deco lamps and fluted cornices and a serviceable billiard room. It was a big old building and covered with soot, but it was attractive in a gloomy and indestructible way.

Inside, among the souvenirs and seamen's necessities like gloves and twine and sun-glasses and slippers, there was political crap and propaganda about Chinese soldiers fighting in Vietnam, but masked as 'Frontier Guards in South China'. I noted down the captions. *Comrade Hu Yaobang was wielding his writing brush* [photo of Politburo member posing with big writing brush] *to write a few words calling on the officers and fighters of the frontier guards 'to be able to wield both the pen and the gun to make our country and people rich'* and under a different photograph, showing five soldiers squinting at some bushes, *All officers and fighters of the 'Heroic Hard Sixth Company' rendering battle achievement in defending Laoshan battle.*

I had a beer and kept walking and thought: These people were giving us a hard time over Vietnam? They were still fighting the Vietnamese – and probably getting their asses kicked, because nothing is more indicative of a war going badly than valiant propaganda like this. If a country shouted that it would fight to the last drop of blood that usually meant that it was ready to surrender; and in China, as a general rule, you could regard nothing as true until it had been denied. Anything officially denied was probably a fact.

I continued walking, across the metal bridge in front of what had once been Broadway Mansions, and over the creek to Huangpu Park, on the Bund, where the rest of the nineteen-twenties buildings still stood. I fantasized that there were certain cities in the world that could succeed only by becoming gross parodies of what they were – or of what people expected them to be (like a tall person who has no choice but to learn basketball), and that Shanghai was one of them.

The sign on the gate of the park gave a historical note:

This park was guarded by police of the International Settlement and Chinese were refused admittance. To add insult to injury the imperialists in 1885 put up at the gate a board with the words 'No Admittance to Dogs and Chinese'. This aroused among Chinese people popular indignation and disgust which finally compelled the imperialists to remove the board.

In another place the popularity of the park was remarked on:

Admissions total over 5 million a year. On holidays it sometimes has a sightseer density of 3 persons to the square metre.

In Chinese terms this crowd-praise was wonderful: in the west people are stifled by a crowd, but in China they feel propped up, and only the worthiest attractions have millions of visitors.

But that was not for me. I walked on, and took shelter in a cool building beyond the Bund which had stained-glass windows – not a church, but a bank or counting-house, because the windows showing Burne-Jones-like maidens were labelled *Truth* and *Wisdom* and *Prudence*. The foyer had a dome and a vaulted ceiling and onyx pillars and a black marble floor. I thought to myself: This is just the sort of place that would have had the shit kicked out of it during the Cultural Revolution.

To test my suspicion I asked a man – Mr Lan Hongquan, who worked there, as it was now a government office.

I said, 'Isn't it amazing that this place survived the Cultural Revolution.'

'It almost didn't,' Mr Lan said. 'In 1967, the Red Guards burst in and splashed paint everywhere. They completely covered the windows and these marble walls with paint – it was black paint. You couldn't see anything of these decorations. The job was so big and expensive that it took ten years to clean up – it was only finished last year.'

Quite a way up that street I came to the Shanghai Municipal Foreign Affairs Office, where I had an appointment with the Chief of the Propaganda Division – such was his title – and his assistant. This was Mr Wang Hou Kang and Miss Zhong.

'A very nice house,' I said, in the palm court of this mansion.

'It belonged to a former capitalist.'

He then told me that there were 164 joint-ventures with twenty countries. I expressed surprise, but didn't ask any more questions, because I had been told by wiser minds that most of these joint-ventures were still in the discussion stage; and it would have been embarrassing to Mr Wang if I had asked him how many had borne fruit – the number of joint-ventures in operation was very small.

Because I had been bucking the traffic all day, I said, 'Do you think that Chinese people will ever have their own cars?'

'Very few will. And not for pleasure but business. What we want to do is make and sell cars to other countries. The export market – that's what interests us.'

I asked him what changes had struck him since Deng Xiaoping's reforms had taken effect.

'Magazines are more colourful – more open. More picturesque, I can say. And there is the writing.'

'About politics?'

'No, about sex. Before, people never wrote about sex, and now they do.'

Miss Zhong said, 'Sometimes it is very embarrassing.'

'People dare to express themselves through stories,' Mr Wang said. 'That is new. And people can engage in discussions without being labelled "rightist" or "counter-revolutionary" or "bourgeois" if they said certain things.'

'So no one calls anyone a paper tiger any more?'

'There are still paper tigers. Paper tiger is more a philosophical concept,' Mr Wang said.

We talked about money after that. He said, 'Things have certainly changed. Take me, for example. I earned ninety-two *yuan* a month in 1954 and did not get a salary increase until 1979.'

'But did prices rise in the years when your salary didn't change?'

He laughed. I had not said anything funny. But there are many Chinese laughs. His was the one that meant: *You are asking too many questions*.

The subject of clothes was not contentious.

Mr Wang said, 'After Liberation people cherished simple clothing. They identified the blue suits and the blue cap with revolution. People wore them and felt like revolutionaries. They were sturdy clothes and they were cheap – people felt thrifty wearing them. They made people equal.'

'Why have they stopped wearing them?'

'By and by, some people wanted to wear more colourful clothes. But they were afraid. There was an idea prevailing that if people wore colourful clothes they would be part of the bourgeoisie.' He laughed. His laugh meant: *I don't believe that myself*. 'They remembered the Red Guards who used to go out with scissors. They cut your cuffs if they were too wide or too narrow. They cut your hair if it was too long.'

'Do you think that will come again?'

And I saw the marching Red Guards, with their long scissors and their fiendish grins, marching down Nanjing Road, on the look-out for flapping cuffs or flowing locks. They raised their long scissors and went *Snip-snip! Snip-snip!* I realized that a passionate and crazed teenager with a pair of scissors is much scarier than a soldier with a rifle.

Mr Wang said, 'I think the answer is definitely no.'

'You seem pretty sure,' I said.

'Yes, because the Ten Years' Turmoil' – he used the current euphemism – 'went so far. It was so big. So terrible. If it had been a small thing it might have returned. But it involved everyone. We all remember. And I can tell you that no one wants it back.'

The wisest thing that anyone can say is 'I don't know,' but no one says it much in China, least of all the foreigners. The exception to this in Shanghai was Stan Brooks, the American consul-general. He had a steady gaze and was not given to predictions or generalizations. He was from Wyoming and had been in China off and on since the nineteen-seventies, when Mao's intimidating bulk still influenced all decisions and turned most of his colleagues into lackeys.

'I called them "The Whateverists",' Mr Brooks said, basing it on the Chinese term *fanshi*, whatever. 'Their view was that whatever Mao said about this or that was correct. Some members of the Politburo have paid the price for being Whateverists.'

I said that I had been amazed by changes in China – not just superficial changes, such as clothes and traffic, but more substantial ones, such as the way people talked about politics and money and their future, and the way they travelled. They had only been allowed to travel for the past five years, and now they went everywhere – in fact, a lot of them wanted to travel outside China and never come back.

'We have visa problems with some of those people,' Mr Brooks said. 'They go to the States to study and they get jobs and stay on. Thousands will never come back to China.'

'You must have guessed that China would change,' I said, 'but did you imagine that it would look like this?'

'Never,' he said. 'I had no idea. We could see that a new phase was opening up, but we weren't expecting this.'

'Weren't there political scientists writing scenarios or projections?'

'Not that I know of. If they were, they certainly didn't foresee this. It took everyone by surprise.'

And Mr Brooks's view – also very sensible – was that since this hadn't been foreseen it was impossible to know what would follow it.

'We are witnessing China in the middle of a turbulent passage,' he said. 'No one can put his hand on his heart and say what is going to happen next. We just have to watch closely and wish them well.'

But over dinner – and now there were twelve of us at the consulate dining-table – the subject of Chinese students staying on in America came up.

'Excuse me,' said a thin elderly man, clearing his throat. This was Professor Phan, formerly a member of the History Department at Fudan University in Shanghai.

There was an immediate silence, because these were the first words the professor had spoken; and the suddenness of his soft voice made everyone self-conscious.

'My children saw the Red Guards humiliate me,' he said, in a gentle and reasonable way. 'Can you blame them for choosing to stay in Minnesota?'

And then Professor Phan was the only one eating, while the rest of us gaped. He had speared a small cluster of Chinese broccoli – he was unaware that he had become the centre of attention. He seemed to be talking to the woman on his left.

'I was in prison for six years, from 1966 to 1972,' he said, and smiled. 'But I tell my friends, I was not really in prison for six years. I was in for three years – because every night when it was dark and I slept, I dreamed of my boyhood, my friends, the summer weather, and my household, the flowers and birds, the books I had read, and all the pleasures I had known. So it was only when I woke up that I was back in prison. That was how I survived.'

There was another silence while he ate what was on his fork; and then he saw that everyone was listening.

He said that he believed that Nixon's visit to China had something to do with his release, because some of the people accompanying Nixon in 1972 showed an interest in political prisoners and had asked to visit prisons.

'Usually we got one thin slice of meat a week. If the wind was strong it blew away. But just before President Nixon's visit we started to get three pieces. The prison guards were afraid that he might visit and ask how we were being treated.'

Professor Phan had studied at Queens' College, Cambridge, and had lived in England from 1930 to 1939. There was a shyness in the way he spoke that made his intelligence seem even more powerful, and he had a slight giggle that he uttered just before he said something devastating. He seemed about seventy-five, and I had the feeling that though prison had aged him it had also in a way strengthened him. I should say this was a frequent impression I had in China, of former political prisoners. Their hardships and isolation, and even the abuse they suffered, never seemed to have weakened them. On the contrary, they were tougher as a result, and contemptuous of their captors, and not only strong in their convictions but also outspoken.

In that respect, Professor Phan was typical, but not less impressive for that. He giggled softly and said, 'Americans have no cause to fear the Chinese – none whatsoever. The Chinese are interested in only two things in the world – power and money. America has more power and money than anyone else. That is why the Chinese will always need the friendship of America.'

It was clear that he was speaking with the ultimate cynicism, a bleak despair. He giggled again and called Mao 'the Old Man', and he repeated something that Mr Brooks had said to me, about Mao being like a feudal emperor.

'In prison we had to read the Old Man's speeches,' Professor Phan said, and smiled sweetly. 'Four volumes. Sometimes they made us recite the speeches, and if you got a word wrong the guards would become very angry and you'd have to start all over again. Apart from that we did nothing. We sat on the stone floor all day, like animals. I longed to go to bed, and sleep, and dream of the past.'

Someone said, 'What was your crime, professor?'

'My crime? Oh, my crime was listening to the radio – American and English language broadcasts.'

After dinner I accompanied him home – he did not live far away, and it was a pleasant summer night.

'This humiliation you spoke of –'

I didn't quite know how to begin; but he knew what I was asking.

He said, 'One night, in September 1966, forty Red Guards showed up at my house. Forty of them. They came inside – they burst in, and there were both men and women. They put me on trial, so to speak. We had 'struggle sessions'. They criticized me – you know the expression? They stayed in my house, all of them, for forty-one days, and all this time they were haranguing me and interrogating me. In the end they found me guilty of being a bourgeois reactionary. That was the crime. I was sent to prison.'

'What was the sentence – the length, I mean?'

'Any length. I had no idea when I would be released. That was the worst of it.'

'Forty Red Guards – that's very scary. And they were at your house for almost six weeks! Did you know any of them?'

'Oh yes. Some of them were my students.' He gave the same gentle little giggle and said, 'They are still around,' and disappeared into his house.

On my walks in Shanghai I often went past the Chinese Acrobatic Theatre, a domed building near the centre of the city. And I became curious and attended a performance; and after I saw it – not only the tumblers and clowns and contortionists, but the man who balanced a dinner service for twelve on a chopstick that he held in his mouth – I wanted to know more.

Mr Liu Maoyou was in charge of the acrobats at the Shanghai Bureau of Culture. He had started out as an assistant at the Shanghai Library, but even at the best of times things are quiet at the city library, since it is next to impossible – for political reasons – for anyone to borrow a book. The librarian is little more than a custodian of the stacks. He jumped at the chance of a transfer and joined the Bureau of Culture, and he accompanied the Chinese acrobats on their first tour of the United States in 1980.

'We call it a theatre, because it has an artistic and dramatic element,' Mr Liu said. 'It has three aspects – acrobats, magic, and a circus.'

I asked him how it started.

'Before Liberation all the acrobats were family members. They were travellers and performers. They performed on the street or in any open space. But we thought of bringing them together and training them properly. Of course, the Chinese had been acrobats for thousands of years. They reached their height in the Tang Dynasty and were allowed to perform freely.'

Mr Liu said this with such enthusiasm that I asked him how he felt about the Tang Dynasty.

'It was the best period in China,' he said. 'The freest time – all the arts flourished during the Tang era.'

So much for the Shanghai Cultural Bureau, but he was still talking.

'Before Liberation they were doing actions without art-form,' he said. 'But they have to use mind as well as body. That's why we started the training centre. We don't want these acrobats to be mind-empty, so after their morning practice they study maths, history, language and literature.'

He said that in 1986 thirty candidates were chosen from 3,000 applicants. They were all young – between ten and fourteen years old, but Mr Liu said the bureau was not looking for skill but rather for potential.

'We also have a circus,' he said. 'Also a school for animal training.'

This interested me greatly, since I have a loathing for everything associated with performing animals. I have never seen a lion-tamer who did not deserve to be mauled; and when I see a little mutt, wearing a skirt and a frilly bonnet, and skittering through a hoop, I am thrilled by a desire for its tormentor (in the glittering pantsuit) to contract rabies.

'Tell me about your animal training, Mr Liu.'

'Before Liberation the only training we did was with monkeys. Now we have performing cats –'

'Household cats? Pussy cats?'

'Yes. They do tricks.'

It is a belief of many Chinese I met that animals such as cats and dogs do not feel pain. They are on earth to be used – trained, put to work, killed and eaten. When you see the dumb laborious lives that Chinese peasants live it is perhaps not so surprising that they torture animals.

'Also pigs and chickens,' Mr Liu said.

'Performing chickens?'

'Not chickens but cocks.'

'What do the cocks do?'

'They stand on one leg – hand-standing. And some other funny things.'

God only knows how they got these pea-brained roosters to do these funny things, but I had the feeling they wired them up and zapped them until they got the point.

'What about the pigs?' I asked.

'The pigs do not perform very often, but they can walk on two legs –'

And when he said that I realized what it was that was bothering me. It was that everything he said reminded me of *Animal Farm*; and the fact that it was a fable of totalitarianism only made Mr Liu's images worse. He had described a living example of the moment in that book when oppression is about to overtake the farm. There is terror and confusion at the unexpected sight: *It was a pig walking on his hind legs.* And Orwell goes on:

> Yes, it was Squealer. A little awkwardly, as though not quite used to supporting his considerable bulk in that position, but with perfect balance . . . And a moment later, out from the door of the farmhouse, came a long file of pigs, all walking on their hind legs . . .

I was thinking of this as Mr Liu was saying, '– and lions and tigers, and the only performing panda in China.'

He said that the animals and the acrobats often went on tour – even to the United States. Many of the acrobats worked in the United States. In 1985, a deal was made whereby Chinese acrobats would join Ringling Brothers Circus for a year or two at a time. In the first year there were fifteen, and in 1986 there were twenty hired-out Chinese acrobats working in America.

I asked Mr Liu about the financial arrangement.

'I don't know exactly,' he said, 'but Ringling Brothers Circus pays us and we pay the acrobats.'

'How much does Ringling Brothers pay you?'

'About $200 to $600 a week, depending on the act. For each person.'

'How much do you pay the acrobats?'

'About 100 *yuan*.'

Twenty pounds sterling.

Talk about performing pigs! I wondered how long people would be willing to allow themselves to be treated as exportable merchandise. For some it was not long: the very week I had the conversation with Mr Liu a man playing the role of an acrobatic lion disappeared in New York. Months later he still had not been found.

On my last day in Shanghai I tried to figure out what it was that I hated about big cities. It was not only the noise and the dirt and the constant movement – the traffic and the bad tempers; the sense of people being squeezed. It was also the creepy intimation of so many people having come and gone, worked and died; and now other people were living where those had died. My impression of wilderness was associated with innocence, but it was impossible for me to be in a city like this and not feel I was in the presence of ghosts.

This became a strong feeling of mine in Chinese cities. I kept thinking: Something awful happened here once, and I shuddered. And it was probably a feeling that was enhanced by the refusal of the Chinese to talk about ghosts, since they were officially forbidden to discuss such ludicrous things. In the same way, the Chinese allow people to practise religion providing they don't talk about it; but no one who has any religious belief is admitted to the Chinese Communist Party – that is one of the party's basic rules.

Shanghai seemed haunted to me. It was full of suggestions and whispers of violence. It was a city in which irrational murders had been committed – not just in the narrow brown rooms of tottering buildings, but in the streets and alleys, and even in the parks and flower gardens. In the end I was impervious to its charms, and it became a rather diabolical place in my imagination. Or was it that the Shanghainese were very articulate and that they told harrowing stories?

I heard some terrifying stories at Fudan University, and that campus was full of ghosts. It did not, at first glance, have the look of a place of learning. From the outside it looked like a Chinese factory – the same scrubby hedge and sharp fence, the same yellow walls and guarded gate and adjoining settlement of dusty half-built buildings, and barracks-like teachers' quarters and the villagey huts nearby – tailor, laundry, vegetable-seller, butcher, noodle shop, bicycle-mender. It all had the doomed and arbitrary appearance of a Chinese factory town, developed on impulse, unplanned and built on a shoestring, cutting every corner possible.

But this was a slightly misleading impression, because inside the hedges and walls it was shady and orderly, and even a little sleepy – or perhaps reflective – and as if to indicate the seriousness of their intentions the students had, not long ago, vandalized their forty-foot statue of Chairman Mao. They had scratched out the motto on the plinth that had once read LONG LIVE CHAIRMAN MAO!

That statue was one of the souvenirs of the Cultural Revolution. At that time students did not apply to Fudan. There were no entrance exams. Instead, suitably violent and fanatical youths were sent from their factories and work-units in order to persecute the hapless teachers. Coming to class and spending the morning making your teacher parade up and down wearing a dunce cap was regarded as a serious endeavour by the students – who were not by any means all Red Guards. They were simply young and enjoyed the idea of turning the university upside-down.

It is a compelling idea – standing a society on its head, putting children in charge, declaring a ten-year holiday, gaoling and tormenting parents and authority figures, painting the streets red, chanting, settling scores with old enemies and refusing to study. But it does not take longer than a few seconds to see that it is totally impractical, not to say dangerous, and that any society having to endure it would become stupider, more brutish, slower, less subtle, backward and insecure.

'I'll give you an example of the English lessons,' a university official told me. 'The students would show up in class, make their greeting to the portrait of Chairman Mao, and then when the teacher began speaking they would interrupt. "This is a waste of time." "This is an imperialist subject." "What is the point of studying English?" That sort of thing.'

Mr Liu's attitude towards Chairman Mao was that the old man had really gone off in the late nineteen-fifties. I had heard this before – they suggested that he was gaga but they meant an extreme form of senile dementia.

'You think he was crazy?' I said.

'Let's say he made many mistakes,' Mr Liu said.

'Tell me one or two.'

'All right. In 1957 the President of Peking University – who was a close personal friend of Mao – went to see him. His name was Ma Yinchu. He said, "There are 500 million people in China. We must do something about the population before it is too late." Well, people say Mao was like an emperor. That is not so. But he had certain characteristics – like a sage, delivering wise sayings. He was very angry with President Ma for questioning him – for even bringing up this subject of population. He said, "What is the problem? A man is born with one mouth but has two hands to feed that mouth."'

'Is that a wise saying?'

'It is a silly saying,' Mr Liu said. 'President Ma left feeling frustrated. He resigned his post and just stayed home reading books after that. That was Mao's first big mistake – not doing anything about the population, when he was warned.'

'Can you give me some more mistakes, Mr Liu?'

'Two more. He always spoke about collective leadership and group decisions, but in fact that was all false. There was no democracy at all. That was a serious contradiction. And it was a mistake for him to use his personal popularity to sway the people. In the end this was a corrupting thing, because he manipulated them.'

The President of Fudan is a shy brilliant woman named Xie Xide, a Smith College graduate (class of '49) and MIT PhD. Her intelligence and her education and her original research in the field of physics were no help during the Cultural Revolution – it is a matter of record that they were held against her. She was shipped out of Shanghai to a factory, where she assembled radios during the day and studied Mao's thoughts at night. The thoughts were set to music. Doctor Xie was required to sing them. Was it any wonder that on the wall of her apartment there was a dramatic piece of calligraphy, two characters, *jing song*, a sort of idealist's epigram that exhorts people to be like a pine tree (*song*) that not even a strong wind can bend (*jing* covers that whole defiant image). These characters were inscribed by Fang Yi, a former vice-premier in the Central Government and vice-chairman of the Academy of Sciences. He was a man noted for having a mind of his own.

President Xie has a pronounced limp, and it is whispered that she was tortured during the Cultural Revolution. But her own shyness made me too shy to ask a brutal question – and anyway there were many examples of people who were physically mistreated by Red Guards. One of Deng Xiaoping's sons, Deng Pufang, was thrown out of a window. His spine was snapped and he is still in a wheelchair.

I asked in an oblique way about the university students' fanaticism, because Professor Phan had told me that he had been held for forty-one days by them in the struggle sessions at his house.

'The university students were very bad,' President Xie said. 'The young schoolchildren were bewildered – they hardly knew what was going on. But by far the worst were the high-school students.'

I said nothing, because I wanted her to say more. She had a soft but very distinct voice.

'Here at Fudan the students humiliated their teachers,' she said. 'But in the high schools it was not unknown for students to beat their teachers to death.'

I said that perhaps it was not really a political puzzle at all, this violence – that it might be a psychological one, and that the aberration lay in the lost childhood of the Chinese people. I asked whether the psychology department ever dealt with this decade of frenzy and mass hysteria.

'There is no psychology department,' she said.

That was the problem, really – that the Chinese dealt with the past the way they did their peculiar privacies, by drawing a veil over it and not assigning blame or responsibility except to a handful of scapegoats. Ancient history in China was lively and immediate, but more modern history receded and blurred as it became recent, and what happened ten or fifteen years ago was all silence and shadows. No wonder there was an official policy forbidding people to believe in ghosts.

But Shanghai, even bursting at the seams, was a real city, and the fact that it was haunted only made it seem more citified. Also its ships and its civic pride and sea air and all its colleges reminded me of Boston. I had it in my mind to stay longer, but one day in Shanghai I met the Wittricks and the Westbetters. They had just arrived in Shanghai yesterday and they were leaving tomorrow.

'We're going to Canton,' Rick said. 'Why don't you come along? It's thirty-six hours. Scenery's supposed to be breath-taking. And Canton's gorgeous.'

I thought: What the hell, and said OK.

5

The Fast Train to Canton

It was always like a fire-drill, getting on or off a Chinese train, with people panting and pushing; but the journey itself was a great sluttish pleasure for everyone – a big middle-aged pyjama party, full of reminiscences. It seemed to me that the Chinese had no choice but to live the dullest lives and perform the most boring jobs imaginable – doing the same monotonous Chinese two-step from the cradle to the grave – and because of that, these people were never happier than when on a railway journey. They liked the crowded compartments and all the chatter; they liked smoking and slurping tea and playing cards and shuffling around in their slippers – and so did I. We dozed and woke and yawned and watched the world go by.

This was the last stop on the tourists' trip before they reached Hong Kong, and I was glad to see some familiar faces.

'See this piece in the *China Daily*?' Ashley Relph asked and showed me the paper.

Under the headline MIRACLE SURGERY FOR WORKER WHO LOST LIMB it described how a man had been more or less devoured by his stitching machine in a clothes factory, and his arm had been severed. Just reading that gave me the anxious twinges I associated with a castration complex, but there was more. The poor fellow had been rushed to the hospital and in a landmark surgical operation his arm had been sewn back on, 'and he is now receiving therapy to learn how to use it again'. The article also mentioned how fingers and toes had been sewn on to workers who had lost them. It had always worked.

It's a great society for mending things, I thought. There was no need for a man to be put on the occupational scrap-heap simply because his arm had been chopped off. You found a way to reattach the arm and you sent him back to work. The epoch of invention ended 1,000 years ago, and these days the Chinese were perfecting a technique for making-do and mending. This was not invisible mending. It was always obvious when a thing had been patched – it was a society of patches. They patched their underwear and darned their socks and cobbled their shoes. They rewrote their slogans and painted out the Thoughts of Chairman Mao, and come to think of it that was a form of patching, too. But Mao had spoken repeatedly of the evils of wastefulness: 'Thrift should be the guiding principle in our government expenditure . . . corruption and waste are very great crimes . . . never be wasteful or extravagant.' An entire section of his Thoughts is entitled *Building Our Country Through Diligence and Frugality*.

One of the great differences between China under Mao and China under Deng was that the Mao mania for patching and mending had begun to subside, pride in poverty was regarded now as old hat, and the Dengists liked things that were brand-new. New clothes were now so cheap that no one had to waste time mending them. Yet I was sure that it was this make do and mend philosophy that had inspired these medical advances and miracles with amputees.

The news items gave me the creeps, though. I read a report about a man whose penis had been sewn back on. Fifty other men had had the same operation in China, 'and 98 per cent of them found their penis functioned again,' the *China Daily* stated. Some of the men had what was called 'one-stage reconstruction of the penis', which was not a reattachment but a whole new dick cobbled together from spare parts – a piece of rib, a skin graft, some loose tubes. A survey showed that most of the men were able to father children. 'A father who went through the one-stage reconstruction of the penis even mailed his daughter's photo to us,' Professor Chang, the master-mind of this technique, said.

The strangest case of human mending occurred not long ago in Shenyang. This was also reported in the *China Daily* under the confusing headline, TRANSPLANTED LEG SAVES GIRL'S ARM.

> Eleven-year-old Meng Xin's left arm and leg were severed in a train accident.
>
> To save her, the six surgeons used part of her severed leg to make a forearm to which they attached her hand.
>
> Following the 18-hour operation Meng's skin on her transplanted forearm returned to normal, and her transplanted fingers have recovered their sense of touch.
>
> She can clench her fist and move her left arm.

And yet these mending operations are not surprising to anyone who has looked under the bonnet of an old Chinese bus, or closely scrutinized the welds in a Chinese steam locomotive, or watched a Chinese street tailor or cobbler at work. I was sure that it was the Maoist philosophy of frugality that had inspired brilliant medical advances and miracles with amputees. You only had to see the amazing contraption of hosepipes that filled the trains with water at the larger railway stations to realize that it was inevitable that such people would in time be able to rig up a new penis for an unfortunate Chinese castrato.

Ashley was still watching me reading the paper. Handing it back to him, I said, yes, wasn't it remarkable?

'Lom mistair,' he said, and winked at me. 'It's the CIA, isn't it? You're an agent, you tell people you're a journalist because that's good cover. You go sniff-sniff-sniff and get people blabbing, and then you lock yourself in your room and write a report.' He laughed. 'That's all right. I don't care! I won't tell anyone.' And he looked out of the window. 'Jesus, I am so sick of this country – I can't wait to get back home. Chinese food – every day – Chinese food. And these people!'

'The Chinese?'

'Naw, they're all right. They're bloody *small*, though,' he said. 'I was thinking of the tour here.'

They were in the corridor, watching China go by. It was not very pretty here. The industrial suburbs of Shanghai continued for almost 100 miles, until the train pulled into Hangzhou. Marco Polo had mentioned Hangzhou – it was one of the boasts of this tourist-paradise: lake, temples, hotels, restaurants, noodle stalls, take-your-picture booths. It was a help to have Marco Polo's praise as a blurb on your brochure ('the greatest city which may be found in the world'), but even that did not make the place sparkle for me. And I had always wondered why Marco Polo, who talked about everything and supposedly went everywhere, never mentioned either the Great Wall, or the fact that the Chinese drank tea, in his *Travels*.

Ashley said the tourists were driving him mental, and he brought me up to date. The most obnoxious man and Wilma, the bald woman, had become lovers. There had been a fight in the French compartment, and one of them – who was bringing a legal action against another – had joined the American group, Wittricks and Westbetters. Blind Bob was terribly bruised as a result of his Mister McGoo stumbling. Rick Westbetter was planning to write a letter to President Reagan, about Chinese duplicity. The Australians were feeling cranky, but of course they were relieved to be heading for Guangdong, since south China was closer to Australia. Bella Scoons was telling herself that the distance was no more than four trips to Kalgoorlie. The Cathcarts had made themselves unpopular by refusing to pay for a beer one hot day because 'We've paid for this trip already and that beer ought to be free.' They made an issue of the one *yuan* (fifteen pence) and just sat and broke out into a virtuous sweat. Morthole had added to his rock collection: he could hardly heave the sack of them. And Kicker said ironically, 'How about a tomb? We haven't seen a tomb today!'

'I'd like to show that fucker a tomb,' Ashley said.

They were all tired and crabby. You need a good night's sleep, I wanted to say. It was like school, like an outing; it had gone on too long. *Day thirty-seven*, Miss Wilkie was writing in her journal.

'It's 10,000 miles we've done,' she said, '10,000 miles. And believe me it hasn't been a picnic.'

This was Zhejiang Province, the old eternal China – no fashion shows here, no spivs, no 'Shansh marnie', no talk of microchips and Reforms.

This was mostly paddy fields, and green shoots standing stiffly in black goop. It was an open, almost treeless landscape of bumpy ground and sharp-featured hills and greeny-blue mountains; tea, and rice, and bursting blue vegetables, reeking canals, tile-roofed huts, trampled dirt-roads, coolie hats, and everyone dressed in the same style of pyjamas.

The Zhejiang hills – the Kuocang Shan – were streaky: slashes of white and green, with claw marks and jagged ridges. There were no shade trees. Shade is a unnecessary luxury in an agricultural country and stunts the crops. In the unhindered sunshine the landscape was austerely tended and harshly fertile, and familiar things like trees and huts were so out of scale that the people looked miniaturized.

Everything they did was connected with food – planting it, growing it, harvesting it. The woman who looks as though she is sitting is actually weeding, those children are not playing – they are watering plants, and the man up to his shoulders in the creek is not swimming but immersed with his fish-net. The land here has one purpose: to provide food. The Chinese are never out of sight of their food, which is why as a people arrested at the oral stage of development (according to the scholar of psychohistory, Sun Longji) they take such pleasure in fields of vegetables. I found the predictable symmetry of gardens very tiring to the eye, and I craved something wilder. So far, China seemed a place without wilderness. The country had been made over and deranged by peasant farmers. There was something unnatural and neurotic in that obsession. They had found a way to devour the whole country.

Hunger had made them ingenious. At Jinhua the train stopped for a while and I saw a three-decker van for carrying pigs; animals in China always seemed to be kept in a space their own size. What could be crueller? I suppose the answer was: lots of things – an intellectual forced to shovel chicken-shit, a Muslim forced to keep pigs, a physicist ordered to assemble radios, an historian in a dunce cap, a person beaten to death for being a teacher. Next to these Cultural Revolution atrocities a pig in a poke was not really very bad, though it may have contributed to other forms of heartlessness. It was a very hot and humid day, and the pigs were whimpering in their racks as the train passed.

The background was mountainous, the foreground as flat as Holland – square pools of rice-shoots, and the roads no more than long narrow tracks. This landscape had no date – the people dressed as they always had; and it was impossible to date it by looking closely at tools and implements. I saw a thresher that looked like the first thresher in the world: a rigged-up whacking paddle hinged to a stick; and the buffalo yokes, the wooden plough, the long-fingered rakes and the fishermen's nets were all ancient designs. By sundown we had done 400 miles and we had never been out of sight of bent-over farmers or cultivated fields. Every surface had been cultivated, but it was spring and so even these cabbages had beauty.

I began talking with a Chinese man named Zhao who had just visited his girlfriend in Shanghai and was heading back to Changsha in Hunan.

'I took her out to a restaurant and I ordered dishes to impress her. Duck, chicken, fish – everything. It cost me twenty *yuan*!'

That was about £4 and for a moment I thought: *So what?* and didn't understand the anguish on his face.

Zhao said, 'That's a week's pay for me! I couldn't eat. I went to bed that night and I couldn't sleep.' He clenched his fists and hammered with them. 'Twenty *yuan!* I was cursing. I still feel bad.'

'I'm sure she appreciated it,' I said.

'Yes,' he said. 'She is a simple girl. She is a country girl. She is pure.'

Just as the landscape altered and became hillier, the sun went down. A couple from Macau – Manuel was Portuguese, Veronica was Chinese – were in my compartment. Veronica was skinny, with a small schoolboy's face and a schoolboy's haircut. She pouted for a while in the upper berth and then we all went to sleep. But I had never really got used to sleeping among strangers and so I woke up in the middle of the night and read my *Jin Ping Mei* and noticed once again that it was packed with foot-fetishism and bondage games. I glanced up and saw Veronica staring down at me from the upper berth.

At dawn, under a pink sky, the train stopped at Zhuzhou, and Zhao got out to change for the train to Changsha.

I said goodbye to him. I was grateful for something he had told me – that on a railway line outside Changsha was Shaoshan, the village where Mao Zedong had been born.

'Everyone used to visit that village,' he said. 'Now no one does.'

One of these days I'll go there, I thought. Zhao had given me careful directions.

This Canton train now turned south. With mountains always in the distance we tracked across the rice terraces to Hengyang, where the railway divides, one line to Guangxi, the other to Guangdong – the Two Kwangs, as they were once known.

The landscape had changed since Shanghai – not only its configuration (we were now among steep hills), but the methods of farming (these teetering, brimful terraces). The people here wore large wheel-like hats and lived in brick houses, with porches, about six families to a house. And some of the houses looked grand and ambitious, with columns supporting the porch-roofs and dragons moulded on the waterspouts of the eaves.

Every available flat space was planted. Beans grew at the margins of the rice terraces, and there were cabbages on the hillsides, and spinach and greens at the edge of the roads. The earth had been moved and manoeuvred so that everything – and especially the crumpled hills – looked man-made. The hills seemed a way of growing food vertically, like having fields on ledges and shelves to economize on space. The trees were tall and spindly, so that they would take up the least amount of room.

'Was that Hengyang?' Manuel said.

I told him it was.

'That was the place where Li Si – the Emperor Shi Huang's minister – was sawn in half, for burning the books in 213 BC.' He smiled into his bristly beard. 'The interesting thing is, he was sawn in half *lengthwise*.'

He had left Portugal and had planned to be in Macau for about two years; but five years later he was still there. He wondered whether he would still be there when Macau was handed back to the Chinese in 1999. He said he was impressed with what he had seen in China – it was his first visit. But he smiled again.

'Maybe after five years all this could be turned upside-down.'

'Are you optimistic?'

'You know the saying? An optimist speaks – what?'

'Chinese,' Veronica said.

'No. An optimist speaks Russian. A pessimist speaks Chinese.' Then he frowned. 'That doesn't sound right. I think it's an optimist speaks Chinese, a pessimist speaks Russian. That doesn't sound right either.'

We debated this. I said, 'Have you heard of the man who said, "I speak English to my valet, French to my mistress, and German to my horse"?'

'And Chinese to my laundryman,' Manuel said.

'And Portuguese to my cook,' Veronica said.

With the whole day to kill we tried to devise the itinerary for the longest railway journey in the world. It began in Portugal: Bragança–Lisbon–Barcelona–Paris–Moscow–Irkutsk–Peking–Shanghai – Hong Kong.

We came to Chenzhou, an industrial city in a mountain valley, with high, sharp, grey-green peaks all around it. And at noon we passed through Pingshi, on the Hunan-Guangdong border. The cliffs had the look of temples, with vertical sides that might have been fluted and carved. But they weren't; this was simply the pattern in the basalt. Here the boulders were as huge as hills and there were pagodas on them.

'Pagoda is a Portuguese word,' Manuel said. 'We say *pagode* in Portuguese – it means noise. I suppose they associated noise with these structures.'

Mandarin was also Portuguese, he said – from *mandar* (to be in charge); and the Japanese *arrigato* (thank you) had come from *obrigado*.

I went to the dining-car and took a seat next to a Chinese man in order to avoid Kicker ('First thing I do when I go home is have a big steak . . .'). We were passing through low jungle, but even so rice and corn were being grown under the thin trees. I thought: There are no old trees in China – at least I hadn't seen any.

The food was not good, but to give my meals a point I invented a system for nominating a dish of the day. I had spent too many days eating unmemorably. This was a Cantonese train, with the distinctively wet and sticky cuisine – mushrooms, chicken, sweet-sour fish, greasy vegetables. I chose the eels as my dish of the day.

While I was eating I remembered another occasion, six years before, when I was eating with a Chinese youth – a pompous one who was the son of a well-placed official, a so-called cadre-kid.

I had talked politics with him and he had said in one of his rebuttals, 'I am a member of the proletariat – and you are not. You are bourgeois.'

I mentioned this to my fellow diner, Mr Zhu.

'What does "proletariat" mean?' he asked.

I explained it.

He shook his head. 'No. I am a higher class than that. I am a white-collar worker.'

We talked about foreigners, because the dining-car was full of the tourists. Zhu said that unlike Chinese all foreigners were very excitable. We also had very loud voices. And we were gullible.

We discussed the Chinese proposition *We can always fool a foreigner.* Zhu said it was true, while I maintained that it was gloating and self-delusion. It was not even half-true, but I had yet to meet a Chinese person who did not believe it deep down. I said that most foreigners suspect that the Chinese believe this, which makes the Chinese misapprehension even worse. 'Consider the China pride and stagnant self-complacency of mankind' Thoreau wrote at the end of *Walden*.

Later, at Yingde, under the wrinkled mountains there were pools of lotus flowers and shaggy green slopes of bamboo. You might mistake this for wilderness, but no: the bamboo is eaten and used for baskets and house-building, and the lotuses are not growing wild – they are farmed and harvested for their roots. That was another dish of the day: dessert of sliced lotus root in syrup.

All day, beside this track, another track was being laid: a new one, for heavy freight, to Hong Kong, in anticipation of 1997.

I sat by the window and looked out, through the flicking rain. A boy was riding his buffalo home, and the sound of the train made pigs scatter under the banana trees, and it was so lush the train brushed against the tall tasselled weeds that grew beside the track. I saw clusters of deep-green bamboos, and women chopping firewood, and men smearing the wood frames of houses with mud to make walls. And peeling blue-gums, and a herd of buffaloes under some lofty cliffs of orange clay. It was a very wet province, Guangdong, and very distinctive for not looking exhausted: it was fertile, orderly, and energetic, and yet everything and everyone I saw had a specific purpose, which seemed to me very tiring to the eye – nothing random or accidental. Some minutes before we reached Canton the train stopped and a large blue dragonfly hovered near my window. That was perfect – the Chinese dragonfly shimmering in the lushness of Guangdong.

It was very hot in the train, in the nineties, with high humidity. Some passengers had collapsed, others were gasping. I hated arriving in Canton, because it meant I had to take off my pyjamas. It was raining hard in Canton. Cyclists in plastic shrouds darted through the downpour. I had not been prepared for the traffic or the commerce – all the radio and television shops, the taxi drivers who listened to Hong Kong rock music on their radios, the luxurious hotels like the White Swan, where Chinese went to look at the waterfall in the lobby, the 1,147-room Garden Hotel, the biggest in China, the China Hotel (its motto, *For the Merchant Prince of Today*) advertising 'A well-steaked reputation . . . succulent jet-fresh prime US and New Zealand corn-fed beef . . . Our steaks have a delicious reputation' – which also goes to show how far the Chinese will go to please foreigners, since the Chinese on the whole find a simple cooked steak a barbarous and tasteless meal that is appreciated by primitive folk like Mongolians and Tibetans.

No one I met remarked much on Canton. They spoke of Hong Kong and how it was going to be radically altered by Chinese control. I did not believe that. I did not think it would change. My feeling was that Canton was quickly turning into Hong Kong, and in most respects it was impossible to tell the difference.

The Chinese in Canton seemed well aware that making money and hustling in the Hong Kong manner was what mattered most. They could be mocking, too, about the government's solemn pretensions. One of the party slogans – written on billboards in

Canton – WAS LOOK TO THE FUTURE! (*Xiang qian kan.*) But the word for future (*qian*) sounds the same as the word money (*qian*) even though the character is radically different. So the current pun in Canton was LOOK TO THE MONEY!

Some Chinese in Canton asked me what I wanted to see there. I said, 'How about a commune?' and they almost split their sides laughing. The Chinese laugh is seldom a response to something funny – it is usually *Ha-ha, we're in deep shit* or *Ha-ha, I wish you hadn't said that* or *Ha-ha, I've never felt so miserable in my life* – but this Cantonese boffo was real mirth. The idea of visiting a commune anywhere in Guangdong province was completely ridiculous. There were none! And didn't I know that Deng Xiaoping had officially declared the commune experiment to have been a failure? Didn't I know that everyone was now paddling his own canoe?

I said, 'I was here six years ago and went to a huge commune outside Canton. Everyone said it was a model commune. It was a success. Factories. Rice fields. Fruit trees. A canning industry. I went to a woman's house and she had a radio, a television, a refrigerator –'

'She was the only person in the commune who had those things! It was a trick to impress you!'

'I just want to know what's there now,' I said.

'It's all been broken up into *geti hu*.'

Single-unit households, that is: every family for itself, or the family business.

'Is it working?'

'Yes, much better than before.'

'So if I go out there and ask the people how things are they'll say, "Wonderful."'

'That is correct.'

I said, 'How will I know they're not trying to impress me? Maybe that's a trick, too.'

'No, no, no,' this Chinese man said. 'Nowadays, people tell you what is in their heart. They are not afraid any more.'

'But they swore to me that the model commune I saw was running perfectly.'

'What did you expect them to say?'

That was a good point. Why should they belittle it to a foreigner, especially when it was such a loss of face to do so?

'That commune was so large,' my Chinese friend said, 'that a person had to take a train to see the head of the committee.'

'Is that a figure of speech?'

'Yes. It is a joke.'

For uninteresting reasons I was unable to visit the commune and compare my impressions with what I had seen in 1980. What I remembered best was visiting the woman who had the big dusty television (with a red shawl over it: cloth television-covers are still very popular in China), and listening to her spiel about this being a workers' paradise, and then going outside and watching children feeding white ducks in a green creek. But I swore that the first chance I got I would visit a commune and look at it closely for changes.

The changes were obvious in Canton. For one thing it was full of tourists. Some of these people were extremely elderly and infirm. They said they were looking forward to the Great Wall.

'Is there wheelchair access on the Great Wall?' they asked each other. 'Is there a ramp? Is there disabled parking? Is there a handicap entrance?'

It amazed me that people so frail should have risked being so far from home. But they were confident and curious, and I admired their pluck.

On the other hand, Canton was one of those places in the world where the hotels are so good and so all-encompassing that a guest need never leave: all the shops, events, colourful clothes, rugs, restaurants and everything else are right there in various parts of the air-conditioned building. And it is one of the facts of life in China today that the hotels are as great a tourist attraction as any of the temples or museums.

People went to Canton for many reasons, but the most interesting one I heard was from seven skinny youths who had come from Hong Kong to go ten-pin bowling.

I didn't laugh. Brainlessly banging cannon-balls down a varnished ramp and watching the pins go bopping seemed like fun to me. It was a hot afternoon and Canton was a big screechy place.

I loitered at the bowling alley but didn't play. I met an American named Barton, an oil man, who was supervising the drilling of wells. Were they offshore? He didn't say; he was rather circumspect, rather Chinese in fact, as if he suspected me of being engaged in industrial espionage.

Barton had been in Canton for four years, and before that had been in the Persian Gulf, which he had hated. But he hated China, too – his test wells had not paid off, though some others had. And yet the oil price was so low it hardly seemed worthwhile looking. It was certainly proving expensive. He told me several things I had not known – that China was a huge oil-producer, that it had a surplus because there were so few motor vehicles in China (and the power plants and most of the trains were fuelled by Chinese coal) and that China exported crude oil and gasoline to the United States. (Gasoline and fireworks are China's biggest exports to the United States.)

The shrinking oil-exploration schemes had meant a cut-back in Barton's mode of life, though. His wife and children lived in Hong Kong. The family used to get together twice a month. Now they met only once a month. It was pretty tough, Barton said, but necessary.

'I've got two kids to put through college. I need this job, I need the money – all the *gweilos* here do.'

Most of the expatriates used that expression when they referred to themselves. It was south China and Hong Kong self-mockery and meant 'foreign devil'.

'I was offered a job in Singapore,' he said. 'It was also oil-related. I probably should have taken it, but that place is too strict. I can't stand Lee Kwan Yew. He's a shit. They can have him. I'll take Deng any day.'

Barton laughed the phlegmy, fruity laugh of the chain-smoker.

'Know what we call Lee Kwan Yew? Hitler-with-a-heart. Har! Har!'

As someone who had had his own problems with 'Harry' Lee, I thought this description was funny and apt. And I was also struck by Barton's seriousness.

I was able to tell Barton my own Chinese oil-drilling story. In 1968, the Chinese embassy in Uganda brought a troupe of Red

Guards to Kampala to put on a show. There were acrobats and accordion-players and jugglers, all wearing red armbands; but the highlight of the evening was a Red Guard ballet about drilling for oil in one of the coldest and dreariest parts of China – Daqing, in the Manchurian province of Heilongjiang.

In the heat of the Ugandan night they mimicked frostbite and hypothermia as they danced and drilled through layers of ice and rock. They dropped with exhaustion and were on the point of giving up altogether – no oil.

They were harangued all this time by Red Guards (dancing, chattering, shaking their fists) and at the lowest point, when they had all but abandoned the effort of drilling, one of the Red Guards produced the *Little Red Book* and began reading Mao's Thoughts. He read from the chapter, 'Self-Reliance and Arduous Struggle'.

He showed his big square teeth and yelled, 'What is work? Work is struggle! There are difficulties and problems in those places for us to overcome and solve. We go there to work and struggle to overcome these difficulties. A good comrade is one who is more eager to go where the difficulties are greater!'

This cheered up the dancers dressed as riggers and drillers (they wore big bandage-like mittens and had rags on their feet). They were stirred by Mao's thought and, as a chorus chanted 'Great Helmsman . . . Reddest of the Red Suns rising in the East', the drillers went back to work and at last struck oil, a great gusher. This was expertly simulated with lights and back-projection, and over all of it a portrait of Chairman Mao shimmered as the Red Guards cheered. Oil! Mao's Thoughts! Prosperity! Workers serving the people! Overcoming difficulties!

Now all that was over and the oil-workers are, typically, harassed Americans, separated from their families, quite well paid and trying to put their kids through college.

At the Trade Exhibition, which is an immense bazaar of Chinese merchandise and the pride of Canton, I met a disgruntled man from Hong Kong, one Mr Tan, who was visiting his Cantonese relatives. He loved his relatives and was very loyal and dutiful, but he hated the Chinese attitude towards Mao. I had taken Mr Tan to be an unassuming soul, but he was full of invective.

'Mao kept China in the dark for almost thirty years,' he said. 'That's why these goods are substandard.'

I said that some of the merchandise looked well made to me – the bicycles, the wrenches, the carpets. And though the electric appliances looked dangerous and ugly, the beaded bags, the screwdrivers, the canned food and the textiles were all great bargains.

'It is not enough to make these things,' Mr Tan said. 'These people are in the dark. They think they know the world. They know nothing!'

It was even more mocking the way he said it in his Cantonese way, *Dey know nutting!*

'Mao was a joke. He was so stupid. And they believed him. Ha!'

'Everyone says it's different now,' I said.

'It looks different, but it is the same. You know why? Because they are the same.'

That cynicism was characteristic of the people the Chinese called 'Hong Kong Compatriots', and it was compounded of doubt and fear. It was voiced most strongly in Canton, because Canton was the closest equivalent in Chinese terms to Hong Kong. The anxiety was contagious. Most people in Canton wondered – and with reason – *What next?*

I looked for people who might have a clue. The most knowing was of course an American banker who had been in Canton for about an hour and a half. But he had been there before. His name was Arthur Fliegle, and he had a sort of sales-pitch in everything he said, that sounded so convincing – at least *he* sounded convinced – that it seemed to reek of insincerity. But he was on the boil, and so I listened.

'Forget the hotels, forget the Friendship Stores and gift shops, forget the restaurants and bowling alleys – all the tourist-related stuff,' Fliegle said. 'That will go its own way. It earns some money, but it's no big deal.'

'But the Chinese are trying to attract tourists,' I said.

'Forget it. That's a detail. They want investment. So look at it – look at the rest. The oil. The industry. The joint-ventures. Want to hear an interesting statistic? We're dealing with about 200 joint-ventures through my Hong Kong bank. Guess how many of those 200 are currently operating – I mean, actually off and running?'

I said I couldn't guess.

He raised two fingers. 'Two. That's all. And neither of them is making any money.'

'But everyone talks about joint-ventures.'

'They're whistling in the dark. Most companies have withdrawn their top people. They had highly paid executives in China, but they haven't been making any money. So they pull out their expensive American yuppies and they put in Joe Chen from Hong Kong – you know the guy, middle-aged, brown suit, plastic brief-case. They say "Go for it, Joe!" and he makes a dive, hits a brick wall and staggers back. "Go for it, Joe!" they yell again. And he hits the wall again. But so what? He's only costing $20,000 or $30,000 a year. That's the kind of guy operating now. The six-figure executive is gone.'

To provoke this man Fliegle I said that the Chinese seemed very confident about doing business.

'I'm not talking about them – I'm talking about investor confidence, and that seems to be ebbing away. That's why the next three or four years are so crucial. Already companies have pulled out. They aren't philanthropists or idealists. They want to make money, and if they don't make it they'll leave. At the moment, China's in a big expansionist phase, but so far there hasn't been much of a return – nothing to justify great hopes or big investments. The bubble might burst, and if it does it's going to be hell here. We'll know inside five years whether it's going to work.'

I found what this man said interesting, because he had no political ideas at all – he was all practical and unsentimental about the quickest way to make a buck. It fascinated me to think that there were many Chinese who were just the same.

Some Chinese had begun to rob graves. One of the commonest and most frequently condemned crimes in south China – where the best graves were – was relic-smuggling: digging up armour, weapons, pots, bronzes, silver, and ornaments, and bringing them to Hong Kong. In just two years, from 1984 to 1986, over 100 instances of smuggling had been foiled by the Chinese police – and 20,000 antiques recovered. These were not just family treasures but items filched from Tang and Han Dynasty tombs in Hunan. In some instances, it was a medieval kind of vandalism – farmers trampling on Han lyres and flutes because they had tiger motifs inscribed on them which the farmers found 'inauspicious'. Or the sixty tombs in Hengyang County which were destroyed by pig-keepers who used the mausoleum bricks to make pigsties. But the majority fell into the category of smuggled goods.

Typically the valuable contraband is hustled to Hong Kong by boat, or in trucks hidden under loads of Chinese cabbages. The destination is nearly always Hong Kong – none of this stuff is ever sold in China.

There are almost no antiques of any value, or any real age, for sale in China. It is illegal to sell anything older than 150 years – that is, the corny, imitative and degraded Early Qing. For Tang celadons, Ming bowls, even ancient terracotta and neolithic figures, Hong Kong is the place, and Hong Kong is busier now than it has ever been, because the smuggling is so intense.

'Nowadays the Chinese know it's valuable,' an antique dealer told me. 'They used to sell it to the state, but they don't any more – the state prices are too low. And it's this new attitude. Everyone's in business. Everyone is digging. They're looking for another Xian, another terracotta army – but this one they're going to sneak into Hong Kong – you'll see it in the shops in Hollywood Road and Cat Street. Already I am seeing the most incredible pieces – you wouldn't see them in the V and A, I'm not kidding. They are looting tombs, stealing from graves, digging holes. There has never been a period like this.'

It was very easy to say what China wasn't. It wasn't a frenzied and fanatical slogan-chanting mob of workers and peasants. It wasn't very political – people rolled their eyes and began to yawn at the mention of Mao. It wasn't particularly well built and indeed had some of the shoddiest-looking blocks of flats I had ever seen. It wasn't a country with lovely cities – and even much of the countryside looked torn apart and scalped. It wasn't very orderly, it wasn't quiet, it wasn't democratic. It wasn't what it had been – particularly here in Canton. That was obvious.

But it was hard to say what China was. Perhaps there was an intimation of hope in its complexity, but it was maddening for me to sit there watching the Cantonese rain come down and not to know what this all meant. And then I got a big dose of people attitudinizing – there was probably more of it in Canton than anywhere else, because Canton had more foreign visitors – and I thought: I'll just write it down and keep my own mouth shut, and I'll keep moving through China, going everywhere the train went, to the highest and lowest places, the hottest, the coldest, the driest, the wettest, the emptiest, the most populous, that was the only way, and afterwards I'll make up my mind.

A few days before I left Canton I met a woman who had been there, she said, many times. She was also leaving, but she was going in a different direction. Her name was Lisa Packard. She lived in Hong Kong. She had been visiting China for a dozen years, off and on, and now she was sick of it. She was in her mid forties and she seemed to me an enterprising person, with enough cultural and commercial interests to keep her busy. And she seemed well connected.

I agreed with her that things had changed, and I asked her whether she remembered the year that had happened.

'Remember the year?' she laughed. 'I remember the *week* things changed. There was a speech by Deng. Everyone responded to it. The Chinese are experts at interpreting jargon, and they knew he was saying something significant. It was one particular week in 1984, and after that everything was different.'

She said that sourly, so I said, 'But there have been a lot of improvements.'

'I don't think so,' Lisa said. 'I hate the changes. Now, all they want are trinkets and toys – colour TVs, cameras, watches, recorders, refrigerators, motor cycles. They're greedy, they're starting to be very crooked, they don't trust each other, they lie. Remember how you used to hear how they'd give you back your used razor blades? "Oh, we don't need these. We have razor blades of our own." So honest! So straight! So Chinese!'

I said that was a directive of Mao's from the *Little Red Book*. The Three Main Rules of Discipline for soldiers – but also for party workers – were: 'Obey orders in all your actions'; 'Do not take a single needle or thread from the masses'; and 'Turn in everything captured'. He had also made rules such as 'Speak politely', 'Return everything you borrow', 'Do not swear at people', and 'Do not take liberties with women'. Was this disillusionment with Mao a reason for this change in conduct?

Lisa said, 'Their excuse is that they have to get things while they can. They've only had a few years of this free system. But they know that China has periods of violent change. No one had foreseen this period. No one can foresee when it might end. So they are absolutely frantic. They feel it could all end tomorrow, and so they are grabbing with both hands. That's what they say when I ask. "If we delay we might never get another chance."'

'Surely that's an understandable attitude for people who have had their asses kicked for the past thirty years. And all the sermons they've had to listen to!' It often seemed as though Chinese life was one long sanctimonious drone of warning and advice and it was often hard to distinguish the moralizing edicts of the Chinese Communist Party from the corn-pone saws of Elbert Hubbard. Not only Mao, but his followers as well, had created a whole anthology of pious parables, from The Foolish Old Man Who Removed the Mountains to Lei Feng the Model Soldier.

'I'm talking about real corruption, the worst kind – party corruption,' Lisa Packard said. 'Where only the high party members get privileges – they go abroad, they get into five-star hotels, they have access to hard currency. The rest of the people are out of luck. But the army is watching. The army isn't sharing in any of this. A soldier has no means of making extra money, he is not part of the economy, he simply watches people come and go.'

I had heard that before; only the army – still sentimentally called the People's Liberation Army – had the key to China's future, because no one could govern without the army's consent. And the PLA was notoriously conservative.

'The army is watching, and what does it see? People who are spiritually hollow, spiritually bankrupt. At least with fat, crazy old Mao they had a kind of faith – even idealism and a sense of working together. They always used that Chinese expression, "working together". There was a unity in that, but it's totally lacking now. They're not nice, they're not polite. I think they're lost and it will all end horribly for them.'

But far from dampening my ardour, what Lisa Packard said only made me eager to plunge back in. Anyway I was sick of this rain. I heard there was no rain at all in Inner Mongolia and that the crocuses were popping up all over distant Gansu; so I planned a long trip by train through the westernmost provinces of China – so ambitious a trip that I had to enlist the help of the Railway Board. They were suspicious but they said that if I went to Peking they would discuss it with me. I needed permission, they said.

The tourists were leaving China for good – some had gone already, the Wittricks, the Westbetters, laden with souvenirs (lacquer, carpets, chopsticks, brassware, fans), and the Cathcarts were already back in Bexhill on Sea.

Kicker and Morris had not left the bar of the White Swan. Kicker said, 'The guys back home will never believe it when I say I screwed a bald woman.'

He was chuckling softly. His laughter always reminded me that he had a metal plate in his head. Then he squinted at me.

'But I was a Marine,' he said. 'We fuck anything.'

He had met a young Japanese woman in Canton – had just passed by her open hotel room, started shooting the breeze with her and ended up in bed with her. Kicker was sixty-seven years old and had the face of a rapist. But his features softened as he recalled the encounter – just yesterday, it was, on the fourth floor.

'It was real nice,' he said. 'That gal gave me more loving in those six hours than I had in fifteen years of marriage.'

Morthole was looking on. He was very drunk. He was alone. He had not made any friends on his long trip. He asked me what I was planning to do. I told him: Head north – more China.

'More tombs,' he said. 'More chopsticks. More pagodas. What are you doing?'

'Trying to get the hang of it,' I said.

'And you're going by train? It'll take ages!'

'It'll give me a feeling of accomplishment.'

Morthole laughed. He did not seem to me very bright, but I had never said much to him. I had merely noted the times when he had gone in search of stones, and I had marvelled at the satchelful he had collected. His prize was a chunk of the Great Wall – he wondered whether he would be able to smuggle it through Customs at Canton Railway Station.

Each of those tourists had surprised me in one way or another. It made me think that you never really know anyone until you have travelled 10,000 miles in a train with them. I had sized them up in London, but they were all both better and worse than they had seemed then, and now they were beyond criticism because they had proved themselves to be human. Morthole, the recluse and rock-collector, had a surprise for me, too. I had thought him an illiterate and I had not taken him very seriously – or his bag of rocks.

'Do you know *The Excursion*?' he said.

I said I didn't know what he was talking about. What was this, some China sightseeing tour to the high spots?

'William Wordsworth,' he said. 'I learned it at school.'

'Oh, *that Excursion*.'

Morthole raised his glass and said:

> 'An irksome drudgery seems it to plod on,
> Through hot and dusty ways, or pelting storm,
> A vagrant merchant bent beneath his load,
> Yet do such travellers find their own delight . . .'

Oh, God, I thought, and all this time I've been patronizing this poor bastard.

But speaking of travellers finding their own delight, I decided that day to leave Canton. I went to bed thinking how China exists so distinctly in people's minds that it is hard to shake that fantasy loose and see the real thing. It was not quite the same as looking for igloos in Alaska, or grass skirts in Tahiti, or big blubber-lipped Ubangis in Africa; but it was similar. And it was as wrong to lean on the fake Chinese imagery that comes third-hand to every westerner as it was to believe in the wholesome air of poverty.

I had a nightmare. I woke up in a sweat as the nightmare ebbed away: I was on a mobbed street, full of toothy and unfriendly faces, and felt trapped and suffocated in a big city. It was a Chinese city – a Chinese nightmare. I thought: Most of my nightmares are Chinese nightmares. On its most ordinary-seeming street, this unravelling republic had sights to scare the hell out of me. But I was growing fond of its gorgeous insects.

6

Train Number 324 to Hohhot and Lanzhou

It had been a very bad month on China's western railway, where wild yaks on the line accounted for some delays, and sandstorms were frequent. Just before I set off I read in the *China Daily* that 330 miles of track had been buried by the worst sandstorms for twenty years. The report was precise in its tale of woe: a force twelve gale had raged for forty-eight hours, and the 'eye-blinding sandstorm' had dumped 100,000 tons of sand on the track, stranding forty-seven trains and closing the line for nine days, during which 10,000 rail passengers were evacuated. People died in the storm. People were injured. Vast prefectures of Gansu and Xinjiang were cut off.

But in the way it was ignored by the world, and even ignored by most Chinese (it was just a tiny news item) and in the way it was quickly remedied, it was a very Chinese disaster.* After the death and destruction, shovels were distributed, the trains were dug out, the tracks disinterred, and new sand-barriers erected – fences this time, instead of grass clumps. The Chinese had their political

*The 1976 earthquake in China, hardly noticed by the world, killed more than 250,000 people, and 16 million Chinese died in the 1957–9 famine.

dilemmas, and the technological side of Chinese society was a mess ('communications' was an inappropriate word for toy telephones, morse code and scribbled notes), but if it were possible for the Chinese to shovel themselves out of trouble they succeeded brilliantly. Digging was a national preoccupation and during the Cultural Revolution – as my friend Wang said – everyone had his own hole, in case of war. Come to think of it, the Great Wall too was a sort of digger's masterpiece. And the old fable that Mao always cited, The Foolish Old Man Who Removed the Mountains, was the digger's gospel – the point was that the old man was not foolish at all and that the Chinese could move mountains (even the metaphorical ones of imperialism and feudalism) by digging.

When the line was clear I left for Hohhot, in Inner Mongolia. I was not alone. A small portly gentleman had been assigned to me. He had the face of a sea-lion – not an unusual face in China. English-speaking was not one of his skills, but he was fluent in Russian, a language that mystifies me. His name was Mr Fang. We were travelling together as a result of a discussion I had had with the Railway Board, but these discussions were more in the nature of 'struggle sessions'.

A delegation had come to my hotel and delayed me with politeness and abused me with flattery, blackmailing me with such phrases as 'famous writer', 'important person' and 'foreign friend'. Indeed, I was so important and dignified that I could not possibly travel alone on this journey to the west, but would have to be provided with an entourage.

I said that I usually travelled alone, and that I made a virtue of it, and I refrained from saying that if I was in need of a travelling companion it certainly would not have been a huge goofy man like Mr Zhong, with his sinister laugh and his slurping way of eating.

We were in the restaurant of my hotel, Mr Zhong, Mr Fang and Mr Chen. Mr Zhong blew the surface of his tea, then sucked it in and gurgled it inside his cheeks, and gulped it. And his way with noodles was worse, and noisier: he made his mouth into a suck-hole and woofed them through it in a wet twisted hank. His gasps made me feel violent towards him.

So far, Mr Fang had not said anything; and Mr Chen only put in a word now and then to be helpful.

'There is no earthly reason why anyone should come with me.'

Mr Zhong went *schhhllooopp* with his tea, and chewed it loudly, and then said, 'To give you correct information.'

'I think I'm capable of getting correct information on my own,' I said. 'I've done a little travelling, you know.'

'But not in China.'

'In China, as a matter of fact. Six years ago. Down the Yangtze.'

'The Chang Jiang,' he said, giving me correct information, as if I didn't know what the Chinese called the damned thing. Like all pedants, at heart he was just being stubborn and obstructive.

'And Peking and Canton.'

'Beijing and Guangzhou,' he said woofing noodles.

'I'm giving you their English names, Mr Zhong. We don't say Hellas for Greece, or Roma for Rome, or Paree, if we're speaking English. So I don't see the point –'

'I must come with you,' Mr Zhong said.

Never, I thought.

'We will leave tonight,' he said.

Over my dead body, I thought.

'I will help you,' he said.

'Believe me, it's extremely kind of you to offer,' I said. 'But I don't need your help.'

His face was big and pale. He smiled at me and said, 'I can carry your bag.'

I said, 'Did you go to a university?'

'Oh, yes. Jiaotong University. I studied engineering.'

'So you're trained for a different job – not for carrying bags.'

'My English is very good. I can be your interpreter.'

'I want to improve my Chinese.'

'I can help you with that,' he said. 'And you can teach me some more English, and about literature, and about your country.'

'I'm afraid that's out of the question,' I said.

'You must be looked after properly.'

'I don't want to be looked after,' I said. 'I just want to take the train and stare out the window.'

'Oh, no,' he said. 'We must do our best. You are our responsibility. And we can talk.'

Why wasn't Mr Fang saying anything?

'I may not want to talk,' I said. 'I may want to sit and read. I may want to look out of the window.'

Mr Zhong put his face against his teacup, averted his pale lips, and whooshed at it. I had taken a dislike to him very early in the discussion – as soon as we were introduced, in fact – because he was a person whose banter sounded to me like a reprimand. I had left some papers in my room and he had said, 'Don't get lost!' and 'Don't disappear!'

'You are very generous to offer to look after me, but I can manage alone,' I said. 'I may not want to talk to anyone. And I don't want any of your kind assistance.'

There followed a rapid conversation in Chinese, Mr Fang doing most of the talking. I had been fascinated by his sea-lion's face, his sorrowful eyes and downturned mouth. He spoke with insistence and authority, and he had seemed very intelligent when he had been listening.

Fattish and insolent-looking Mr Zhong went on slurping his noodles and sucking his tea, as Mr Fang spoke. One of Mr Zhong's slurps was actually a form of reply. I decided that he looked brattish and spoiled, and I guessed that he had been a Red Guard, from the way he nagged.

He said quietly, 'Mr Fang says he will go with you.'

'Why?'

'Because he does not speak English.'

'I don't want to walk around with him either,' I said, imagining Mr Fang breathing down my neck.

'He will simply sit,' Mr Zhong said.

'But in another compartment,' I said, 'because I would like to meet other people.'

'He will occupy another compartment,' Mr Zhong said.

'If he doesn't talk to me, and he doesn't walk around with me, and he doesn't travel in the same compartment,' I said, 'I don't understand why he wants to come with me.'

'To make sure you are comfortable. Hospitality. You are our guest. Ha-ha!' Mr Zhong's shouting laughter was cruel and accusing.

I said, 'Mr Fang is head of the department. He is obviously very busy. He has a desk, a chair, and work to do. He has to write reports. He has a family – right? Wife? Children?'

'Two females.'

'Okay. So wouldn't it be a lot more convenient if he didn't come with me? I can hire local guides – it's cheap enough.'

'Perhaps. But this is the Chinese way.'

Mr Chen was becoming anxious. He signalled to me with his eyes, saying: Enough, no more, leave off.

That was how I came to be travelling with this small silent man on the train to Hohhot. The fact was that the authorities had got wind that I was travelling in China, and afraid that I would snoop, and that I'd rat on them afterwards, they stuck me with Mr Fang. Interestingly, this episode was probably the most irritating thing that happened to me in China, and they could have made me very happy if they had decided not to haunt me in this way and attempt to obstruct me with this nanny-like official.

When we were alone on the train and rolling through Hebei Province and its endless rice fields, I asked Mr Fang in Chinese whether he spoke English.

'Not well,' he said in Chinese, and it was then that he divulged his fluency in Russian. He had taught Russian literature and language at a technical college in Peking.

'Evgen Onegin,' he said. 'Pushkin. Chekhov. Gogol. Dostoievski.'

'Turgenev. Tolstoy,' I said, and he nodded. 'Bulgakov. Mayakovsky.'

Saying these names was like holding a conversation. But it was a short conversation. I had made a thing about not wanting to sit around talking English, and so they had called my bluff by sending this Russian speaker.

I was grateful that I had been spared Mr Zhong. I had not wanted to travel with any official, but at least Mr Fang was a gentle soul. He offered to carry my bag, and then he offered to heave it into the luggage rack; I said I could manage. His own bag was very small. Because the Chinese don't own much, they travel light. And Mr Fang's bag contained a large book and not much else.

'Pushkin?' I asked.

He laughed and showed me. It was an English-Chinese dictionary. I looked up a few obscene words, but there were none in it. I riffled the pages and saw a word, a definition, and a sample sentence in italics: *Because of the calumnies of the enemy, Lu Xun was compelled to fight harder*.

It was a twelve-hour journey to Hohhot, but this was a long-distance train, going on to Lanzhou, so we left at midnight. We were joined by two jolly Cantonese who were going to Datong to change trains for the Taiyuan line. They were going, they said, to Pinghe, to an open-cast mine – one of the largest in China.

I looked on the map.

'I can't find Pinghe.'

'It's not on the map yet.'

That was another Chinese conundrum – that they could build cities faster than they could print them on maps, and build railways quicker than they could show them with black lines.

'The whole province of Shanxi is a coal seam,' one of the men said. Heavy equipment was his speciality. He said that 2,000 men were digging and that coal would be produced soon.

'What sort of a place is Pinghe?'

'It is a horrible place,' the second man said, with a smile. 'It is flat and windy. There are no trees. There is dust. It is desert.'

They were travelling with enormous amounts of luggage, but they explained that most of it was food, since there was no food in Pinghe. There was nothing in Pinghe except coal.

They dragged themselves and their provisions off the train early the next morning, and soon after that we entered Inner Mongolia – a bare dusty landscape, with low stunted-looking trees, and square-sided settlements made of smooth mud, and goats, and mongrels, and people hacking at furrows and bashing weeds, and here and there was the occasional horseman. It was one of the regions the Chinese described by wincing and calling it 'the grasslands' – and they prayed they would not be sent to work in such a region. On the other hand, it was a fact that the Hans had displaced the Mongolians here – the expatriates and exiles had taken over.

As we rounded a bend, the engine came into view – a big black locomotive, squawking and blowing out smoke and steam, a fat kettle on wheels. The air was so still on the Mongolian plain that on the straighter stretches the smoke from the engine passed my windows and left smuts on my face, and I was eighteen coaches from the smoke-stack.

By hot yellow noon, the landscape had wrinkled mountains behind it, but they were bare and blue, and some nearer hills were only slightly mossy. There were no trees. There were ploughed fields everywhere, but nothing sprouting. In the villages there were mud walls around every house. You would not have to be told you were in Mongolia – this was about as Mongolian as a place could possibly be.

I found Mr Fang staring dejectedly out the window and, feeling sorry for him, I asked him about his Russian teaching.

'I liked it,' he said, 'except for the Red Guard period.'

'What happened then?'

'From 1966 until 1972 there were no classes. I stayed at home and read books.'

'Why? Had you been criticized?'

'Criticize' was the jargon-word for forty-six of them howling at you or even beating you.

'Yes. They said I was a revisionist.' In a plaintive way, he said, 'Maybe it was true. I did not understand Marxist-Leninist theory.' He turned to me and added, 'They didn't understand it either.'

'Afterwards, did you feel bitter?'

'No. I said nothing. They were young. They didn't know anything. That whole period was a disaster.'

He was riled by the memory, so I left him alone. But my curiosity impelled me to go back, because I couldn't understand how it was that he had spent all those years at home, reading books. I said, 'You mean, you were just sitting there, turning pages?'

He shook his head. 'I was carrying rocks.'

It was forced labour, he explained. The whole technical college had been moved to a remote place called Mengjin, just north of Luoyang, in Henan Province; and there they had built a bridge over the Yellow River.

'Most of these railways were built by intellectuals who were sent to the countryside,' he explained. 'That's why they took so long. What did we know about it?'

He was disgusted, he said. In the fifties Japan and China were about equal, he went on. In the sixties Japan developed and China went backward. 'Now look at the difference!'

I did not agree with his analysis, but instead of contradicting him I asked, 'Would you like China to resemble Japan?'

'Frankly no.'

We were still at the window. As the mountains receded into the distance, the houses became more frequent and piled up and uglier – the unmistakable sign in China that a city is not far off. There was a wide dry river-bed, a depleted tributary of the Dahei river, and tall gawky trees – Mongolian trees, like fakes, unconvincing because they are wholly out of place and too feeble to serve any purpose. Anyway, most trees I had seen in China seemed purely symbolic. I saw distant water-towers and chimneys, and not far off a dust cloud. Beneath that dust cloud was Hohhot, the capital of Inner Mongolia.

It was not really a city – it was a garrison that had been plonked down in the Mongolian prairie, and every building in it looked like a factory. It had been planned and much of it built by the Russians, but even its newer structures looked horrible – the hotel, the guesthouse, the department stores. I wondered whether it looked this way because of the Mongols themselves – what did tent-dwelling nomads know about city planning? But no, it was not inhabited by Mongols. It was all Hans in short-sleeved shirts, pouting as they cycled on Hohhot's streets.

'What do you want to see?' Mr Fang said.

'I want to see a Mongol,' I said.

'There isn't time.'

He explained that all the Mongols were over there, in the grassland, in the rugged range they called the 'Great Green Mountains'. The horsemen, the wrestlers, the archers, the yakherds, were absent from Hohhot. They lived in the wild, which was their right these days as a so-called minority.

I declined a visit to Yijinhuoluo, the tomb of Genghiz Khan (1162–1227), which the Chinese built recently as a sop to Mongolian national pride. It is a whitewashed yurt, in concrete, in the middle of nowhere.

'I want to see how people live here,' I said.

Mr Fang took me to the 'Five Pagoda Monastery', which was a

stack of defaced Buddhas, still showing traces of Cultural Revolution vandalism. But it was high enough for seeing the roofs of the old town, and the crooked lanes, and the minarets of the mosque.

'Let's go there,' I said, pointing.

But Mr Fang manoeuvred me into the car and we drove out of town to the tomb of Wang Zhao Jun, on a man-made hill 150 feet high. He urged me to admire the ingenuity of the hill – think of all the digging!

'I would like to see some people,' I said.

He took me to a pagoda, a lamasery, and then to the mosque.

'How many Muslims are there here?' I asked a man in a skullcap.

'Thousands.'

'Have any been to Mecca?'

'One,' he said. 'The government sent him last year.'

The mosque was decorated in the Chinese style, with curved tile roofs and red-painted eaves. In the centre of the main building high above the door there was a painted clock-face – a large one, that gave the mosque the look of a railway station. But this was all painted, and even the time was painted on it. The time was perpetually 12.45. No one knew why.

The following day I sneaked downstairs, skipped breakfast, and was on my way out the front door of the hotel when Mr Fang hurried towards me, making a noise. It was a kind of laughter. By now I was able to differentiate between the various Chinese laughs. There were about twenty. None of them had the slightest suggestion of humour. Some were nervous, some were respectful, many were warnings. The loud honking one was a sort of Chinese anxiety attack. Another brisk titter meant something had gone badly wrong. Mr Fang's laugh this morning resembled the bark of a seal. It meant *Hold on there!* and it stopped me in my tracks.

'Where are you going, Mr Paul?'

'For a walk.'

Mr Fang conferred with his Hohhot deputy. My walk was given official sanction, and I was driven about 100 yards to the People's Park and released. It was not a large park. It was surrounded by high walls. Its artificial lake had dried up. It was very dusty. Here, I walked. Even at this early hour there were Chinese couples smooching. The poor things have nowhere else to go in China, except public parks. I said to myself: It is wrong to expect too much from a Mongolian city.

Mr Fang and his deputy were waiting for me by the turnstile at the exit gate.

'You enjoyed your walk?'

'Very much,' I said.

'Now what would you like to do?'

'I think I'll go back and get washed,' I said. 'I need a shave.'

Mr Fang laughed in consternation, and told me to wait. And he held another conference with his Hohhot deputy, while I stood, frowning at the city. There were no clouds overhead. The sky was blue, the earth brown, the air smelled of dust. It was a typical Mongolian day.

Mr Fang gestured for me to get into the car. We drove across town to what I first took to be a factory and then realized was a hotel. It smelled of peeling paint and rotting carpets. I was escorted to a room where there were barber chairs and sinks. A young man approached holding a towel and twitching it.

Mr Fang said, 'He is very young and inexperienced, but he will try.'

The young man smiled and worked open the cut-throat razor that he had been concealing with his towel.

'I can shave myself,' I said, and did so, using one of the sinks.

Mr Fang laughed: nervous admiration and a sort of pent-up anxiety. I could tell he was worried by what I would ask to do next. I spent the rest of the day trying to elude him and his deputy, and at last in the market I succeeded. It was late in the afternoon. We were all (Mr Fang, his deputy, and the driver) admiring a stack of vegetables, and when I saw they were transfixed by a shaggy mound of blue cabbages I slipped away.

I found the bird-sellers and had an urge to buy every one of their birds and let the poor things go. There was once a Chinese festival which encouraged such practices, 'The Liberation of Living Creatures'. The Chinese are bird-mad. They pay large sums for the rarest birds, and they keep them in tiny ornate cages, or else they eat them. This is not bird-fancying exactly; they covet the birds but they are not sentimental about them. At the Hohhot bird market there were people carrying home finches that had been stuffed into small plastic bags, and the new owners simply clutched them in their sweaty hands. I said it was a little hard on the birds, but they showed me that they had compassionately poked holes in the plastic bags.

There were rosefinches and hawks, and the most popular bird looked like a plover, with a ringed neck and brownish wings. But when I heard it sing I knew it was not a plover. One of the bird-sellers wrote down its name and I discovered later it was a Mongolian lark. It seemed a hell of a fate for such a musical bird to be snatched from its freedom in the immense grasslands and clapped into a tiny bamboo cage. But there are worse fates. One of the culinary perversions of France is making larks into pâté and spreading them on toast.

Later, when Mr Fang found me, he introduced me to several officials. They had been sent to Hohhot from Peking. Everyone I had met in Hohhot, except the Muslims, had been sent from Peking. It was just another unpopular post, but no one complained. I did find it odd that after two and a half days in Mongolia I still had not met an ethnic Mongolian. Everyone I asked had the same explanation – a vague wave of the hand and a mutter, 'Over there,' meaning somewhere in the yellow emptiness of the grasslands.

When we left Hohhot, and were waiting for the train to arrive I reminded Mr Fang of our agreement not to travel together in the same compartment. He said that was fine with him. There was a commotion behind us – fifteen shuffling men escorting a high official across the platform. They were seeing him off. He was a stern skinny man in a blue cap and blue baggy suit; his shapeless clothes alone marked him out as a hardliner – the conservatives (always referred to in China as 'leftists') still have not abandoned their Maoist look of austerity, and this one had an unusually fearsome look, as if daring anyone to laugh at his flappy pants.

His underlings were effusive in the insincerely solicitous way that arouses either contempt or pity – or indifference, as in the case of this official. All this bootlicking hardly made him blink, and he turned his back on them as they slurpingly said goodbye.

When I found my compartment, this man was in it, already seated and making tea. I had come to see that there was even a 'leftist' way of making tea. The real hardliners carried old chubby jam-jars and reused the tea-leaves again and again, seldom changing them but letting them pile up until the jar was half-full of sodden leaves. I put a pinch of green tea into the teacup that was provided free by China Railways – surely he knew that? – and poured the hot water from the thermos, also provided free of charge.

'Hallo,' I said. 'How are you?'

He nodded, saying nothing.

'Are you going to Yinchuan or Lanzhou?'

He stared at me.

'I'm going to Lanzhou,' I said, and in English, 'God, you're a friendly guy. But don't mind me – I'm just going to curl up with this book.'

It was *The Gobi Desert*, by Mildred Cable, an account of her Chinese travels in the twenties, when she went up and down the deserts of Turkestan in a horse-drawn cart.

The sun reddened and dissolved into the dust of the Mongolian plain as we set off, jogging westward. In the morning the blue baggy man was gone, and I guessed he had got off in the Mongolian city of Baotou.

We followed the course of the Yellow River, its big loop in Mongolia and its straighter progress in the stricken province of Ningxia. No one had a good word for Ningxia, and I could see why. It was a parched and windblown place, with a tiny population, many of them the tenaciously backward-looking Hui people – Muslims. Privately the Chinese regarded them as filthy and superstitious, but publicly they praised their quaint habits. The Chinese felt rather guilty about the Hui people. Knowing of the Hui horror of pigs and pork, officials in the time of the Cultural Revolution put Huis in charge of pigsties and made them pigherds and bacon-slicers.

We had left the sparse plains and grassy mountains of Mongolia, and were now among big, bulky, Irish-looking mountains, scattered with sheep and goats. All the slopes were worn-down and stony, with gullies and ravines and chopped-out sluices and quarries – as if some time in the remote past water had rushed through this place and taken every live thing away, and the topsoil too. It was spectacular desolation.

The plain returned again and was as flat as a billiard table. The railway tracks were dead straight, and the steam locomotive pulling the train poured soot behind it. I kept the window closed when I realized that the black flakes were accumulating on me and Mildred. I decided that this landscape of straight lines had inspired people to build houses with lots of right angles – flat roofs and straight square walls. There seemed something melancholy in such enormous distances, and yet nearly everything that was ploughable had been ploughed. But I did not see anyone in those hot fields. The sun moved slowly through the high blue sky, and beneath it everything looked torpid, in tones of light brown. There were very few towns, but each one was a dismal anticlimax: square factories, square houses.

The gulping, wheezing steam engine, with its characteristic rattles and shakes, released a dragon of black smoke and it steamed onward through Ningxia. And once from the upraised track I saw a town that was all bungalows and yards – like a parody of an American suburb; indeed, like my home town, Medford, made out of mud.

In the dining-car the wind made a low fuzzy moan through the rusty window screens. It was lunchtime, and we all had our snouts in the rice bowls. It was greasy spinach today, and little withered worms of pork, and knuckles of nameless meat.

I shared my table with Mr Lu, on his way to Lanzhou. He was in his twenties, and college-educated. Perhaps it was because we were in the dining-car that he began saying how people behaved very greedily and selfishly these days.

'They say, "Everyone else is doing it – why shouldn't I?"'

I said, 'Presumably it's because the lid is off, and people have more freedom.' And I said that I had read that it was usually the case that when tyranny was relaxed people behaved more recklessly – sometimes sudden freedom brought chaos. But that wasn't an argument against freedom.

'I don't know,' Mr Lu said. 'But we have never seen this sort of thing before. The Chinese even in bad times behaved very responsibly so as not to shame their families. But now it's every man for himself.'

I said that on the whole I had found the Chinese very polite and helpful.

'It depends on how old they are,' Mr Lu said. 'The worst ones are those who were about ten or fifteen at the start of the Cultural Revolution. They were robbed of everything. They had no childhood, no education, no family, no training, no happiness at all. They are about thirty or forty years old now, and they are very angry – angry with everyone. They feel cheated. I know a woman in Lanzhou who said, "If the City Council doesn't give me an apartment I'll go find one, and I'll move in, and I won't budge." I told her that was illegal. She said, "I don't care." That's not Chinese. But she was about thirty-five. She had lost everything in the Cultural Revolution. We are living in a very strange time.'

'This train isn't so strange,' I said.

He smiled at me. He said, 'Not long ago on this train I saw an incident. A man in Hard Class was lying across one seat. That means he was taking up three sitting-places. The other passengers were angry. But the man would not move. Finally, they got a policeman, who told the man to move.

'The man said no. The policeman said, "Move."

'"What are you going to do about it?" the man said.

'Of course, the policeman could do nothing if the man didn't co-operate. But that was very unusual – very un-Chinese. This man was thirty or so – that explained it to me. The lost generation. The interesting thing is that he did not move. The policeman went away. He had failed. He had even tried to use logic. "You bought one ticket, but you are using three seats" – that sort of thing.

'"I don't care," the man said. "So what?" That's the attitude among that age-group.'

'Do you think it's serious?'

'Yes. And it frightens me,' Mr Lu said.

Mr Lu asked me where I was going. I told him that I was headed into Xinjiang, and he made a face – a slight smile of pain. He said he had no desire to go into the desert. The cities of Turfan and Urumchi held no interest for him.

'If I had the time and the money I would go to Hangzhou or

Suzhou,' he said, expressing the common Chinese wish to go to a place where there were a million other tourists. 'Or Guangzhou,' he added – another Disneyland.

But to the question 'Where would you go?' the Chinese I spoke to rarely named a place that was outside the Great Wall, reflecting the ancient fear and prejudice that it was all monkeys and hairy bastards and savages beyond the Wall.

There were two dozen Chinese college students on the train, going to Lanzhou from Peking to take part in a swimming meet. They were going Hard Class and they seemed to enjoy being tumbled together in the dormitory coaches. At their technical college they lived just like this, eight to a room, with laundry hanging everywhere, and they slept on shelves that went up the wall.

As we passed from Ningxia into Gansu I talked to them. Some were shy and some frisked like kittens and others just glowered at my nosy questions. I asked most of them whether they believed in life after death. All of them said firmly no.

'But most Americans do,' one said, and the rest of them agreed that this was so.

I had asked them that because we had begun by talking about dreams. They told me dreams they had – about guilt, persecution, being naked, being pursued.

'Everyone has those dreams,' I said. 'I used to dream about being chased by a monster that looked like a huge potato. And I still have dreams about suddenly realizing that I have to take an important exam that I'm unprepared for.'

We were talking in English, which they spoke very well. In fact, one of the boys – unusual for a college student – was westernized (in the Chinese way) to the extent that he had had his hair curled. It was the fashion in large Chinese cities that summer, among people who had money – men and women. Taxi drivers affected a Liberace coiffure, their hair permed and fluffed up, and sometimes lightly tinted. But it was not so common as to go unnoticed. Outside The Phoenix Beauty Salon in Shanghai, and Peking's Golden Flower Perma Parlour there were always baffled people pressed against the front windows, watching the dandified young men getting their hair curled.

That curly-haired student said he didn't have any dreams at all, presumably on the assumption that dreaming was too old-fashioned a preoccupation for such a stylish trend-setter as him.

Anyway, I left the subject, and left their coach, but later when I was looking at the rubbly landscape I was joined by one of the girls who said that she had had a dream that was worrying her.

'Three dreams, I mean. But all of them were about my father and my brother.' She had a delicate face and anxious eyes, and she spoke in a shy but determined way. Obviously she had not wanted to tell me this dream in front of all the other students. 'In the first dream my father killed my brother with a stick. In the second, he hanged my brother. In the third, he shot him What does it mean?'

'Is your father violent?'

'Very violent,' she said.

'What about your mother?'

'My mother passed away six months ago.'

'When did you start having these dreams?'

'After she died.'

'You live in Peking?'

'No. I study in Peking, but my home is in a country area, near Wuhan. It is a very large house – nine rooms, in a very remote place. It is also a very strange place. There are groves of bamboo all around it. Do you know the sound that bamboo makes?'

I nodded: it was one of the creepiest sounds in the world, the wind making the bamboo stalks rub and mutter.

'It is an old house,' she said. 'My mother died in it, and my father lives there with my younger brother. My father is not only violent. He is also very unhappy. I am afraid. Do you think my dream will come true?'

I said that she probably felt guilt for having gone to Peking to study. Her mother had been a restraining influence, and she wanted to protect her brother.

'The last time I saw my brother he was unfriendly. It was Spring Festival. I was glad to see him, but he refused to go for a walk with me.'

This was all very gloomy, and I tried to think of something to say, but before I could she spoke again.

'I think something terrible is going to happen,' she said. 'My father is going to kill my brother.'

Actually I felt the same thing, but I didn't say so. I told her not to worry but to go home fairly soon, to see her brother and try to gain his confidence.

She said, 'This dream is telling me that I must get a job in Wuhan, near my home.'

This corner of Gansu had the look of a landscape which had been bombed. But the craters and foxholes and exploded-looking ravines were the work of wind and water – wind, mostly, because this was semi-desert. The Yellow River was motionless and soupy, and the hills were the colour of cornbread and just as crumbly.

Once when I was talking with the students I saw Mr Fang eyeing me. I knew he had been sent to keep me in line, and I was waiting for a chance to ditch him; but I felt a little sorry for him, in whatever report he had to write about my behaviour or the subjects of my whispered conversations on the trains, because the poor man spoke only Russian. His sea-lion face often made him seem sad.

I found one of the teachers and discovered her to be just about my age. Her name was Professor Shi. In 1967, when she was a student, she was an ardent supporter of the Cultural Revolution and volunteered to travel from Peking to Anhui Province to work on a tea plantation. She abandoned all ideas of further study and picked tea for six years.

'I think it was like the Peace Corps,' she said.

'No,' I said. 'The Peace Corps was innocent and inefficient, and we weren't under any pressure to join. But going into the countryside in China was a big Maoist campaign.'

'I asked to go,' Professor Shi said, somewhat avoiding my point about her being pressured. 'I wanted to live like a peasant.'

'Did you succeed?' I asked. In Africa, in the sixties, I had had the vague idea of going native and living in a mud hut, and to that end I left my Peace Corps house and moved to an African township – in a two-room hut. But it hadn't worked. My African students thought it was undignified and my neighbours were afraid of me. Foreigners who moved into huts were either crackpots or spies.

Professor Shi said, 'In the beginning it was wonderful. We had competitions to see who could pick the most tea. The hard part was not the picking or the bending. It was that you had to carry a heavy bag the whole time, full of tea-leaves.'

There were no lights at this tea plantation. But there was a stream, so these youngsters from the city decided to build a dam and put in a generator. This certainly resembled a Peace Corps project – the outsiders deciding that what these peasants needed were some of the comforts of home – juice, especially.

'We worked very hard for a year building the dam. At the end of that time, when it was finished, we set aside one night for the lights to be turned on and for the electricity to flow. I remember it very well. That night, when the electricity came on, I stood and cried – I was so happy. Others were crying too.

'The old electrician from the work-unit said, "You're tough Peking boys and girls. Why are you crying? This is just a simple dam and simple electric power and a few flickering bulbs."

'He was wrong. We had done it all ourselves, with our own hands. Like picking the tea. That was why we cried.'

I was affected by her story, although I had been somewhat annoyed by her comparison between the Red Guards and the Peace Corps. But I saw that there was a connection, and both had emerged at the same time.

She had fallen silent. She had told me her good memory. She then said, 'Later it was different. I became a teacher in 1974 and the Red Guards came to check up on us. They told us what to teach. They bullied us and they were very tough. I was trying to teach English. They didn't like it. They said it was bourgeois and useless. That's when I changed my mind about the Cultural Revolution.'

As an English teacher she said she understood Mao, because she had read Percy Bysshe Shelley. I said, '*What?*'

'Mao was a political revolutionary,' she said. 'But he was also a romantic poet. That was the problem.'

She saw the old man as a sort of dreamer in baggy pants – scratching out his poems with his goose-quill pen and leading shiny-faced youths into the fields to harvest rice and grain. But the old romatic, perhaps like all romantics, was not only impractical, but also selfish and egotistical, and by the sixties he was around the bend, too. This was a far cry from the young idealist Shelley, and not much like the old leech-gatherer, Willy Wordsworth.

'He was also a tyrant, wasn't he?'

She said she didn't know about that. It was painful to think about recent history. She too wanted to go to the United States – to study, and for a change of pace.

It was now late afternoon, and damp and grey. The crumbly hills had caves cut into them, and every slope looked like a prehistoric settlement. It was not an optical illusion: this province was full of troglodytes knuckle-walking along these ledges and into the caverns they had chopped out of the hillside.

A young man was watching them with me. I took him to be one of the students on the swimming team, but he said no, rubber was his business – he made tyres. Lanzhou was a centre of rubber manufacturing.

I said, 'That's interesting,' and he seemed rather sceptical, and smiled at me as if defying me to find anything interesting at all about tyres or rubber.

'What about contraceptives?' I asked.

And then he asked me to explain what the word meant. This required gestures as well as a delicate description, but he got the point.

'I don't make them,' he said. 'But we have these things in China – for birth control. One-Child Policy, you know?'

I did not say so, but it seemed to me that people living five to a room was a form of birth control. In a country without any privacy and with very few trees it was a wonder than any children were conceived.

But this subject reminded him – his name was Mr Chang – of an experience he had had in Peking.

Mr Chang said, 'I was walking down the street. A man stopped me and said, "Want a girl?"

'I told him no.

' "She's very nice. Five *yuan*."

' "I am not interested," I said.

'He said, "I can get you a very dark and private corner in the park, so that you can be alone with her."

'I said that I did not want her, but what about my friend? You see, I was looking after an American delegation of rubber dealers. One of them even asked me if there were girls. It is forbidden. But there are girls.

'"That is out of the question. We do not want an American."

'I said, "Why not?"

'"They are too big in their penis. The girl is Chinese. She is very small. It will hurt her too much."

'I told him he could think about it.'

Mr Chang giggled, perhaps wondering whether he had gone too far – after all, I had told him I was an American. It was also very unusual that he should tell me this story. He covered himself by telling it in a disapproving way – sort of pious and lurid at the same time.

The pimp told him not to go away, while he consulted the girl.

'And then he came back and said, "She says she will do it with the American, but it will cost twenty *kwai*"' – that meant hard cash.

Then Mr Chang looked very worried. Would I take him for a pimp? After all, it seemed as though he had been negotiating with this sleazy man – and pimping was a capital offence: a bullet in the back of the neck.

Very angrily, Mr Chang said, 'We must rid China of such people!'

Already the train was slowing down in the deep ravine, and ahead Lanzhou lay smoking and steaming on both banks of the Yellow River.

7

The Iron Rooster

Lanzhou is a city in a valley of the Yellow River, and so it is long and narrow and hemmed in by mountains. There were hundreds of brickworks and smoking kilns on its outskirts, and it was brick-coloured, the same shade as its clayey landscape. It was damp and muddy this afternoon in early summer. Since ancient times it had been one of the gateways to China, the last place to change horses and buy provisions before heading for the outer limits of the empire. The next large settlements were in Turkestan, and beyond them was Europe. It still looked like a city on the frontier, with the patched and botched appearance of all Chinese cities – no trees to speak of but plenty of tall factory chimneys and power-lines. Most of the oil in Xinjiang was refined here, and it was whispered that in Lanzhou they made atom bombs. If one accidentally went off in this remote mud-coloured place, who would know?

Some of those chimneys were the minarets of mosques. This was the eastern limit of the Muslim world that had its other centres in Turfan and Kashgar and Khotan, at the edges of China. The mountains were bare and stony. The city's bleakness gave it a tidy look. The river was so shallow that there was no boat on it larger than a sampan, and the water was like cocoa, the same orangey brown. Some men on the banks flung nets in and dragged out tiddlers, which they pinched in their fingers and saved. Another group of men used its banks for curing goatskins – dousing them and then jumping up and down on them on the rocks. The rocks and stones were smooth, some were flat, the sort you find on the sea-shore. This was once part of the inland sea that had flooded towards the Pacific and created the Yangtze Gorges and dumped its sediment to make the whole of east China.

After a few days in Lanzhou I discovered that it had the same labyrinthine lanes in one section that Peking had – small cool courtyards, and tile roofs on which weeds had taken root, and carved doorways; and the squatting children and sweepers who always existed in those old neighbourhoods. The temple at Five Spring Mountain was tended by a terrified monk, who stammered at my questions and pleaded with me to go away. At the base of the ancient but derelict pagoda there was a shooting gallery – kids with air-pistols whacking away at tattered targets. In that same vandalized hillside, with its painted pavilions, there was a circus – daredevil motor cyclists speeding up the vertical walls of a jangling cage, while the Chinese gaped and refused to applaud.

The rest of Lanzhou looked as though it had been built the day before yesterday, in the nineteen-fifties, when the railway west was also built, under Russian guidance. The city did not have a prosperous air, and yet the stores were full of merchandise and the markets piled with vegetables. This was a railway junction to which trains came from every direction in China. Lanzhou had fish from the China Sea, and fruit from Guangdong, meat from the north and dried apricots and raisins and prunes and nuts from Xinjiang in the west. It also had televisions and refrigerators, the two most coveted appliances in China.

I read a story in Lanzhou in the magazine *Chinese Literature* (Autumn, 1986). It was by a well-known short-story writer, and Minister of Culture, Wang Meng, and was called *The Wind on the Plateau*. It was clumsy but enlightening, a story about a family in the new consumption-conscious China. Zhao the teacher has changed his life from the austere one he was living in the sixties and seventies. He has bought property and owns a TV and a refrigerator. He believes his life is just about perfect.

> Yet his son was far from satisfied with things as they were. He wanted video equipment, a musical door-chime, a motor cycle and a rubber dinghy. Why not go out and get an air-conditioner made in Australia?

This seemed to me one of the oddest shopping lists I could imagine, but it was a fairly accurate picture of the current state of craving. But I kept thinking: A rubber dinghy?

Meanwhile, Mr Fang was still traipsing after me, and when I sauntered so did he, and when I lollygagged he just stood nearby looking futile and sorrowful. But one day in Lanzhou he came in very handy. I was passing a public toilet and saw a number of large plastic drums on the pavement outside. They stank so badly I asked what was in them. No one seemed to know, but then Mr Fang materialized behind me and spoke one of the few English words he knew.

'Urine,' he said.

There were sixty-three five-gallon drums arranged in rows, waiting to be collected. This hardly noticed feature of Chinese life – urine collection – puzzled me. Mr Fang was pitifully eager to help me understand its purpose. He knew nothing about it himself, but between us, and using his dictionary, we tried to unravel the mystery.

Inside this public toilet, over the urinal, was a sign: *We would like good quality urine, so please do not put anything in – no spitting, no paper, no cigarette butts.* And another sign said: *This urine is used for medicinal purposes.*

Mr Fang and I accosted a man coming out of the john and asked him what it was all about.

'They are saving this urine for medicine,' he said. 'I don't take it myself, but it's very good medicine.'

What was this medicine intended to cure?

'I don't know,' he said.

I asked him whether it was used for fertilizer.

'Oh yes,' he said. 'That too.'

As we talked, passers-by threaded their way through the 315 gallons of human piss reeking in sticky drums on the pavement.

I thought Mr Fang would feel useful if I gave him a job to do. He had been looking very demoralized. I asked him to find out what this urine collection was all about. He went away and returned with a ragged scrap of paper on which was written the single word *enzyme*. He said a doctor had written it down. But I was still dissatisfied.

I subsequently discovered that it was used in endocrinology and that hormone crystals were sublimated from it. The Chinese had been using human urine in sophisticated medicine for a thousand years and in ancient China treated a number of conditions including impotence, hypogonadism, and dysmenorrhea. These urine hormones also straightened out hermaphrodites. Steroids and pituitary hormones were also isolated from the urine. It was also news to me that present-day fertility drugs are extracted from the urine of menopausal Italian nuns.

The trouble was that because I had enlisted Mr Fang's help he believed that I had softened towards him and he was eager for more work on my behalf. Was there anything more I wanted him to do? he wondered. I couldn't think of anything until the day I went to Lanzhou Station to buy tickets for Turfan and Urumchi and saw a squabbling crowd of people, and rather insolent and sneering ticket-sellers, and one man told me he had been at the station all day (it was now 4.00 in the afternoon) and still didn't have a ticket. So I asked Mr Fang if he would buy the tickets. He said: 'Gladly!' and gave me his chattering laugh – it called attention to his relief – and he went to work. Later in his Confidential Memo titled *Theroux Paul*, Mr Fang perhaps scratched with his quill pen: *Very interested in urine.*

We left Lanzhou at about midnight – the best time of day for catching a long-distance train. You board, hand over your ticket and go to bed; and within a few minutes you're jogging along, sound asleep. When you wake up you've gone 500 miles.

This was the train that the man in Peking had called the Iron Rooster, which was like calling it 'the cheapskate express', because the people who ran it were penny-pinchers. But that was just prejudice, a way of maligning a minority, a dig at the Uighurs. In most respects the train was no better or worse than any of the others I had taken in China. And the penny-pinching was not unusual – austerity, and mending and patching, were among the commonest features of Chinese life. Luxury, even simple comfort, had been condemned as decadent, and so inconvenience, plainness, and roughing it had come to be accepted as virtues. Only recently – within a few years – had anyone confessed to wanting creature comforts and pretty colours. But that did not strike me as immoderate. It was a society that was pledged to austerity that was probably the most prone to going on binges.

So, philosophically, the name didn't fit. But in every other respect this thing was an Iron Rooster. It squawked and crowed and seemed to flap, as steam shot out of its black boiler and it shook itself along the tracks. It was a big clattering thing, with bells and whistles, that went its noisy and cocksure way westward, into the desert of what used to be called Turkestan.

I slept like a log. The train was not particularly crowded. Mr Fang was installed in another compartment. I had expected a stifling coach, but it was chilly on the train. I needed the China Railways horse-blanket.

I woke at 6.00, in darkness. Everywhere in China is on Peking Time. It had been light until 9.00 at night in Lanzhou. I read Mildred Cable on the Gobi Desert and realized that I was just passing a point the Chinese had once called the Gate of Demons, because beyond it was the howling wind and wasteland of which they had an acute terror ('Some told of rushing rivers cutting their way through sand, of an unfathomable lake hidden among the dunes, of sand hills with a voice like thunder, of water which could be clearly seen and yet was a deception'). I read for an hour. At 7.00 it was still dark, the sun behind the distant mountains. We came to a small station called Shagoutai, where the only living things were a muleteer and his mule – the animal loaded with water-bags and waiting behind the level crossing.

They were dark, treeless, grassless ranges of mountains, and they were folded like thick quilts. They were black, because they were backlit by the unrisen sun. Near Lanzhou I had thought the mountains were like *shuijiao*, 'water-dumplings'. The same smoothness, and folds, and crimp marks. I loved the sight of the wilderness of dumplings. But in this semi-desert, with far-off hills, no image came so easily to mind. The nearer hills all had cave entrances in them – the arched doorways of the cave-dwellers of Gansu. It was a strange rocky province, and so long and narrow I knew I would be travelling through it tomorrow. Like Qinghai, the adjoining province to the south, Gansu was notorious for being a place where political prisoners were sent, the Chinese Siberia. Security was a simple matter, because there was no escape through the desert. Only forty years ago travellers on this route – and at just about this spot in Gansu – were met by a large stone tablet with the inscription EARTH'S GREATEST BARRIER. Meaning the Gobi.

The landscape changed, all at once, into everything, at the town of Wuwei. The Iron Rooster was in a deep cool valley, and there were wet mountains a few miles away, and beyond them a great ridge of brown mountains, and higher and farther still on the distant horizon a long range of snowy mountains. So blue and white were these mountains of ice that the range itself had the look of a sword blade. There were arid patches too, between the snowy peaks in the distance and the green valley in which we were travelling.

These mountains to the south were the Datong Shan, several of them 20,000-footers, just inside the province and sometime penal colony of Qinghai, at the edge of the Tibetan Plateau.

I had been warned that this train trip west would be barren and boring. It was not. I was beginning to understand that the empty parts of China are the most beautiful, and some of them, like these valleys, very fertile. It was a chain of oases along the northern arm of the Silk Road. Its utter emptiness was so rare in China that it seemed startling to me, and where there were gardens and trees it was almost lush. Large herds of sheep grazed among the stonier stretches, nibbling at hanks of grass; and there were mules, and crows, and mud-walled towns. In one place I saw six camels, big and small, placidly watching the train go by. The mules were indifferent to the train. They were braying and biting and mounting each other, honking and showing their teeth as they hauled their hoses into place.

The train was full but not crowded. The dining-car was nearly always empty, perhaps because most of the passengers were Uighurs – Muslims – and the Chinese menu was about as porky as it could be. And the other dishes could not possibly have been halal, which is the Islamic version of kosher – implying ritual slaughter. Because business was so bad, the chef usually chatted, asking me what I wanted. How about some chicken and prawns? Or shredded pork? Or pork balls? Or diced pork and doufu? Or fish with ginger? Cauliflower with dried shrimp? Sautéd cucumber?

Like many features of Chinese life the food had glorious names, and each dish its own identity and pedigree. But in practice it was almost impossible to tell apart – not only the same taste, but the same colour and stringiness.

By mid afternoon the train was moving across a flat green plain between two ranges of low mountains, the Qilian Shan and the Helan Shan. In places I could see the crumbled sections of the Great Wall. Where the land was flat it was intensively cultivated, and in places there were tall, slender and rather redundant-looking poplars. The Chinese, averse to planting shade trees, favoured the skinny symbolic tree that doubled as a fence. The idea of The Forest was alien to China. It only existed in northern Heilongjiang province – the Manchurian north-east; and I had heard that even the little that remained was being cut down and made into chopsticks and toothpicks and ping-pong paddles.

In most other countries, a landscape feature was a grove of trees, or a meadow, or even a desert; so you immediately associated the maple tree with Canada, the oak with England, the birch with the Soviet Union, and desert and jungle with Africa. But no such thing came to mind in China, where the most common and obvious feature of a landscape was a person – or usually many people. Every time I stared at a landscape there was a person in it staring back at me.

Even here in the middle of nowhere there were people and settlements. The villages were walled in, and most houses had walls around them: mud smeared over bricks. They were the sort of stockades that are frequent in Afghanistan and Iran – at the far end of this Silk Road – and probably a cultural hangover from the memory of marauders and Mongol hordes, the Central Asian nightmare.

The day had turned very hot. It was now in the nineties. I saw eighteen sheep crowded into a little blot of shade under a frail hawthorn tree. Children cooled themselves by kicking water in a ditch. Farmers with lampshade hats planted crops by pushing one sprout at a time into the ground, a process that had a greater affinity to needlepoint sewing than to farming, as though they were stitching a design into the furrows. And though there were black peaks and mountain ranges on both sides of the train, the land ahead fell away, and it was as if we were approaching the ocean – the land dipped and had the smooth stony look of the sea-shore. It was the hottest part of the day, but even so the land was full of people. Hours later, in an immense and stony desert I saw a man in a faded blue suit, bumping over the stones on his bike.

Then there were sand dunes near the track – big soft slopes and bright piles; but the snowy peaks in the distance still remained. I had not realized that there was anything so strange as this on this planet.

I was eating dinner in the empty dining-car at about 8.00 that night when we came to Jiayuguan. What I saw out the window is printed on my mind: in the summer dusk of the Gobi Desert, a Chinese town lay glowing in the sand, and rising above it, ten storeys high, was the last gate in the Great Wall, the Jia Yu Watch-tower – a fortress-like structure with pagoda roofs; and the train slowed at the Wall's end, a crumbled pile of mud bricks and ruined turrets that the wind had simplified and sucked smooth. In the fading light of day, there was this ghostly remainder of the Great Wall, and what looked like the last town in China. The Wall went straggling west, but it was so small and destroyed it looked like little more than an idea or a suggestion – the remnants of a great scheme. But my excitement also came from seeing the red paint on the gate, and the yellow roof, and the thought that this train was passing beyond it into the unknown. The sun slanted on the grey hills and the desert and blue bushes. Most of what I saw was through the blurring haze of the day's dust, and the intimation at sunset was that I would fall off the edge of the world as soon as it got dark.

On my way back to my compartment I passed the Hard Class compartment, in which Uighurs were praying – kneeling on mats and facing south-west towards Mecca between the berths; and Chinese were brushing their teeth, and glugging tea, and hanging up laundry; and very loud Arabic music blasted from a portable stereo. Some people were sleeping and many were sighing, and a few spitting and hoicking. A card game was in progress, and a furious argument. Nearby a young girl placidly nursed her baby. The floor was thick with spittle, orange peels and peanut shells and tea dregs. More men entered gargling from the washroom.

Someone grasped my arm. The light was bad but I saw he had a big nose and wavy hair and a brown suit with bell-bottoms, a style that had become popular that year in the oases of the Xinjiang desert.

'Shansh marnie?'

It was the Uighur catch-phrase: *Change money?*

The Uighurs were officially designated a Chinese minority, and Xinjiang was their own autonomous region. They were a Turkic-speaking people, the remote descendants of nomads whose kingdom existed here 1,200 years ago, and many of them looked like Italian peasants. It was no wonder that Marco Polo found them a friendly and fun-loving people. They were overwhelmed by the Mongol hordes in the thirteenth century, and were drafted into the army of this khanate. They converted to Islam, they adapted the Arabic script for their language, they were conquered by the Chinese several times, and several times rebelled, most recently a hundred years ago. There are about 4 million of them in Xinjiang and they seemed totally out of sympathy with the Chinese and often mocking. Their world was entirely separate: it was Allah, and the Central Asian steppes, a culture of donkey carts and dancing girls. They ate mutton and bread. They were people of the bazaar, who – familiar with outlandish travellers – were travellers themselves. For the first time since the People's Republic was founded they were allowed to travel.

They were the people who lurked outside the Friendship Stores in Peking and Shanghai, and stood discreetly outside the tourist hotels, looking like exchange students from a Mediterranean country. They usually wore dark suits and ties and platform shoes. They wore watches and sun-glasses. Their Chinese was seldom fluent – but that was excusable; it was rare to find any Chinese person who spoke Uighur. Yet their history as a people had taught them to count in fifty languages. Numbers, after all, are the language of the bazaar. And they had two words of English.

'Shansh marnie?'

'How much?'

'One dollar, four *yuan*.' The official rate was three.

'Say six.' I was bargaining for the sake of it, and because it was such a novelty to encounter a black market in this upright, no tipping, no favours, anti-corruption economy. What this Uighur and I were doing was sinning; and it felt delightful.

'No six.'

'Five.'

'No five. Four.' He also had bushy eyebrows and a big chin.

He asked me how many dollars I wanted to change. He took out a pocket calculator and said that over a certain amount he could give me a better rate. The train rumbled on towards Anxi. I lost interest in haggling and had no interest at all in changing money at the black market rate. What fascinated me was his tenacity in sticking to this rate of one to four. For him it was like a magic equation. But this Uighur was no fool. Two months later the Chinese government devalued the *yuan* to exactly this rate.

That night the train crossed the Ravine of Baboons (Xinqxinq Xia) which had always been regarded as the frontier of Chinese Turkestan.

'The desert which lies between Anxi and Hami is a howling wilderness, and the first thing which strikes the wayfarer is the dismalness of its uniform, black, pebble-strewn surface.' That was Mildred speaking. And reading her book reminded me that I was missing one of the glories of this region by not visiting the caves at Dunhuang – Buddhas, frescoes, holy grottoes; the sacred city in the sands. But I intended to go one better, by visiting the lost city of Gaocheng (Karakhoja) whenever this train got to Turfan.

I had gone to bed in a strange late twilight amid a rugged landscape; and I woke, slowly jogging in the train, to a flat region of sand and stones. Farther off were large humpy sand dunes which had the appearance of having softly flowed and blown there, because there was nothing like them nearby. The dunes were like simple gigantic animals that went blobbing along through the desert, smothering whatever they encountered.

Soon a patch of green appeared – an oasis. Once there was

merely a road linking the oases – but 'once' meant only thirty years ago. Before then it was a rough route, what remained of the Silk Road. But these oases were not metaphors for a few trees and a stagnant pool. They were large towns, well watered from underground irrigation canals, and grapes and melons were grown in great profusion. Later in the day the train stopped at Hami. The Hami melon is famous all over China for its sweet taste and its fragrance; and Hami was no insignificant place, although now it was what remained of the fruit-growing communes of the fifties and sixties. It had known great days, and had had a khan until this century. It had been overrun by Mongols, by Uighurs, by Tibetans and Dzungars. It had been repeatedly reoccupied by the Chinese since the year 73, the Later Han Dynasty, and had been a Chinese city from 1698 onward. Nothing of this remained. What had not been damaged in the Muslim Rebellion of 1860–70 had been flattened in the Cultural Revolution. The Chinese had a facility for literally defacing a city – taking all its characteristic features away, robbing it of its uniqueness, cutting its nose off. Now what Hami was best known for was its pig-iron.

The peaks beyond it and farther up the line had patches of snow on their ridges that lay like saddle-blankets, squarish and flat. But down here in the train and on the desert it was very hot – over a hundred degrees in the train and hotter outside. The sun burned down on the sand and stones. There were a few gullies, and in the oldest and deepest ones which were sheltered perhaps a dead *wutong* tree, and here and there clumps of camel-thorn, the only identifiable weed, apart from the spikes of grey lichens. We were heading towards a dusty range of hills that was surmounted by a blue range of mountains, and beyond that, rising up, were more mountains, which were bright with snow patches and ice slides – long streaks that might have been glaciers.

They were the first sight I had of the Bogda Shan, the Mountains of God. They were very rugged and very high, but their snow was the only lively feature of this place. Beneath those mountains there was nothing but desert, 'the howling wilderness', which this afternoon was too bright to stare at. Rainfall is unknown here, and most of those mountains seemed little more than a vast poisoned massif – a lifeless pack of rock. It is the dead centre of Asia.

The Iron Rooster moved along at about thirty miles per hour, as it had been doing for two and a half days; moving slowly as the landscape grew even stranger. That was a good thing. If the train had been moving any faster it would have been impossible for me to comprehend the changes in the landscape, from the rice fields and little hills to the great bare mountains. A plane ride from Lanzhou to here would have been a shock, and from Peking would have been very bewildering. A plane from anywhere else would have been like space travel – some interplanetary mind-bender.

I paced up and down in my pyjamas, among slumbering Uighurs, and occasionally had a beer. A pint cost about ten pence.

Because we were on Peking Time, the hottest part of the day was 4.30 in the afternoon, and it remained light enough to read until almost midnight.

In this oddly lighted world of snow and sand, the stone mountains reddened and rushed up to the train. In the distance was a green basin, 500 feet below sea-level, the lowest place in China, and one of the hottest. Another oasis, the town of Turfan. Round about there was nothing else but 100 miles of blackish gravel, and Turfan itself was twenty miles from the station. I got off the train here.

Turfan ('one of the hottest places on the face of the earth') was an extremely popular oasis about 400 years ago. Before then it had been a desert town overrun by successive waves of nomads: Chinese, Tibetans, Uighurs and Mongols. The Silk Road established it as a great oasis and bazaar, but after that – from about the sixteenth century – it was all downhill. And after it was finally left alone by the war-lords and the Manchus, a new marauder appeared in the shape of enterprising archaeologists, and the few frescoes and statues that remained after more than 2,000 years of continuous civilization were snatched and carried away to places like Tokyo, Berlin and Cambridge, Massachusetts.

Such a place seemed to me unmissable. The station was at the edge of the depression. All I could see were telephone poles in the stony desert, and the huge purply-red range called the Flaming Mountains. The town of Turfan did not reveal itself until I was almost on top of it, and even then it seemed less like a Chinese town than a Middle Eastern one – it was straight out of the Bible, with donkeys and grape arbours and mosques, and people who looked Lebanese, with brown faces and grey eyes, the men in skullcaps, the women in shawls.

The desert was almost unbelievably horrible-looking – bouldery and black, without a single green thing in it. And it seemed as though if you walked on those stones you would cut your feet. In some spots it looked like an immensity of coal ashes, with scatterings of clinkers and scorched stones. In other places it was dust, with rounded mounds piled here and there. The mounds I discovered were part of the irrigation system called the *karez*, a network of underground canals and boreholes that had been used successfully since the Western Han Dynasty, about 2,000 years ago. There were also parts of this desert surrounding Turfan that had the same undersea look, as of an ocean floor after the tide went out for good. Everyone called it the *gobi*: the waterless place. Rainfall is unknown in Turfan.

In this shallow green valley in the desert, in which all the water came from underground, there were no high-rise Chinese buildings, and most of the houses were small and square. There were grape arbours suspended over most of the streets – for the shade and also for the prettiness of them. This town is the chief source of Chinese grapes – there is even a winery in Turfan – and thirty varieties of melon grow in the area. That intensifies the relief of having come from one of the wildest deserts in the world. Turfan is the opposite of everything that lies around it, with its water and its shade and its fresh fruit.

Mr Fang still tagged behind me, keeping his distance, sometimes speaking an ominous sentence.

One of the most ominous for the traveller in China is: 'It is a new hotel.' That sometimes struck fear into my heart. It implied peeling wallpaper, plush chairs, exposed wires, lights that didn't work, a hairy carpet, hard beds and a bathroom with no water, loose tiles, sticky glue on the sink, no shower curtain, and a cistern you had to fix yourself by twisting the ballcock. The doors were usually stuck on the fake-wood cabinets, the curtains were thin, the door-knobs loose, the coat-hangers misshapen, the telephone didn't work, and neither did the radio. There was always a colour television and a bunch of plastic flowers. Such places smelled of fish-glue and failure, and they were terribly expensive. In all cases in China I preferred an old hotel. They weren't pretty but they worked.

But Mr Fang said the old place in Turfan was full, and he put me in the new, as yet unnamed, hotel. It was half-finished, and it was empty. Its odour was powerful: fresh cement. In the rubble of the courtyard there was a fountain which contained hot dust and a stiff little mouse. I stood, a little dazed from the heat, and heard a donkey bawl.

Because of Peking Time, they ate breakfast at 9.30, lunch at 2.00, and dinner at 9.00 in the evening. What are civilized hours in a place like Sandwich, Massachusetts, are very inconvenient in Chinese Turkestan. I woke hot and hungry at about 6.00 in the morning, and I had no appetite in the evening. But the eating hours were official and inflexible, and the local people woke late and went to bed late. Nothing I could do persuaded anyone to galvanize himself early in the cool part of the day.

'We will miss breakfast,' Mr Fang said.

'Does that matter?'

'We must have breakfast.'

I thought: What good are you? But it was not only that mealtimes were sacred. The food was paid for and therefore had to be eaten. And the Chinese are an oral people – that was another reason. Most of all, the Chinese are at their freest when they are eating. A meal is always a relief and a celebration.

Yet I never wanted breakfast – noodles, thin rice gruel, meat dumplings, maybe mushrooms, and warm milk. As a foreigner I might be offered orange soda or a Pepsi with my breakfast noodles.

In Turfan I bought the local raisins made from white grapes – the best in China; and apricots. And I sat in my room, eating that stuff and drinking my Dragon Well green tea and writing my notes, until Fang and the driver had had their fill of gruel, and then we set off, down the dusty roads.

It was often a furnace. But on the mornings it was overcast it was pleasant, with low cloud and the temperature only in the nineties. I liked the town. It was the least Chinese place I had seen so far, and it was one of the smallest and prettiest. There were very few motor vehicles, and it was quiet and completely horizonal

It was a Uighur town, with a few Chinese. There were also Uzbeks, Kazakhs, Tadjiks and Tungus around the place, in high boots and bow-legged in the Mongolian fashion. They were leathery-faced, and some looked like Slavs and some like gypsies, and most of them like people who had lost their way and were just stopping briefly in this oasis before moving on. Half the women at the Turfan bazaar had the features of fortune-tellers, and the others looked like Mediterranean peasants – dramatically different from anyone else in China. These brown-haired, grey-eyed, gypsy-featured women in velvet dresses – and very buxom, some of them – were quite attractive in a way that was the opposite of oriental. You would not be surprised to learn that they are Italians or Armenians. You see those same faces in Palermo and Yerevan.

Their gazes lingered, too. And some women came close and reached into the velvet and withdrew rolls of banknotes from between their breasts and said, 'Shansh marnie?'

They put this Chinese money into my hand – the money was still warm from having been in their deep bosoms – and they offered me four to one. They had gold teeth and some looked like foxes, and they hissed at me when I said no.

It was wonderful, that market in Turfan, just what you would expect of a bazaar in Central Asia. They sold embroidered saddle-bags, and leather holsters, and home-made jack-knives, and baskets and belts. The meat market dealt exclusively in lamb and mutton – no pigs in this Islamic place; and there were stalls selling shish kebabs. Much of the produce was the fresh fruit for which Turfan is well known – water-melons and Hami melons and tangerines. And there were about twenty varieties of dried fruit. I bought raisins and apricots, almonds and walnuts: it struck me that dried fruit and nuts was caravan food.

There were tumblers and fire-eaters at the Turfan Market, too, and a man doing card tricks on an overturned wheelbarrow. There was something medieval about the market – the dust and the tents, the merchandise and the entertainers, and the people who had gathered there, the men in skullcaps, the women in shawls, the shrieking children with wild hair and dirty feet.

*

Nothing puts human effort into better perspective than a ruined city. 'This was once a great capital,' people say, pointing to fallen walls and broken streets and dust. Then you stand in the silence of the lifeless place and think of Ozymandias, King of Kings, covered by a sand dune and forgotten. It is very thrilling for an American to consider such a place, because we don't yet have anything that qualifies – only ghost towns and fairly insignificant small cities, but nothing like the monumental corpses of once-great cities that are known in the rest of the world. Probably American optimism arises from the fact that we don't have any devastated cities. There is something wearying and demoralizing about a lost city, but it can also give you a healthy disregard for real estate.

Gaocheng was perfect in its ruin and decrepitude. It had been a renowned city for well over 1,000 years, and now it was a pile of dust and crumbling mud. So far it had been spared the final insult – tourists – but one day, when the Iron Rooster turned into a streamlined train, even they would find this place, east of Turfan, twenty-five miles into the desert. It had half a dozen different names – Karakhoja, Khocho, Dakianus (from the Roman Emperor Decius), Apsus (Ephesus), Idikut-Shahri (King Idikut's Town) and Erbu (Second Stop). Gaocheng had come to be its accepted name, but it hardly mattered, because there was not much left of it. Yet enough remained for anyone to see that it really had been an enormous place, a city on a grand scale, which was why it looked so sad. It had the melancholy emptiness of all great ruins.

Its walls and fortifications were mostly gone, but the ones that still stood made it seem a remarkable citadel. It had been an ancient capital of this region, and then a Tang city, and then a Uighur city, and at last the Mongols had captured it. The Uighurs didn't want the place destroyed, so they had surrendered without a struggle and let the Mongols take charge, as they had over the rest of China. It was the period of Mongol rule, the Yuan Empire of the thirteenth and fourteenth centuries, when the first westerners began travelling widely in China – among them, Marco Polo.

By then Gaocheng was Muslim. It had previously been Buddhist. It had also been a centre of Christian heretics – first Manichaean, then Nestorian. It is impossible to consider these heresies without reaching the conclusion that they make a certain amount of sense. The Manichaeans, followers of the Persian prophet Manes, believed that there is good and evil in all humans, and that life is a struggle between these interdependent opposites, the light and the dark, the spirit and the flesh. The Nestorians were Christians who had been declared heretics for denying that Christ could be human as well as divine. They went on to argue that Mary was either the mother of God or the mother of the man Jesus; but she couldn't have it both ways. For this the Nestorians were persecuted, after the Council of Ephesus (in present-day Turkey) and they ended up, in the seventh century, at the last stage of the Silk Road, deep in China, where the first Nestorian church was founded in 638, in Chang'an – Xian.

What made this all the more fascinating to me was that there was nothing left – no church, no heretics, no books, no pictures, no city. There was only the sun beating down on the mud bricks and the broken walls, and all the religion, trade, warfare, art, money, government and civilization had turned to dust. But there was something magnificent in the immensity of this dumb ruin. I kept on seeing this desert as a place where an ocean had been, a gigantic foreshore of smooth stones and seaside rubble; and this city of Gaocheng was quite in key with that, looking like a sandcastle when the tide had floated most of it away.

The only live things here were goats. The frescoes and statues had been stolen – and sold or else removed to museums. Farmers had dismantled many of the buildings so that they could use the bricks, and when the local people found pots or vases or amphoras (and they were good ones, for there was both Greek and Roman influence at Gaocheng), they used them in their kitchens, so that they wouldn't have to buy new ones.

I went to a nearby village of Uighurs and asked them whether they knew anything about Gaocheng. 'It is an old city,' they said. The people I asked were brown-faced, hawk-nosed men in skull-caps, whose village was shady and totally off the map. They had donkeys, they had a mosque and a small market, but they didn't speak Chinese or any other language but Uighur. The place was called Flaming Mountain Commune, but that was merely a euphemism. The village had gone to sleep. The women watched me through the folds in their black shawls, and I saw one who looked exactly like my Italian grandmother.

Mr Liu, my guide, did not speak Uighur, though he had lived not far away for twenty years. I had the impression that these desert-dwelling Uighurs did not take the Han Chinese very seriously. When we started away there was a thump against the side of the car, and the driver slammed on the brakes and chased after the laughing kids. He made a fuss, but no one came to help – no one even listened. And then, a further insult. He stopped to ask directions to an ancient burying-ground, the necropolis at Astana, and when he put his head out of the car window two children stuck feathery reeds into his ears and tickled him. They ran away, as he got out and raged at them.

'They are very bad boys,' Mr Liu said, and he glowered at me when he saw that I was laughing.

The corpses in the underground tombs at Astana were 600 years old, but perfectly preserved, grinning, lying side by side on a decorated slab.

'You want to take a picture of the dead people?' the caretaker asked me.

'I don't have a camera.'

She paid no attention to that. She said, 'Ten *yuan*. One picture.'

Mr Liu said, 'I hate looking at dead bodies,' and hurried up the stone stairs, fleeing the burial chamber.

When he was gone, the caretaker said, 'Shansh marnie?'

I hated to leave Turfan. It was the first town I had seen in China that didn't look Chinese, and I wondered why this was so. It was the hottest place I had been, the lowest, the strangest, in the middle of nowhere, with sulky old men and rapacious women and stone-throwing kids. I didn't find any of it threatening – in fact I liked seeing people resisting Chinese dullness, and setting their faces against humourless and canting politicians. It was unusual that such a place had managed to keep its pride and its culture intact, even if its culture was little more than melons and tambourines and Islamic prostrations. It was a green island in lifeless wilderness: very exciting to get here on a train, and even better that it was a gasping, drooling steam train.

I took that same train out of Turfan, Mr Fang by my side, and headed west through the desert towards Urumchi, which everyone called 'Woolamoochie'. It is only 100 miles or so, but the trip is slow because of the circuitous passage through the Tian Shan – the Heavenly Mountains. The series of intersecting valleys contains some of China's most beautiful scenery – cliffs, mountain streams, boulder-strewn gullies and deep gorges. The train labours through each of the twelve tunnels and then bursts into one of these valleys in the blinding Xinjiang sunshine and the rushing water of the Baiyang river drowns out the gasps of the locomotive.

At one point a black and white crane, five feet tall, gathered itself up and leaped out of the suds of the fast river, folded its legs and neck and beat itself slowly towards the cliffs. After several hours of these brilliantly lit valleys and bouncing clouds, the tracks straightened and we headed across brown desert to the large smoking city of Urumchi, the last place in China that is reachable by train. The next big town west of this is Alma-Ata, in the Soviet Union Republic of Kazakhstan. Horsemen and nomads don't recognize national frontiers. There are plenty of Kazakhs in Urumchi, along with Tartars, Uzbeks, Tajiks and Mongols; but more than a third of the city's population is Uighur, and the railway station is in the Uighur style, the station sign in the Uighur script.

It is almost impossible to find any traveller offering a kind word for Urumchi. What began as a Han outpost on the Silk Road developed into a T'ang trading centre and then was captured by Huns and finally Mongols. It became the capital of Chinese Turkestan, but with a strong Russian flavour. For most early travellers it was the first stop in China and something of a disappointment ('no one leaves the town with regret'), because it was lacking in any cultural interest. The treasures, the tombs, the lost cities – all the good places to loot – lay farther east. Urumchi was merely political. Here were the offices, the interrogation centres, the gaols, the bureaucrats, the spies. That was the case at the turn of the century, and at the time of the Russian Revolution, and it is pretty much the case now.

It had a certain ugly charm, this city of 1.5 million people, very few of whom were Han Chinese. It was surrounded by big brown mountains, and it had wide streets and shish-kebab parlours. Many shops had rare animals strung up outside. It was very hot in the daytime and one of the popular recreations was playing pool and billiards under the trees – there were pool tables all over Urumchi, in the open air.

Mr Fang disappeared when we reached the hotel, but his place was taken by Mr Yang, who – when I asked about Russians – said there was a large Russian community here which dated from the nineteen-thirties. I had just missed their Easter celebration – the Chinese government had given them permission to hold it for the first time since Liberation.

There were so many different ethnic groups in Urumchi that I wondered what the Cultural Revolution had been like.

'It was very bad here,' Mr Yang said. 'But the minorities were not interested. They did not participate in the Cultural Revolution. Very few of them were Red Guards.'

'If they didn't participate, then they must have been persecuted,' I said.

'Oh yes,' Mr Yang said, readily agreeing. 'They were persecuted! Islamic religion was declared illegal. Praying was illegal. Mosques were considered bad. The Red Guards went in and smashed up the mosques. And people were punished.'

'How did they punish the Muslims?'

'They made them raise pigs.'

Typical, I thought; and perfect in its way. It was always said that the Chinese under Mao were a forgiving bunch – believers in redemption and re-education. But it seemed to me uniquely vindictive to make physicists assemble crappy radios, and to force literature teachers to hoe cabbages or shovel chicken-shit, and to put Muslims to work in pigsties. That was on the same order as putting hysterical schoolkids in charge of the middle schools; the result was easily predictable, and in the event the little brats persecuted their teachers and passed in blank examination papers to prove they were good Maoist anti-intellectuals.

'I'll bet the minorities didn't like that very much,' I said.

Mr Yang shrieked with laughter. It was the Chinese laugh that means: *On the contrary!*

He said, 'They wanted to protest, but they didn't dare. They wanted to have a counter-revolution!'

'Do they want to have a counter-revolution now?' It was a delicate question, because there were always rumours of Uighur discontent; and anyone who saw these frowning, disapproving and uncooperative Uighur faces all over Xinjiang could easily reach the conclusion that here were people who were not entirely sold on the aims of the People's Republic.

Mr Yang laughed again, a slower warning honk that meant: *Do not ask that question.* But that particular laugh was also a noise I interpreted as a complex *yes.*

But I was stuck with Mr Yang. He asked me what I wanted to see in Urumchi.

I said, 'Something memorable.'

We drove to Nanshan, the South Mountain Pasture. It was only twenty minutes out of Urumchi but it looked like western Uganda, a great green plain with the Mountains of the Moon rising out of it, several snow-capped peaks. What distinguishes these mountain-sides from any others in China are the spruce forests, tall, cool and blackish-green. On some of the meadows there were goatherds and shepherds with their flocks, and Kazakhs living in mud-smeared huts and log cabins. There were yurts, too, and near them men wearing fur hats with earflaps, and boots and riding britches; and women in shawls and dresses and thick socks. They looked like Russian babushkas, and unlike the Chinese these women were long-nosed and pot-bellied. They tended vegetable gardens near their cabins, and they had donkeys and cranky dogs and snotty-nosed kids who, because of the cold, also had bright red cheeks.

To avoid talking to Mr Yang for a while I walked fast up the slope and found a waterfall. Beneath it, in the stream, there was ice – big yellow crusts of it, and solid thick shelves of it frozen to the rocks. Twenty minutes down the road the townsfolk of Urumchi were perspiring and playing pool under the trees, and here it was freezing.

I found a Uighur, Zhu Ma Hun – 'Hun' means 'mister' and the rest was the Chinese version of the Muslim name Juma (Friday – the sabbath). He seemed to claim that he had been the Chinese ambassador to Syria, but he may have meant that he worked in that embassy. His Chinese was as limited as mine. On the other hand, he spoke Turkish and Arabic as well as his native Uighur.

He said he came from Tacheng, on the border of Soviet Kazakhstan, about 500 miles from Urumchi and about as far out as anyone can live in China and still be regarded as Chinese. That gave me an idea.

'You're not Chinese, are you?'

'Yes! I'm Chinese!'

He was big and friendly, fat-faced. He might have been a Turk, a Smyrna merchant, or a pasha with a big paunch. He said he had been to Mecca on the Hadj.

We were strolling along the mountain road. We passed a public toilet – the Chinese tend to erect them in the middle of all beauty spots – and though we were forty feet away the thing gave off an overpowering stink. Every public toilet I saw in China was so vile it was unusable. Every foreigner mentioned them; the Chinese never did – not because they were fastidious but because they were ashamed and phlegmatic, and preferred to suffer in silence.

'I think you don't have many of those in the States,' Zhu Ma Hun said.

'Right,' I said, thinking he meant the brick shit-house, but I saw that he was pointing to a yurt, where an old nomad – possibly a Tadjik – was lugging a bucket of water.

'But do you have *any* tents?' he asked.

'Not as many as you,' I said.

The Chinese idea of a picnic box-lunch is an assortment of dry sponge cake and stale cookies. Mr Yang had given me a box in the car, and I had not realized what was in it until I was some distance up the mountain. I fed the whole thing to some cows.

That afternoon, still hungry, I looked for something to eat in the market at Urumchi. My favourite street food was a kind of stuffed pancake called *jiaozi* or else fried dumplings. But the treat here was lamb kebabs and flat loaves of bread they called *nang*, probably the same as the Urdu word *nan*, familiar to anyone who has eaten in an Indian restaurant.

There are so few western travellers in Urumchi that Uighurs become animated when they see them. They stare, they gabble, they proffer dried fruit and bunches of fresh grapes. One man tried to interest me in his medicine: dried and splayed lizards (for high blood pressure), deer antlers (for potency) and snakes, frogs, birds' beaks and a hideous little bundle of twiggy things which he said were the umbilical cords of donkeys.

'They are very good for you,' he said vaguely, when I asked what they were for.

The traders in the market, selling the carpets that are woven in Urumchi and the clothes that arrive by train, were either bearded men in skullcaps or fat women in brown dresses. They held up their merchandise, they beckoned me over, but whenever I got close they breathed on me and snatched my wrist and spoke the Uighur greeting.

'Shansh marnie!'

There were more dead animals elsewhere in Urumchi. It is a measure of how deep in the hinterland Urumchi is that there are still many wild animals in the surrounding countryside. At one shop I saw the usual snakes and dried lizards and umbilical cords, but also wolf pelts, fox furs, half a dozen bearskins and the carcass of an eagle – a white-shouldered imperial eagle (so my bird book said), with a wing-span of about six feet. This beautiful bird was a great deal bigger than the Uighur woman selling it.

'Do you want to buy it?' she said.

'What would I do with it?'

'You take the feathers and rub them on your skin. It's good medicine.'

'What about this?' I said, pointing to the skull of a gazelle, to which two lovely horns were attached.

'Medicine. Grind it into powder. It makes you strong.'

There were any number of western scientists who claimed that traditional Chinese medicine could be efficacious; but what this woman was saying – and the man in the market with his donkeys' umbilical cords – was surely complete nonsense?

I was prepared to believe that the Chinese had the herbal solutions to high blood pressure, and that acupuncture had its practical uses; but when they scrunched up a dead owl and said, 'Yum, yum – good for your eyes!' I wanted to say 'Bullshit.' If I didn't it was only because I didn't yet know the Chinese word for it.

There are a handful of tigers in China, some in Hunan, some in the far north-east. Needless to say, they are an endangered species. There is so little food for them that when they're very hungry these tigers will eat insects and frogs. In a copy of a Chinese magazine (*China Today*) I read the following:

> The [Chinese] tiger is a kind of treasure. The hide of the tiger can be made into an expensive coat. The bones, the kidneys, the stomach and the penis are very valuable medicine. The medicine made from the ribs of the tiger is a very good and effective medicine for curing rheumatoid arthritis.

It was bad enough that they were killing the few animals they had left, but they were doing it for the stupidest reasons. It was probably true that the most accurate epitaph for creatures that have become extinct is: *It Tasted Good.*

I tried to get Mr Fang to teach me how to say, 'That is merely a superstitious belief with no scientific basis to support it,' but we got nowhere. He asked me why I wanted to be able to say this, and I mentioned the Chinese habit of making the lovely little Asian barred owlet into soup. He said there were two reasons for that: they tasted good and they were good for your eyesight.

He was bewildered that anyone with sense should care for the life of a bird or an animal. I did not argue with him. The Chinese themselves often lived in such cramped and uncomfortable conditions that they could hardly be expected to sympathize with animals that lived the same way. Indeed, the way the Chinese lived and died bore a remarkable resemblance to their animals.

Mr Fang surprised me further by saying, 'Mr Jiao wants to see you.'

'Who is Mr Jiao?'

'General Manager of the Urumchi Branch of China Railways.'

'How does he know I'm here?'

'I told him,' Mr Fang said, and looked sad in his sea-lion way. 'He wants you to eat with him.'

Mr Jiao Xiku was a dark, tough-looking man from the far-eastern province of Shandong. He had a short neck and a broad face, and as the evening advanced and he drank more and more Xinjiang white wine, his dark face was suffused with a kind of alcoholic blush and his eyes became smaller and very red, like two boiled berries.

We were joined by his assistant, Mr Jie, who – because he was an underling – did not say very much. After the formalities ('We are honoured to have you') I realized that this would be a large meal. The cold dishes were set out and ignored; that meant there were about a dozen more courses to come.

I asked Mr Jiao about the railway. What were the problems in building and maintaining it? He said the worst problem was the wind, the sandstorms that often grew to force nine or ten. A cold wind met a hot wind in the *gobi* and caused great turbulence. And then there were the tunnels through the Tian Shan – they had taken years to cut.

'You see, we did all this by ourselves. We had no help.'

'I thought the Soviets helped,' I said.

'They planned the line to Urumchi. They did the survey – but it was an aerial survey. They didn't foresee all the difficulties. And of course our friendship with them was broken in 1960.'

'So you were on your own then?'

'Yes. And what made it especially hard was that they took all their materials away. The tracks, the equipment, the wood, everything. Just loaded it and took it across the border. And they took their plans, too! Rolled up their plans and went home with them. No one helped us!'

'But you stuck to the original plans?'

'We had no choice. We kept to the same route and finished the line in 1963.'

I said, 'The line is headed straight for the Soviet border.'

'That was the idea,' Mr Jiao said. 'And we're still building.'

'You're going to connect the line to one in the Soviet Union?'

'Yes. At Alataw Shankou [the Dzungarian Gate]. We have built as far as Usu. There's some dispute about who is supposed to build the connecting line, but we expect it to be done by 1990.'

Then Mr Jie piped up, 'There used to be a slogan, THIS YEAR URUMCHI, NEXT YEAR THE BORDER!'

'When was that?'

'In 1958.'

Meanwhile, dishes of food were being put on the table, and sampled, and replaced with others. There was peppery Xinjiang chicken, and lamb, and cucumbers with red peppers, and mushrooms and white fungus, and the best dish I had in China, which was chili duck smoked in jasmine tea, rubbed with rice wine, air-dried, sprinkled with scallions, steamed and then deep-fried. I made a note of the name: *zhang cha yazi.*

'You like the duck,' Mr Jie said, noticing my greed and heaping my plate with more.

I said, 'If I met someone who could make that dish I would marry her.'

The two men stared at me and nodded, which was probably what I deserved for the silly remark.

To change the subject I said, 'Do Hans ever marry Uighurs?'

'Very seldom. You see, the Uighurs are afraid that if they marry outside their people it will reduce their numbers. They try to avoid it. Of course, sometimes a Uighur man marries a Han girl. But a Han man cannot marry a Uighur girl.'

'What do you mean, "cannot"?'

'It is against the law. The government forbids it.'

I guessed that he meant the Xinjiang Uighur Government. This was an autonomous region, with its own peculiar laws and its own parliament in Urumchi.

'Anyway, they're Muslims and we're not,' Mr Jiao said.

He said that he had been in Urumchi for twenty-eight years – had come as a sort of pioneer in a voluntary Maoist scheme. I asked him whether he spoke Uighur.

'Very little,' he said.

'It's a very hard language,' Mr Jie said. He had been in the region for thirty-one years – he was also from the east, Dalian, on the Gulf of Bohai.

Both men shared the Han conceit, like the British in India, which this Chinese rule in Xinjiang strongly resembled: better that these local folks learn to speak Chinese than that we should grapple with their language.

We were still eating. It was local food, they boasted. And I realized as we reached the last of the dishes that they were paying me the highest possible compliment: it was a meal without rice or noodles or bread. Such stodge was usually offered to plump out a poorer meal; but this was all delicacies.

'Will you go back home when you retire?'

'No, I'm staying here,' Mr Jiao said. 'My children are here. This is my home now. I will die here.'

We talked about the best railway routes through China. They said they liked going to Xian, because it took in the most interesting parts of China and was the most atmospheric.

'You're talking about the Silk Road,' I said. 'Ancient history.'

Mr Jiao said, 'Yes. Recent history is not very interesting.'

Remembering what Mr Yang had said about the Cultural Revolution in Urumchi I asked whether it was true that it had been violent here.

'It was very bad,' Mr Jiao said. His eyes had become very red and tiny. He made a sweeping gesture with his dark hand. '*Very* bad.'

'Did it disrupt the trains?'

'Yes! For twenty-four days at one time. That was in 1968. But there were lots of disruptions and much worse things. You see, the Red Guards were not one group. There were a number of different factions. Two factions were fighting in Urumchi.'

'Fighting in what way? You mean arguing?'

'First it was arguing – over the correct interpretation of what Mao had said. One work-unit claimed to be better Maoists than the other. They accused the others of being rightists. And then after the arguments got them nowhere, they fought with guns. Yes, guns. Bang-bang. People died.' His eyes went weepy-looking – but it was the wine. 'It was very bad.'

'Do you think it will come back – a second Cultural Revolution?'

'Absolutely not!' he thundered. 'Never!'

'Did Mao ever visit Urumchi?'

'No. Too busy, I think,' he said, and glanced at Mr Jie. 'But Zhou Enlai came here and travelled all over.' He said it in the affectionate way that Chinese always referred to Zhou. 'And recently Deng Xiaoping visited here. He had a good time. He was really impressed.'

By now we were all drunk enough to talk about war and friendship. I mentioned the Japanese and said I thought they were planning to take over the world by dominating its economy because they had failed to do so by military means. And how did it feel as a Chinese to be occupied again by a nation that had been driven out in the nineteen-forties?

'We have a saying in China,' Mr Jiao said. '"You can't attack everyone, so you have to be careful of everyone."'

The last dishes were taken from the table. Mr Jiao stood up a little unsteadily and we thanked each other. There were no other formalities; no small-talk; no lingering. Nothing is more abrupt than the end of a Chinese banquet.

In succeeding days I discovered that this part of Xinjiang was being opened up for oil-exploration. Already it was producing an enormous amount of oil – some oil was being exported to the United States. To the south-east, in the Lop Nor desert, atom bombs were being tested. There had even been a noisy protest in Peking by university students, but the police had put a stop to that, and the atomic testing had continued.

Most of China's minerals came from Xinjiang, and from the numerous radar dishes on the mountains it was easy to conclude that strategically it was an important area. I went to factories and became gloomy, seeing women painstakingly making silk carpets with very ordinary designs: one square yard a month, a whole year to make a not-very-pretty carpet. And there were jade-carvers in Urumchi who were doing something similar, taking weeks to make fifty-dollar grinning Buddhas in jade, or six months of cutting and polishing to make a jade dish. I had the impression the stuff didn't even sell particularly well.

No one seemed to mind. Urumchi was in a little time-warp, everything happening late. Breakfast was at 9.30, dinner at 9.00 at night. At about 10.30 every night the sun broke through the clouds and shone brilliantly until after 11.00, and then at midnight the whole place suddenly went cold.

I went into the desert to look at camels, and then north-east to the Bogda Shan, with their peaks like rocky steeples, and then to Tianchi, the Heavenly Pool, a lake about 2,000 feet up a mountainside. Above it, the snowy peak of Bogda Feng (18,000 feet) and the other peaks in the range looked like the lower jaw of a wolf, white and black fangs in a long angular jaw. There were noodle stalls and

Young Pioneers and Chinese tourists at the end of the road, but fifty feet beyond that there was no one – nothing but whispering pines and birds singing. I had not seen anything prettier than this, and while such a piny wilderness did not look Chinese, it did not look European either: the settlements on the road and in the woods were Mongolian yurts and cabins and tiny villages with those same bow-legged horsemen in boots, and women wearing shawls, and red-cheeked children. I spoke Chinese to a man who might have been a Kazakh and he just laughed.

I met a Chinese man named Mr Ching near the lake. He had given himself the English name 'Tom' after reading *The Adventures of Tom Sawyer*, and when he had done so everyone in his office decided to do the same thing. He worked in the Agricultural Bank in Altay, in the distant north of Xinjiang, in a little corner of China that was pinched by Russia on one side and Outer Mongolia on the other.

In that place, Tom Ching said, 'We have Mike, Julian, Jan, Wayne and Bob.'

Tom said he was thirty-four, which was just the age of the generation that had been involved in the Cultural Revolution – he would have been about sixteen at the height of it. But had the Cultural Revolution penetrated to the remote town of Altay?

'Oh, yes!' Tom said. 'We had it there. I was in middle school.'

'Did you have Red Guards?'

'Yes. I was a Red Guard! In my own school! I was an organizer!'

Tom Ching wore a yellow sweater and Chinese blue jeans and white sneakers. He carried a portable radio and a plastic hold-all stencilled *Shanghai.* All this was regarded as stylish. All he lacked was sun-glasses.

I said, 'Did you criticize your teachers for being rightists?'

'Yes!' he said eagerly.

'Did you have a little red book?'

'Yes. The quotations of Chairman Mao.'

'Did you sing songs?'

'Oh, yes. "The East Is Red" and the others – all the songs.'

'Did you criticize running dogs and people who took the capitalist road?'

'Yes!' Why was he smiling?

'Did you break things in Altay?'

His face fell. He paused a moment and peered at me, looking sheepish, and took a deep breath. He said, 'You were in China then, eh?'

8

Train Number 104 to Xian

Chinese trains could be bad. In twelve months of travelling – almost forty trains – I never saw one with a toilet that wasn't piggy. The loudspeakers plonked and nagged for eighteen hours a day – a hangover from the days of Maoist mottoes. The conductors could be tyrants, and the feeding frenzy in the dining-car was often not worth the trouble. But there were compensations – the kindly conductors, the occasional good meal, the comfortable berth, the luck of the draw; and, when all else failed, there was always a chubby thermos of hot water for making tea.

Yet whatever objections I could devise against the trains they were nothing compared to the horrors of air travel in China. I had a small dose of it when I left Urumchi for Lanzhou – there was no point in retracing my steps on the Iron Rooster. I was told to be at the airport three hours early – that is, 7.00 in the morning; and the plane left five hours late, at 3.00 in the afternoon. It was an old Russian jet, and its metal covering was wrinkled and cracked like the tinfoil in a used cigarette pack. The seats were jammed so closely together that my knees hurt and the circulation to my feet was cut off. Every seat was taken, and every person was heavily laden with carry-on baggage – big skull-cracking bundles that fell out of the overhead rack. Even before the plane took off people were softly and soupily vomiting, with their heads down and their hands folded, in the solemn and prayerful way that the Chinese habitually puke. After two hours we were each given an envelope that contained three caramel candies, some gum and three sticky boiled sweets; a piece of cellophane almost concealed a black strand of dried beef that looked like oakum and tasted like decayed rope; and (because Chinese can be optimistic) a toothpick. Two hours later a girl wearing an old postman's uniform went around with a tray. Thinking it might be better food I snatched one of the little parcels – it was a key-ring. The plane was very hot, and then so cold I could see my breath. It creaked like a schooner under sail. Another two hours passed. I said: *I am out of my mind.* An announcement was made, saying in a gargling way that we would shortly be landing. At this point everyone except the pukers stood up and began yanking their bundles out of the racks; and they remained standing, pushing, tottering and vaguely complaining – deaf to the demands that they sit down and strap themselves in – as the plane bounced, did wheelies on the runway and limped to Lanzhou terminal. Never again.

'What you think of Chinese airplane?' Mr Fang asked in a rare burst of English.

'Lamentable.'

'Thank you!' he said. 'Maybe we take plane to Xian?'

'You take the plane. I'll take the train.'

'Tomorrow?' he said hopefully.

'Tonight.'

Mr Fang seemed weary. If I tired him out he might leave me alone. He was not actively offensive; but it made me uneasy always to see him ten steps behind me, silently looking on, clutching his dictionary, and now probably looking up the meaning of the word 'lamentable'.

There was a dwarf at Lanzhou Station – an exceedingly small dwarf, less than three feet tall. At first I thought he was a child, but he had a wrinkled face, and a sort of frowning and anxious expression; a tiny hat, tiny slippers. He walked very briskly. That was the first giveaway – children never walk with such conviction.

And then people began to stare. I followed this dwarf through the station.

People pointed, some shrieked and called out. A Chinese man fumbled with a camera but was not quick enough to take a picture. A child saw him and yelled to his mother. And then, strangest of all, he was seen by a group of about fifteen deaf-and-dumb people. They were enthusing noiselessly and wildly signalling – pointing at the stern little man. They tried to surround him as they gesticulated and mimed their fascination, not realizing how grotesque they were in their dumb-show ridicule, and that this dwarf was just a person on his way home. Then there were hoots of laughter, from Chinese who found the deaf-and-dumb people funny and the dwarf hilarious. The dwarf hurried away, while the people stared at these handicapped people who were speaking to each other like Siamese dancers, flicking their fingers. The Chinese never seemed to hide their interest in anything. They stared frankly – when I opened my wallet they peered in, when I unzipped my bag a crowd gathered to look at my laundry. They were seldom alone; usually they were part of a watching crowd, which made it all possible. They were riveted by the freakish and the pathetic.

In front of Lanzhou Station there were about thirty young people standing in a long line, just at the exit door. They carried red banners with gold characters inscribed on them, and long streamers, and placards and flags. They were silent, standing patiently, like mourners. And I thought perhaps they *were* mourners, awaiting a catafalque from Train 104. It was 11.00 at night, and as this was Lanzhou, very chilly and damp.

'What are they doing, Mr Fang?'

'They are welcoming the delegates,' he said, without hesitation.

'Which delegates?'

'From the conference.'

'Which conference?'

'There are so many conferences,' he said.

I felt I was being fobbed off with a lame explanation. I pressed Mr Fang a bit harder.

'Perhaps an agricultural conference,' he said.

His 'perhaps' made me suspicious. I then suspected that they were striking, protesting, making some sort of fuss. If so, that was interesting, because fusses and strikes were never reported in the *China Daily*. In fact, the demand of most demonstrations – when they occurred, which was rare – was that the demonstration be reported in the Chinese news.

'What do those signs say, Mr Fang?'

'I can't read them without my glasses.'

'Please put on your glasses,' I said. 'I am very curious.'

'Ha! Ha! Ha!' he howled, pushing his glasses on and leaning forward. 'Ha! Ha! Ha!'

This grunting mirthless laugh meant: *I have just made a jackass of myself.*

Then he removed his glasses and became very solemn. Chinese laughter often had a sobering effect. It was more than explanatory; it was also cathartic.

'They are advertising a hotel.'

'One hotel?'

'Many hotels.'

'How many?'

'Many, many,' he said sadly. 'When the passengers come out of the station they will look up and see the banners. This one offers good food, that one offers good rooms, this one is nearby. They are in competition. They are doing it for business.'

Mr Fang was surprised that such go-ahead commercial sense existed in distant Gansu. And I think it was news to him so many restaurants, guesthouses and hotels were available in Lanzhou. It suggested more than the free market; it hinted at bourgeois ideas and competitive instincts.

I said, 'They are taking the capitalist road!'

Mr Fang replied coldly, 'We do not use that expression any more.'

He always winced when I trotted out expressions such as 'class enemy' (*jieji diren*) and 'running dog' (*zou gou*).

We bypassed the clamour of 200 travellers trying to push through the Hard Sleeper turnstile, and we knocked at the Soft Sleeper Waiting-Room door. The room attendant admitted us and showed us to the overstuffed chairs. I made a mental note to add antimacassars to my list of antiquated Chinese manufacturing (washboards, quill pens, corsets, back-scratchers, fish-glue, spittoons, steam locomotives), and I asked Mr Fang for his dictionary.

'Capitalist road' was in it under 'road', and so was 'running dog' ('a lackey, a flunkey, a stooge'). I looked up *ziyou*, 'freedom, liberty', and found a series of definitions, each with its own explanatory sentence. I copied the most interesting ones into my notebook.

> Citizens of China enjoy freedom of speech, correspondence, the press, assembly, association, procession, demonstration, and the freedom to strike.
>
> Bourgeois ideas must not be allowed to spread unchecked.
>
> The petty bourgeoisie's individualistic aversion to discipline.
>
> Liberalism is extremely harmful in a revolutionary collective.
>
> We can't decide this matter for ourselves; we must ask the leadership for instructions.

This official Chinese dictionary, reprinted by the state publishing house in 1985, contained definitions and illustrations that all contradicted life in China, in fundamental ways. I thought: When that book is revised and rewritten I will believe that China has changed. It was clearly out of date, but like much else that was said – the guff about Marxist-Leninism and the Guiding Spirit of Mao's Thought – it was ineffectual. Such sentiments were dead but they wouldn't lie down.

Around midnight, the train drew in. There was a commotion outside as the hotel touts and agents jostled for attention. I went to the sleeping-car. Mr Fang vanished. I found my berth and discovered that no one else was going to Xian. The sleeper was empty. This was the rarest situation on a Chinese train, and one to be relished. Such circumstances were almost luxurious and definitely cosy. My own gooseneck lamp, plastic flowers, thermos, pillow, quilt and comforter. There was a table-cloth on the little side-table, and a five-foot crocheted antimacassar on the seat-back.

The only disquieting part of it was the music. I couldn't twist the knob with my rubber-band trick, so I took out my Swiss Army knife and unscrewed the loudspeaker from the ceiling, disconnected it, replaced the plate and was able to read in silence. I was reading Lu Xun's *The True Story of Ah Q* because a Chinese woman had said that the story revealed the Chinese national character. So far it was about Ah Q's pompousness, foolishness, pretence and cowardice – and he had the farcical misapprehension of Mr Pooter. Was that the point?*

I read on, soothed by the ponderous motion of the train, and the melancholy cry of the steam whistle.

There had been a bucket of dead eels next to the hopper in the toilet cubicle. I had glimpsed the creatures in the middle of the night. That was memorable – and a good thing, too, because the next morning I went to the dining-car and asked what was on the menu, and the chef said, 'Eels!'

He said the train was operated by the Qingdao Railway Board, and had just come from the coast. It made a great loop through China, bringing with it Shandong specialities – seafood, jelly candy, and China's best beer.

We were still in Gansu, going south-east towards Shaanxi (not to be confused with Shanxi, a bit north-east), and we had just left the town of Tianshui. The landscape was unlike anything I had seen in Xinjiang or even the rest of Gansu. It was the carefully constructed Chinese landscape of mud mountains sculpted in terraces which held overgrown lawns of ripe rice. The only flat fields were far below, at the very bottom of the valleys. The rest had been made by the people, a whole countryside that had been put together by hand – stone walls shoring up the terraces on hillsides, paths and steps cut everywhere, sluices, drains, and carved-out furrows. There was more wheat than rice here, and bundles of it were piled, waiting to be collected and threshed – probably by that black beast up to his nose in the buffalo wallow.

The whole landscape had been possessed and shaped and put to practical use. It was not pretty, but it was symmetrical. You

---

*'Ah Q typifies all those who compensate themselves for their failures and set-backs in real life by regarding them as moral or spiritual victories' (*Selected Works of Mao Zedong*, Vol. I, p. 282).

couldn't say 'Look at that hillside', because it was all terraces – mud-walled ditches and fields, and mud-walled houses and roads. What the Chinese managed in miniature with a peach stone, carving it into an intricate design, they had done on a gigantic scale with these honey-coloured mountains. If there was an outcrop of rock they balanced a rice paddy on it, and the steps and terraces down the steep hills gave them the look of Mayan pyramids. There had not been much of that in the west of China. It was huge, the sort of complicated mud kingdom that insects created, and it was both impressive and appalling that everything visible in this landscape was man-made. Of course you could say that about any city in the world, but this wasn't a city – it was supposed to be the range of hills above the river Wei; and it looked as though it had been made by hand.

The river itself was muddy, flat, shallow, full of sandbanks this time of year.

'There are no fish in the Wei,' a man told me at Baoji, the railway junction where we stopped at noon. And then he loudly cleared his throat and spat a gob on the platform and in a reflex of politeness scuffed it with his shoe.

Everyone hoicked, everyone spat, sometimes dribbling, sometimes in a trajectory that ran like candlewax down the side of a spittoon. They tended to spit in waste baskets or against tree-trunks; but not even a government campaign restrained some from spitting on floors, and I saw people spit on carpets, always remembering politely to grind it with their foot.

I noticed on the platform at Baoji how they walked scuffingly, sort of skating, with their arms flapping, with narrow jogging shoulders, or else hustling puppet-like, with their limbs jerking. They minced, they plodded, they pushed, keeping their hands out – straight-arming their way – and their heads down. They could look entirely graceless – unexpected in Chinese.

And they talked very loudly in that deaf, nagging and interrupting way, as if no one ever listened to them and they had to shout to be heard. The radios and televisions were always turned too loud, the volume at maximum. Why? Was there a national deafness, or was it just a rather unfortunate habit?

They left doors open – that was a national habit. And they liked sitting in their underwear on the train. They were naturals for relaxation, and could turn even the shortest journey into a pyjama party. They were very tidy in the way they dressed and packed their bags, but they were energetic litterers and they were hellish in toilets. It was strange seeing a neatly dressed mob leaving a railway car that they had befouled.

They spat, they shouted, they stared and undressed; and yet with all this they seldom quarrelled. They were extremely shy, modest, timid even, and naive. 'Modesty helps one to go forward,' Mao said, 'whereas conceit makes one lag behind.' On trains they often looked contemplative.

We were now through the Wei Gorges, and after Baoji the land opened up and became flatter. It was spread with wheatfields in which people were scything and bundling and carting away the stalks. It had grown very hot and hazy, and though it was humid, too, this mid afternoon the fields were full of people, because of the harvest. They stood chest-high in the wheat, and they disappeared when they bent over with their sickles.

The villages here were tumble-down, but even the poorest houses had tall TV antennas. In some countrified places there was that other Chinese conundrum, of ugly tenements and barrack-like buildings in a pastoral setting. We stopped at Xianyang, where China's first emperor had 460 of his critics buried alive,* and then we crossed the Wei again – too shallow here for even the smallest boat – and through more wheatfields to the city of Xian.

The first sign of the city proper is the high wall around it, like a medieval fortification, built in the Ming Dynasty (fourteenth century) and recently restored. It has crenellations and sentry posts and towers with windows designed (like those on the Great

---

*Mao was often accused of being like the first emperor, Qin Shi Huangdi. His reply (in 1969) was: 'Well, and what was so remarkable about Qin Shi Huangdi? He executed 460 scholars. We, we executed 46,000 of them! . . . You think you insult us by saying we are like Qin Shi Huangdi, but you make a mistake, we have passed him a hundred times!'

Wall) for the width of crossbows. And like the Great Wall, it was built as much to keep some people out as to keep others in. The Xian city wall was high and bulky, and the train passed the North Gate, which looked like a temple, with red beams and a large arched roof. Near it was a big banner with two-foot characters, saying BE DISCIPLINED AND OBEY THE LAW.

Xian Station was new, the streets were broad, the city was well organized; it was as though it was designed to be visited. As the capital of the brilliant but brief Qin Empire and the starting-point of the Silk Road, it had always been regarded as a visitable city. Even 8,000 years ago, people lived here in reasonable comfort – the proof was at the excavated neolithic site at Banpo, nearby. Its most glorious associations are with the first emperor, Qin Shih Huangdi, the man who unified China, burned the books, built the Great Wall, standardized the laws, currency, roads, weights, measures, axle lengths and written language, and ordered the terracotta warriors to be made. That was well over 2,000 years ago, though the warriors weren't found until twelve years ago.

'When I was young, no tourists came to Xian,' Mr Xia told me, as we walked around town. He was thirty years old, a local guide. 'There were some visitors and foreign experts from East European countries. But we never saw Americans.'

'When did they start coming?'

'Obviously, after the terracotta army was found. Then, people were very interested. More and more things were unearthed. In 1980 some diggers found the bronze horse and chariot. People wanted to see these things.'

That was wonderful for the Chinese. They probably realized that the value of a tourist lies in his attention-span. Sightseeing is perfect for a dictatorship – China is surely not anything else, politically speaking. The tourist visits, sees the sights, and when they've all been seen it's time to go. The non-sightseer lingers, ignores the museums, asks awkward questions, fills people with alarm and despondency and has to be deported. Also, typically, the non-sightseer is not a big spender and in his or her unregulated way is quite a dangerous person to have around.

I hated sightseeing in China. I felt the Chinese hid behind their rebuilt ruins, so that no one could look closely at their lives. And the rebuilding was poor – usually botched and too sloppily painted. The places were always impossibly crowded and noisy. The Chinese were so desperate in their courtships that they went on tourist outings in order to hide and canoodle. Every holy mountain and famous pagoda had more than its share of motionless couples hugging and (sometimes) smooching. It was no good saying a particular place was hideous or pointless. It was the ritual of visiting – the outing – that mattered.

Xian was one of the few exceptions I found. It was genuinely interesting and pretty, and rather a stately and dignified place – different in that respect from most other Chinese cities, which were sooty and badly made and industrial. But Xian knows it is important. Hotels were being put up quickly to accommodate tourists, and in what had been for hundreds of years a very provincial city, off the beaten track, people seemed aware of the city's new celebrity as a tourist attraction.

The stallholders of Xian are relentless in their hectoring. They plead, they beg, they bargain. They sell cast figures of the warriors, and mats, and puppets cut out of cow-hide and horrible little coasters, and they push them in your face and shriek, 'Ming Dynasty!'

Tourists and the Free Market Economy arrived at about the same time, which meant that the first tourists found rapacious individuals waving handicrafts and haggling.

A small proportion of the merchandise is not junk. It is stuff from attics and old chests, the family jewels, knick-knacks that have been around for years, filthy little incense burners, cracked jade seals, tobacco boxes made out of hammered silver, rags of silk, very old and beautiful clothes made of silk or embroidery, and bonnets, jade wine cups, old brass padlocks, wooden images of gods and goddesses, silver fingernails, elaborate hairpins, perfume jars, snuff containers, pewter jars, pretty teapots, chipped dishes and plates, ivory chopsticks. mortally wounded vases.

Entirely off their own bat the Chinese turned the Free Market into a flea market. The trinkets and treasures have come out of the woodwork, and the stallholders or improvisational market people have become pestering hagglers for the first time in the People's Republic.

A thought that occurred to me back in Xinjiang was that the Uighurs were reverting to what they had always been – travellers, nomads, bargainers, inflexible Muslims and 'shansh marnie' people. So it was elsewhere, too. Scholars who had had to pretend to be political parrots for the sake of Mao were reforming themselves into that old distinguished class of scholar gentry; and gamblers and drinkers were re-emerging, and so were family farmers, and tinkers, and pot-wallopers, and little businessmen; and these folks living at the margins of the big cities – the market traders. Especially them.

What choice had they? Politics was closed to them. They couldn't emigrate. They couldn't criticize the government. The Communist Party was like a Masonic order, just as mysterious a brotherhood, possibly sinister, and just about unjoinable – you had to be chosen, and the most supine and robot-like yes-men were the likeliest candidates.

In such circumstances, who wouldn't dig out the family silver and flog it to tourists?

'This is old – *very old!*' they squawked. 'Qing Dynasty! Ming Dynasty! Fifty *kwai*! How much you pay? Make me an offer!'

That fascinated me. No fixed prices, no fixed location, no overheads. Just a wild-eyed person clutching my arm and pushing a string of old beads at me.

What made the whole enterprise even more interesting was that the stuff ranged from certifiable treasures to outright fakes. I went to Mount Li to look at the man-made hill which is probably the tomb of the first emperor – and it is probably just as likely that the tomb was looted in 206 BC, the year his dynasty ended.

A man lurking in the market near that hill hissed at me and pointed to a bulge in his shirt, indicating that he had something wonderful inside.

'You want to sell me something?' I said.

He shushed me, making a worried face. And with great caution he showed me what he had. It was a brass jar, with a lid, about five inches high, with markings on it.

'Two hundred *yuan*,' he said.

I laughed at him, but he persisted. 'Look,' he said. 'The sides. The top. Look closely.'

There were erotic carvings on it, five sexual positions, tiny inscriptions, and bits of flummery and decoration. Also, I could see that it was old – not ancient, but old. Qing. Nineteenth century. Maybe a little earlier than 1850. Dao Guang period, according to my book.

'I'll give you fifty.'

He laughed at me, harder than I had laughed at him.

'What is it?'

'For special medicine,' he said, and leered.

He meant aphrodisiacs – what else would you put in such a thing?

He dropped his price to 150 and then to 100. Then I showed him eighty *yuan* in Foreign Exchange Certificates and our illegal bargain was sealed. It was not a treasure, but it was unusual, and it was a damned sight more interesting than the dusty hill on the tourist itinerary.

The fakes were not difficult to spot, but the whole idea of people knowingly selling fakes said a great deal for this new burst of Chinese enterprise. Sometimes they were little stone statues, often they were clumsy bronze copies, but the majority of the bogus merchandise was marble or limestone heads or carvings which had been made to look as though they had been hacked off a temple wall. 'Very old', the traders said. 'Song! Ming! Qing!' They quoted high prices and dropped them. Fifty other people were selling identical stuff, but that did not stop anyone from claiming they were ancient, when – it was very obvious – they had all been made in a factory that specialized in fakes.

A very large market, selling all these things – fakes, treasures, and flea-market knick-knacks – had just been specially built and recently opened adjacent to the site of the terracotta army. It is the government's way of admitting that such freelance traders are here to stay. Some stalls have roofs and are rented for a small fee; but the rest of the market is in the open air, set up on tables and benches.

'When the foreigners come, business is very good,' a man told me, after selling me a pretty perfume bottle for about sixty pence. 'But the Chinese people don't buy these things. They don't like antiques.'

They are proud of the terracotta warriors, though (yet are not above looting them: in June 1987 some Chinese looters were caught trying to sell a warrior's head to a foreign dealer for $81,000 in Xian; the death penalty was a certainty). When I went, there were thousands of visitors looking at them and very few of these people came from overseas. The majority were Chinese tourists, who had come great distances in rickety buses that had been hired by their factory or co-operative or work-unit. They were poorly dressed and perspiring in the summer heat; they hurried to and fro in little trotting groups; they grinned for pictures, striking poses in front of the hangar-like building that houses the warriors. They were photographed by foreign tourists, and some of them returned the compliment – or insult – and took pictures of the tourists.

The terracotta warriors (which cannot be photographed) were not a disappointment to me. They are too bizarre for that. They are stiff, upright, life-sized men and horses, marching forward in their armour through an area as big as a football field – a thousand of them, and each one has his own face and his own hair-style. It is said that each clay figure had a counterpart in the emperor's real army that was scattered throughout the Qin Empire. Another theory is that the individual portraiture was meant to emphasize the unity of China by exhibiting 'all the physical features of the inhabitants of mainland east Asia'. Whatever the reason, each head is unique, and a name is stamped on the back of every neck – perhaps the name of the soldier, perhaps that of the potter-sculptor.

It is this life-like quality of the figures – and the enormous number of them – that makes the place wonderful, and even a little disturbing. As you watch, the figures seem to move forward. It is very hard to suggest the human form in armour, and yet even with these padded leggings and boots and heavy sleeves, the figures look agile, and lithe, and the kneeling archers and crossbowmen look alert and fully human.

This buried army was very much a private thrill for the tyrant who decreed that it be created to guard his tomb. But the first emperor, Qin Shi Huangdi, was given to grand gestures. Until his time, China was fragmented into the warring states, and bits of the Wall had been put up. As Prince Cheng, he took over from his father in 246 BC. He was thirteen years old. Before he was forty he had subdued the whole of China. He called himself emperor. He introduced an entirely new set of standards, set one of his generals – and many of his convicts and peasants – to work building the Great Wall, abolished serfs (meaning that, for the first time, the Chinese could give themselves surnames) and burned every book that did not directly praise his achievements – it was his way of making sure that history began with him. His grandiose schemes alienated his subjects and emptied his treasury. Three attempts were made to kill him. Eventually he died on a journey to east China, and to disguise his death his ministers covered his stinking corpse with rotten fish and carted him back to be buried here. The second emperor was murdered, and so was his successor, in what the Chinese call 'the first peasant insurrection in Chinese history'.

The odd thing is not how much this ancient ruler accomplished, but that he managed it in so short a time. And in an even shorter time his dynasty was eclipsed by chaos. Two thousand years later China's rulers had remarkably similar aims – conquest, unity and uniformity.

The rare quality of the terracotta warriors is that unlike anything else on the tourist route in China, they are exactly as they were made. They were vandalized by the rebellious peasants in the year 206 BC when these people invaded the tomb to steal the weapons – crossbows, spears, arrows and pikestaffs (they were all real) – that the clay warriors were holding. After that they lay buried until in 1974 a man digging a well hit his shovel against a warrior's head and unearthed it. They were disinterred. They are the one masterpiece in China that has not been repainted, faked and further vandalized. If they had been found before the Cultural Revolution instead of after it, they would undoubtedly have been pulverized by Red Guards, along with all the other masterpieces they smashed, burned or melted down.

Chinese tourists also flock to Xian to see the Hua Qing Pool, a sort of Tang Dynasty resort that is associated with the two-week arrest in 1936 of Chiang Kai-shek, the so-called 'Xian Incident'. They crowd around the sign saying THIS IS THE WINDOW THAT CHIANG KAI-SHEK JUMPED OUT OF and say, 'Where are the bullet holes?'

They go to the Big Goose Pagoda, the Drum Tower, the Temple

of the Recumbent Dragon, and the Banpo neolithic site, where a sign reads:

> People in this primitive society with low productivity couldn't understand the structure of the human body, living and dying and many phenomena of nature, so they began to have an initial religious idea.

They go to the Great Mosque, Qingzhen si, where many people still do have religious ideas. This mosque was founded 1,200 years ago and has been enlarged, vandalized, demolished and rebuilt many times since. It was in the process of being restored when I visited. I asked an old man how many believers there were in Xian. He said there were hundreds and that a few dozen had been to Mecca. He also said that during the Cultural Revolution the mosque had housed animals – pigs, mainly, which seemed the most popular way of insulting Muslims. When I left him he said, 'We are Sunni. Not Shi'ites. No Khomeni. Ha! Ha!'

That was a 'Ha-ha' I hadn't heard before, and it seemed to mean: *Death to the infidels*.

Walking among the gates and pillars with their Arabic inscriptions I saw an old man.

'*Salaam aleikum*,' I said. 'Peace and blessing be upon you.'

'*Wa-aleikum salaam*,' he replied, returning the greeting. 'Are you from Pakistan?'

'No. America.'

'Are there Muslims in America?' he asked, using the word *Mussulmen* in his Chinese.

'Yes. Quite a few,' I said. 'Why did you think I was from Pakistan? Did you think I looked like a Pakistani?'

'Maybe,' he said, and shrugged. 'I don't know. I've never seen one.'

9

The Express to Chengdu

I became sad, looking at Mr Fang's lopsided expression of longing, one eye screwed up and one spiky patch of his hair sticking up. He could be so silent. He merely followed me, perhaps hoping that I would do something wrong. He looked so grateful when I asked for his help. Now we were in the Soft Class Waiting-Room at Xian Station, killing time with magazines, and I became sadder when I saw him trying to work out with a dictionary a page in *China Products Monthly*. I had the same magazine, and that page was an ad for 'Jiangsu Ceramics' – small ugly statues of angels, Santa Clauses, snow-covered churches, Mickey Mouses, choirboys with lyres; and what Mr Fang was trying to read described the ceramics as *Ingeniously conceived! Vividly modelled! Freshly coloured! Boundlessly interesting!*

He looked up and smiled at me, which depressed me even more, because I suspected that he was sad. Then I decided that he was not sad at all. He was like so many other Chinese – reserved and fatalistic and steeling themselves against disappointment. Yes, the Great Wall was a masterpiece and the Tang Dynasty had been glorious and they had managed to thrash the Japanese, and they invented poison gas, toilet paper and the decimal point; but they also had a long history of convulsions and reverses. Never mind that they forgot they invented the mechanical clock. Look at the upheavals that had taken place in just the past hundred years: the Taiping revolt, the humiliating colonialism by Europe and Japan, the Boxer Rebellion, the fall of the empire in 1911, the republic of Sun Yat Sen, the battling between Chiang Kai-shek's Guomindang and Mao's communists, the Sino-Japanese war, the Great Leap Forward and all the other witch-hunts and hysterical purges that followed the emergence of the People's Republic, culminating in the Cultural Revolution. Who wouldn't be uneasy? And these sudden agonies were undoubtedly the reason that few people ever showed confidence in the future. It was better not to think about it. And it was a loss of face to seem disappointed, which was another reason the Chinese never opened presents in front of the gift-giver (nor commented on the present, no matter how large or small), and why their impulse when startled was always to laugh.

Mr Fang, who was a Russian specialist, and had lectured on Pushkin, and acted as interpreter in Moscow and Leningrad at a time when the Russians and the Chinese had been comrades, had been howled at in the nineteen-sixties for teaching a bourgeois foreign language and forced to carry boulders in a sort of chain-gang. And now he was shadowing an ungrateful American through Central Sichuan. Instead of screaming 'What next!' he looked up and shyly smiled.

He pretended not to see me board the train, but I called out to him, 'I'll see you in Chengdu.'

The train pulled out at about 5.30 in the bright early evening, and passed the wheatfields and the harvesters. It also passed a great number of mounds and tombs and tumuli, probably all of them looted (though no one took treasures to the Government Antique Exchange any more, where they were paid a pittance for the object which was then sold for a high price at a state shop). I had heard at my hotel that another pit near Xian had just been excavated and was full of yet more terracotta figures. I asked for information on this, but either no one knew about it or else they had decided to keep it a secret.

As the sun drooped and the steam train went *chik-chik-chik-chik-chisssss* at a siding, a dark perspiring Chinese man threw the compartment door open and entered dragging four big bags.

'I am from Kowloon,' he said.

He looked very sick. He was out of breath, he fumbled with straps and zippers. He jangled a bunch of keys that hung on a chain from his thick leather belt. His track shoes stank. He constantly said 'Sorry' both in Mandarin and English. His eyes were narrow wounds.

'I drink too much last night.'

He abruptly left his bags and ran out of the compartment. When he returned, he cleared his throat and said, 'I vomited in the toilet.'

Another man entered the compartment. This coming and going was quite usual. Travellers sauntered through the train looking for empty berths and free seats. When they located one they paid a surcharge on their ticket and claimed the place. An empty compartment did not stay empty for long; and the coming and going went on all night, too.

This new man was youngish and rather tough-looking, beefy-faced, with a big belly and big feet.

'I want to sleep here,' he said, slapping the berth on which I was sitting.

'This is mine,' I said. 'I am sleeping here.'

He didn't like my saying that. He was in a sort of uniform – army pants and a khaki jacket. He had the look of a pushy, bullying Red Guard. There was no question in my mind but that he was a party hack.

I ignored him and continued to write in my diary, pleasant thoughts about Xian. This Red Guard grumbled to the man from Kowloon.

'He says he has to sleep there,' the man from Kowloon said.

'Sorry,' I said.

Because I had been in the compartment first, and this was my berth, I had the use of the table, and this corner seat. I knew he coveted it when the man from Kowloon said, 'He has to write his report.'

'I have to write my report,' I said.

'His is very important.'

'So is mine.'

'His report is for the government.'

'Then it must be a load of crap.'

'He is not writing about a road,' the man from Kowloon said.

The two men took out cigarettes and filled the compartment with smoke. I told them to cut it out – a recent ruling on China Railways had said that people could smoke only with the consent of other passengers. It was late, and hot, and stifling in this small compartment.

'It's against the rules,' I said.

They put their cigarettes away and began to talk – very loudly, shouting in fact, because the man from Kowloon had the Hong-Konger's characteristically poor command of Mandarin, and the Red Guard was from Urumchi in Xinjiang and spoke a rather debased version of Mandarin. This language problem didn't stop them yakking, but it meant that most of the time they were interrupting each other and repeating things constantly. I opened the window because of the heat. Smoke from the engine blew in and gagged me, and the *chik-chik-chik* made my teeth rattle.

'He says he has to write his report.'

'First I have to finish mine,' I said.

'He wants to smoke.'

'Smoking isn't allowed in the compartment unless everyone agrees,' I said. 'I don't agree.'

'He wants to know why there is a smoking-box on the wall,' said the man from Kowloon, clicking an ashtray on the wall.

'Why not ask the *fuwuyuan* or the *lieche yuan*?' I said, because these room attendants were passing our door.

'Each room has smoking-boxes,' the Red Guard said to me, in an intimidating way. 'What are they for?'

'For putting out cigarettes,' I said, trying to stare him down.

'We must have co-operation,' he said.

This meant: Stop being a pain in the ass.

'For the sake of friendship,' he said.

This little formula was spoken through gritted teeth.

'I am minding my own business, so why don't you mind yours?' I said. 'Fish-face.'

I went back to my diary, but their shouting back and forth made it impossible to concentrate, so I went to the dining-car. It was past eight o'clock – late by Chinese standards (they usually ate dinner before 6.30 or 7.00) – but the menu was recited to me in the usual way, and I ordered. No food came. I asked why.

'There are some foreigners on board,' the waiter said.

'I'm a foreigner.'

'But you are alone,' he said. 'We must wait for the group.'

We stopped at Baoji, the junction, which we had passed a week before; but this time we turned south towards Sichuan. No food came. It was after 8.30. The waiter said, 'Foreigners . . . Group.'

I told him I was hungry and to bring the food soon. 'Dying of hunger' was a phrase sounding like *ursula*. Still no food came.

Then the group of foreigners appeared: fourteen chunky Swedes, with sunburned arms and whitish hair. One had a video camera. As he poked it and whirred it, the others put their elbows on the sticky dining-car tables. Their guide bought all the beer, before I could order any. Then the food came – to them and finally to me. It was after nine o'clock. The Swedes ate slowly, trying to pincer their slippery noodles. Then the train stopped at Liangkou with such a jolting halt the noodle bowls shot into the Swedes' laps.

'I'm still hungry,' I said to the waiter. 'Is there any more food?'

'We have some sausages.'

'Pork?'

'No. Horse.'

I had four of them. They were not bad. The meat was dark and tough, with a strong smoky taste.

When I got back to the compartment it was full of men – the man from Kowloon, the Red Guard and three others. The corridor was crowded with men in pyjamas, and children squawking, and some card-players. The fans rattled and buzzed; so did the train.

'He is from Xinjiang,' the man from Kowloon said. 'He is a student. He wants to know your name.'

'My name is Paul. He is sitting on my bed. I want to go to sleep.'

This disapproving tone had the effect of emptying the compartment very quickly. We turned the lights out, but the three others – a new man had joined us – went on shouting at each other in the darkness.

There was no dawn. The mist grew lighter, thinned slightly, and as we passed at that early hour from Shaanxi into the vast populous province of Sichuan, small knobby trees became visible, and so did the faint outlines of mountains and hills; and people appeared as small dark brush-strokes in this simple Chinese water-colour.

The mist hung over the mountains, and as the sun heated it and made it thinner, a greenness came into it, and there was a lushness, the rice fields, beneath it. It was like looking at a landscape through etched glass, seeing everything blurred, and now and then getting a clear glimpse of the beautiful contours of mountains, of fields and valleys. The sharpest line was the path that always led around the hillside, a packed narrowness that looked bright and baked. In this blur, people were hoeing, and cycling, and leading hairy pigs to market.

The landscape was softened by the mist, but when the mist all burned away what had seemed idyllic looked senile. And the farmers had a hard routine this humid summer morning. Chinese farming is back-breaking, but it is some consolation to know that these days the farmers are well-off – much better off than any teacher or factory worker. The free market has helped them by guaranteeing them good prices; they no longer have to sell at fixed and punitive prices to the state. We had only gone a few hundred miles, from Shaanxi into Sichuan, but we had moved from a wheat-growing region to paddy fields. It was more southerly here, and wetter and warmer.

That was another virtue of the train in China. It allowed one to make visual connections in a place that was otherwise full of shocks and bafflements. Every other mode of travel made the country seem incomprehensible. Well, even on a train it was incomprehensible at times. But doing it this way helped. It wasn't one countryside: it was a thousand landscapes and hundreds of crops. Sometimes, an hour passed and everything was different.

Now there were cornfields, and harvesters flinging ears of corn into gunny sacks, and browsing buffaloes, and a brownish goose with an orange beak standing in the middle of a flooded field, and women yoked to buckets, and a human scarecrow – a boy frightening birds by using a long stick with blue streamers on it; and a man on the bank of a canal, fishing Chinese-style, a rod in each hand.

I could not understand the Red Guard's Chinese, so I asked the man from Kowloon whether he would translate my questions.

He said, 'I am interested myself!'

'What does he do for work?'

The Red Guard was sulking in his bed.

'He works in an institute – agricultural. No. Language institute. In Urumchi.'

'I was in Urumchi.'

'He says, many people go to Urumchi.'

I said, 'What language does he teach at this institute?'

'He doesn't know the answer to your question.'

'Does he speak foreign languages?'

'He says he works there –'

The Red Guard was gabbling in his berth.

'– he is not a teacher.'

'What is his job?'

'He is a cadre.'

An official. Why did they use this French word? Probably because they hated the word 'official' – it smacked of feudalism and the class system.

'Is he a member of the Chinese Communist Party?'

'He is.'

One of the few.

'Ask him when he joined.'

'When he was eight years old.'

'That's impossible.'

Gabble, gabble.

'When he was sixteen, he says. He joined the party then.'

'Ask him if he was a Red Guard.'

'Yes, he was a Red Guard.'

I was pleased that I had spotted him. But why did he *still* look like one?

'Ask him if he was in the Gang of Rebellion.' These brutes, the *Zaofan Pai*, were said to be the toughest, most thuggish of the Red Guards. They did battle with the *Bao Huang Pai* (Emperor's Gang) until long after the Cultural Revolution ended.

The question was translated, but with a mutter of 'That's enough questions' the Red Guard slid off his berth and hurried into the corridor, clacking his plastic sandals.

Nearer Chengdu, the man from Kowloon said that this was his

first trip to China. His name was Cheung. He was exactly my age – he showed me his passport so that I would see his name written: we had the same birthday.

'The Year of the Snake,' I said.

He was married, he had three children. He was a taxi driver in Kowloon and had come to China for the same sentimental reasons that so many overseas Chinese had in making the journey. And practical reasons, too: the discounts, the freebies, the brotherly goodwill, the ease in making arrangements as a Foreign Compatriot, and all the other angles that went under the general heading of ethnic nepotism. In Xian he had met some Chinese taxi drivers and they had bought him enough beer to get him plastered.

'In ten years you'll be able to drive your taxi from Kowloon into China.'

'Yes,' he said. 'But I don't want to.'

'Chinese taxi drivers make money – didn't they tell you that?'

And because no Chinese could afford to ride in a Chinese taxi, the customers were always foreigners. This was what the party would call a pernicious influence, and I agreed. Chinese taxi drivers, as a breed, seemed to me stubborn and grasping. And they weren't particularly skilful drivers. It was very rare to spend any length of time in Chinese taxis and not experience an accident – usually your taxi crashing into a cyclist.

Cheung said, 'They have to earn seventy *yuan* a day. After they make that amount on the meter they get a percentage of the rest. But they only have to work eight hours. In Hong Kong we all work twelve hours. It's a very hard life. Food is expensive, rent is expensive, everything costs too much.'

'Maybe the Chinese government will straighten things out when they take over Hong Kong.'

'No. They will ruin it. No democracy.'

'There's no democracy there now. It's a British colony. The Governor-General is appointed. And the strange thing is,' I said, because I had suddenly realized what a political anachronism Hong Kong was, 'very few people actually speak English in Hong Kong.'

'We speak Cantonese.'

'That's the point. It's part of Guandong province, really. British culture didn't sink in. It's all Cantonese.'

Cheung did not want to argue. He said, 'I don't care. I am going to the United States.'

'You mean, for good?'

'Yes. I have a sister in San Francisco. I also am getting a visa from the American embassy in Hong Kong.'

'Will you be driving a taxi in the States?'

'No. I will get a job in a restaurant.'

'A Chinese restaurant?'

'Of course. There are many. In Chinatown.'

'Have you ever been to the United States?' I asked.

'No,' Cheung said. 'But I have spoken to my friends. I can earn $800 a week.'

'Doing what?'

'Maybe cooking.'

'What do you mean, "maybe"? Can you cook?'

'I am Cantonese. I can cook Cantonese food, I think.'

'Why not stay in Hong Kong?' I said. 'Are you really afraid that things will change when the Chinese take over?'

He thought a moment, then said, 'In Hong Kong is too hard work. America is better. Better living.'

'Why not England?'

'I don't want England. Not good living.'

'Have you been to England?'

'No. But my friends tell me.'

He was packing up his gear. It was near 11.00 in the morning, and rice fields slid by in this green steamy place. We would be in Chengdu soon. Anyway, Cheung was sick of my questions. But I was fascinated by this man who had already decided to chuck his life in Hong Kong and emigrate to a wonderful new existence in America – a little paradise called Chinatown, where Chinese people fitted in, earned American salaries and never had to integrate or make any concessions to this big sheltering republic. It also interested me that this British colonial had rejected Britain.

'Who is the Prime Minister of Britain?'

'I don't know.'

'Who is the leader of the Chinese people?'

'Deng Xiaoping.'

'Who is the President of the United States?'

This puzzled him for a moment, but only a moment. 'President,' he began thoughtfully, and drew a breath. 'Nixon.'

Nixon had been out of office for eleven years.

'You think Nixon is president of the United States right now?'

'Yes. I think so. I like him. Do you like him?'

'Not very much.'

'Which party do you support? Liberty Party, or the other one?'

'Liberty Party,' I said. 'We call them Democrats.' But Mr Cheung was not listening. He had hoisted his bags for our arrival in Chengdu. I said, 'By the way, who is the Governor-General of Hong Kong?'

'Sir Something,' Mr Cheung said, and hurried off the train.

I looked into a mirror at a dark, noisy, garage-like restaurant called 'Pockmarked Mother Chen's' (Chen Ma Po, home of hot bean curd) and saw Mr Fang staring at the back of my head. After my bowl of bean curd was served to me I was given a plate of hot dumplings. I liked them, but I hadn't ordered them. They weren't on the menu; they had been bought at a stall.

'That man bought them for you,' the waiter said, pointing to the back of the room.

But by then Mr Fang had gone. He had been very observant over these past weeks: he knew of my fondness for dumplings. But he had never mentioned it. I was touched by his gesture, but then I became suspicious. What else had he noticed about me?

The bean curd was flavoured with oil and onion and chopped pork and flakes of red pepper the size of a thumbnail. The fried dumplings were filled with spinach. The rice was damp and lumpy, but that didn't matter – Chinese rice was made in huge tureens, so it was always stodgy. This was the Chinese equivalent of a fast food joint. People popped in for a quick meal and they hurried away. Near me a blind man sat with his guide-boy – the blind man had a tight grip on the boy's wrist. And satisfied eaters, having finished, were blowing their noses in their fingers, or hoicking loudly, or spitting on to the floor.

Turning away from the sight of a man taking aim for a spittoon – was I a silly, ethnocentric, old fussbudget for finding a brimming spittoon unwelcome in a restaurant? – I saw a woman watching me.

'Are you an American?' she asked, hopefully, in English.

Her name was Mrs Ji. She said she was pleased to meet an American, because she had recently visited the United States – seeing relatives – and had had a wonderful time. She had spent most of the time in Seattle, but had also been to Los Angeles, San Francisco and even Las Vegas, where she had gambled and broke even.

In Shanghai I had met a Chinese woman who told me that the sight of Chinatown in Boston had depressed her. It seemed to her fatuous and antediluvian, a sort of Guangzhou ghetto. Didn't these people know better than to behave like sheep? I asked Mrs Ji if she felt any of that exasperation.

'I know what she meant,' Mrs Ji said. 'I don't like American food, so I ate at a lot of Chinese restaurants. They were all bad. And the so-called Sichuan restaurants – no good at all.'

'But not much spitting,' I said. 'These spittoons –'

'We spit too much,' she said. 'The government is trying to stop it.'

The anti-spitting posters were everywhere, but it was really a campaign to encourage spitters to aim rather than to discourage spitting. The message was: Use a spittoon.

After a while – I was asking Mrs Ji about her family – she told me that she was divorced.

'My husband met a younger woman a few years ago,' she said, and volunteered the information that she herself was forty-eight years old.

'Was it easy to get a divorce?'

'Very easy.'

'Are there many divorced people in China?'

'Many.'

She didn't elaborate, and anyway it was a delicate subject. It was well known that there were a number of stresses in Chinese society: the shortage of money, the crowded households, the bureaucracy, the one-child family, and the husband and wife – quite a large proportion – who were separated for reasons of work: different factories, different cities, and sometimes different provinces. And many divorces resulted from the pairings-off between peasants and intellectuals during the Cultural-Revolution.

Perhaps my questions made Mrs Ji self-conscious. After being so candid, she became quite prim and hurried away – had she seen someone watching? I paid for my lunch and went for a walk.

Chengdu had a number of Buddhist temples and pretty parks. It was one of the many Chinese cities which in the past twenty years had lost its city walls and battlements and beautiful gates; but conversely it was one of the few which had a towering statue of Chairman Mao on its main street. In the course of time, those statues would be broken up. Chengdu's Mao statue was one of the largest in China. It had not been vandalized or pulled down. Mao's liking for the poetry of Du Fu meant the Tang poet's cottage in a Chengdu park is now a national shrine. But the city was oversized and charmless, and though some of its markets and shop-houses remained, too many of them had been torn down to make room for workers' barracks and tower blocks.

Encouraging people to live in big cities and tall buildings made it easier to control their lives. Of course Chinese cities had always been crowded, but the policies of the People's Republic had robbed them of any interest and made them plainer and reminded people that they were merely screws in the vast machine. I had an inkling of this walking around Chengdu, getting the railway-induced kinks out of my muscles. Chinese cities made me feel small and insignificant: they were not places to loiter in. They were the corners of the greater labyrinth, and it was impossible to go very far without coming upon a barrier – the road ended, or there was a roadblock, or a checkpoint. No wonder people mobbed the railway trains. And it was not surprising that when the Chinese visited places like Seattle or San Francisco their inclination was to stay.

I passed the Sichuan People's Hospital one day, walking on the outskirts of Chengdu. It was a busy place, or perhaps I had got there during visiting hours; anyway, a great number of people were coming and going. Fruit and vegetable stalls had been set up across the street from the hospital, where people could buy presents for the patients. But among those stalls were half a dozen medicine-men, selling potions that ranged from the outright quackery of antlers and bird-bills and snakeskins, to herbal remedies that were accepted in many Chinese hospitals. It was an appropriate place for the quacks, and they apparently operated on the assumption that if someone was not happy with his treatment at the state hospital he could supplement his medicine with lizards and powdered deer antlers.

Mr Fang followed me everywhere, in his hesitant way, hanging back apprehensively, and smiling when I caught his eye. But it was always a smile of fear.

I walked past a family planning poster – a large billboard near the centre of Chengdu. It showed a Chinese leader welcoming the birth of one baby girl (the parents handing it over for approval). The slogan underneath said CHINA NEEDS FAMILY PLANNING.

When I turned around and addressed Mr Fang the poor man yelped. Then he recovered himself and laughed. His laugh said *Sorry for screaming!*

'That man looks familiar,' I said. 'Is that Zhou Enlai?'

'Yes. It is Zhou.'

'Why him on a family planning poster?'

'People like him. People respect him.'

'Why not Mao Zedong?'

'On a family planning poster!' Mr Fang said. He was right to find it absurd. After all, Mao had encouraged the Chinese to breed like rabbits. 'Not so good,' Mr Fang said.

I asked him whether people had a more respectful attitude towards Mao or Zhou these days.

'For myself, I prefer Zhou. And I think many others do, too. But I cannot speak for them.'

'Why do you prefer Zhou, Mr Fang?'

'He was honest. He was a good man. Also during the Cultural Revolution he suffered much.'

'Was he criticized?'

'Not in public, but within. It was worse. People know that.'

Before I set off again, I said, 'Mr Fang, why don't you go back to the hotel and rest? It's not necessary to follow me.'

'It is the Chinese way,' Mr Fang said.

The parks in Chengdu attracted the newer sort of Chinese youth.

Observe the young couple entering People's Park in a suburb of Chengdu one June afternoon. The first thing that strikes you about the man is that he does not look anything like the man in the family planning poster. He is smoking a king-sized cigarette – it dangles from his lips – and in his hand he has a suitcase-style cassette recorder and radio, and the screechy music (probably a Hong Kong tape) thumps against it and drowns conversation and frightens the dusty starlings. The fellow wears a T-shirt saying *Cowboy*, and the motif on the shirt is a long-nosed man in a ten-gallon hat. He also wears tight blue jeans and platform shoes with womanish high heels. His hair has been professionally curled – the Canton fashion spread to Shanghai and has recently reached Chengdu. He wears sun-glasses. He swings his radio and puffs his cigarette.

His girlfriend (if she were his wife he would not be trying so hard to impress her) wears a pink dress. It is light and fluttery. She might have made it herself. She also wears the nylon knee-socks that younger women favour, and high-heeled shoes, and sun-glasses with rhinestones on the frames.

This is their day off. They are spending it in the park, Later on they will look for a tree and hide behind it for a session of old-fashioned smooching. The parks and the boulevards are full of such couples. They are the new people in the People's Republic – the inheritors. But their motto is *Get it while you can*.

I asked Mr Fang whether he had seen them. He said he had. He was very disapproving of these youngsters.

'It is the fault of the Cultural Revolution,' he said. 'They saw that it was a disaster. For that whole time there was disruption. No one obeyed. That is why, now, these young people have no manners, no discipline and no ideas.'

'You sound angry, Mr Fang.'

He did not reply. He laughed – a sharp, stuttering and explosive laugh. That meant he was very angry.

He had said he disliked modern Chinese stories. He meant he was out of sympathy with them. Who were these spoiled brats and spendthrifts who appeared in the pages of *Beijing Literature* and *Harvest* and *Monthly Literary Miscellany*? Actually they were just the sort of youngsters you saw every day in the public parks, trying to be cool, which mean mimicking western ways – sun-glasses, curled hair, platform shoes, knee-socks, flared trousers, blue jeans, transistor radios, earphones and, for a lucky few, motor cycles. They even had to have a fancy brassiere, probably the most superfluous garment in China.

In Xu Naijian's recent (1985) story, *Because I'm Thirty and Unmarried*, the so-called spinster is told by her girl cousin, 'What kind of bra is this you're wearing, so big and ungainly? Get yourself one of those bras from Xinjiekou. They're a nice shape – made in Guangzhou. You're so out of date . . .'

The puzzling conflict that arises when a Chinese person is faced with choosing between the east and the west was expressed by the Chinese traveller Liang Ch'i-ch'ao. In *Travel Impressions of Europe* (1919), he wrote:

> Of course we may laugh at those old folks among us, who block their own road of advancement and claim that we Chinese have all that is found in western learning. But should we not laugh even more at those who are drunk with western ways and regard everything Chinese as worthless, as though we in the last several hundred years have remained primitive and have achieved nothing?

As Mr Fang walked along with me (but a few steps behind me) we passed a refreshment stand and heard loud singing – one uproarious voice trying to manage a twangling Chinese song. The singer, a man, was seated at a table, his back turned to us. His two companions, who were sober, wore terrified smiles. The man was at the final stage of Chinese drunkenness: red-faced, singing and drooling. Another bottle of beer and his eyes would swell up, he would gasp for breath and soon be out cold.

'That is also a result of the Cultural Revolution,' Mr Fang said. 'What does he care? He has lost all discipline. He has no pride. It is bad behaviour.'

Then the man stood up, still singing, and staggered a little. He turned aside. He did not see me, but I saw him. It was Cheung, the taxi driver from Kowloon.

10

The Halt at Emei Shan: Train Number 209 to Kunming

The biggest statue of Buddha in the world, and probably the ugliest, is three hours down the main Chengdu-Kunming line at Leshan, a riverside town. The Buddha and the surrounding temples make it a place of pilgrimage. The statue sits in a niche as big as a gorge, at the confluence of three rivers. It is said that this Buddha was erected there 1,200 years ago because the turbulence created by the meeting rivers had drowned so many boatmen. Even now I could see men battling through the suds in their sampans as I watched.

But it was less an object of veneration than an example of the Chinese fascination with freakishness – the very big, the very weird, the highly unusual. This Buddha's ears were twelve feet long. Chinese tourists frolicked on his feet. You could park a car on the nail of his big toe. Close up he was Brobdingnagian – big, plain, disproportionate – with weeds growing from his cracks. From the river I imagined he did not look so grotesque. There were dragon-boat races on the river that week: more freakishness – oarsmen throwing panicky ducks into the water and then chasing them in the luridly painted boats.

There were dragon-boat men in the restaurant at Leshan. They were singing and swilling beer and engaged in drinking contests (the loser had to clip clothes-pegs to his ears, so that he would look like a total jackass). For lunch I had the specialities of this pleasant town – frogs' thighs and green bean seeds, and then I went to the holy mountain at Emei. Like Leshan, Emei is also a place of pilgrimage. It is considered an act of piety to climb the mountain – holiness at 10,000 feet, on this penultimate staging-post to even holier Tibet.

I met a group of eight elderly pilgrims at Emei. They were all in their seventies and carried backpacks – ingenious wicker baskets – and walking-sticks and food bundles. They were the classic instance of smiling and portable pilgrims.

'Where do you come from?'

'From Xitang.'

Over 300 miles away, in the north-east of Sichuan.

'Why did you come here?'

'To pray to our God.'

'And we are now going to Wuhou Temple in Chengdu,' one old woman said. 'To pray.'

The women wore a sort of nun's cap – a starched white cloth carefully folded and pinned; and they had thick socks, like leg-warmers, and like the men they leaned on hiking-staffs. They were bluff and hardy and very good-humoured. Some of the women smoked pipes, and one chomped on a cigar. The men wore cloaks with big sleeves. They said they had climbed to the top of the mountain. None of them wore anything sturdier than sandals or cloth slippers.

China has five holy mountains. It is the Chinese Buddhist's wish – and the wish of many foreign hikers – to climb them all. The trouble is that, being holy and being Chinese, they have been trampled for thousands of years. They have steps cut to the summit, and noodle stalls along the way, and kiosks selling post-cards, monks selling strings of beads, hawkers, fruiterers and professional photographers who charge one *yuan* per pose. And along with the tough grannies toiling towards the top, there are the Americans in their Chinese T-shirts, the Chinese in their American T-shirts, the Germans wearing rucksacks, and the French clutching the guidebook that says *Chine*. None of this makes the mountain less holy, but it makes the climb less fun.

For some reason, Emei was full of monkeys – frowning rhesus monkeys. They pestered pilgrims and snatched food and rode on the necks of their owners in a lazy and confident way, with their legs dangling over the chest. They picked their teeth as they rode along. On a back road near Emei I saw a man giving his monkey a piggy-back, as he cycled – just like a father and child.

I stayed at what was described to me as the Railway University at Emei – it was Mr Fang's doing. Actually it was the Institute of Communications, and it had 30,000 students. I was in the guesthouse, which, being new and 'modern', had the bizarre touches that the Chinese reserve for their most expensive structures. And when these structures venture out of the realm of Chinese architecture altogether they acquire things like concrete umbrellas on the terrace, velvet padded walls, fuse boxes in the dining-room, murals of pandas, cactuses in the bathroom as a sort of suggestion that there is no water, very scary-looking bare wires protruding from the wall, water-stains on the ceiling which take on the appearance of caricatures, and in the smallest rooms the most enormous sofas. The reflecting pool is another feature of such places. These pools were very entertaining – you never knew what you might find in them: dead fish, shoes, a bicycle wheel, rusty cans, chopsticks; but never anything as dull as algae. The one at Emei was full of water, and in the water a very large mirror that had plopped off the wall and shivered to pieces in the pool.

'What do you think of the guesthouse?' Mr Fang asked me.

'Excellent,' I said. 'I want to stay longer.'

But the cook sized me up and did one of the cruellest things any cook can do in rural China: he made me western food – what he conceived to be western food. Undercooked potatoes, pink chicken, boiled cabbage, and something so odd I had to ask its name.

'Bean –'

His English was like his cooking: strange mimicry. But I eventually found out what he was trying to tell me: Wiener schnitzel.

Yet I enjoyed the place. I had felt the same in Inner Mongolia, at

Jiayuguan, Turfan and Urumchi – the wilder and emptier parts of China. I had had enough of Chinese cities. But this was pleasant, and it was possible to take long walks through the countryside, watching people hoeing or pigs wallowing, and in the far-off villages the little kids doing homework in copybooks in front of the thatched-roof huts.

The railway halt at Emei was at the end of a long muddy road, and a market nearby sold fruit and peanuts to the pilgrims waiting patiently, leaning on their walking-sticks, for the train. And then, above the sound of sparrows and the whispers of bamboos, a train whistle blew. I liked these country stations, and it seemed perfect to sit there among the rice fields in the hills of Sichuan until, right on schedule, the big wheezing train arrived to take me away, south into Yunnan. It was twenty-four hours to Kunming, and the train was uncharacteristically empty: I had a compartment to myself, and this one – because of the intense and humid heat – had straw mats instead of cushions.

'There are 200 tunnels between here and Kunming,' the conductor said when he clipped my ticket. No sooner had he got the words out of his mouth than we were standing in darkness: the first tunnel.

We were among tall conical hills that were so steep they were terraced and cultivated only half-way up. That was unusual in China where land economy was almost an obsession. And the day was so overcast that waterfalls spilled out of the low cloud and paths zigzagged upwards and disappeared in the mist.

So many tunnels meant that we would be among mountains the whole way – and hills and valleys, and narrow swinging footbridges slung across the gorges. The ravines were spectacular and steep, and the mountains were close together, so the valleys were very narrow. All of these magnificent geographical features had meant that the railway line had been difficult. In fact many of the engineering problems had been regarded as almost insurmountable until the early seventies when, with a combination of soldiers and convicts – a labour-force that could be shot for not working – the line was finally finished.

The line could not go through the mountains of the Daxue range, and so it crept around their sides, pierced their flanks, and rose higher and circled until it had doubled back upon itself. Then you looked down and saw the tunnel entrances beneath you and realized that you had not advanced but had only climbed higher. Then the train was in a new valley, descending to the river once again. The river was called the Dadu He, 'Big Crossing'. It was wide and greyer than the sky above it. For most of its length it was full of boulders. Fishermen with long rods or ancient fish-traps sat on its banks.

These were the densest, steepest mountains I had seen so far, and the train was never more than a few minutes from a tunnel. So, in order to read or write, I had to leave the lights burning in the compartment. One moment there was a bright valley with great white streaks of rock down its sides, and gardens near the bottom and vegetable patches sloping at an angle of forty-five degrees, and the next moment the train would be roaring through a black tunnel, scattering the bats that hung against the walls. This was one of the routes where people complained of the length of the trip. But it was easily one of the most beautiful train-trips in China. I could not understand why tourists went from city to city, on a forced march of sightseeing. China existed in all the in-between places that were reachable only by train.

'What do you want for lunch?' the chef said. This dining-car was empty, too.

'This is a Sichuan train, right?'

'It is.'

'I will have Sichuan food then.'

He brought me Sichuan chicken, hot bean curd, pork and green peppers, green onions stir-fried with ginger, soup and rice – a four-*yuan* lunch – and I went back and had a siesta. There were countries where train-journeys were no more than a period of suspense, waiting to arrive; and there were countries where the train-journey was itself an experience of travel, with meals and sleep and exercise and conversation and scenery. This was the latter. When I woke up in mid afternoon I saw that the mist and cloud had dispersed. The long hooting train had passed from low steep mountains into higher broader ones.

I sat by the window and watched the world go by. Four black

pigs, each one a different size, trotting in a file along a hill path. Some hills scarred with eroded gullies and others covered with scrub pine – the first pines I had seen in China. Deep red valleys, the soil laid bare, and green bushy hills. The river was now the same red as that clayey soil. There were junipers at railway stations, fluttering and bowing, for it had now become windy. And five ranges of mountains in the distance, each with its own shade of grey, according to how far off it was. In a pretty valley-town called Shamalada, beyond the solid houses and tiled roofs ten naked children turned somersaults on a mudbank and plunged into the red river. It was not late, but the sun slipped beneath the mountains and then the valleys were full of long cold shadows, as if the slopes had dragging cloaks.

Just before darkness fell, at the head of one valley, I saw a terrace below the line – a cemetery. It had a big stone gateway and a red star over the gate. That red star usually meant it had something to do with the People's Liberation Army. This one had fifty graves – rectangular stone boxes with flowers beside them. Except for the Muslim regions, like Xinjiang, or the Hui province of Ningxia, it was unusual to see cemeteries in China – new ones, at any rate. A cemetery is regarded as a waste of space. The dead are cremated and the ashes are put on a shelf in the family house, along with the tea-leaves, the vase of plastic flowers, the photograph of Su Lin at the factory outing to Lake Hong, the combination thermometer-and-calendar and the needlepoint portrait of a white kitten playing with a ball of yarn.

I enquired about the cemetery.

The Head of the Train (*lieche zhang*), a man named Mr He, said, 'Those are the graves of the men who died while building the railway. It took ten years, you see.'

Those ten years, from the early sixties to the early seventies, coincided with the period of patriotic fervour and intense jingoism. It not only had the largest number of self-sacrificing soldiers and workers, but also an enormous number of political prisoners. The efforts of these passionate people produced the Chengdu-Kunming line.

I slept, but fitfully, for each time the train entered a tunnel the compartment howled with its noise and filled with smoke and steam from the engine. In the morning we were among bulgier, wetter mountains – the Yunnan valleys are cool throughout the year, because most of the province is at a high altitude.

A bad-tempered attendant banged at the door at 7.00. But knocking was only a formality. After a few knocks she used her own key to open the door and she demanded the bedding. 'Hurry up! Get out of bed! Give me the sheets! Do it now!' I thought: What nags these people can be.

'Why are the *fuwuyuans* in such a hurry to collect their bedding?' I asked the Head of the Train, Mr He.

He said, 'Because the train does not stay long in Kunming. Just a matter of hours, and then we turn around and go back to Chengdu.'

That was why they were nags: they were overworked.

Mr He had risen through the ranks. He had been a luggage handler, a conductor and a cook – all jobs at roughly the same salary-level, about 100 *yuan* a month. He had joined when he was twenty – he said he hadn't had any education ('not much chance of it in the sixties') and I took that to mean that he was a casualty of the Cultural Revolution. He had chosen the railways because his father had been a railwayman. Now he was in total charge of this train.

'I was promoted by being appointed,' he said. 'I didn't apply for it. One day they simply came to me and said, "We want you to be the Head of the Train," and I agreed.'

I asked him about travellers, because it seemed to me that one of the features of China now was the large numbers of people going cross-country.

'Yes,' he said. 'Especially in the last three or four years. Many travellers, of all kinds.'

'Do they give you problems?'

'What do you mean?'

'Do they drink too much? Do they shout, or quarrel, or make disturbances?'

'No. They keep order. We don't have those sorts of problems. In fact, we don't have many problems. My job is easy. The Chinese obey the rules, on the whole. That's our nature.'

'What about foreigners?'

'They obey the rules,' Mr He said. 'Very few people break them.'

'Are you a member of a union, Mr He?'

'Of course. The Railway Workers' Union. Every worker is a member.'

'What does the union do?'

'It offers opinions about conditions of work, and it discusses problems.'

'Does the union discuss money?'

'No,' he said.

'If conditions of work are bad – let's say if you're not given time for a nap or for meals – and if the union's opinions are not respected, would you consider going on strike?'

After a long pause, Mr He said, 'No.'

'Why not? Railway workers go on strike all the time in Britain and the United States. There is a right to strike in China – it's in the constitution.'

He rubbed his chin and became very serious.

'We are not serving capitalists,' he said. 'We are serving the people. If we go on strike the people won't be able to travel, and that will hurt them.'

'That's a good answer, Mr He. But now there are capitalists in China. Not only tourists from western countries, but also the Chinese themselves are accumulating wealth.'

'To me they are all passengers.'

'I'm a capitalist myself, I suppose,' I said.

'On my train you are a passenger, and you are welcome. Ha!' This 'Ha' meant: *Enough of this line of questioning!*

'Mr He, you mentioned you have a son.' A child of six, in a school in Chengdu, was what he had said. 'Would you like him to follow you and your father and work in the railway?'

'I'll tell you frankly – I would. But it's not my choice. It's up to him. I can't tell him what to do. At the moment he wants to be a soldier in the army.'

In the corridor the passengers were flinging their luggage out of the windows on to the platform at Kunming.

*

The Chinese flock to Kunming to gape at the colourful natives – twenty-three separate minorities, all gaily dressed in handsomely stitched skirts and quilted jackets, boots and head-dresses. They come from the far-flung parts of Yunnan to sell their pretty embroidery and their baskets. They are attractive and a bit wild and look uncompromisingly ethnic. Mao's stern grey policies were merely a hiccup in their multicolour tribalism. For the Chinese, the minorities in Yunnan are somewhere between hill-billies and zoo animals.

What exactly do these minority people themselves think? Are they rebellious or downtrodden? Do they crave autonomy? Their numbers are very small: only 5,000 Drung people in Yunnan, only 12,000 Jinuos and twice that number of Pumis. The Uighurs and the Yi people were another matter – there were millions of them. At about the time I was in Yunnan there were uprisings and riots among Soviet minorities – in Kazakhstan and Kirghizia. I could imagine that happening in China – perhaps a Muslim rebellion like the one that raged through Xinjiang in the nineteenth century. And I could imagine the same result: it would be ruthlessly suppressed.

People also go to Kunming to visit the petrified forest ('We call this one Chicken Tree – can you see why?') and to see the polluted lake and the temples above it which are so relentlessly visited they are practically worn away from the successive waves of trampling feet, and those temples that aren't are buried under ice-cream sticks and candy wrappers and half-eaten mooncakes.

I went for walks. I even managed to lose Mr Fang for a few days. I went to an exhibition commemorating the tenth anniversary of the death of Zhou Enlai. There was a sort of Zhou Enlai cult growing in China. It was also the tenth anniversary of the death of Mao, but no such exhibition had been mounted for him. Of the thirty-odd photographs in the Zhou exhibition only one showed Mao Zedong – in 1949, Liberation Year: Mao very small, Zhou very large.

At an antique shop near the exhibit I saw a very shapely bronze incense burner – a water-buffalo. It stood among the junk jewellery, the broken pocket watches, the old forks with twisted tines, the Yunnanese tobacco pouches. I asked how much?

The price he quoted was $17,000.

I was still laughing as I strolled through the market in the Kunming back-streets. It was there that I worked out a way of eating Chinese dumplings without risking infectious hepatitis or cholera or bubonic plague (there had been outbreaks of this medieval life-shortener in northern Yunnan and Qinghai). There were few dishes tastier than freshly fried or steamed Chinese dumplings, and they were tastiest in the open-air markets. But the plates they were served in were washed in dirty water, and the chopsticks were simply wiped off and reused.

My hygienic answer was to ask for them in a piece of paper – and to provide my own paper. And the chopsticks could be made safe by scorching them in the cooking fire – holding them in the flames for a few moments to kill the germs. But as a matter of fact many travellers in China carry their own chopsticks.

My favourite spot in Kunming was the park at Green Lake – though it was an unprepossessing park, with a go-kart track, a children's football field, and a pathetic circus in two brown tents (the star attraction was a tortured-looking bear pacing in a tiny cage). The lake itself had disappeared, dried out, grown weeds and grass: there was no water at all in it.

But that area had become the meeting-place for people who wanted to kill time by singing, putting on plays or operas, or making music. It seemed very odd to me at first, the people in little groups – twenty or thirty such groups scattered throughout the park; and each gathering of people producing a play or listening to someone singing. There were duets, there were trios, and many were accompanied by men playing violins. Often the duet was an old man and an old woman.

'They are singing a love-song,' a bystander told me. His name was Xin. He agreed with me that it was very touching to see these people performing.

He said, 'For ten years we hated each other and were very suspicious. We hardly spoke to each other. It was terrible.'

He meant the Cultural Revolution, but didn't say it. Like many people he could not bear uttering the mocking words.

'This is like a dream to these people. The old ones can hardly believe it. That's why they are here. To talk and to remember.

They don't want to forget the old songs. This is their way of remembering.'

What made it especially unusual was its exuberance, because the Chinese are very shy and rather self-conscious, and find it an agony to be set apart and stared at (which was why the Red Guards' struggle sessions were so painful and so often ended in the suicide of the person struggled with). The fact that they were performing solos was a measure of their energy and confidence. It was a great deal easier to stand alone and sing if you were happy.

Some of them were telling stories in dialogue form, others were playing traditional songs. At least half the groups of old people were performing the Yunnan version of Peking opera, called *dian xi*.

The most ambitious one I saw involved four or five singers who stood under the trees and acted out a sad love-story from Zhejiang called 'Flower Lamp' (*Hua Deng*).

'This is known all over China,' Xin said, and he explained it.

It concerned a young man, Liang Shanbo, and his lover, Zhu Yingtai. The plot was not unlike that of *Romeo and Juliet*. The lovers' families were so opposed that it was impossible for the two to meet without using a subterfuge. Liang had the clever idea of dressing up as a woman (the man playing Liang in the park used a fan to suggest this), and in this way gained access to the lovely Zhu. The romance blossoms, but both families are against the marriage. After some complications ('The plot zigzags,' Xin said) they realize they cannot marry. Zhu kills herself. Liang sings a pathetic love-song on her grave, and then he kills himself. The end.

The motley groups in the park in Kunming liked this one best of all. It was performed among the bamboos, and accompanied by old violinists in faded blue jackets and caps. But even the skinniest old man and the most elderly woman wore animated expressions – and they were all playful. Of all the people I saw in China, they were the happiest.

The trouble with China was that it was overrun with people and – except for the occasional earthquake or sandstorm – I rarely saw examples of man's insignificance beside the greater forces of nature. They had moved mountains, diverted rivers, wiped out the animals, eliminated the wilderness; they had subdued nature and had it screaming for mercy. If there were enough of you it was really very easy to dig up a whole continent and plant cabbages. They had built a wall that was said to be the only man-made object on earth that could be seen from the moon. Whole provinces had been turned into vegetable gardens, and a hill wasn't a hill – it was a way of growing rice vertically. Some of the ruination was not deliberate; after all, in Chinese terms prosperity always spelled pollution.

That was how I felt until I reached Yunnan. Then I saw the more familiar situation – and one I found more subtle and energizing – people dwarfed by nature, crowded by jungle, hemmed in by the elements, rained on and battered by the unpredictable tantrums of heaven and earth.

I saw such landscapes on my way to Vietnam. Kunming is only 200 miles from the Vietnam border. Looking at a map one day I saw a railway line leading south, and I looked for Mr Fang to arrange a journey on it. Wasn't he shadowing me in order to offer Chinese hospitality? Hadn't he urged me to give him something to do? How thrilled he was when I asked him to translate for me, or commiserated with him about the spivs and the louts and said, 'I blame their parents!'

But when I asked him to get me permission to take the narrow gauge railway to the border, he turned ashen.

'It is forbidden,' he said.

'The line is open as far as Bao Xiu,' I said. I had checked in the railway timetable – there were two trains a day.

'But you are a foreigner.'

'You said that you would help me. If you don't help me, what is the point of your being with me, Mr Fang?'

'I will try.' I knew he meant it, because he seemed very rattled: he was steeling himself to see a higher official.

That same night Mr Fang came to me and said that permission had been approved for me to take the train south. But the line into Vietnam had been severed in 1979, so I would have to content myself with a journey about a third of the way – to Yiliang – and then come straight back. I said that was fine with me.

'Mr Wei will go with you.'

'Who is Mr Wei?'

'You will see tomorrow.'

The train left at 7.00 in the morning; Mr Wei was at the station. He had already bought the tickets, and before I could say anything he was apologizing for the train – just a little one, he said, tiny coaches, steam engine, uncomfortable seats, no dining-car. Mr Wei was a small, malnourished-looking man in his thirties. But he was not as sulky as he seemed – he was merely nervous. He said he hated these little trains and these jungly places.

I wanted to tell him that I liked seeing examples of man's insignificance beside the greater forces of nature. But I decided not to. I had bought a pound of peanuts in Kunming market and spent the early part of the trip eating those until Mr Wei relaxed.

The French had built this line. At about the turn of the century, after they had consolidated their hold on Indo-China, they decided to open up the interior. There was money to be made by selling French products in these Chinese provinces. And there was a great deal the French wanted to buy – silks, minerals, furs, leather goods, precious stones. And they had a vague idea of extending their influence into China. The railway was finished in 1910, and until fairly recently it was easier to ship goods to Kunming from Shanghai via Hanoi than it was cross-country.

Mr Wei didn't think much of this train, but it was practically ideal – like the best kind of sleepy branch-line train that creaked through the countryside. Europe and America had got rid of them, but they still sauntered through China. People played draughts and smoked the big lengths of bamboo pipe that looked like drain-pipes. They were all farmers – no sun-glasses or platform shoes here, no Guangzhou brassieres or cassette recorders.

After a while, Mr Wei began talking. He said, 'I missed out on my education,' and I knew he was referring to the Cultural Revolution, so we talked about that. 'I hated it,' he said. 'It was bad in Kunming.'

'Because they smashed the temples?'

'Not only that. They fought. One factory fought another factory. They fought in the streets – people screaming. They had sticks, they had guns. They set fires. People died.'

'Hundreds or thousands?'

'I don't know. Hundreds maybe.'

'Were you a Red Guard?' He was just the right age – about thirty-five.

'No,' he said, almost vehemently. 'I didn't like them.'

'Do you think they are bad men when you see them now, the ones who were Red Guards?'

'Now? No, I don't. They are not bad men. They were protecting Mao. That's what they said. Each one thought he could do a better job. That's why they fought.'

'They killed people, though.'

'We can't blame them for that. That is the responsibility of the leaders.'

That was the usual line, and a useful one too: all the blame had been put on the Gang of Four. Having such scapegoats was probably another example of Chinese economy. What was the point in tearing the country apart when in a ritualistic way (the trial had been televised) all the blame could be put on four people who were then promptly purged.

When we had gone ten miles Mr Wei (who I now realized was no lackey) relaxed and pointed out the sights. That was Running Horse Hill (Pao Ma Shan), where there was a complex of buildings called the Fire-Bury Works (*Huozang chang*): the local crematorium.

'People send the dead body to the works,' Mr Wei said. 'The men put gasoline on the body. They burn it. They get ashes. They put the ashes in a small box. The people take it home and put it on a desk.'

'Everybody does this?'

'Most people do it. A few take the ashes to the mountains – to a Buddhist temple. But we take it home. I have my mother's sister in a box.'

These burial rites of the Chinese were bad news to American entrepreneurs of the 1970s who tried to export coffins to the People's Republic. In the same fortune-hunting spirit, in the nineteenth century, the Sheffield Silver Co. sent vast shipments of forks and spoons to China hoping to tempt the Chinese away from their chopsticks.

Beside the line were beehive huts which, when I looked closer, were actually tombs. Mr Wei said that thirty or forty years ago people were buried like that; but no more.

I saw people walking through the cool yellow woods, and farmers on their way to market who had stopped near the railway to wash their vegetables in the ditchwater – which was foul. In a shady spot a man was unhurriedly tearing open a buffalo's throat, slaughtering it. The creature was on its back, with its legs in the air, and its wounded neck was bright red, with a bib of flesh hanging down, and its blood running into the railway ditch.

An old woman got on the train at one of the many small stations. She had a little girl with her, and then a younger woman joined her. She had a baby slung over her back.

We fell into conversation – Mr Wei translating their rustic Yunnanese dialect. It seemed that the young woman had given birth to a little girl. But she and her husband were disappointed. They decided to take the drastic step of having another child. As soon as the woman became pregnant she was fined 1,000 *yuan*, a penalty called a *fa kuai*; but she paid up willingly in the hope that the child would be a boy. It was indeed a boy.

These were the poorest people imaginable – lined faces, threadbare clothes, cracked hands, and wearing bonnets and broken slippers. And the woman had stumped up what was for most city-dwellers a year's wages to have a second child. (The fact that the second child in China is nearly always a boy leads many people to conclude that female infanticide is quite common.)

'The city people don't have extra children,' Mr Wei said. 'They are happy with one. But the country people want more children – to help them with their farming and also to look after them when they are old.'

The One-Child Policy was instituted in 1976, and seemed to work well, although the population has continued to grow at unanticipated rates. The fear these days is that there will be a great number of old people in China at the end of the century – a sort of mushroom effect; and that the one-child family will create a nation of small spoiled brats. Already there is a creature in China which has appeared for the first time in vast numbers: the fat, selfish little kid with rotten teeth, sitting in front of a television, whining for another ice cream.

The train was travelling in a narrow groove cut just below the summit of these pretty hills, and buttresses had been built to prevent landslides. They hadn't worked. Man was insignificant here. Nature gave him a very hard time. Well, that was the way of the world, wasn't it? It was unnatural that other Chinese people had turned a dramatic landscape into a cabbage patch.

Mr Wei said that he had managed to get a few years' education in the technical institute in Changsha. His Cultural Revolution job had involved mending box-cars in a factory in Kunming. He said he hated the work and was no good at it. He had always wanted to go to university and he had spent all those years holding a welder's torch and cursing.

I said that I planned to go to Changsha myself and wanted very much to visit Mao's birthplace, Shaoshan, near that city. Had he been there?

'I went ten years ago. In 1976.' He made a face.

'What did you think?'

'I didn't like it,' he said. 'It is not good for the people. It is a bad place.'

'But Chairman Mao was born there.'

'I know,' he said, enigmatically.

'Wasn't he a good leader?'

'Mao did harm. The Cultural Revolution delayed our development. Shaoshan is not a good place.'

He told me that with such solemnity that I was determined to go there.

'Which Chinese leader do you respect the most?'

'Deng is not dead yet, so he might make mistakes. Better to mention a dead one. Zhou Enlai is liked by many people.'

'Do you like him?'

'Yes. Very much.'

'Where is his village?'

'It is Huai'an, in Jiangsu Province' – far away, in the east, some distance north of Shanghai.

'What do you think of Zhou's village?'

'In my heart I like it. I would like to go there.'

'Why do so many people respect Zhou?'

'Because he worked hard for the Chinese people.'

'Isn't Deng Xiaoping working for the Chinese people?'

Mr Wei frowned. 'As I said, he is not dead yet. There is still time for him to make mistakes.'

As the sun climbed towards noon and the foliage thickened by the tracks the landscape became tropical – bamboos and bird-squawks. And some houses came into view. They were not Chinese houses. They were stucco, with green shutters and heavy verandahs – just the sort of houses that you see in the French towns of Vietnam. I had seen such houses in Hue and Danang and in the back-streets of Saigon: it was French government housing, for the colonial officers – in this case, railway personnel. It was so strange, this touch of Frenchness, deep in the hills of Yunnan, still intact – still lived-in – after almost a century.

And that was Yiliang. A sign at the station said THE PEOPLE'S RAILWAY IS FOR THE PEOPLE (*Renmin Tielu Wei Renmin*).

'I'm hungry,' I said.

'You cannot eat here,' Mr Wei said.

What?

Before I could complain, he rushed me out of the coach and on to the platform. My feet had hardly touched the ground before I was on my way back to Kunming – I was still breathless when we were underway. I had scarcely seen Yiliang. And I had wanted to stroll around the old French town, look into the houses, talk to the people, loiter in the market.

Mr Wei said he had just been following orders. It was Mr Fang who explained. I had insisted on taking this train, although the train was off-limits to foreigners, because foreigners were not allowed in the deep south of Yunnan – the Chinese were fighting the Vietnamese on the border; it was a security risk. But Mr Fang had explained that it was the train I was interested in, not the towns. And so the railway authorities had said that, as long as I did not stop in any of the towns to look around or eat, I could take the train. But at a certain stage of the journey I had to stop and be spun round and sent straight back to Kunming, without looking left or right. That was how I took the train without violating the law. It was a very Chinese solution.

11

The Fast Train to Guilin: Number 80

The young girl and boy entered the railway compartment holding hands, which was very unusual. But they had a Chinese explanation.

'We got married this morning,' the boy said. 'We are going to Guilin for a few days.'

Honeymooners! He was in his twenties – very thin, rather furtive, but stylishly dressed in a leather jacket and pointy shoes. She wore a dress. In a train a dress was just as unusual as hand-holding. It was blue satin, with a fringe of lace, and though it matched strangely with her yellow ankle socks and red shoes, the hemline was high enough so that I could see her legs. It was not their shapeliness that interested me, it was their very existence. Women's legs are a rare enough sight in China for them to be a complete novelty.

'Do you want me to go into a different compartment?' I asked. 'I'd be glad to.'

'Why?' the boy said.

'So that you can be alone.'

'We can be alone up here,' the boy said, flinging his bag on the upper berth and hoisting his bride on the one opposite.

And there they sat until long after we left Kunming Station. It was late evening, about 9.00, and this was perhaps their first night together. It was certainly their first as man and wife. Was I sincere in saying that I'd be glad to leave them alone in the compartment? Of course I wasn't. I was trying to get the measure of this place; but its bigness often baffled me. I needed luck in trying to uncover the truth, which was why I looked into women's handbags when they opened them just to see what was inside; and opened drawers in people's houses, and read their mail, and searched their cupboards. When a man took out his wallet I tried to count his money. If a taxi driver had his sweetheart's snapshot pinned to his dashboard I scrutinized it. If I saw someone reading a book or magazine I noted down the title. I compared prices. I copied down graffiti and slogans that I saw on walls. I got people to translate wallposters, particularly the ones that gave the sordid details of a criminal's career (these details were set out and advertised just before the doomed man was shot). I memorized the contents of refrigerators, of travellers' suitcases, I remembered the labels in their clothes (White Elephant tools and Pansy Brand men's underwear and Typical sewing-machines stick in my mind). I searched brochures for solecisms and collected Rules of the Hotel for Guests (example: 'Guests may not perform urination in sink basin'). And just for the record, I asked endless pestering questions. So, really, would I willingly pass up a chance to spend the night with a honeymoon couple?

They smoked, they muttered a little, they rattled magazines. I wrote:

> 10.16 pm. No activity from the honeymooners. Contented breathing. Could be snores. One might be asleep. Anticlimax.

The cigarette smoke bothered me, and on this banged-up train of the Shanghai Railway Board, nothing worked. The fan was dead, the lock had been torn off the door, the arms had been twisted off the seats, the luggage rack was broken, and the window could not be raised. This last matter was the most serious: the compartment was now very hot and smoky. It was a good thing that the honeymooners were either asleep or else ignoring me, because

I took out my Swiss Army knife and unscrewed the window locks, removed the window frame, levered the window up six inches, then put the hardware back on, so that no one would suspect I had tampered with it. Dire punishments were threatened for anyone who messed with the train, and if you even chipped your China Railways teacup you were charged for it.

There was silence all night in the upper berths. Nothing to report except that I seemed to have more proof that the Chinese were very phlegmatic.

I woke to find myself in the rocky province of Guizhou, all pyramidal limestone hills and granite cliffs. The landscape was green and stony, like Ireland, and the people lived in rugged Irish-looking stone cottages, and houses with rough-hewn beams. They were the strongest houses I saw in China, and around them, marking the limits of their land, were beautifully built drystone walls, symmetrical and square.

Among these great slanting slab-like hills there was very little arable land, and not many flat places for farming. The gardens were made by balancing walls and building terraces, and by all the other useful things that could be made from the chunks of stone – bridges, aqueducts, roads, dykes and dams. The villages were thick with villas and two-storey houses (it was rare in the country to find more than one floor), all of them stone-built, with slate roofs. And their grave-mounds were just as solid and built with the same granite confidence: the cemeteries were miniature versions of the villages.

While the honeymooners nipped down to the dining-car for the breakfast of rice gruel and noodles, I ate some bananas I had bought in Kunming and drank my green tea. We passed Anshun ('once the centre of the opium trade') and we stopped a while at Guiyang, where I met Mr Shuang.

Mr Shuang was in his late sixties, plum-faced and whiskery, with a shapeless cap and a red armband that showed he was a railway worker. But he was a retired man who out of boredom had gone back to be a platform supervisor.

'I was sick of staying at home,' he said. 'I've been doing this job for half a year. I like it. But I don't need the money.'

He said he earned 130 *yuan* a month.

'What do you spend it on?'

'I don't have children or a family, so I buy music.' He smiled and said, 'I love music. I play the harmonica.'

'Do you buy Chinese or western music?'

'Both. But I like western very much.'

'What kind?'

He said in a neatly enunciating way, 'Light orchestral music.'

That was the kind that was played in the train and in the railway stations when they weren't playing Chinese songs. They played 'The Skaters' Waltz' and 'Flower Of Malaya' and selections from *Carmen.*

'Do you get many travellers in Guiyang?'

'Unfortunately, very few people come here. This province was closed to foreigners until 1982. Some people pass through but they don't stop. And yet we have many places to see – some very nice temples, and the Huangguoshu Falls and the hot springs. Please come back to Guiyang and I'll show you around.'

It seemed that the more remote and countrified the place in China, the more hospitable the people were.

For the onward journey the honeymooners had changed their clothes: he wore a jacket and sun-glasses, she wore a tweed skirt. They smoked and slumbered. Maybe this fatigue meant it was the end of their honeymoon?

By mid afternoon we were in the south-east of Guizhou, among greener hills showing the scars and broken terraces of having once been farmed. The route to Guilin was roundabout, because of all the mountains. They were an obstruction, but they were very pretty – velvety and shaggy with grass and trees. It was much hotter now, and most of the train passengers were asleep, barely stirring at Duyun; that place looked like Mexico, with a big yellow-stucco station and palm trees under a clear blue sky.

Farther south the landscape changed dramatically: the grey hills here were shaped like camel humps, and chimney-stacks, and stupas with sheer sides. They were the oddest hills in the world, and the most Chinese, because these are the hills that are depicted in every Chinese scroll. It is almost a sacred landscape – it is certainly an emblematic one. It had happened all at once: the hills looked squarish and ancient, like a petrified city. We had entered a new province, Guangxi, and from here to the city of Guilin, 200 miles or more, it was all the landscape of the Chinese classical paintings.

It was a rice-growing area, but there wasn't much water available. This was probably the reason I saw such ingenious pumps and irrigation in Guangxi. I saw about ten different kinds of water-movers. I saw the chain-pump being pedalled by two children. This pump, Professor Needham says, is unchanged in its design since its invention in the first century AD. All the pumps I saw were mechanical – no motors, no hoses even. The largest and weirdest was a gigantic spoon, about ten feet long, and made of wood, which a woman used to move water from a lower field to a higher one. She didn't simply lift and dump the water; she scooped and splashed very quickly, and it was like a laborious form of playing.

Amid these limestone stacks and buttes there was a limestone village with the same look of eruption. But there was no railway station to serve these stone houses – not even a platform, nor a level crossing. The village was in a low place and its muddy streets were in shadow. What was remarkable was the number of horses in the place. People were buying and selling them, riding them, tethering them to trees, hitching them to carts. It was market day, late afternoon, and the traders were winding things up. For the next little while along the railway tracks I saw pony carts making their way home. It was unusual to see Chinese horsemen, but I enquired and discovered that these were people of the Miao minority, who are fairly numerous in Guangxi – there are 5 million of them altogether. The Chinese are respectful of such people, but are more mystified by their customs and habits than they are by those of westerners. They stared, fascinated, but still they didn't understand. They never seemed to understand the strengths of these little nations in their autonomous prefectures (Guangxi had two minority states within its borders), and so they never seemed to take the minorities seriously. They treated them like exotic pets.

An eerie sight in Guangxi were the caves in those grey limestone hills. The hills had come to look like fat columns and towers, and the caves made them seem hollow. Later I learned that Guangxi is full of caves. Some are underground dripping caverns, but these above-ground things – many of them at any rate – had been converted into homes. The strangest ones looked like gaping mouths, with white stalactites showing like teeth.

In a shallow pool among those tower-like hills there was a grey and white crane, the sort the Chinese regard as an auspicious bird, representing long life. The train startled the bird and off it went, soaring and circling as we rumbled on, through a painting of mountains that was being endlessly unrolled.

In the kitchen of the dining-car, a young woman was scrubbing pots and singing.

I know that you love me
I am waiting
But where do you want me to go?

The pot she scrubbed with a stiff brush was nearly as big as she was. And the kitchen was a primitive thing: it was black, with a black coal stove, and a cracked sink. At mealtime it looked more like a blacksmith's forge than a kitchen. The meals on this train had been terrible. Lunch had been bad dried fish, disgusting fatty ham, rancid prawns and rubbery rice. But I had my bananas and I still had peanuts I had bought back in Sichuan.

As I loitered, listening to the kitchen girl singing, a young man introduced himself. He was Chen Xiangan, from Shanghai. He worked in the dining-car. He spoke no English at all. He asked me, Could I help him with his problem?

'Gladly,' I said.

'I want you to give me a name – an English one.'

That was not an unusual request. English names were coming back into fashion, now that people were reasonably sure they wouldn't be attacked by Red Guards as bourgeois capitalist-roaders and harbingers of revisionism for calling themselves Ronny and Nancy.

'It must sound like my Chinese name,' he said, and that was when he told me he was called Xiangan.

I pondered this. Xiangan sounded Irish to me – like Sean or Shaun. I suggested that but then told him that Sam was simpler, and Sam Chen seemed like a good Shanghai name to me.

He thanked me, and later I saw him pushing a food trolley. He wore only a T-shirt and blue underpants and an apron. He was saying over and over again, 'Sam Chen, Sam Chen, Sam Chen.'

In her nasal twanging voice the kitchen girl was still singing her love song.

I know that you love me
I am waiting . . .

We came to Mawei, a station amid the limestone stacks and dark pine trees. There was no town. There were villages scattered nearby. The passengers dashed off the train and rushed outside the station where, at tables, about fifty people were selling fresh plums – yellow and purple ones, and dusty bananas, and round water-melons. This was the longest stop I ever made at such a small place, and I was sure it was deliberate – a fruit-buying stop.

The honeymooners bought a water-melon. They crawled into one berth and cut it open with a jack-knife and ate it with a spoon, taking turns and slurping. It was like sex. For once the girl had stopped chain-smoking her Gold Medal cigarettes, and once they were together, eating this water-melon on the rumpled bunk, they stayed together.

The kitchen girl was still singing, plonkingly and with feeling.

I know that you love me
I am waiting . . .

At sundown we entered the heights above a wide valley that was darkened and in shadow, because of the setting sun. The valley's rim was all rounded peaks that were slowly blackening, but the other side was distant, perhaps thirty miles across. The sky slumped into this space as the sun passed behind the far hill, and the valley was so deep I could not see its floor, only shadows that made it look bottomless. We were still climbing, but before we got all the way up, the orange and all the flamboyant fire of the sunset had vanished. Then night fell and we were travelling in darkness.

I lay on my mat in the heat and read *Kidnapped*, and dropped off to sleep at about 11.00. The lights were still on when I woke again and fixed the sliding door with a rubber band. The lights went out. I heard that melon-eating sound again from the berth above, where the honeymooners were lying together. But I knew it wasn't that – they had finished their melon hours ago. And yet this was a rich satisfying sound, with a deep breath, like the sigh you hear from someone with a hearty appetite. They were devouring each other in the dark.

They were still at it, at 4.00 in morning, when the train arrived at Guilin.

'In China, we have a saying,' Mr Jiang Le Song said. *'Chule feiji zhi wai, yangyang duo chi.'* Looking very pleased with himself, he added, 'It rhymes!'

'We call that a half-rhyme,' I said. 'What does it mean? Something about eating planes?'

'"We eat everything except planes and trains." In China.'

'I get it. You eat everything on four legs except tables and chairs.'

'You are a funny man!' Mr Jiang said. 'Yes. We eat trees, grass, leaves, animals, seaweed, flowers. And in Guilin even more things. Birds, snakes, turtles, cranes, frogs, and some other things.'

'What other things?'

'I don't even know their names.'

'Dogs? Cats?' I looked at him closely. I had overheard a tourist objecting to the Chinese appetite for kittens. 'You eat kittens?'

'Not dogs and kittens. Everybody eats those.'

'Raccoons?' I had read in a guidebook that raccoons were also popular in Guilin.

'What is that?'

Raccoon was not in his pocket English-Chinese dictionary.

He became very confidential, glancing around and drawing me close to him. 'Maybe not lackeys. I have never heard of eating lackeys. But many other things. We eat' – and he drew a meaningful breath – 'forbidden things.'

That had rather a thrilling sound: *We eat forbidden things.*

'What sort of forbidden things?'

'I only know their Chinese names – sorry.'

'What are we talking about?' I asked. 'Snakes?'

'Dried snakes. Snake soup. They are not forbidden. I mean an animal that eats ants with its nose.'

'Scaly anteater. Pangolin. I don't want to eat that. Too many people are eating them,' I said. 'It's an endangered species.'

'Would you like to eat forbidden things?'

'I would like to eat interesting things,' I said, equivocating. 'How about sparrows? Pigeons? Snakes? What about turtles?'

'Those are easy. I can arrange it.'

Mr Jiang was young. He was new to the job. He was a little too breezy. He had the joky and insincere manner of someone who has been dealing with elderly foreigners who enjoy being joshed as they are being deferred to. I felt this obsequiousness was a deliberate ploy to undermine me.

I had told him I didn't want to go sightseeing, and yet within an hour of our meeting he took me to the caves outside Guilin, where there were hundreds of shuffling Chinese tourists.

'What are we doing here?' I asked.

'I am so sorry,' he said. 'We will leave immediately. I thought you might want to see our famous Reed Flute Cave.'

What was the point of looking at these humdrum and hackneyed marvels? And having just come through hundreds of miles of Guizhou and Guangxi I had seen enough rock formations to last me a lifetime. I had liked them because I had felt I'd discovered them for myself – I hadn't been led there by someone burbling, 'Look!'

'Let's look at them,' I said.

Like so much in China on the tourist route – like the terracotta warriors and the Ming Tombs – the Reed Flute Caves were discovered by a man digging a well. This fellow's shovel opened the way to a vast limestone cave, with chambers and corridors and grottoes. That was in 1959. Lights, signposts, balconies and stairways were installed, and then it became domesticated and acceptable to the Chinese.

It looked grotesque and Disneyish, a piece of natural vulgarity – a tasteless act of God. It could have been made out of polyester or papier mâché. It dripped. It glugged. Chunks of slimy limestone dropped from the ceiling. It was the spelunker's version of Sunset Strip or the Shanghai Bund. People crowded through it, skidding on the greasy floor, listening to a guide explaining its variety of crazy shapes.

'We call this the Lotus Rock. This is the conch-shell. This is the elephant's foot – can you see why? This is the carp . . .'

I ditched Mr Jiang and Mr Fang and went down to the river Li to look at the boats. Some of the houseboats were for hire, so I took one, which was owned by two old women. We floated downstream, past some lumpy and lovely stone hills and temples. After some time they said they couldn't go any farther or else they wouldn't be able to pole the boat back. But the river winds south, to other rivers, the Gui Jiang and Xi Jiang, and then to Canton. I asked them whether they had been that far.

'Yes, but not in a boat like this.' They had the gargling and quacking Cantonese accent, and their Mandarin was nearly as bad as mine. 'We went in a big boat.'

'Why not this one?'

'You would never get back in this one.' She meant you couldn't pole upstream from Canton to Guilin. Well, that was reasonable.

But I became possessed by the idea of taking a small boat – say, a collapsible kayak – to China, and setting it up in a place like Guilin, and paddling from river to river, and sleeping under trees. It would be a way of seeing the country from an entirely different angle, and of avoiding people like Fang and Jiang. And when I got sick of it I would simply go gurgling into the estuary of one of these muddy rivers, and then into the South China Sea.

Taking a break from the arduous poling the old women moored our boat to the south bank of the Li, near a fishing village. In the shallows were simple raft-like boats made of six or seven big curved bamboos lashed together, and also sampans and houseboats. There were cormorants on many of the boats. The women called the birds *wang* and also *yu-ying*.

The first western traveller after Marco Polo described these birds. This man was the missionary Friar Odoric, from Friuli in Italy. He left his Franciscan convent in Udine in the year 1321 to travel in the east for three years. He went barefoot. He was very tough, very pious, and severe with himself. He wore a hairshirt the whole time.

After travelling thirty-six days from the coastal town of Fuzhou, he stayed with a man who said to him, 'Sir, if you would see any fish being caught, go with me.'

That was 660 years ago, but the Chinese haven't changed their methods of using cormorants for fishing; and so Friar Odoric's description still stands.

> Then he led me to the bridge, carrying in his arms with him certain dive-doppers or water-fowls [cormorants], bound to perches, and about every one of their necks he tied a thread, lest they should eat the fish as fast as they took them . . . He loosened the dive-doppers from the pole, which presently went into the water, and within less than the space of one hour, caught as many fish as filled his three baskets; which being full, my host untied the threads from about their necks, and entering the second time into the river they fed themselves with fish, and being satisfied they returned and allowed themselves to be bound to their perches, as they were before.

A boat near ours had seventeen of these birds roosting on it. A young boy sluicing out a muddy bucket said that the birds cost 300 or 400 *yuan* each, but the two old women said the true figure was closer to 1,000. Whatever it was, between £100 and £200 was a huge amount, and so the birds must really earn their keep. These fishermen used them by placing a ring around the birds' necks to prevent them from swallowing the fish.

So far, I had felt the Chinese were rather cruel to animals; but they are also practical. It was not just cruel but also very stupid to abuse these valuable creatures. It was all right to torment pigs by stacking them in carts when you took them to market, or to herd buffaloes into freight-cars and ignore their piteous moos when they were being sold, or to tie chickens into bundles, so that the buyer could carry them home; but an expensive cormorant had to be coddled. A man on one boat was scratching a bird like a cat, and playing with it affectionately, and another man was feeding his flock and stroking their feathers and nuzzling them.

All these birds were exiles. They are the great cormorant (*Phalocrocorax carbo*), the only one used for fishing, and are caught in the distant coastal province of Shandong. They had been brought here in baskets on a freight train.

When we continued on our way, poling the houseboat, I took the port side with one of the poles. But the boat slid into a fast current, and although I was twice as big as my poling partner, I wasn't much use. The other old woman relieved me and when I was out of their way they propelled the boat harmoniously and swiftly back to town.

The next day I saw another side to Mr Fang. I was asking Mr Jiang my usual questions about the Cultural Revolution and he was replying in a rather bland and non-committal way when Mr Fang began speaking very fast. I was sure he was reprimanding the young man.

'What did you say?' I asked.

'I told him to tell the truth,' Mr Fang said. 'It is important to know the truth about the Cultural Revolution. Foreigners must be told. We must face the facts. It was a disaster, so what is the point of smiling and pretending we don't care?'

That was very good. In a quiet way Mr Fang was stubborn and truthful, and I knew that he despaired of the vacillating yuppies like Mr Jiang.

Mr Jiang struggled to tell me something, but he was only twenty-two. He said he didn't have a very clear memory of the Cultural Revolution.

'I know my father was regarded as too right-wing,' he said. 'My family was sent for re-education, to a remote place, to plant rice. My father had been an English teacher in a middle school. The family worked on the land, learning from peasants, for six years. It was very hard for them. I was too young to notice. For the first year we had no house. We lived in a sort of barn – a place where grain was stored. We had no crops. We ate the local leaves and roots, living like animals.'

'Is your father angry about it?'

'He doesn't talk about it,' Mr Jiang said.

'Never?'

'Never. Nothing. He doesn't say anything.'

'Why not?'

'Because it was a bitter period.'

Mr Fang said, 'He is making a mistake. He should talk about it. He should tell these people what it was like.' And with his sad swollen face turned on me Mr Fang said, 'Disaster.'

It was a few days before I saw Mr Jiang again, and in that time I walked the streets and browsed in the market (it was full of exotic birds and pretty turtles, all languishing in cages). I took a tourist boat down the river Li to Yangshuo, past the droopy, dumpy, limestone hills – more like cones and camel humps than hills; and these rise straight out of their dull reflections in the green river. The boat was crowded, the tourists were bumptious – 'What a place for a condo!' 'They should call that one "Dolly Parton Hill"!' – but the place was so weirdly pretty nothing else mattered. Among these blunt hills and bamboos, there were children swimming, and men fishing, and buffaloes wading in the river up to their noses, occasionally ducking and snaffling weeds off the bottom.

Even in the rain, even with rambunctious tourists, it was sixty miles of magnificence. At Yangshuo the boat turned slowly, giving a sort of panning shot of the small town on the low bluff of the river. The stone landing-stages had elegant roofs, and colourful Chinese stood waiting for the boat to put us ashore. But as the passengers disembarked the town exploded, and we were mobbed by traders and marketeers and old women waving bamboo back-scratchers. They had been waiting for two days for the boat to arrive, and time was of the essence: tourists did not linger in Yangshuo.

Wrinkled Chinese men in black pyjamas and lampshade hats balanced shitting cormorants on their shoulders, and when tourists took their picture they demanded a fee of one *yuan*. There were people selling kites, pot-holders, aprons, napkins, fans, and carved salad bowls. I was attracted by pairs of hand-made eye-glasses, the kind that transform anyone who wears them into a Chinese scholar. I bought a pair. I bought a silver box and an old wooden puppet's head. It was a typical tourist market – mostly junk, some charming handicrafts, and a few treasures from damp attics, being sold illegally. The tourists seemed surprised by the Chinese ferocity in pricing and bargaining. Surely after decades of isolation and communism these people ought to be a little naive? They had no right to know the real value of the stuff on their stalls. As was frequently the case in China, it was the tourists who were naive. The traders hardly budged from their prices, and when the tourists shouted at them, the Chinese hissed back. There were no bargains, even in this distant bend in the river Li, on the muddy riverbank. It was true of China in general, and was perhaps a key to their survival. I thought: The Chinese wake up quickly.

That night Mr Jiang emerged from behind a potted palm at my hotel to introduce me to a small monkey-like man.

'Our driver,' Mr Jiang said.

'Qi,' the man said, and smiled. But it was not a smile. He was only saying his name.

'I have fixed everything you requested,' Mr Jiang said. 'The driver will take us to Taohua – "Peach Flower Restaurant".'

The driver slipped on a pair of gloves, and whipped the door open for me. Mr Jiang got into the front seat, beside the driver. The driver adjusted his mirror, stuck his hand out of the window to signal – although we were in a car park and there were no other cars in sight – and drove into the empty road. After perhaps fifty yards he stopped the car.

'Is there anything wrong?' I said.

Mr Jiang imitated a fat man laughing: 'Ho! Ho! Ho!' And then in a bored voice added, 'We have arrived.'

'There wasn't much point in taking a car, was there?'

'You are an honoured guest! You must not walk!'

I had learned that guff like this was a giveaway in China. When anyone spoke to me in this formal and facetious way I knew I being taken for a ride.

Before we entered the restaurant, Mr Jiang took me aside and said, 'We will have snake soup. We will have pigeon.'

'Very nice.'

He shook his head. 'They are not unusual. They are regular.'

'What else are we having?'

'I will tell you inside.'

But inside there was a fuss over the table, a great deal of talk I did not understand, and finally Mr Jiang said, 'This is your table. A special table. Now I will leave you. The driver and I will eat in the humble dining-room next door. Please, sit! Take no notice of us. Enjoy yourself!'

This was also an unmistakable cue.

'Why don't you join me?' I said.

'Oh no!' Mr Jiang said. 'We will be very comfortable at our little table in the humble dining-room reserved for Chinese workers.'

This was laying it on a bit thick, I thought; but I was feeling guilty about this meal, and eating good food alone made me feel selfish.

I said, 'There's room at my table. Please sit here.'

'OK,' Mr Jiang said, in a perfunctory way, and indicated that the driver should follow his example.

It was quite usual for the driver to be included – in fact, it is one of the pleasures of Chinese life that on a long trip the driver is one of the bunch. If there is a banquet he is invited, if there is an outing he goes along, and he is present at every meal along the road. It is a civilized practice, and thinking it should be encouraged I made no objection, even though the driver had taken me only fifty yards.

'Special meal,' Mr Jiang said. 'We have crane. Maybe a kind of quail. We call it *anchun*. We have many things. Even forbidden things.'

That phrase had lost its thrill for me. It was a hot night, this young man seemed unreliable to me, and I was not particularly hungry.

'Have some wine,' Mr Jiang said, pouring out three glasses. 'It is osmanthus wine. Guilin means "City of Osmanthus Trees".'

We gulped our wine. It tasted syrupy and medicinal.

The food was brought in successive waves – many dishes, but the portions were small. Perhaps sensing that it would go quickly, the driver began tonging food on to his plate.

'That is turtle,' Mr Jiang said. 'From the Li river.'

'And that is forbidden,' he said, lowering his voice. '*Wawa* fish – baby fish. Very rare. Very tasty. Very hard to catch. Against the law.'

The fish was excellent. It was a stew of small white lumps in fragrant sauce. The driver's chopsticks were busily dredging it for the plumpest fillets.

Mr Jiang crept closer and mumbled a word in Chinese. 'This is muntjak. From the mountains. With onions. Forbidden.'

'What is a muntjak?' I asked.

'It is a kind of rabbit that eats fruit.'

As all the world knows, a muntjak is a small deer. They are regarded as pests. You see them on golf-courses outside London. Marco Polo found them in the Kingdom of Ergunul and wrote, 'The flesh of this animal is very good to eat.' He brought the head and feet of a muntjak back to Venice.

I sampled the pigeon, the snake soup, the muntjak, the crane, the fish, the turtle. There was something dreadful and depressing about this food, partly because it tasted good and partly because China had so few wild animals. These creatures were all facing extinction in this country. And I had always hated the Chinese appetite for rare animals – for bear's paws and fish lips and caribou's nose. That article I had read about the Chinese killing their diminishing numbers of tigers to use – superstitiously – as remedies for impotence and rheumatism had disgusted me. I was disgusted now with myself. This sort of eating was the recreation of people who were rich and spoiled.

'What do you think of this?' I asked Mr Jiang.

'I like the turtle with bamboo,' he said. 'The muntjak is a bit salty.'

'You've had this before?'

'Oh yes.'

'What does the driver think?' I said. I was trying to describe to myself the taste of the snake and the crane and the pigeon. I laughed, thinking that whenever someone ate something exotic they always said 'chicken'.

The silent driver, endlessly stuffing himself, made a dive for the turtle, tonged some into his bowl and gobbled it. He did the same to the *wawa* fish.

'He likes the fish,' Mr Jiang said.

The driver did not glance up. He ate like a predator in the wild – he paused, very alert, his eyes flicking, and then he darted for the food and ate it in one swift movement of his claw-like chopsticks.

Afterwards, slightly nauseated from the forbidden food, I felt like a Hindu who has just eaten hamburger. I said I would walk home. Mr Jiang tried to drag me into the car, but I resisted. Then, hiding his sheepishness in hearty guffaws, he handed me the bill: 200 *yuan*.

That was four months' salary for these young men. It was a huge amount of money. It was the foreigner's airfare from Guilin to Peking. It was the price of two of the best bicycles in China, the Flying Pigeon Deluxe. It was more than a night at the Great Wall Sheraton. It represented a good radio. It was two years' rent of a studio apartment in Shanghai. It was the cost of an antique silver bowl in the bazaar at Turfan.

I paid Mr Jiang. I wanted a reaction from him. There was none. That was for form's sake. The Chinese make a practice of not reacting to any sort of hospitality. But I persisted.

'Is the driver impressed with this meal?'

'Not at all,' Mr Jiang said. 'He has eaten this many times before. Ha! Ha!'

It rang in my ears – one of the few genuine laughs I heard in China.

It meant *We can always fool a foreigner*.

I was the hairy big-nosed devil from the back of beyond, a foreigner (*wei-guo ren*) whom the Chinese regard as the yokels of the world. We lived in crappy little countries that were squeezed at the edges of the Middle Kingdom. The places we inhabited were insignificant but bizarre. Once the Chinese believed that we tied ourselves into bunches so that we would not be snatched away by eagles. Some of our strange societies were composed entirely of women, who became pregnant by staring at their shadows. We had noses like ant-eaters. We were hairier than monkeys. We smelled like corpses. One odd fenestrated race had holes in their chests, through which poles were thrust when they carried one another around. Most of these notions were no longer current, but they had given rise to self-deceiving proverbs, which sometimes seemed true. And then the laughter was real.

12

The Slow Train to Changsha and Shaoshan 'Where the Sun Rises'

I boarded the Changsha train at Guilin station and found it rather empty and haunted-looking. It was an old-fashioned train with antiquated coaches. It had come from a strange place, too – Zhazhang on the coast of Guangdong, heading for Wuhan on the Yangtze. It was just after sundown, but very hot. I put on my pyjamas, started reading *Kidnapped* and went to sleep dreaming that I was on this very train.

In my dream the train stopped at a station in a darkening landscape among leafless trees. It was a big wooden building, not like any I had seen, with high roof-tops and balconies. I knew this was not my destination and yet I got off the train and went inside the place. The walls were whitewashed, there were potted palms here and there, and the tracks went across the lobby – two or three platforms near the ticket windows. I found this very confusing.

'What station is this?' I said, meaning to make a note for my diary.

A Chinese man said, 'Ask the people here.'

There were workers in greasy overalls hammering the tracks. They were black – or rather, half-Chinese, half-black.

Someone near them said, 'This station was built by the British.'

None of the black workers spoke English. In Chinese one of them said, '*Zhi shi shenme difang Kong Fuzi*.'

This made no sense to me. I looked closely at the men. They were like the blacks in old Hollywood movies, light-skinned, with pale eyes, and a penetrating gaze.

I realized that I had been there too long and that my train was leaving. I became panicky. Some tourists blocked my way. A stout woman confronted me.

'Are you Paul Theroux?'

'No,' I said, and slid past her.

I went in the wrong direction, to Track Seven. My train was on Track Five. I ran back and forth.

One of the tourists was laughing at me, and another said, 'The British named this station after Confucius.'

In the nick of time I caught my train, and I woke up perspiring in the rocking berth. It was midnight. The coal smoke and clanging at the window was the coal smoke and clanging from my dream.

The train arrived in Changsha before dawn. The wide streets were hot and dark. Mr Fang was just behind me, murmuring.

'What's wrong, Mr Fang?'

'Trains!' he said, and he laughed. At that hour of the morning it was a terrifying laugh. He made the noise again and said, 'Trains!'

He was weakening.

It was not only the train that bothered Mr Fang; it was also Changsha itself. The city was associated in the minds of all Chinese with the memory of Chairman Mao. Mao had been born nearby, at Shaoshan. He had been educated here. He had taught school here. He had helped found the Communist Party in Changsha, and had given speeches and recruited party members. Changsha was his city and Hunan his province. For years and years, whenever the Chinese had permission to travel they came here in a pious way, as homage to Mao, and they finished the tour by journeying to Shaoshan.

Mr Fang was sick of Mao, sick of political talk, disgusted with political emblems and songs. He was not interested in the party either. He wanted to get on with his job – he had work to do in Peking. It would have been the height of rudeness for him to say that he was sick of following me around on this trip, but I knew he was at the end of his tether. He groaned when we boarded trains these days, and his cry of 'Trains!' at Changsha Station convinced me that he was on the point of surrender.

Another train and more Mao: that was Fang's nightmare.

His distress put me into a fairly good frame of mind. And I was glad to be here. All along I had intended to visit Mao's birthplace and interrogate the pilgrims. No one seemed to have a good word for Mao these days; but what did they think in Changsha?

'He made very few mistakes, and the mistakes were very small,' Mr Ye said, showing me the Mao statue at the birthplace of Chinese communism. The statue was gigantic – Mao in an overcoat and cap, waving.

'Are you proud of him?'

'Yes!' Mr Ye said defiantly. 'We are proud of many things he did.'

Mr Shao said, '*Most* of the Chinese people are proud of him. A few don't agree.'

'Deng Xiaoping called him a great man!' Mr Ye protested.

I said, 'Shall we go to the Mao Museum?'

'It is closed,' Mr Shao said.

'Really? Why is it closed?'

The men fell silent, and their silence meant: Don't ask.

'What about the middle school where Mao taught?' I said.

Mr Ye frowned and said, 'It is ten kilometres from the city. We can drive by it, but we cannot go in. It is not very interesting.'

People used to make pilgrimages here!

'I suggest we go to the Hunan Museum of History,' Mr Shao said. 'There is a woman in it who is 2,000 years old.'

She lies naked in a lucite coffin filled with formaldehyde, her face is hideous from decay and dissection, her flesh is pruny white and her mouth gapes open. She died in the Han Dynasty after eating a water-melon. The seeds taken from her stomach are on view. Indeed, her stomach is on view – all her internal organs are in jars. The Chinese throng this museum for much the same reason that, as a schoolboy, I used to go to the Aggasiz Museum at Harvard. I was fascinated by the pickled head of a gorilla in a big jar and the way one of his jelly-like eyes had come loose and floated to the top of the jar. Horror-interest.

One of the pitfalls of long journeys is the tendency of the traveller to miniaturize a big city – not out of malice or frivolity, but for his own peace of mind. Confronted with stony-faced and charmless Chinese cities I tried to simplify them and make them interesting to me. Changsha was a good example of that. I knew it had several universities, a number of technical institutes, hospitals and medical schools – most Chinese cities were equally well equipped. They are a tribute to China's determination to be self-sufficient, healthy and literate. And such projects and institutions are seen as so necessary that the Chinese cannot understand why African and other Third World countries indulge themselves in meretricious enterprises like luxury airports or super highways. The Chinese are contemptuous of showy projects and regard aid-recipients who spend money this way as pathetic and backward. On the whole, the Chinese are baffled by people who are unwilling to make sacrifices. That is admirable. But it is very tiring constantly to be subjected to Chinese sacrifices. After the twentieth hospital and fortieth university campus I began to give them a miss.

So Changsha was rather more than Maoist memories and the 2,000-year-old pickled woman; but the rest was not compelling. I found it hard to distinguish the hotels from the colleges and the hospitals from the prisons. Chinese architecture, which is all-purpose and excruciating, makes it almost impossible to tell these places apart. One of the most common experiences a foreigner has in China (outside the three or four major cities) is of waking in a dreary room, seeing the water-stained ceiling, torn curtains, dented thermos bottle and rotting carpet, and not knowing whether you are a student, a guest, a patient, or a prisoner.

That is changing. I met four men from the Hunan Provincial Tourism Bureau in Changsha, and when one of them – Mr Sun Bing – said, 'We are the Selling and Marketing Department of this outfit,' I was convinced it was changing fast.

'We want foreign friends to know what a wonderful province this is,' Mr Li said.

'Because of Chairman Mao?'

'Not only that,' Mr Zhang said. 'Our great secret is Wuling Yang.'

'Another politician?'

'A region. More beautiful than anything in Guilin.'

'Limestone hills?'

'Of course, but better shapes,' Mr Sun said. 'More interesting. Bigger. Plus woods and birds.'

'And minority people,' Mr Chen said.

'Very colourful minority people,' Mr Sun added. 'Altogether a most attractive package.'

Rap on, I thought. I loved this. Four new Chinese, selling their province's scenic wonders. And again I thought: The Chinese wake up quickly.

'People know nothing about this now,' Mr Zhang said. 'It is a secret. No one goes there.'

'Why not?'

'Because there is no hotel. But one is being built. And when it is, this region will be famous all over the world.'

Mr Li said, 'Hunan is a lovely province. People must know it better. We compete with other provinces, but we have everything. Until now visitors did not come here to look at the scenery, but they are starting to.'

And saying this he led me to a table, where we had a long meal of Hunanese dishes – the best food in China, in my opinion. This banquet consisted of frogs' legs, turtle, duck, tripe, sea-cucumbers (which are actually sea-slugs), soup and vegetables – no rice, no noodles: that sort of stodge was for people with cruder palates. I knew that it was a blatant attempt to win my approval, and I was touched by their innocent belief in the dynamics of feasting the foreign devil. The Chinese can be deeply unsubtle, stage-managing a bowel-shattering banquet before asking a favour. Or is that subtle? Anyway, they have found that it works. But I would gladly have praised the hills of Hunan without a third helping of frogs' legs.

'Until now visitors did not come here to look at the scenery,' Mr Li had said. How true. They had come as pilgrims, first to walk the seventy-five miles west to Shaoshan, and then – after the railway line was built in the late sixties – to take the strangest train in China. They had come believing the Cultural Revolution slogan, THE SUN RISES IN SHAOSHAN (*Taiyang cong Shaoshan shengqi*), which was a metaphor for Mao Zedong's having been born there. The Chinese had once named themselves 'Shaoshan' in Mao's honour, and I ran into at least one Li Shaoshan.

In the sixties there were several trains every hour. Now there is one train a day. It leaves at 6.00 in the morning from Changsha and arrives three hours later at Shaoshan. It returns from Shaoshan in the evening, just an old puffer on a forgotten branch-line, which had outlived its purpose.

The road had always been popular, even after the train was running regularly. It was not only the best way for Red Guards and revolutionaries to prove their ardour, but long walks were part of Mao's political programme – the 'Forge Good Iron Footsoles' scheme. The idea was that all Chinese citizens were to have sturdy feet during the Cultural Revolution, because when the Nameless Enemy tried to invade China the evacuation of cities might be necessary. Mao filled the people with a war-paranoia – that was the reason they were required to make bricks, dig trenches and bunkers and bomb-shelters. They were also ordered to have hard feet and to take twenty-mile hikes on their days off in order to give themselves 'iron footsoles' ('All I got were blisters,' my informant Wang told me). It was to this end that they trekked for four days on the road from Changsha to Shaoshan, sleeping in peasants' huts and singing 'The East Is Red', 'The Sun Rises In Shaoshan'. They also sang ditties that had been set to music from the Selected Thoughts, such numbers as 'People Of The World, Unite And Defeat The US Aggressors And All Their Running Dogs!' with its stirring last line, 'Monsters of all kinds shall be destroyed.' My favourite song from the Selected Thoughts, one I was assured had enlivened the marches along the Shaoshan road with its syncopation, went as follows:

> A revolution is not a dinner party,
> Or writing an essay, or painting a picture,
> or doing embroidery;

The Slow Train to Changsha and Shaoshan

It cannot be so refined, so leisurely and gentle,
So temperate, kind, courteous, restrained
and magnanimous.*

A revolution is an insurrection,
An act of violence by which one class
overthrows another.

They sang them on the trains, too. They flew flags. They wore Mao buttons and badges, and the red armband. It was not a trivial matter. It compared in size and fervour to Muslims making the Hadj to Mecca. On one day in 1966, a procession of 120,000 Chinese thronged the village of Shaoshan to screech songs and perform the *qing an* with the *Little Red Book*.

Twenty years later I arrived at the station in an empty train. The station was empty. The unusually long platform was empty, and so were the sidings. There was not a soul in sight. The station was tidy, but that only made its emptiness much odder. It was very clean, freshly painted in a limpid shade of blue, and entirely abandoned. No cars in the car park, no one at the ticket windows. A large portrait of Mao hung over the station and on a billboard was the epitaph in Chinese: MAO ZEDONG WAS A GREAT MARXIST, A GREAT PROLETARIAN REVOLUTIONARY, A GREAT TACTICIAN AND THEORIST.

That was delicate: nothing about his being a great leader. Mao's dying wish (obviously ignored) was to be remembered as a teacher.

I walked through the village, reflecting on the fact that nothing looks emptier than an empty car park. There were many here, designed for buses; they were very large and nothing was parked upon them. I went to the hotel that was built for dignitaries and I sat in the almost-empty dining-room, under a Mao portrait, eating and listening to people spitting.

The tide was out in Shaoshan; it was the town that time forgot – ghostly and echoing. And so it fascinated me. It was actually a pretty place, a rural retreat, with lovely trees and green fields, and

---

* 'These were the virtues of Confucius, as described by one of his disciples', runs the commentary in Mao's *Selected Works*. So Mao was also criticizing Confucius for not being of a revolutionary spirit.

a stream running through it that topped up the lotus ponds. In any other place an atmosphere of such emptiness would seem depressing; but this was a healthy neglect – what is healthier than refusing to worship a politician? – and the few people there had come as picnickers, not as pilgrims.

Mao's house was at the far end of the village, in a glade. It was large and its yellow stucco and Hunanese design gave it the look of a hacienda – very cool and airy, with an atrium and a lovely view of its idyllic setting. Here Mao was born in December, 1893. The rooms are neatly labelled: PARENTS' BEDROOM, BROTHER'S ROOM, KITCHEN, PIGSTY, and so forth. It is the house of a well-to-do family – Mao's father was 'a relatively rich peasant', clever with money and mortgages, and he was a money-lender of sorts. There was plenty of space here – a big barn and a roomy kitchen. Mrs Mao's stove was preserved ('Do Not Touch') and a placard near it read: *In 1921 Mao Zedong educated his family in revolution near this stove.* And in the sitting-room: *In 1927 meetings were held here to discuss revolutionary activities.*

It was not like visiting Lincoln's log cabin. It wasn't Blenheim. It wasn't Paul Revere's house. For one thing it was very empty. The few Chinese nearby seemed indifferent to the house itself. They sat under trees listening to a booming radio. There were girls in pretty dresses. Their clothes alone were a political statement. But this handful of people were hardly visible. Its emptiness meant something. Because when it was heavily visited Shaoshan had represented political piety and obedience, now that it was empty it stood for indifference. In a sense, neglect was more dramatic than destruction, because the thing still existed as a mockery of what it had been.

It had the fusty smell of an old shrine. It had outlived its usefulness, and it looked a little absurd, like a once-hallowed temple of a sect of fanatics who had run off, tearing their clothes, and had never returned. Times have changed. Towards the end of the Cultural Revolution, the pseudonymous Simon Leys visited China and in *Chinese Shadows*, his gloomy and scolding account of his trip, he wrote that Shaoshan 'is visited by about three million pilgrims every year'. That is 8,000 a day. Today there were none.

If Shaoshan was embarrassing to the Chinese it was because the whole scheme had been to show Mao as more than human. There was an obnoxious religiosity in the way his old schoolhouse had been arranged to show little Mao as a sanctified student. But the building was empty, and there was no one walking down the lane, so it didn't matter. I had the impression that the Chinese were staying away in droves.

One stall sold postcards. There was only one view: *Mao's Birthplace* (the house in the glade). And there were a few Mao badges. It was the only place in China where I saw his face on sale, but even so it was just this little badge. There were also towels and dishcloths, saying *Shaoshan*.

There was a shop in the Mao Museum.

I said, 'I would like to buy a Mao badge.'

'We have none,' the assistant said.

'How about a Mao picture?'

'We have none.'

'What about a *Little Red Book* – or any Mao book?'

'None.'

'Where are they?'

'Sold.'

'All of them?'

'All.'

'Will you get some more to sell?'

The assistant said, 'I do not know.'

What do they sell, then, at the shop in the Mao Museum? They sell key-chains with colour photographs of Hong Kong movie actresses, bars of soap, combs, razor blades, face cream, hard candy, peanut brittle, buttons, thread, cigarettes and men's underwear.

The museum did try to show Mao as more than human, and in its eighteen rooms of hagiography Mao was presented as a sort of Christ figure, preaching very early (giving instructions in revolution by his mother's stove) and winning recruits. There were statues, flags, badges and personal paraphernalia – his straw hat, his slippers, his ashtray. Room by room, his life is displayed in pictures and captions: his schooldays, his job, his travels, the death of his brother, the Long March, the war, his first marriage . . .

And then, after such languid and detailed exposition, an odd thing happens in the last room. In Number Eighteen, time is telescoped, and the years 1949–76, his entire chairmanship, his rule, and his death, are presented with lightning speed. There is no mention of his two other marriages, nothing about Jiang Qing. Non-persons like Jiang Qing and Lin Biao have been air-brushed out of photographs. The nineteen-sixties are shown in one picture, the mushroom cloud of China's first atom bomb in 1964. The rest of the decade does not exist. There has been no Great Proletarian Cultural Revolution. The Mao Museum was founded in 1967, at the height of it!

But by omitting so much and showing time passing so quickly the museum gives the viewer a bizarre potted history of Mao's final years. In the previous rooms he looks like a spoiled child, a big brat, scowling and solemn. In this final room he develops a very unusual smile and on his pumpkin face it has a disturbing effect. After 1956 he seems to be gaga. He starts wearing baggy pants and a coolie hat, and his face is drawn from a sag into a mad or senile grimace. He looks unlike his earlier self. In one picture he is lumberingly playing ping-pong. In 1972 and after, meeting Nixon, Prince Sihanouk, and East European leaders, he's a heffalump, he looks hugely crazy or else barely seems to recognize the visitor grinning at him. There is plenty of evidence here to support what the Chinese say about him all the time – that after 1956 he was not the same.

Mao had set out to be an enigma and had succeeded. 'The anal leader of an oral people,' the sinologist Richard Soloman has said. Mao can be described but not summed up. He was patient, optimistic, ruthless, pathologically anti-intellectual, romantic, militaristic, patriotic, chauvinistic, rebellious in a youthful way, and deliberately contradictory.

Shaoshan said everything about Mao: his rise and fall; his position today. I loved the empty train arriving at the empty station. Was there a better image of obscurity? As for the house and village – they were like many temples in China, where no one prayed any longer; just a heap of symmetrical stones representing waste, confusion and ruin. China was full of such places, dedicated to the memory of someone or other and, lately, just an excuse for setting up picnic tables and selling souvenirs.

*

Mr Fang was sitting in the hotel lobby with his head in his hands. He did not look up when a man near him hoicked loudly, spat a clam on to the floor and scuffed it with his foot.

'I'm leaving, Mr Fang.'

He raised his head and looked at me with his swollen eyes.

'Where are you going?'

'Canton for a while. Then Peking.'

He groaned. 'By train?' he asked. His lips were dry.

'The People's Railway is for the people,' I said, recalling the slogan I had seen in the Yunnan town of Yiliang.

This made him wince. He said, 'I am fifty-six years old. I have travelled a great deal. I was a Russian interpreter. I have been to Leningrad and other places. But I have never taken so many trains all at once. I have never slept on so many trains – I don't sleep at all. Trains, trains.'

'A train isn't a vehicle,' I said. 'A train is part of the country. It's a place.'

'No more,' he said, not listening.

'I'm going to Canton.'

'I must go with you,' he said. 'But we can take a plane.'

'Sorry, no planes. Chinese planes frighten me.'

'But the train –'

'You take the plane,' I said. 'I'll go by train.'

'No. I go with you. It is the Chinese way.'

He looked miserable, but I had very little sympathy for him, He had been sent to nanny me and breathe down my neck. He had been discreet – he had not got in my way; but who had asked him to come? Not me.

'Go back to Peking,' I said. 'I can go to Canton myself.'

'After Canton,' he said, 'are you taking more trains?'

'I don't know.'

'Planes are quicker.'

'I'm not in a hurry, Mr Fang.'

He said nothing more. I was glad: without even trying, I had outlasted him. He was at his wits' end, he hated trains now, he had suffered the torture of sleep-deprivation. He was dying to go home.

And yet he followed me on to the express to Canton the

following night, and he sat behind me in the dining-car. He looked physically ill and to make matters worse the dining-car quickly filled up with some high-spirited tourists, whose plane had been cancelled.

They were the sort of good-hearted Americans who, at an earlier time in the history of American tourism, used to go to Pike's Peak. Now it was China. They went shopping. They were bussed to temples where they also shopped. They talked a great deal, but not about Chinese culture. They said, 'Joe senior died and she remarried twice more. She was an awful alcoholic.' They said, 'Bananas are good for you. They feed on carbohydrates.' When someone among them mentioned Canton they said, 'You can go bowling in Canton!'

But they were not more talkative than the Cantonese in the dining-car, nor were they any louder. In a circumspect way they were appreciative.

The waiter put down a dish of green vegetables.

'Who's going to eat this?' a hearty woman said.

'What is it?' another woman asked.

'My son would eat that,' said a third woman, peering at it.

'Is it spinach?'

'It's a type of spinach,' a man said.

'Never mind!' a man from Texas cried. 'The streets are safe! My poor wife's from west Texas and she didn't see a city until she was twenty-three years old. But I could put $10,000 worth of gold on her and send her into the street and she'd be perfectly all right. Because this is China, not Texas.'*

'But don't touch the water,' the hearty woman said.

'It tastes like LA water,' someone said. 'I'm not used to it.'

'It tastes like Saginaw water,' a young woman said. 'It's the chlorine. I had a cup of coffee there once and it was awful. I says,

---

* Was a vindictive Chinese god listening to this? Perhaps. Exactly a year later, on 20 June 1987, a man from Texas was murdered on this very train by two Chinese men. The victim's name was Ewald Cheer. The motive was robbery ($186). He was the first American to be murdered in China for forty years. His killers were quickly found guilty and executed.

"What's wrong with this coffee?" But it wasn't the coffee. It was the water.'

Her friend – or perhaps her husband – said, 'Outside Saginaw, in hick towns like Hemlock, the water's real nice.'

'Boy, am I glad I didn't bring nylons!' the hearty woman said. 'Did you think China was going to be this hot?'

'It's hot here, sure,' said the man from Texas. 'But up north it's freezing. It's all snow and ice. That's a fact.'

'He's bringing more food,' someone said.

'Jesus, do you think that has a name?'

A woman said in an announcing voice, 'I'm going to tell all my friends who are going on a diet to go to China – I mean, the ones that are real picky about their food. They'd slim down good!'

'But the real picky ones wouldn't go to China,' the young woman said.

As I left the dining-car I heard someone say in an anxious voice, 'My question is, what do they do with all these left-overs?'

A Cantonese man had entered my compartment. He was panting, fossicking in his knapsack. He looked simian and strange. He spoke no language but his own. He climbed into the upper berth and rattled his bags. I turned the light out. He turned it back on. He slurped tea out of his jam-jar and harumphed. He noisily left the compartment and returned wearing striped pyjamas. It was midnight and yet he was still leaping back and forth, once narrowly missing my glasses with his prehensile foot as he used the table as a foothold. I went to sleep and woke at about 3.00 in the morning. The man was reading, using a flashlight, and muttering softly. I slept very little after that.

I felt just as grouchy as Mr Fang in Canton, and so I decided to stay awhile and not make any onward bookings. It is wrong to see a country in a bad mood: you begin to blame the country for your mood and to draw the wrong conclusions.

I had once laughed to think that there were luxury hotels in Canton, with delicatessens and discotheques. The Chinese there had taken up weight-lifting; they had body-building magazines. The White Swan Hotel had hamburgers and a salad bar. The China Hotel had an air-conditioned bowling alley. Now it did not seem odd to think that people would go to China to shop, to eat, or to go bowling.

Mr Fang said nervously, 'No more trains?'

'Not at the moment.'

'Maybe you will go home?'

'Maybe.'

Was he smiling?

'I will take you to the station,' he said. 'Chinese custom. Say goodbye.'

'That's not necessary, Mr Fang. Why not take the plane back to Peking?'

'There is one leaving tomorrow morning,' he said. He was eager.

'Don't worry about me,' I said.

He seemed reluctant, but he said no more. I bought him a picture book about Guilin and that evening, spotting him in the lobby, I gave it to him. He did not unwrap it. He slipped it under his arm, then gave me his sad sea-lion stare and said, 'Yes,' and shook my hand. 'Bye-bye,' he said, in English, and then abruptly turned away. It is not a reminiscing race, I thought. He kept walking. He did not look back.

Then, because this was Canton, I went bowling.

13

The Peking Express: Train Number 16

And then there were a number of public events that shocked the country. I did not set off immediately. It is so easy to be proved wrong in China. No sooner had I concluded that China was prospering and reforming, that people were freer and foreign investment rising, than the country was in crisis. True, some aspects of China never changed – the rice-planters bent double, the weeder on his stool, the boy pedalling his 2,000-year-old irrigation pump, the buffalo-man, the duckherd. But in the months before I left Canton to resume my Chinese travels, the *yuan* was devalued by 30 per cent – instead of three to the dollar there were now almost four; and the black market in hard currency was very brisk, and the most common greeting was 'Shansh marnie?' People were criticized for wanting to go abroad and a law was passed requiring potential students to post a bond of 5,000 *yuan* – an enormous sum – before they could study in another country. Foreign investment dropped by 20 per cent, and Deng Xiaoping criticized Chinese manufacturers for producing shoddy goods that no one wanted.

And the students demonstrated, for the first time since the Cultural Revolution. The demonstrations were orderly, but the defiance implicit in such illegal gatherings was seen to be a sign of chaos. The Chinese horror of disorder made them seem important, though I felt the parades and demands were mostly half-baked. Traditionally, December and January have been regarded by the Chinese as appropriate months for disruption, and so there was a ritual end-of-term element in the demonstrations, high spirits, funny hats, a measure of farce. The grievances were numerous, and on posters and in the chanting the students demanded press freedom, electoral reform, a multiparty system, and official permission to demonstrate. Banners were flown reading WE WANT DEMOCRACY. They demanded sexual freedom and better food in the university cafeterias. Eight cities were affected, and the size of the demonstrations varied from a few hundred students in Canton to well over 100,000 (and an equal number of spectators) in Shanghai, which came to a standstill for a full day.

The Chinese government, with its liking for scapegoats (so much more economical than a full-scale witch-hunt), blamed one man for the country-wide outbreak. This was Dr Fang Lizhi, an astrophysicist and vice-president of the National Science and Technical University in Hefei. He had been very busy. He had written articles in *China Youth News* criticizing students for having 'low democratic consciousness'. He lectured his own students at Hefei, and just a month before the demonstrations he had addressed students at Jiaotong University in Shanghai.

Dr Fang's message was a mixture of noble sentiments and platitudes. Among other things, he said, 'Men are born with rights – to live, to marry, to think, to receive an education,' and that the only way for China 'to transform the feudalistic ideas and gradually approach modern standards in thinking' was for its intellectuals 'to demonstrate the strength they possess'. He implied that government leaders were not above criticism.

'Democracy can be achieved only gradually through consistent effort,' he said. 'There is nothing to be afraid of. Criticizing government leaders is a symbol of democracy. I hold the view that we may criticize leaders.'

The abusive term for such sentiments is 'bourgeois liberalism' – a sort of selfish and privileged complaining. Soon after Dr Fang gave the speech, the *People's Daily* attacked 'the trend towards bourgeois liberalization'. In the Chinese mind a person who holds liberal views is a rightist and a person who toes the party line most strictly is a leftist.

Dr Fang was vilified. Taiwan was blamed for fomenting trouble. The government papers said it was partly the work of 'professional hooligans'. In Shanghai a worker at a lacquerware factory was arrested as a counter-revolutionary for establishing his own political party, the *Weimin* (Defend the People) Party. He was the only member of this party, but still it was no joke. Starting your own party meant that you intended to overthrow the Chinese Communist Party. That was treason and the penalty for it was a bullet in the neck.

The very fact that the demonstrations were mentioned in the news was a sign that the government was alarmed. It was fairly well known that one of the demands of the Peking students was that the demonstrations should be reported in the newspaper. Disturbances of any kind had been hushed up in the past. At first the government sent water trucks to Peking's Tian An Men Square at 4.00 in the morning. The paving stones were drenched and the ice that resulted seemed like a guarantee that the students would fall down when they tried to march. But 3,000 students appeared later that morning and kept their footing, and when thirty-four were arrested and hauled off to be interrogated another demonstration was mounted; more signs, more slogans, and the thirty-four were released.

The most worrying thing for the government was that in Shanghai both factory workers and students – not natural allies – had come together and marched in the same parade. To ingratiate themselves with the factory workers, the government blamed the students. The mayor of Shanghai addressed a large gathering of students and was heckled. 'Who elected you?' a student called out. That was regarded as very shocking, because it is a total lapse of taste to suggest that someone like the mayor (who is appointed by the Central Committee) is a party hack.

The demonstrations were peaceful. Furthermore, they were essentially supporting Deng's policies of reform. 'Bourgeois liberalization' was just what the government had been encouraging. But the government did not want to be seen this way, permitting arch-unrepentant capitalist-roaders, behind-the-scenes reactionaries, harbingers of feudalism, running dogs, those 'left in form but right in essence', and promoters of the right-deviationist wing – to use the convenient Chinese categories – to flourish. It was, as far as I could see, the most recent example of the Chinese not knowing when to stop – first the government, then the students.

There was a suspicion that behind it all was a power struggle in the Chinese leadership. The students were being manipulated, not by Dr Fang (who was fired from his university job and then expelled from the party), but by leftists who wanted to discredit the reforming rightist Mr Deng. Or was it the rightists who were inciting the students in order to provoke the leftists into over-reacting?

I decided to find out for myself.

On a hot muggy winter day in Canton I went to Zhongshan University, south of the city on the opposite bank of the Pearl River, to see whether the students were still rioting. They were not. It was very placid under the eucalyptus trees. The students were cycling and punching volleyballs and jogging. They were doing their laundry, they were smooching, they were studying. Some of them stared at me. They had few inhibitions. They even talked about the demonstrations. They said their own professors were critical of the government and especially the official policy of suppressing or misreporting the news.

'How do they know it's misreported?' I asked.

'Because we know the truth,' a student said. 'We listen to Hong Kong news here.'

The Hong Kong stations came in loud and clear in Canton, and some Hong Kong newspapers circulated in the city, as well.

A student who called himself Andrew – he was a Cantonese fellow named Hen To – said, 'I'll tell you anything you want to know about the demonstration here.'

I liked his attitude, but there was not much to tell. He said the students in the south were complacent and money-minded, not furiously political as in the north.

'We only had 200 students in our demonstration,' he said. 'After they made a fuss here they marched to the government offices in town and sang songs. It wasn't much – not as big as Shanghai or Peking.'

'What did the students say they wanted?'

'Democracy and reform,' Andrew said.

'But China is changing very fast,' I said.

'That's what the old people think,' he said. 'We young people say it is changing too slowly. But that is the government policy. They want China to look stable, so that foreign investment will be encouraged. No one will put money into China if there are riots.'

I asked him his plans.

'I'd like to take up business,' he said. 'Import and export.'

'You might make a lot of money.'

'I hope so.'

'Then you'll become a capitalist-roader.'

'Maybe,' he said, and snickered. 'I think we have a lot to learn. We want to use the good features of capitalism but not the bad ones.'

'Is that possible?'

'We can try.'

That was the new thinking – TO BE RICH IS GLORIOUS, politically an OK slogan. It was the philosophy of the young, of the rising students, and even of many farmers. It was the essence of Deng's thinking, too. It was in total opposition to Mao's philosophy, and it was one of the reasons Shaoshan had no visitors.

Andrew saw himself as an individual, with his own needs and desires. He didn't say what every student had said for the past thirty-five years when asked about their ambitions: 'Serve the people.' He said 'business', 'money', 'import-export'. He was fairly open-minded. He studied hard. He liked his fellow students. He lived in a room with seven others and did his homework in the library. His favourite author was Mark Twain. In the film theatre on campus (built by a Hong Kong tycoon named Leung) he had seen *On Golden Pond*, *Superman* and *Rambo*.

I said that *Rambo* represented everything that I loathed.

'But he is strong,' Andrew said. 'His body is interesting. The way he looks. The things he does.'

That was a point, the freakishness of it; but I said, 'Do you realize that it was about Vietnam?'

'Yes.'

'So doesn't that make it a reactionary, bourgeois, violently imperialistic movie?'

Andrew shrugged and said, 'We don't take it that seriously.'

He was twenty-one years old. His parents, as teachers, had been singled out during the Cultural Revolution.

I said, 'They were the Stinking Ninth.'

'Yes,' he said. He knew exactly what I meant. Mao decreed nine categories of enemy: landlords, rich peasants, counter-revolutionaries, bad elements, rightists, traitors, foreign agents, capitalist-roaders, and – the stinking ninth – intellectuals. It is a strange list, because it seems to embrace the whole of humanity.

His parents had been rusticated – sent shovelling. They had fared better than the brother of my friend Miss Chung, who had been locked in a broom cupboard right here at Zhongshan University by Maoists. His crime was that he was the son of a man who had once been a Guomindang politician. He was kept in the broom cupboard for two years and, after a severe interrogation, hanged himself.

I told Andrew the tale. He said that it was not an unusual story. Well, that was true enough, but it made me feel once again that wherever I was in China I was among ghosts.

'Do you believe in ghosts?' I asked.

'No,' Andrew said, and I could tell that he meant it.

He wasn't superstitious, he wasn't spiritual, and he certainly wasn't political – there was no future in Chinese politics. He was practical. His was the first generation in China to grow up with no dogma – no emperor, no gods, no chairman; no Taoisms, no Maoism, no Buddhism. Nor had Andrew's generation been touched in the least by Christianity. Democracy was such a long shot that Andrew had not bothered to take part in the students' demonstrations. His realism was a kind of glumness.

That night I wondered what would become of him. But of course it was very obvious. If he went into business and made some money he would prosper in a small way and raise a one-child family. He would not use expressions like 'Serve the people'. He would regard himself as an intellectual (*zhishi fenzi*), the term the Chinese use for anyone who does not work with their hands. If he was self-employed, as he wanted to be, he would probably work hard. On holidays he would visit hotels like mine, where they had 'holiday specials' – Christmas banquets, New Year's parties ('free hats, favours, racket-makers') and a 'New Year's Day Champagne Brunch Buffet' at 28 *yuan* a throw.

One of the worst aspects of living in brisk dictatorial China is that you seldom have an accurate idea of what is really going on. It is not that the Chinese government is inscrutable. Lazy travellers and visitors love Chinese mysteries, but the Chinese are quite knowable. And Chinese bureaucrats are among the most scrutable and obvious on earth. And yet anyone must find the Chinese media obfuscatory and unforthcoming. The Chinese people manage to keep abreast of events by depending on telepathy and whispers, and by the Politburo hyperbole: if a high official is said to have a cold he's likely been fired, if he is 'convalescing' he has been exiled, and if he is 'extremely ill' he is about to be murdered.

And liberal does not mean liberal or open-minded. The connotations of the term, which is based on the Chinese characters for freedom (*ziyou*), are entirely negative, implying licence or licentiousness. A Chinese official and most American Republicans would agree on what the word liberal implies. For Mao it was a term of abuse.

Meanwhile, the fuss over the students had not died down – the government was still ranting. But there was no public defiance. The Chinese had that squinting wind-in-the-face expression that they assumed when they were at their most resigned. No one on earth is more silent than a silent Chinese. I asked my usual provocative questions, but made little headway. I was sure a power struggle was in progress, because Deng Xiaoping, aged eighty-three, had still not named his successor.

A Hong Kong student at Canton Station told me, 'The government has denied that there is any problem.'

'Then there must be a problem,' I said. 'Never believe anything in China until it has been officially denied.'

We were waiting for the Peking Express on this humid winter night in Canton. It was said to be one of the best trains in China. (This was the old Huguang Railway line.) It was a thirty-six hour trip – two nights on the train, which went 1,500 miles, passing through five provinces, bisecting China from bottom to top and crossing the Yangtze river at Wuhan.

Some visitors to China laugh when you tell them you're taking a two-day trip on a train, and then they are delayed for five days at a Chinese airport, waiting for the fog to lift. Everyone who takes a plane in China has an airline tale of woe.

The only bad moment the train passenger has is on the platform, when the other passengers are boarding. Which ones will be in your compartment? It is a much more critical lottery than a blind date, because these people will be eating and sleeping with you. I had seen lepers on trains, and bratty children, and on the way to Guilin a man travelling with five parrots and no cage.

I watched the people boarding. The old woman in the padded jacket, carrying a lunch tin – some pungent stuff in there, chicken-foot stew, Cantonese cow tendon, and highly prized rotten eggs wrapped in seaweed. There was a spiv in sun-glasses with a radio, a man with three suitcases and a crate of bananas; a salesman with his case of samples – rubber bungs, probably; three ornery moustached men wearing high-heeled shoes; a small family – haggard father, mother with pin-curl perm, and spoiled child snatching at things that moved. The harassed, spiky-haired student, the fat-faced party hack in the Mao suit, the secret drinker with swollen eyes, the pretty girl travelling with her dragon-like grandmother, the plump boys in new eye-glasses from Hong Kong, the physics prof on his way to a conference, the loud-voiced Chinese-American who speaks only a few words of Cantonese but uses them on everyone, the middle-aged Japanese couple, looking wrinkle-proof but anxious, the students returning from overseas loaded with duty-free presents, western clothes and a musical suitcase, the skinny, smiling and lovably ineffectual-looking soldiers of the People's Liberation Army – it is impossible to feel threatened by soldiers whose uniforms are four sizes too big.

I was assigned to a compartment with some salesmen. One was the Chinese version of Willy Loman, and the other a frisky man who smiled too much and said, 'I'm in machine tools,' just as his American counterpart would do. There was a third man who was practically invisible, reminding me of how the Chinese to a large extent have perfected the art of living at close quarters.

Mr Yeo, the machine-tool man, admired my sweater ('Nice one. Good quality. Very warm. You'll need it in Peking') and was full of direct questions: 'You're – what? About thirty-five? Any children?'

He handed me an envelope of pemmican, as a sort of get-acquainted gift, shared his tea with me, and accepted a chocolate bar in return. I thought he might be exhaustingly friendly, but he slept through most of the trip and snored loudly. The Willy Loman character also slept a great deal, but woke at 4.00 in the morning and did lazy calisthenics, wagging his head and slapping his fore-arms. He was in feedstuffs and cereals. His luggage filled the luggage shelf – both boxes and suitcases. He was very solemn except when I caught his eye. Then he broke into a laugh and gave me a broad smile. His laugh was urgent and meant: *No questions, please!* As soon as he turned away he frowned. That was also very Chinese.

The first night there was a tremendous amount of snoring in our compartment. From time to time it woke me with its flapping wind. It was louder than the clanging wheels of the train. But I slept soundly the rest of the time, and didn't get up until 9.00.

The train was so cold that morning that the windows were streaming with condensation. I shaved in cold water – but it was always cold – and in mid morning we arrived at Changsha, where I had been some months before on my way to Mao's birthplace. It had been steamy and dismal in the summer. In the winter it was smoggy and brown and much uglier. The words 'a Chinese city' had acquired a peculiar horror for me, like 'Russian toilet', or 'Turkish prison', or 'journalist's ethics'. In the cold rain of winter, with the cracked and sooty blocks of flats, the muddy streets, the skinny trees and dark brown sky they are at their very worst.

But this city was the signal for the attendants to stoke the fires, and as soon as the coach was reasonably warm the passengers threw their clothes off and clomped around in plastic shoes and wrinkled pyjamas. They propped themselves in the draught between the coaches and brushed their teeth. Some practised kung fu in the corridors.

The dining-car was crowded at lunchtime. Although there were no tourists on the train and everyone wore old clothes – shouting and spitting and blowing smoke into each other's face – they were also flinging money around. I guessed that they were mainly Cantonese, on this profitable business route: Guangdong was a producer of goods and Peking a lucrative outlet. These scruffy passengers were all in business. The man next to me paid almost twenty *yuan* for a meal for himself and his wife. Call it £3 and it doesn't seem much; but it was nearly a week's pay. He was a grizzled man with matted hair. He smoked and ate at the same time – chopsticks in one hand, cigarette in the other. His small boy did not eat. This little irritant dug out all the toothpicks from the plastic holder and threw them on to the floor; then tipped over a glass of water; and then began smacking an ashtray against the table and squawking. He was about five or six. His father laughed at this obstreperousness – very un-Chinese. But that was not the only uncharacteristic behaviour in this rowdy train. It was also full of drunks, and not only beer-drinkers, but also old men getting plastered on the rice wine they had brought with them.

I read and dozed and woke up in the north of Hunan, at the city of Yueyang, which was a grey town surrounded by fat shadowy mountains. A few hours later we came to Wuhan. I had been there once before, in 1980. It had seemed to me a nightmare city, of muddy streets and black factories, pouring frothy poisons into the Yangtze. It was bigger than I remembered it, but not so black. There were dozens of high-level cranes putting up new buildings, including a hospital.

The Yangtze is almost a mile wide at Wuhan, and on its banks it has landing-stages and flights of steps that resemble the ghats on the Ganges. On the Hankou side there were also many new buildings, and there were cars in the streets – I remembered the wagons and carts, pulled by old women. The buildings and the traffic jams were not necessarily improvements, but they made a difference. Modernization did not make any Chinese city look less horrific; many cities looked more so as a result of building schemes.

It was cold enough in Wuhan for people to be wearing mittens and boots. That was what the salesmen in my compartment were wearing when they got out, pulling their suitcases through the windows. They did it clumsily. They were bemused by the sight of a girl walking along the platform carrying a dead fish.

Before we pulled out of Wuhan the sleeping-car attendant roused me and said I had to move.

'You are in the wrong berth,' she said.

'I am in the right berth,' I said. I knew she wanted to move me, but I saw no reason why she should put me in the wrong. I made her compare my ticket with the berth number, and I created a hoo-hah, so that I would have the satisfaction of hearing her apologize.

'It is a mistake,' she said, ambiguously, and led me to a compartment which held a man, a woman and an infant.

'How old is that baby?'

'Two weeks.'

The baby was snoring. After a while it began to cry. The man took a bottle out and fed it, and the child's mother left the compartment.

That was how it went. The man did everything for this baby, which was rapped in a thick quilt like a papoose. The man fed it, changed it and dandled it. The woman hung around and lazed, and several times I saw her sleeping in the Hard Class coach that adjoined ours. Perhaps the woman was ill. I did not want to ask. The man took charge.

'It's a boy,' he said, when he was feeding it.

I hadn't asked.

He was a doctor. His wife was also a doctor. He worked in Peking, his wife in Canton; and he had gone to Canton to be present for the birth. Now they were all going back to Peking for a few months – the woman's maternity leave. There were feeding bottles, baby powder and cans of soluble milk formula all over the compartment. They used disposable nappies which they discarded in a bucket under my bed. I did not mind; I like the milky smell of babies, and I was very touched by the love and attention that this man gave the child.

I read on my bunk while the man burped his baby and the woman looked on. I drank Cantonese sherry. It was like being in a cabin in the woods with this little family. For dinner I had the speciality of this train, 'Iron dish chicken pieces' – a hot iron platter of chicken, sizzling in fat. The dining-car was very congenial – steam, shouting, beer fizzing, cigarette smoke, waiters banging dishes down and snatching empty plates away.

The two men at my table were young and half drunk. I liked these crowded dining-cars rushing through the night, and the food being dished out, and people stuffing themselves.

'We sell light-bulbs and light-fittings,' one of the men said. 'We're heading home after a week's selling.'

'Where is home?' I asked.

'Harbin.'

'I am going there,' I said. 'I want to see the ice festival and the forest.'

'It's too cold to see anything,' the other man said. 'You will just want to stay in your room.'

'That's a challenge,' I said. 'Anyway – how cold is it?'

'Twenty-two below – Fahrenheit,' he said, and he poured me some of his beer and clinked glasses.

By then I had taken for granted the friendliness of the Chinese. Their attentions were sometimes bewildering, as when they leaned over my shoulder trying to read what I was scribbling into my notebook, or pressed their damp faces against my book, fascinated by the English words. But their curiosity and goodwill were genuine, and in general they were hospitable towards strangers and reasonably candid.

'Do you travel much?' I asked.

'Yes. All over. But not outside,' the first man said. 'I'd like to but I can't.'

'Where would you go?'

'Japan.'

That surprised me. My reaction must have shown on my face, because the Chinese salesman wanted to know what I thought of his choice of country. I said, 'I find the Japanese can be very irritating.'

'The Americans dropped an atom bomb on them.'

'That was too bad, but they started the war by bombing Pearl Harbor, didn't they, comrade?'

'That's true!' the second man said. 'The same day they captured Shanghai.'

It was considered bad manners in China to say disparaging things about any foreign country, particularly with someone who was himself a foreigner. That was why the men cackled. It was naughty to run down the Japanese! It was fun! We sat there yakking until the rest of the people left the dining-car. Then we stopped at Xinyang. We had gone from Hubei Province into Henan. This station was covered in black ice and slushy snow – quite a change from the palm trees and dragonflies of Canton a few days ago.

In my compartment the man was snuggled up with his infant son, and his wife lay sleeping in the upper berth. All night the man attended to the infant. They slept together, the child snickering and snorting the way babies do. From time to time the man swung his legs over and mixed a batch of Nestlé's Lactogen using the tea thermos of hot water and an enamel cup. He was considerate: he did not switch on the light – he used the light from the corridor. The baby's fussing increased and then the father eased the bottle into the baby's mouth and there came a satisfied snorting. The father was very patient. The train stopped and started, was delayed at sidings waiting for a southbound express to go through, and then rattled on to the whistles of lonely freight trains. In the darkness, the man spoke softly to his child, he sang to him, and when the child grew sleepy he tucked him into the berth and crept in beside him.

The muffled sounds in the morning, and the cold draughts – and there was something eerie about the daylight, too – were all produced by the falling snow. The train was battling through this snowstorm: it was beautiful – just as though the train was ploughing through surf in a stormy ocean.

The loudspeaker had come on. The morning exercises were over. The comedy programme with its canned laughter had ended. It was now playing music. The selections from *Carmen* were followed by 'Rhinestone Cowboy', 'Green, Green Grass Of Home', 'Ave Maria', and 'Where Have All The Flowers Gone'.

I drank green tea and watched the storm abate, but as it did the weather seemed to turn colder. The ground was that pale brown of hard frozen earth, the trees stark and slender against the snow. The towns and cities lost their nightmarishness beneath the snow. But nothing else changed; nothing stopped because of the storm. There were donkeys pulling haycarts, workers crowding into factories, children tramping through fields on their way to school (wearing wool caps and carrying bookbags), and lots of people cycled through the snow, down partly cleared roads.

The sky was the colour of ashes. For a few minutes the sun appeared, materializing into a perfectly round but very dim orange, like an old light-bulb that is about to blow. It hung there and then trembled and withdrew into the rags of cloud.

The train was still very noisy. A man was shouting – he wasn't angry, just carrying on a normal conversation. It occurred to me that this is how many prisons must be. The voice of authority was always barking over the loudspeaker, there was always a crush of people, never any privacy. It made travel in China a strange experience for anyone used to silence and privacy.

As we approached Peking, the frozen fields and furrows were emphasized by the snow, and in the coal-yards beside the line men were hacking at coal-piles with picks and shovels. The snow wasn't deep – just a few inches of hard-packed stuff because of the high winds. And then in the distance, through the smoky air, I could see the cranes and derricks of the rising city.

Because it is a flat, dry, northern city, at the edge of Mongolia, Peking has beautiful skies. They are bluest in the freezing air of winter. China's old euphemism for itself was *Tianxia*, 'All beneath the sky' – and, on a good day, what a sky! It was limpid, like an ocean of air, but seamless and unwrinkled, without a single wavelet of cloud; endless uncluttered fathoms of it that grew icier through the day and then at the end of the winter afternoon turned to dust.

Thinking it would be empty I went to see the Great Wall again. Doctor Johnson told Boswell how eager he was to go to China and see the Wall. Boswell was not so sure himself. How could he justify going to China when he had children at home to take care of?

'Sir,' Doctor Johnson said, 'by doing so [going to China] you would do what would be of importance in raising your children to eminence. There would be a lustre reflected upon them from your spirit and curiosity. They would be at all times regarded as the children of a man who had gone to view the wall of China. I am serious, sir.'

The Wall is an intimidating thing, less a fortification than a visual statement announcing imperiously: I am the Son of Heaven and this is the proof that I can encircle the earth. It somewhat resembles, in intention, the sort of achievement of that barmy man who giftwrapped the Golden Gate Bridge. The Wall goes steeply up and down mountainsides. To what purpose? Certainly not to repel invaders, who could never cling to those cliffs. Wasn't it another example of the Chinese love of taking possession of the land and whipping it into shape?

Anyway, it was not empty. It swarmed with tourists. They scampered on it and darkened it like fleas on a dead snake.

That gave me an idea. 'Snake' was very close, but what it actually looked like was a dragon. The dragon is the favourite Chinese creature ('just after man in the hierarchy of living beings') and until fairly recently – eighty or a hundred years ago – the Chinese believed they existed. Many people reported seeing them alive – and of course fossilized dragon skeletons had been unearthed. It was a good omen and, especially, a guardian. The marauding dragon and the dragon-slayer are unknown in China. It is one of China's friendliest and most enduring symbols. And I found a bewitching similarity between the Chinese dragon and the Great Wall of China – the way it flexed and slithered up and down the Mongolian mountains; the way its crenellations looked like the fins on a dragon's back, and its bricks like scales; the way it looked serpentine and protective, undulating endlessly from one end of the world to the other.

On the way back from the Wall I decided to stop at Peking University, where there had been student disruption. The campus was at the edge of the city, in a park-like setting, with pines and little man-made hills and a lovely lake. The lake was frozen. Skinny panting students, with red cheeks and bobbing earflaps, slipped and skated on the ice.

I watched them with an American teacher named Roy who said, 'They *do* have grievances. They want to believe what they read in the papers and hear on the news. At the moment they get it all from the VOA and the BBC. They want to trust their own government – and they don't. They want to believe that the reforms that have begun with Deng are going to continue.'

There were three theories to explain the sudden student

discontent. One: that as Roy said the students really did have grievances. Two: that the government was divided and the students were being used by the liberal elements to test the conservatives. Three: that the disruptions were the work of conservative elements who wanted to discredit the liberals.

I was persuaded that the students had demonstrated on their own initiative. Their grievances were genuine but muddled.

'They were really frightened,' Roy said. 'They didn't think they'd be arrested, but some were. They didn't think the police would push them around – but the police beat some of them and abused others. They know that if it happens again they will be arrested and not released. That scares them. It means they'll be kicked out of the university.'

'The right to demonstrate is written into the constitution,' I said.

'Sure, but it requires five days' notice, and the students have to submit their names in advance,' Roy said. 'So the government will know exactly who the ringleaders are.'

The students were going around and around on the ice, shrieking and skidding.

'There won't be any more demonstrations,' Roy said. 'They're too scared. But it was interesting. They tested their freedoms and discovered they didn't have any.'

The students would not tell me their names – well, who could blame them for being suspicious? They stood on the ice of Weiming Hu and became circumspect when I changed the subject from the weather to their discontent.

One boy told me he was 'a small leader'. He said he was a philosophy student and had been in the demonstration as well as its aftermath, when about 500 students had returned to Tian An Men Square and held a vigil from the night of January the first until the early morning of January the second, when the news came of their fellow students' release from police custody.

'Our teachers support us but they are afraid to say so,' he said. 'Officially they are said to condemn us. But the government misreports everything. They said there were 300 students in the first demonstration when there were actually 3,000.'

I said, 'Do you think this repression is an effect of socialist policies?'

'I am not allowed to answer that,' he said. 'But I can tell you that the trouble with a lot of Chinese students is that they don't have a will to power.'

Perhaps he was quoting Nietzsche from his readings in philosophy. And then I asked whether he thought that the students were too frightened, as Roy had said, to hold any more demonstrations.

'There will be more,' he said. 'Many more.'

A moment later he was gone, and I talked with other students. They were jolly frozen-faced youngsters on old floppy skates. To ingratiate myself with them I borrowed a pair of skates and, seeing me fall down and make an ass of myself, they became very friendly. What did I think of China? they asked. How did American students compare with Chinese students? Did I like the food? Could I use chopsticks? What was my favourite city in China? They were goofy and lovable, with crooked teeth and cold white hands. When I asked them whether they had girlfriends they averted their faces and giggled. They did not seem like counter-revolutionaries.

I had repeatedly requested a high-level meeting – that is, a chance to talk with an important government official. In the past my request had done nothing more than make certain people suspicious. What was I doing in China? they demanded to know. They asked for my itinerary. They were suspicious of me. They insisted that I was important and so they peered at me and followed me and stuck me with Mr Fang who did not know that I was still in China. Now I was on my own. I risked asking for a high-level meeting once more, hoping they would not pounce on me. This time it worked: I was to report to Comrade Bai at the well-known Ministry of Truth in Peking where, I was told, I could ask anything I liked.

I had asked a Chinese friend what questions I should put to the official. He said, 'No matter what you ask him you will find his answers in the *People's Daily*.' In other word, the party line.

The taxi driver who took me to the ministry was impressed by the address I had given him. He said, 'Can you meet American officials like this?'

I told him truthfully that I had never met a really high government official in Washington – that I had never got the urge to meet one. It was only in foreign countries that such things seemed important. But the fact was that I had spent nearly all my time talking to people on trains, or farmers, or market traders, or students. I needed to talk to an official.

'What would you ask this official, if you could?'

The driver said, 'About the future.'

'What *about* the future?'

'Will I be all right? Will the reforms continue? Will we have more democracy? What about prices. And' – he started to laugh – 'how can I get a new licence for my taxi?'

I was met by Comrade Bai, a little fellow in a blue Mao suit, with his hair scraped sideways to cover his baldness. He was smiling and anxious, and breathed noisily through his clenched teeth. He led me to a ministry reception room, with big armchairs. And then he went to tell the high official that I had arrived.

Comrade Hu entered with a flourish, gesturing for me to be seated. He was about fifty-odd, square-faced and unsmiling, and wore a grey western-style suit and a dark speckled tie. He was the new Chinese party man, but slightly rumpled, looking rather uncomfortable in the loosely fitting suit, like an amateur actor playing a part.

His English was good and after our opening pleasantries I asked him about the relations between China and the Soviet Union. He said there was trade between the countries, but there were political obstacles – Soviet aid to Vietnam, the Afghanistan business and troops in Mongolia.

'The Soviets make a big mistake in thinking that their kind of socialism can be exported to other countries,' he said. 'It doesn't work.'

'Can Chinese socialism be exported?'

He took this as a hostile question. He said, 'We do not force our ideas on other people.'

I then asked him a roundabout question, mentioning the government's attitude towards recent events.

'You are undoubtedly referring to the disturbances in Peking and elsewhere by students,' he snapped. 'You must be aware that China is in the first stage of socialism – we are just beginning to develop. We are underdeveloped, and we have to proceed very slowly and carefully. In the countryside the reforms have gone smoothly. But in cities much remains to be done.'

'How long will this stage of socialism last?' I asked.

'Until we achieve our target,' he said, and then began reciting statistics, income figures in dollars and *yuan*. But it was meaningless to say that by the year 2000 the per capita income in China would be, say, £600 a year. What about inflation and food prices and the cost of goods and services?

My questions, I could see, antagonized him. I said, 'Does it seem to you that the Chinese people are too impatient for changes to come about?'

'Some are very impatient,' he said. 'Especially the students. What do these students know about democracy? They are speaking in a very abstract way. They don't have any concrete ideas!'

He kept on talking, not merely to patronize the students but also – it seemed to me – to give a long answer in order to prevent me from asking another question. He was still lecturing me about democracy.

'– and in every country there is a strict definition of democracy. You have yours in the United States. We must have ours in China.'

'So you think these students are really dangerous?'

'The demonstrations could get out of hand,' Comrade Hu said. 'They could bring disorder. If there is no control there could be chaos – everyone doing as he likes. That could provide another Cultural Revolution.'

I didn't see the logic in this. Wasn't it the other way around? If the government kept the lid on and the so-called ultra-leftists succeeded in suppressing the students a Cultural Revolution was much more likely. He was using the Cultural Revolution as a frightener. But I got nowhere in trying to pursue this with him. It only made him increasingly snappish.

'You must read more,' he said. 'You must examine our Four Guiding Principles.'

'I have read them,' I said – that particular pamphlet was in the waiting-room of most railway stations, and I had had plenty of opportunity to read it. 'I was going to ask you about that. Guiding principle number four mentions Marxist-Leninism and Mao's Thought.'

His eyes narrowed at me and he was probably muttering, *'You miserable pipsqueak.'*

'I was wondering which of Mao's thoughts seemed especially pertinent today.'

There was misery on his face as he said, 'I can't summarize Mao's thought. It is too subtle and wide-ranging.' But I pressed him and he said, 'His essay "On Practice" is one which contains the essence of his thought, and that is something we can be guided by these days.'

That essay is an argument for action, I found when I read it later. It is about learning by doing; and 'practising' was like a synonym for living, in this down-to-earth approach to running a society. Mao himself seems to sum up the essay when he says, 'All genuine knowledge originates in direct experience.' It was a struggler's motto: action was everything.

'You must remember that China is unique,' Comrade Hu said. 'There is no model for China. We have to solve our problems in our own way.'

I said, 'Do you think it's a problem that China seeks the west's technology but not its ideology or influence?'

'No problem at all,' he said breezily.

'But there have been negative influences in China that have come with the new technology.'

'We have to educate people to make a distinction between what is good and what is bad influence,' he said.

Like executing 10,000 people in the anti-crime campaign: when people saw the red cross on the picture of the dead man's face they would be properly educated.

'What do you think is especially decadent about western culture?' I asked.

'The music of Beethoven is good, and so are many other things,' Comrade Hu said. 'And I don't think drugs or violence are specifically western. They are by-products. We can do without them – and prostitution, too.'

Thinking of what the taxi driver had said, I asked, 'Will the reforms continue to increase or might they diminish?'

'They will continue as they are,' Comrade Hu said. 'We want to keep our open policy. We want trade with the United States to expand. We believe in reform – we want a growth rate of 7 or 8 per cent.'

When we talked further it was clear to me that this man believed that the sole purpose of political reform was producing economic growth. It had nothing to do with enlightenment or people's minds. If liberalization did not yield prosperity he would just put the screws on again.

We talked about travel in China. He asked me about my experiences, and were they favourable? I said yes, indeed, and gave him a few examples from the various trains I had been on.

Comrade Hu said, 'You have been to more places in China than I have.'

'I'm sure that's not true,' I said.

'It's true,' he said. 'I haven't travelled much.'

'Have you been to Urumchi?'

'No.'

'What about Langxiang in Heilongjiang?' It was a logging town I aimed to visit.

'I have never heard of it,' Comrade Hu said.

'Tibet?'

'No.' He looked very uneasy, and then added, 'But I have travelled abroad a great deal.'

He clawed his cuff in an obvious way and consulted his watch, and so I said that I was grateful for his valuable time, but that I had to go. He rose and took me to the door.

'You have interesting views,' I said. 'I am sure people will be fascinated by them.'

'No, no, no,' he said, smiling for the first time since he had entered the room – but it was of course a smile of anxiety and alarm. 'Don't quote me.'

'Not at all?'

'No. This is a private conversation.'

'What about your mention of Mao's essay "On Practice"? I thought that was rather pertinent.'

'Nothing,' he said, blinking hard. 'And don't mention my name.'

You hideous little wimp, I thought. Before he withdrew I asked him for his card. He frowned and hesitated, and then with great reluctance he handed it over.

Comrade Bai said, 'You heard what he said' – how did he know? – 'don't use his name. And don't mention the Ministry of Truth.'

We were walking outside towards my waiting taxi. I said, 'But what he said was interesting. Why doesn't he want me to write it? You know I'm a writer.'

'Yes. You can write it. But just say "A High Chinese Official".'

What was this, the Ming Dynasty, with all the mandarins scurrying around, whispering and doing it with mirrors? He had not said anything bold – he just did not want to exist and be accountable.

'OK,' I said . 'Can I quote you – that you said that?'

'Ha-ha! Better not!'

I changed the names but as you can see I left that part in. What the hell?

14

The International Express to Harbin: Train Number 17

I wanted to see Harbin at its most characteristic: in the middle of winter, frozen solid. It is in the far north-eastern province – part of what used to be called Manchuria. Now it is Heilongjiang, 'Land of the Black Dragon River'. The Russians refer to the river as the Amur. It is one of the disputed frontiers between the two countries, and over the past twenty years has been the scene of armed conflict as well as low farce – the Chinese soldiers provoking incidents by dropping their pants and presenting their bare bums northward, mooning the Soviet border guards.

The train I took was going on to the border town of Manzhouli and then into Siberia to connect with the Trans-Siberian. I took it because it was the quickest way to Harbin, and also because I wanted to see who was continuing into the Soviet Union. In the event I discovered that very few people were crossing the border. It is the most roundabout route to Moscow, and no one ever goes to Vladivostok.

I left Peking on a cold afternoon, the train travelling through a landscape of black and white – trees and light-poles and furrows set into relief by the snow. The countryside looked like a steel engraving, and it grew sharper and fresher, for the dusty snow of

Peking gave way to a snow of intense brightness in the clearer air of the Chinese hinterland. It was exciting to be heading north in the winter, and I intended to keep going, beyond Harbin to the forests in the north of the province. I had been told there was wilderness there – real trees and birds.

Three swarthy Hong Kong Chinese joined me in the compartment. They said they were cold. They wore thick nylon ski-suits which screeched when they walked or moved their arms, and the noise of the rubbing fabric set my teeth on edge. This sleeping-car was all Hong Kongers in screechy ski-suits. They had travelled non-stop from Kowloon. They had never before been to China, had never seen snow; their English was very poor – and yet they were colonial subjects of the British crown. They did not speak Mandarin. Like most Hong Kongers I had met they were complete provincials, with laughable pretensions. Was it the effect of colonialism? They were well fed and rather silly and politically naive. In some ways Hong Kong was somewhat like Britain itself: a bunch of offshore islands with an immigrant problem, a language barrier and a rigid class-system.

'Going skiing?' I said.

They said no – they had picked these ski-suits up at a cut-price department store in Causeway Bay.

They were looking out of the window at a fat woolly sheep which was nibbling at a hank of brown stubble it had found sticking out of the snow. The sheep glanced up and stared back at them.

What did they think of China so far?

'It's thirty years behind,' one said. This from a person who lived in one of the last colonies on earth. In a political sense Hong Kong had hardly changed since the time of the Opium Wars.

'Thirty years behind what?' I asked.

He shrugged. It was probably something he had read.

'Do you think there's any difference between a Chinese person here and one from Hong Kong?'

'Oh, yes!' several of them said at once, and they were incredulous that I should ask such an ignorant question. But I pressed forward none the less.

'Can you recognize a Hong Kong person when you see one?'

'Very easily.'

'And a person from the People's Republic?'

'Yes,' he said, and when I asked for details he went on, 'The Chinese here have rough faces.'

'What sort of faces do Hong Kong people have?'

'Gentle.'

He said the ways they talked and dressed were all dead give-aways. Well, even I knew that. The Hong Kongers were either overweight or else stylishly skinny. They yelled a lot and wore brand-new clothes and trendy eye-glasses. They fancied themselves up-to-date, and they believed in the myth of their modernity. They were often all elbows, very impatient and demanding. They fussed over each other; they were philistines. A great number of their traits were the result of being British colonials. The colonial system really is paternal in an almost literal way. By treating the people like children it turns into a messy family, and some of the children are favoured, others become spoiled brats, and still others delinquents and rebels.

I did not bore my compartment-mates with this reflection. I simply sat there wondering why they didn't take off their ski-suits.

One of them was engrossed in a palmist's manual. Before dinner, he read my palm.

'That is your star line,' he said. 'Notice it is connected? You are very emotional. That is your life line. You will live to be about eighty or eighty-five.'

'Tell me more.'

'I cannot,' he said. 'I am only on chapter five.' And he went back to his manual.

Dinner in the big steamy dining-car was a noisy affair. At first it was full of Hong Kongers, but they hated the food, found it uneatable, and left in a huff. There were about forty of them altogether on the train. They screeched back to their compartments and stuffed themselves with chocolate cookies.

Their mistake had been in ordering the expensive twenty *yuan* meal. The one for ten was better – no bony fish, no fatty pork, no canned spam; just vegetables and soup. I liked the mob, the nagging waiters, the spilled food, the people stuffing themselves. It seemed like chaos, but really a strict routine was being observed: the progress of the courses could not be interrupted. Most waiters on trains had a sort of surly friendliness. They weren't ill-natured, merely bad-tempered because they worked so hard. They were not servile, they weren't hustling for tips – there weren't any; they were single-minded and offhand without being actually rude. If someone barked at them they barked back.

We stopped at Shenyang and Changchun in the night, and I woke because of the cold and the noise. The attendant had given me a quilted bedroll and a horse-blanket, and yet the train was very draughty. There was snow tracked into the corridor and thick frost on all the windows. When I pissed into the Chinese toilet, which was just a hole in the floor of the train, a great gust of steam shot up, as if I had pissed on a hot stove.

The young men from Hong Kong shivered in the compartment like prisoners in a dungeon. They drank hot water. I offered them some of my green tea (Zhulan brand: *A tea from ancient kings for those with kingly tastes*) but they said no; they preferred drinking hot water. 'White tea,' the Chinese call it; *bai cha.*

At 5.30 in the morning the door banged open and the attendant came in, put down a thermos of water and yelled, 'Get up. Time for breakfast.'

When she had gone I switched off the light and crawled into bed again.

She returned a few minutes later.

'Who turned off that light?' she demanded, switching it on. She stood in the doorway, breathing hard – steam was coming out of her nose and mouth. 'I want the bedding. Now hand it over!'

But the young men from Hong Kong were too cold to surrender it, and I saw no reason to – we weren't due at Harbin for four more hours. It was the usual rigmarole: they wanted to have everything folded and accounted for long before we arrived.

'They need the bedding,' one of the young men said.

'Maybe she wants to wash it,' another said.

'No,' the third one said. Were they talking in English for my benefit or did they normally converse in this almost incomprehensible way (*Dey nee da baydeen*, and so forth)? He explained, 'A Chinese guy told me they only wash it every fourth day, even if four different people use it.'

Later I enquired about this and found it to be a fact. That was why they were so finicky about giving every passenger a clean towel to place over the pillow.

The train attendant came back several more times and eventually just snatched the bedding in the usual way. It struck me that these attendants – usually women – would have made wonderful matrons at English boarding-schools. They were bossy, they were nags, they were know-it-alls; they had piercing voices and no sense of humour; they were inflexible about the rules. They were more than tough – they were indestructible. They kept the trains running.

It was not yet dawn in Heilongjiang, but people were hurrying through the darkness, along snowy paths. I saw about fifty black figures moving through the snow, all bundled up and roly-poly. They were big and small, going to work and to school.

When the sun came up – fire crackling through frost – the sky was clear and the snow a pale northern blue. People cycled through the snow and ice on the uncleared roads and men drove wagons pulled by shaggy horses. The great flat snowfields all had stubble showing through. That was the main difference between this province and Siberia, which was just next door (we were farther north than Vladivostok). This was all farmland, and Siberia was mostly forest and uncleared land. The trip to Harbin was essentially a trip across ploughed fields. The snow was not deep enough to hide the furrows.

In some villages and little towns the houses had the look of Russian bungalows. And their most un-Chinese feature (as peasant huts) was the steeply pitched roof, because of the snow. Some of them were big brick houses with fat chimneys, like old American homesteads, and others were the sort of snug bungalows that I had seen along the route of the Trans-Siberian, made out of wood, and with stove-pipes sticking from the eaves. Not much smoke was coming out of these chimneys. The reason was pretty simple. The frugal Chinese, even in this freezing place, always skimp on fuel, and take a certain pleasure in living in a cold house. Why waste coal, they say, when all you really need is another set of long underwear?

*

In this land of red, wind-chafed cheeks and runny noses, Harbin seemed an unlikely city. It looked Russian (onion-domed churches, villas with turrets and gables, office blocks with pompous colonnades), and it had that strange fossilized appearance that cities have in very cold countries – a sort of dead and petrified shabbiness. Its Russian ornateness was overlaid with soot and frozen slush. Here and there was a Japanese roof or a Chinese ministry or statue – mostly monstrosities, which added to the weirdness of the place, because in addition to their odd proportions, they were also hung with long, gnarled icicles. I liked the city best in the early morning, when it glittered with frost – little prismatic pinpoints on its ugly face.

It was not much more than 100 years old. It was a fishing village on the Songhua river that had been turned by the Russian tsar into a railway junction when he extracted permission from the decadent Qing Dynasty in the eighteen-nineties to make a short cut through Manchuria to Vladivostok. The city went on rising and the various railway lines running after the Russo-Japanese War (1904), and the Russian Revolution. The greedy Japanese presence was powerful – they had planned to take over Asia, beginning here – but their puppet state of Manchukuo lasted only from 1931 until 1945, when the Russians reasserted themselves after the Second World War. Harbin's boast had always been that it was only nine days, by train, from Paris, so it got the fashions and the music and the latest papers long before Shanghai. The striptease and the charleston and dixieland jazz were introduced to China in Harbin in the nineteen-twenties because of the Trans-Siberian link with Paris.

Times had changed. Harbin's sister-city was now Edmonton, Alberta. You guessed that somehow, when you looked at Harbin. There was something in its severity and its dark and funless nights that resembled a remote city in Canada.

And yet in Canada people joke and gloat about the cold. In Harbin and in Heilongjiang in general no one mentioned it except outsiders, who never stopped talking about it. I bought a thermometer so that I would not bore people by asking them the temperature, but the damn thing only registered to the freezing point – zero Centigrade. The first time I put it outside the red liquid in the tube plunged into the bulb and shrivelled into a tiny bead. So I had to ask. It was mid morning: minus twenty-nine Centigrade in the sparkling sunshine. By night-time it would be ten degrees colder than that – so cold in more familiar figures of Fahrenheit that I didn't want to think about it.

I wore mittens and long underwear and thermal boots and a hat with earflaps and two sweaters under my leather jacket. One overcast day of paralysing cold I wore more than that, put on all the clothes I had with me: I turned myself into a big padded and bulging fool, and yet I was still so cold I had to rush inside occasionally and jump up and down. The Chinese were well wrapped up, and some wore face masks, but on their feet many wore no more than corduroy rubber-soled slippers. Why didn't their feet fall off? They were enthusiasts for heavy knitted underwear that gave them elephantine legs, which contrasted oddly with their skinny frost-bitten faces.

They didn't wash, for many reasons, the main one being that they did not have hot water or bathrooms. It hardly mattered; stinks are seldom obvious in icy northern lands. They did not take their clothes off, even indoors – neither their hats nor coats, even when they ate. It was easy to see why. The heating was turned to an absolute minimum – the Maoist doctrine of saving fuel and regarding heating and lighting as luxuries except where they affected production of something like pig-iron or cotton cloth. This constant coat- and hat-wearing, inside and out, had given them some very bad habits. The worst was that they never seemed to close doors, and wherever you went there was a door ajar and a wind like a knife coursing through it.

My hotel was so cold I always wore three or four layers of clothes. It was called the Swan – I thought of it as the Frozen Swan. It had a rock garden and an ornamental pool in the lobby, but the lobby was so cold the fish had died and the plants were stiff and brown. Manchus and Hans sat in thick coats and fur hats on the lobby sofas, smoking and yelling. I was told there was a warmer hotel in Harbin, called the International, but it did not seem to matter to anyone in Heilongjiang whether a hotel was heated or not. The great boast of the hotels was their cuisine and they vied with each other in offering grilled bear's paw, stewed moose nose with mushroom, Mongolian hot-pot, white fungus soup and monkey-leg mushrooms and pheasant shashlik.

I arrived on Christmas Eve – the Russian Orthodox Christmas Eve, at the end of the first week in January. I went to one of the churches, where a shivering moustached man – possibly Russian; he was certainly not Chinese – was draping pine boughs upon the holy pictures and the statues. The interior of the church was sorry-looking and very cold. The next day there was a Christmas service; twenty people chanted, sang and lit candles. They were all Russians and most of them were old women. They had the furtive look of Early Christians, but it was obvious that no one persecuted them. They went about the Christmas service in a morose way and wouldn't talk to me afterward – just crunched away in the icy snow.

Even in January most events take place in the open air. The market is outdoors in the thirty-below temperatures. People shopped, bought frozen food (melons, meat, bread) and licked ice cream. That was the most popular snack in Harbin – vanilla ice cream. And the second most popular were small cherry-sized 'haws' (hawthorn berries) which they coated with red goo and jammed on twigs. The market traders were cheery souls with rags wound around their faces and wearing mittens and fur hats. It went without saying that they spent the whole day outside, and when they saw me they cackled and called out, 'Hey, old-hair!'

It was the Harbin expression for light-haired foreigners (*lao mao zi*), because old people are associated with light-coloured hair. In this regard they have a special phrase for Russians, 'second-class light-hairs' (*er mao zi*), which is intended as a term of disrespect.

A few days after I arrived, the Harbin Winter Festival opened. It was a gimmick to attract tourists to this refrigerator, but it was a good gimmick. Most of it was an exhibition of ice sculpture. The Chinese expression *bing deng* is more accurate; it means 'ice lanterns' and these ice sculptures usually had electric lights frozen inside them.

The whole city of Harbin was involved in it. A sculptor would stack blocks of ice around a lamp-post and then chip away and shave the ice until it resembled a pagoda or a rocket ship or a human being. There was an ice sculpture on every street corner – lions, elephants, aeroplanes, acrobats, bridges; some of them were thirty or forty feet high. But the most ambitious ones were in the People's Park – there were eighty acres of them. Not only a Great Wall of China in ice, but a smaller version of the Taj Mahal, a two-storey Chinese pavilion, an enormous car, a platoon of soldiers, an Eiffel Tower, and about forty more displays, all cut out of ice blocks in which fluorescent tubes had been frozen. Because of the lights these ice sculptures had to be seen at night, when it was nearly forty below. But no one minded. They shuffled around, they slipped and fell, they ate ice cream and goggled at these wonderful examples of deep-frozen kitsch.

'The Russians introduced these ice sculptures,' a Japanese man told me. 'This is not an ancient Chinese art. But the Chinese liked them and developed the knack of making them. And it was their idea to put lights inside them.'

Mr Morioka in his tam-o'-shanter and miracle fibres had taken a sentimental journey back to Harbin. He said you had to come to Harbin in the winter to see it as it really is. The pity was that so few foreigners dared to visit in the winter months.

I said it might have something to do with the stupefying cold.

'Oh yes!' he said. 'I was here in the thirties. I was a student. This was a wonderful place – full of Russian nobility who had no money. Some of them brought jewels and sold them here to keep themselves going. A few lived in style, in those villas that you see in town. But most of the Russians were poverty-stricken emigrés. It was a Japanese city.'

We were strolling through the ice sculptures; through an ice tunnel, down the main street of an ice village, past a pair of ice lions.

Mr Morioka said, 'As you pined for Paris we pined for Harbin.'

'We pined for sex and romance in Paris,' I said.

'What do you think we had in Harbin? We had strippers, night-clubs, Paris fashions, the latest styles – books, songs, everything. This was like Europe to us. That's why our boys used to yearn for the bright lights of Harbin.'

That seemed a very unusual way of describing this Chinese refrigerator, but of course he was talking about Manchukuo, Land of the Manchus, owned and operated by the Sons of Nippon.

'The strippers were Russian. That was the attraction. Some of them had been very grand, but they were down on their luck. So they danced and they performed in the cabaret –'

And as he spoke I could see a roomful of libidinous Japanese with their mouths open, transfixed by a wobbling pair of Russian knockers.

'– and you know, Russian women are very beautiful until they are about thirty or so,' Mr Morioka said. 'These were fine women. Very lovely. I tell you, some of these women were aristocrats. I remember one cabaret singer telling me how she had gone to great parties and fancy balls in country houses in Russia.'

This was an interesting story from the old world, even though it did stink of exploitation. He said that in a Harbin night-club there would be 80 per cent Japanese and 20 per cent rich Chinese. 'Almost no Russians,' he said. 'They couldn't afford it. In Shanghai in the thirties it was fifty-fifty, Japanese and Chinese.'

I wanted to talk to him a bit more, but my feet were so cold I was seriously worried about frost-bite. I apologized and said I had to get out of this park and into a warmer place.

'There isn't much more to tell,' he said. 'It all ended in August 1945, when the Japanese front collapsed. Russian soldiers who had all been criminals and prisoners were unmerciful. They took this city and began raping and murdering. That's another story!'

There were more ice carvings and ice monuments at Stalin Park on the riverbank – walls, fences, lions, turrets, and especially slides and sluices down which people rocketed in sleds on to the Songhua river. There were ice boats with sails and runners, and horse-drawn sleighs. Not many takers – no one had money. But there were plenty of people bruising their ankles on the ice-block helter-skelter.

That made me think that of all the foreign companies that might soon start up in China the unlikeliest was an insurance company. I thought: Who would insure these people? I saw a man skidding at the ice sculptures. He slipped and cracked his head and was dragged into the snow, where he remained inert. It was a country of bare wires and pot-holes. Tourists have been known to disappear down lift shafts and the claims by tourists against the China International Travel Service for injuries, missed cities or sickness are astronomical. The average Chinese factory is a death trap, and yet the Chinese blithely escort visitors through them and past machines that snatch at your hair and poke you in the eye, past gaping holes in the floor and pools of toxic substances and crackling furnaces. Hard hats are not common and few welders I saw wore masks.

My hotel was very cold but very hospitable. It was so friendly it actually aroused my suspicions – like the man who is such a glad-hander you suspect he is picking your pocket. I was on the eleventh floor. WELCOME TO OUR FLOOR! the signs said. That was very unusual. GOOD HEALTH! more said. And many said PROSPERITY AND LONG LIFE!

I asked the floor attendant what was up. He just grinned and said, 'Welcome to our floor!'

'Why are you welcoming me to your floor?'

'I want you to be happy.'

'No one has ever welcomed me to their floor in China,' I said.

'It is a very good floor.'

His insistence in his squawking voice only made me anxious, and so I looked deeper into this and discovered that the previous year there had been a terrible fire in the hotel in which two people died. The eleventh floor had been burned out. The man who had started it was an American businessman. He was said to have been smoking in bed. He was detained by the Chinese and – so I was told – he was confined to a hotel for quite a while, because his company refused to pay the $70,000 damages that the Chinese demanded. And yet no security precautions were taken after the fire. No fire stairs, no smoke detectors, no fire-proof furnishings. All the Chinese had done was print hundreds of cardboard signs to be placed in every hotel room. The sign said: DO NOT SMOKE IN BED.

One day in Harbin I met a Canadian who surprised me by saying that he was delighted to be here. His name was Scotty. He was of course from Edmonton, Alberta, the sister-city.

'But I'm the only Edmontonian here,' he said.

He was a stout and good-humoured man and this was his first time in China. He could hardly believe the notoriety it had given him. He had been to a banquet with the governor and he had met many high party officials in the province. He was the superintendant of a steel forge, on a two-year assignment, and was perhaps on the verge of believing in his importance to the future of Chinese industry. 'It's hard to describe,' he said. 'But I'm a kind of unofficial celebrity.'

'I hope it lasts,' I said, because the Chinese were known to be rather brisk with foreigners they no longer needed. The philosophy of learning from foreigners was spelled out in the nineteenth century by Feng Gulfen. Feng was an adviser to statesmen, a teacher and an advocate of reform. He regarded all foreigners as barbarians but said it was necessary to use them to learn various mechanical skills (shipbuilding and gunsmithing in particular). 'A few barbarians should be employed,' he said, 'and Chinese who are good in using their minds should be selected to receive instruction so that in turn they may teach many craftsmen.' He went on to say, 'We should use the instruments of the barbarians, but not adopt the ways of the barbarians. We should use them so that we can repel them.' These are to a large extent the sentiments of the Chinese government today and the reason for the large number of so-called foreign experts in China. A foreign expert is a barbarian with a skill to impart, but should never make the mistake of believing that he is being invited to stay for an indefinite length of time. They are in China to be used, and when they are no longer useful, to be sent home.

I asked Scotty whether he got homesick. He said he had only been in Harbin four months – not long enough.

'My wife misses grocery shopping and she hates her kitchen,' he said. 'Me? I miss beef. There's no beef here.'

I had not noticed that, but then you usually had to be told what was in a Chinese dish. The Chinese had a way of drawing a culinary veil over even the most obvious ingredients.

'How is your steel forge?' I asked.

'Old-fashioned,' Scotty said. 'So I have to be tough. I'll tell you frankly – I'm cruel. I have to be, to get the quality up. Take today. What did I do? I rejected a whole order. It was worth $20,000 US. Hey, it worried them!'

'Why did you reject the order?'

Scotty became suddenly very enthusiastic about his work and as he talked about forging steel I was convinced that he was the perfect man to send to China – a hard-hat with a mission. He didn't seem the sort of person who suffered fools gladly. If they called him a barbarian I was sure he would return the compliment.

'Every piece of steel has to have a heat number stamped on it. These didn't have a heat number. I just sent them back and said no.' He smiled mischievously and added,'I'll accept the order eventually, when we get the number on it. But they don't know that. That's my secret. Let them stew for a while. Let them think about the foul-up.'

'Was it important, this steel?'

'Sure!' he said. 'Buncha pipe flanges!'

We talked about pipe flanges for a while. It is true that there is not much about pipe flanges to bewitch the imagination and yet we were in one of the downtown hotels where it was warm. When it is minus thirty-eight Centigrade outside it can be counted a pleasant experience to stand in a warm place talking with a fat Canadian about pipe flanges.

All this time in Harbin I was trying to make arrangements to go farther north into the greater desolation of Heilongjiang. I had not known that my destination, Langxiang, was closed to foreigners. But I prevailed upon the Chinese. I said I would behave myself and would not stay long. They said they would consider my request.

While I waited I rummaged in the shops. I bought a pair of gloves, but not a fur hat. Such lovely furs (ermine, sable, fox, mink); such hideous hats and coats. And how awful for a stag to be killed so that its noble forking antlers could be made into buttons for auntie's old coat. I found an ivory object at the Harbin Antiquities Store. 'It is an ancient carving,' the clerk said. 'Of the earth.'

'Impossible.'

How did I know it could not be an ancient Chinese carving of the round earth? Elementary. Until about 1850 the Chinese believed the earth was flat.

It was a pre-war Russian billiard ball, but I bought it just the same.

15

The Slow Train to Langxiang: Number 295

'Is it cold outside?' I asked.

'Very,' said Mr Tian. His eye-glasses were opaque with frost.

It was 5.30 on a Harbin morning, the temperature at minus thirty-five Centigrade and a light snow falling – little grains like seed-pearls sifting down in the dark. When the flurry stopped the wind picked up, and it was murderous. Full on my face it was like being slashed with a razor. We were on our way to the railway station.

'And you insist on coming with me?' I asked.

'Langxiang is forbidden,' Mr Tian said. 'So I must.'

'It is the Chinese way,' I said.

'Very much so,' he replied.

In this darkness groups of huddled people waited in the empty street for buses. That seemed a grim pastime, a long wait at a Harbin bus-stop in winter. And, by the way, the buses were not heated. In his aggrieved account of his Chinese residence, the journalist Tiziano Terzani, writing about Heilongjiang ('The Kingdom of the Rats'), quotes a French traveller who said: 'Although it is uncertain where God placed paradise, we can be sure that he chose some other place than this.'

The wind dropped but the cold remained. It banged against my forehead and twisted my fingers and toes; it burned my lips. I felt like Sam McGee. I entered the station waiting-room and a chill rolled against me, as if my face had been pressed on a cold slab. The waiting-room was unheated. I asked Mr Tian how he felt about this.

'Heat is bad,' he said. 'Heat makes you sleepy and slow.'

'I like it,' I said.

Mr Tian said, 'I once went to Canton. It was so hot I felt sick.'

Mr Tian was twenty-seven, a graduate of Harbin University. There was humour in the way he moved. He was self-assured. He didn't fuss. He was patient. He was frank. I liked him for these qualities. The fact that he was incompetent did not matter very much. Langxiang was a day's journey by train – north, into the snow. He seemed an easy companion and I did not think he would get in my way.

He had no bag. He may have had a toothbrush in his pocket, where he kept his woolly cap and his misshapen gloves. He was completely portable, without any impedimenta. He was an extreme example of Chinese austerity. He slept in his long johns and wore his coat to meals. He rarely washed. Being Chinese he did not have to shave. He seemed to have no possessions at all. He was like a desert Bedouin. This fascinated me, too.

The loudspeakers in the waiting-room were broadcasting the dragon voice of the Peking harridan who gave the news every morning. In China the news always seemed a peculiar form of nagging.

'You are listening to that?' Mr Tian enquired.

'Yes, but I can't make it out.'

'"We must absolutely not allow a handful of people to sabotage production,"' Mr Tian translated the duckspeak from the broadcast.

The announcer was reading a front-page editorial from the *Workers' Daily*. It was the first public acknowledgement that the Chinese Communist Party condemned the student demonstrations. There were other people in the waiting-room but they were talking among themselves instead of listening. They were warmly dressed, in fur hats, wearing mittens and boots. They smoked heavily and from time to time got up to use the spittoon which was the centrepiece of the railway waiting-room.

The shrewish voice was still blaring from the loudspeaker, and Mr Tian blandly helped me to understand it.

'Bourgeois liberalism has been rampant for several years. It is a poison in some people's minds. Some people make trips abroad and say capitalism is good, and paint a dark picture of socialism.'

I said, 'Mr Tian, is anyone else listening to this?'

'No,' he said, and watched a man dribbling saliva on to the floor and scuffing it with his felt boot. 'They are occupied with other matters.'

'Demonstrations have been held in a number of cities,' the voice nagged. 'They are unpatriotic, unlawful, disorderly and destructive. In some cases they have been provoked by foreign elements. They must cease. The Chinese people will not stand by and let lawless students take over. Bourgeois liberalization is something that must be stamped out –'

It went on and on, at such length that it was clear that the government was very worried. The broadcast was full of thinly veiled threats of retribution.

I said, 'What do you think of the demonstrations, Mr Tian?'

'I think they are good,' he said, nodding quietly.

'But the government has condemned them. Don't you think they represent bourgeois liberalism and poisonous influences?'

He shook his head and smiled. His hair stuck up like a roadrunner's. He said, 'These demonstrations show how the Chinese people are thinking.'

'But it's just students,' I said, still playing devil's advocate.

'In some cases there were factory workers,' he said. 'In Shanghai, for example.'

'Some people think that these demonstrations might lead to a conflict between capitalism and communism.'

'We will choose what is best for us,' he said. He had become a trifle enigmatic.

I said, 'Do you ever suspect that you might be a secret capitalist-roader?'

'There is a good and a bad side to everything,' he said.

He did not smile, which was why I suspected him of being

humorous. He could be very mysterious. In other respects he was totally ineffectual. 'Do you want me to do anything?' he would say, but when I made a suggestion – get a ticket, make a phone call, establish a fact – he invariably failed. And yet he went on offering to help me.

The train pulled in, steaming and gasping, just as the sun came up. It had come from Dalian, 600 miles away, and it stopped everywhere. So it was sensationally littered with garbage – peanut shells, apple cores, chewed chicken bones, orange peel and greasy paper. It was very dirty and it was so cold inside that the spit had frozen on the floor into misshapen yellow-green medallions of ice. The covering between each coach was a snow tunnel, the frost on the windows was an inch thick, the doors had no locks and so they banged and thumped as a freezing draught rushed through the carriages. It was the Heilongjiang experience: I crept in out of the cold and inside I felt even colder. I found a small space and sat hunched over like everyone else, with my hat and gloves on. I was reading Lermontov's *A Hero of Our Time* and I scribbled on the flyleaf:

> In the provinces every train is like a troop train. This is like one returning from the front, with the sick and wounded.

Even with three pairs of socks and thermal-lined boots my feet were cold; nor did I feel particularly cosy in my heavy sweater, Mongolian sheepskin vest and leather coat. I felt like an idiot in my hat and fleece-lined mittens, but it annoyed me that I was still cold, or at least not warm. How I longed for the summer trains of the south and the sweltering trip on the Iron Rooster when I had lounged in my blue pyjamas.

Mr Tian said, 'You come from which city in the States?'

'Near Boston.'

'Lexington is near Boston,' Mr Tian said.

'How did you know that?'

'I studied American history in middle school. All Chinese study it.'

'So you know about our war of liberation, Mr Tian?'

'Yes. There was also a Paul who was very important.'

'Paul Revere.'

'Exactly,' Mr Tian said. 'He told the peasants that the British were coming.'

'Not just the peasants. He told everyone – the peasants, the landlords, the capitalist-roaders, the stinking ninth category of intellectuals, the minorities and the slaves.'

'I think you're joking, especially about the slaves.'

'No. Some of the slaves fought on the British side. They were promised their freedom if the British won. After the British surrendered these blacks were sent to Canada.'

'I didn't read about that,' Mr Tian said, as the door blew open.

'I'm cold,' I said.

'I'm too hot,' Mr Tian said.

The cold put me to sleep. I was wakened later by Mr Tian who asked me whether I wanted to have breakfast. I thought some food might warm me up so I said yes.

There was frost on the dining-car windows, ice on the dining-car floor, and a bottle of water on my table had frozen and burst. My fingers were too cold to hold any chopsticks. I hunched over with my hands up my sleeves.

'What food do they have?' I asked.

'I don't know.'

'Do you want noodles?' I asked.

'Anything but noodles,' Mr Tian said.

The waiter brought us cold noodles, cold pickled onions, diced spam which looked like a shredded beach toy, and cold but very tasty black fungus – a speciality of the province. Mr Tian ate his noodles. It was the Chinese way. Even if it was not to your taste, when there was nothing else on the menu you ate it.

'What is that music?' I asked. A tune was playing over the train's loudspeaker. I had heard it before, on other trains.

'It is called "The Fifteenth Moon",' Mr Tian said.

I asked him to explain the incomprehensible words. It was about a soldier who was fighting on the Vietnamese border – just south of where I had taken the train in Yunnan. The soldier was married but his wife was not with him. And yet the soldier thought about his wife a great deal and realized that he was fighting for her – he was triumphant and heroic, because she inspired him. That was a change. A few years ago he would have been fighting for Chairman Mao. It made a little more sense to fight for your spouse and resembled 'Keep The Home Fires Burning'.

'I like this song, but I don't like Chinese music,' Mr Tian said.

'What do you like?' I asked, abandoning my chopsticks and eating the black fungus with my fingers.

'Beethoven. The Ninth Symphony. And I like this.'

Mr Tian opened his mouth and a crow-like complaining came out of it.

> Ah goon Scamba Fey!
> Party say roomee tie!
> Renmanbee da warn hoo-day . . .

'The tune's familiar,' I said. But I could not place it. He was staring at me, challenging me to remember. I said, 'I give up.'

After a while he told me that it was 'Scarborough Fair', sung by his favourite musicians, Simon and Garfunkle. They were very popular at Harbin University and 'Bridge Over Troubled Water' was a much-coveted tape.

After several hours of crossing flat snowfields this train entered a mountainous region. The settlements were small – three or four short rows of bungalows, some of brick and some of mud and logs. They were the simplest slant-roofed dwellings and looked like the sort of houses that children draw in the first form, with a narrow door and a single window and a blunt chimney with a screw of smoke coming out of it.

The toilet on the train looked as though a child had designed it, too. It was a hole in the floor about a foot across. Well, I had seen squat toilets before; but this one was travelling at about fifty miles an hour through the ice and snow of northern China. There was no pipe or baffle. If you looked down it you saw ice streaking past. A gust of freezing air rushed out of the hole. Anyone fool enough to use this thing would be frost-bitten on a part of the body that is seldom frost-bitten. And yet the passengers trooped into this refrigerated bum-freezer. When they came out their eyes were tiny and their teeth were clenched, as though they had just been pinched very hard.

'People ski here,' Mr Tian said at the town of Taoshan, where we arrived at noon. Some passengers got off. They looked like lumberjacks, not skiers. But there were white mountains to the north-west, and the most Siberian touch of all, groves of silver birches.

The train grew colder. What was the point in heating it if it kept stopping and opening its doors? That was the Chinese argument. The same went for the toilet. If a toilet was a hole in the floor with freezing air pouring into the room, there was no point heating the room. If you couldn't heat a room efficiently there was no point heating it at all. That was why the people in this region never took off their long underwear, and why they ate wearing their fur hats.

I was rigid in my seat, reading *A Hero of Our Time* with my mittens on, and turning the pages with my nose. Perhaps the Chinese were thinking, So that's what they do with those long noses! In spite of the shortness of this book I had never finished reading it. I had started it many times. But the hero, Pechorin, is a sort of romantic punk with a death-wish, and the story is told in fits and starts. I came across one of Pechorin's characteristic opinions as we rode along:

> I confess I have a strong prejudice against people who are blind, one-eyed, deaf, mute, legless, armless, hunchbacked, and so forth. I have observed that there always exists some strange relationship between the appearance of a man and his soul, as if with the loss of a limb, the soul lost one of its senses.

This was nonsense. The opposite seemed to me much more likely, that the soul gained a new sense with the loss of a limb, or blindness, deafness or whatever. In H. G. Wells's story *The Country of the Blind* it is the sighted man who is truly handicapped. I was also struck by this passage in the book because there were cripples on the train, and I thought of it again in Langxiang where I met a hunchback who had built his own house, all by himself, and fitted it so that he could carry on his two jobs as a radio repairman and a studio photographer.

We were still jogging along, stopping frequently. And the doors opened and closed with the same pneumatic gasp as those on a refrigerator, each time producing a cold blast through the coach. I hated having to get up, because when I sat down again my seat froze me.

It surprised me to see children standing outside their houses, watching the train go by. They wore thin jackets, no hats or gloves. Many of them had bright red cheeks. They had spiky unwashed hair and they wore cloth slippers. They looked very hardy, and they yelled at the train as it passed their ice-bound villages.

The mountains in the distance were the southernmost peaks of the Lesser Khingan Range, and the foreground was all forest. Most of these settlements were simply overgrown lumber-camps. One of the centres of logging activity is Langxiang. But I had also chosen it because it has a narrow gauge railway which goes deep into the forest and carries logs back to town to be milled.

It was hardly a town. It was a sprawling one-storey village with an immense lumber-yard at its centre and a main street where people with scarves wrapped around their faces stood all day in the cold selling meat and vegetables. One day in Langxiang I saw a man standing behind a square of cloth which held six frozen rats and a stack of rats' tails. Were things so bad in Langxiang that they ate rats and rats' tails?

'Do you eat these?' I asked.

'No, no,' came the muffled voice through the frosted scarf. 'I sell medicine.'

'These rats are medicine?'

'No, no!' The man's skin was almost black from the cold and the dry air.

And then he began speaking again, but I had no idea what he was saying in this local dialect. As he spoke the ice crystals thawed on his scarf.

Mr Tian said, 'He doesn't sell rats. He sells rat poison. He shows these dead rats as proof that his poison is good.'

We had arrived at Langxiang in the middle of the afternoon, just as it was growing dark. This was a northern latitude in winter: night came early. I stepped from the cold train on to the freezing platform, and then we went to the guesthouse, which was also cold – but the clammy indoor cold which I found harder to bear than the icy outdoors. With curtains over the windows and the lights dim it was like being in an underground tomb.

'It's very cold in here,' I said to Mr Cong, the manager.

'It will get warmer.'

'When?'

'In three or four months.'

'I mean, in the hotel,' I said.

'Yes. In the hotel. And all over Langxiang.'

I was jumping up and down to restore my circulation. Mr Tian was simply standing patiently.

'What about a room?' I said.

He said something very rapidly to Mr Cong.

'Do you want a clean room or a regular one?' Mr Tian asked.

'I think I'll have a clean one for a change.'

He did not remark on my sarcasm. He said, 'Ah, a clean one,' and shook his head, as if this was a tall order. 'Then you will have to wait.'

The wind blew through the lobby and when it hit the curtain that had been hung across the main door it filled it like a spinnaker.

'We can have dinner,' Mr Cong said.

'It's not even five o'clock,' I said.

'Five o'clock. Dinnertime. Ha-ha!' This ha-ha meant: *Rules are rules. I don't make them, so you should not be difficult.*

The dining-room in the Langxiang Guesthouse was the coldest room I had entered so far in the whole of Heilongjiang Province. I yanked my hat tight and then sat on my hands and shivered. I had put my thermometer on the table: thirty-six degrees Fahrenheit.

Mr Cong said he was used to the cold. He was not even wearing a hat! He was from the far north, where he had gone as a settler in the fifties to work on a commune which produced corn and grain. Although he was not very old, he was something of an antique in Chinese terms. As a commune worker in one of the remotest parts of China the new reforms were bewildering to him. And he had four children, now regarded as a shameful number. 'They punish us for having more than two,' he said, and seemed very puzzled. 'You might lose your job, or be transferred, as punishment.'

From the utter boredom on Mr Tian's face – but his boredom was a form of serenity – I could tell that Mr Cong and Mr Tian had nothing at all in common. In China, the generation gap has a specific meaning and is something to be reckoned with.

I asked Mr Cong what had happened to his commune.

'It was cancelled,' he said. 'It was dissolved.'

'Did the peasants go away?'

'No. Each was given his own plot to till.'

'Do you think that's better?'

'Of course,' he said, but it was impossible for me to tell whether he meant it. 'Production is much greater. The yields are larger.'

That seemed to settle it. Any policy that increased production was a good thing. I thought: God help China if there's a recession.

The town was in darkness. The hotel was very cold. My room was cold. What to do? Although it was only 6.30 I went to bed – anyway, I got inside with most of my clothes on, and I listened to my short-wave radio under the blankets. That was how I was to spend all of my nights in Langxiang.

I went up the logging line on the narrow gauge railway the next day, but I was disappointed in the forest. I had expected wilderness, but this was filled with lumberjacks cutting and bulldozing trees.

'One day we will go to the primeval forest,' Mr Tian said.

'Let's go today.'

'No. It is far. We will go another day.'

We went to the locomotive shed where we met Mrs Jin, a local guide. The shed was full of smoke and steam, and it was dark; but it was also warm, because the boilers were being stoked and the fire in the forge was blazing. As I walked along Mrs Jin threw herself at me and pushed me against the wall, and then she laughed hysterically, a kind of chattering – one of the more terrifying Chinese laughs. I saw that she had saved me from stepping into a deep hole in which I would almost certainly have broken my back.

I was so rattled by this I had to go outside and take deep breaths. All over this town the snow was packed hard. No street or pavement was clear of ice. They habitually pedalled on the ice, and they had a way of walking – a sort of shuffle – that prevented them from slipping.

'This town is forbidden,' Mr Tian boasted. 'You are very lucky to be here.'

'Are there minorities in Langxiang?' I asked. I was thinking of Buryats, Mongolians, Manchus, and native Siberians.

'We have Hui people,' Mrs Jin said. 'And we have Koreans.'

We found some Hui people – China's Muslims – slitting a cow's throat behind a butcher shop. I could not watch, but being Muslims they were doing it the ritual way, covering their heads and bleeding it so that it would be halal, and therefore untainted.

Before the town darkened and died for the day, we went to a Korean restaurant. It was just a woodframe house, with a stone floor and a fire burning in an open fireplace that was also used for cooking. Four Korean women sat around it eating – all relatives of the owner, who was a younger woman. They wore fur hats and pretty scarves. They were short, and rather dark and square-faced, with big even teeth.

'I can't tell the difference between Koreans and Han Chinese,' Mr Tian said to me.

There were only a few hundred Koreans in town, though there are 2 million of them in China.

'When people come to this restaurant they speak Korean,' one of the women said.

All these women had been born in China, and were married to Koreans, but their parents had been born in Korea. The eldest was about forty and the youngest no more than twenty or so. I wanted to ask them whether they always wore such pretty scarves and hats – and even their coats were stylish – but I did not want to sound patronizing, and in a rare moment of tactfulness I remained silent.

'I'd like to visit Korea,' one of the women said. 'But I don't know where to go. We have no idea where our parents were born.'

'Do you marry Han people?'

'Sometimes. But none of us has ever done so.'

They were whispering and laughing to themselves as they ate, and they asked me questions too – where was I from? Was I married? Did I have children? How old was I? They were smiley types – less phlegmatic and dour than the Chinese. They said they were proud of being Koreans, although all that remained of their culture was their cooking and their language.

Their husbands were lumberjacks and storekeepers. It was just like the Chinese to single them out as a special category. The

Chinese were great makers of ethnic distinctions and could spot a cultural difference a mile away. Muslims have been in China for well over a thousand years and yet they are still regarded as strange and inscrutable and backward, and politically suspect.

All the while in Langxiang my feet and hands were frozen – stinging and painful. My eyes hurt. My muscles were knotted. There was a icy moaning in my head. Mr Tian asked me whether I wanted to see the ski slopes. I said yes and we drove four miles outside town just as the sun slipped below the distant mountains and an even greater cold descended with the darkness.

There on the black and white mountains were ten sluices – frozen chutes cut into the slope. People hauled small boxes up the mountain – they were like little coffins; and then they placed them into a chute and went banging down, cracking from side to side and screaming. I hopped up and down in the cold and said I wasn't interested.

Mr Tian went thrashing up the slope with a splintery coffin and came down showing his teeth. He did it again. Perhaps he was developing a taste for this.

'Don't you like skiing?' he said.

'This isn't skiing, Mr Tian.'

In a shocked voice he said, 'It's *not*?'

But he kept doing it just the same.

I walked down the path and found a shed, a sort of watchman's shack. There was a stove inside. This was a vivid demonstration of heating in Langxiang. The stove was so feeble that there was half an inch of frost on the walls of the shed. The walls (wood and mud bricks) were entirely white.

I kept a record of temperatures. Minus thirty-four Centigrade on the main street, freezing in the lobby, just above freezing in the dining-room. The food went cold a minute after it was plunked down, and the grease congealed. They served fatty meat, greasy potatoes, rice gruel, great uncooked chunks of green pepper. Was this Chinese food? One day I had cabbage stuffed with meat and rice, and gravy poured over it. I had eaten such dishes in Russia and Poland, where they were called *golomkis*.

It was very tiring to be cold all the time. I began to enjoy going to bed early. I listened to the BBC and the VOA under my blanket.

After a few hours I took one of my sweaters off, and one layer of socks, and by morning I was so warm in the sack that I forgot where I was. Then I saw the layer of frost on the window that was so thick I could not see outside, and I remembered.

No one spoke of the cold. Well, why should they? They revelled in it – literally, dancing and sliding on the ice. I saw children in the dark one evening pushing each other off a shelf of ice on to the frozen surface of the town's river. (Other people chopped holes in this ice and drew water from it.) Those children frolicking in the darkness and the perishing cold reminded me of penguins frisking on the ice floes through the long Antarctic night.

When I travel I dream a great deal. Perhaps that is one of my main reasons for travel. It has something to do with strange rooms and odd noises and smells; with vibrations; with food; with the anxieties of travel – especially the fear of death; and with temperatures.

In Langxiang it was the low temperatures that gave me long exhausting dreams. The cold kept me from deep sleep, and so I lay just beneath the surface of consciousness, like a drifting fish. In one of my Langxiang dreams I was besieged in a house in San Francisco. I ran from the front door shooting a machine-gun and wearing headphones. I escaped on a passing cable car – President Reagan was on it, strap-hanging. I was asking him whether he was having a tough time as president. He said, 'Terrible.' We were still talking when I woke up feeling very cold.

That was not the end. I went back to sleep and dreamed that I was at a Christmas party in a large and fashionable house. Nancy Reagan was at the party. Her hair was in big white rollers. She had very thin arms and popping eyes. She said, 'You're so lucky to come from here.' When she said that, I realized that we were on Cape Cod, and perhaps in an idealized version of my own house. She said pathetically, 'I was so poor when I was growing up.' I said, 'I've just had a dream about the President' – and I began to describe my earlier dream within this dream.

Before I got very far, Mr Tian banged on my door and woke me up.

'We are going to the primeval forest,' he said.

We drove about thirty miles, and Mrs Jin joined us. The driver's name was Ying. The road was icy and corrugated and very narrow; but there were no other vehicles except for an occasional army truck. When we arrived at a place called 'Clear Spring' (Qing Yuan), where there was a cabin, we began hiking through the forest. There was snow everywhere but it was not very deep – a foot or so. The trees were huge and very close together – great fat trunks crowding each other. We kept to a narrow path.

I asked Mrs Jin about herself. She was a pleasant person, very frank and unaffected. She was thirty-two and had a young daughter. Her husband was a clerk in a government department. This family of three lived with six other family members in a small flat in Langxiang – nine people in three rooms. Her mother-in-law did all the cooking. It seemed cruel that in a province which had wide open spaces, people should be forced to live in such cramped conditions at close quarters. But this was quite usual. And it was a family under one roof. I often had the feeling that it was the old immemorial Confucian family that had kept China orderly. Mao had attacked the family – the Cultural Revolution was intentionally an assault on the family system, when children were told to rat on their bourgeois parents. But that had faltered and failed. The family had endured, and what were emerging with Deng's reforms were family businesses and family farms.

Kicking through the forest, I asked them whether it was possible to buy Mao's little red book of Selected Thoughts.

'I have thrown mine away,' Mr Tian said. 'That was all a big mistake.'

'I don't agree with him,' Mrs Jin said.

'Do you read Mao's Thoughts?' I asked.

'Sometimes,' she said. 'Mao did many great things for China. Everyone criticizes him, but they forget the wise things he said.'

'What is your favourite thought? The one that you associate with his wisdom?'

'"Serve The People,"' Mrs Jin said. 'I can't quote it all to you, it is too long. It is very wise.'

'What about "A Revolution Is Not A Dinner Party" – can you sing it?'

'Oh yes,' she said, and did so as we marched through the woods.

It was not a catchy tune, but it was perfect for walking briskly, full of iambics: *Geming bushi gingke chifan* . . .

Meanwhile I was bird-watching. It was one of the few places in China where the trees were full of birds. They were tiny flitting things, and very high in the branches. My problem was that I could only use my binoculars with bare hands, so that I could adjust the focus. The temperature was in the minus thirties, which meant that after a few minutes my fingers were too cold to use for adjustments. Yet even in this bitter cold there was bird-song, and the whole forest chattered with the tapping of woodpeckers.

'Mr Tian, can you sing something?' I asked.

'I can't sing Mao's thoughts.'

'Sing something else.'

He suddenly snatched his woolly cap off and shrieked:

> Oh, Carol!
> I am but a foooool!
> Don't ever leave me –
> Treat me mean and croool . . .

He sang it with extraordinary passion and energy, this old, Neil Sedaka, rock-and-roll song, and when he was done he said, 'That's what we used to sing at Harbin University when I was a student!'

There was no wind, and the only sound in the forest was that of the birds – chirping, twittering, pecking the trunks. Mr Tian and Mrs Jin saw some smoke on a hill not far away and decided to go look at it. I carried on plodding and bird-watching. I saw a number of marsh tits and three kinds of woodpecker. I was looking for the chicken-sized great black woodpecker. I saw a pair of tree-creepers making their way up a trunk, their feathers fluffed out. It delighted me to see that these tiny birds were impervious to the cold.

Then I heard the unmistakable crack of a gun going off. I turned around and saw Ying the driver rushing into a thicket and retrieving a dead bird. He had a gun! I tramped back along the path just as he was cramming the bird into his pocket.

'What are you doing?'

'Look, a bird,' he said, fairly pleased with himself. His rifle was a single-shot .22 straight out of a shooting gallery.

'What are you going to do with that bird?'

It was a rosefinch. I had it in my hand now. It was very soft and very tiny, and in this region of dull smouldering cold the dead bird was still warm. It was like holding an extravagant hors d'oeuvre.

Mr Ying perhaps detected a hostility in my voice. He did not reply.

'Are you going to eat this bird?'

He looked down and kicked the snow like a scolded child.

There was nothing to eat. I was sure he was killing the birds for the fun of it.

'Why are you shooting birds, Mr Ying?'

He did not look at me; he was sulking, losing face.

'I don't like killing birds,' I said. 'This is a nice bird. This is a pretty bird. And now it's a dead bird.'

And I was angry, too, because I had not known this gunslinger was behind me, blasting away. I had thought I was in the wilderness. But I had already said too much. Mr Ying looked as though he wanted to shoot me. I put the tiny rosefinch into his hand and I walked away. When I looked back I saw him stamping on the path, making his way to the road. I could not see Mr Tian or Mrs Jin, though I saw what they had been chasing – a tree burning on a hillside, a great thrill, a useless fire.

I went deeper into the forest on my own and saw more birds – great flitting clusters of woodpeckers. You would see as many birds on an average day in Sandwich, Mass., but this was tamed, poisoned, unsentimental and ravenous China, the most populous and domesticated country on earth: on seeing a wild bird the Chinese person invariably licked his lips.

It was an unusual place for China. Pretty birds singing and skittering among tall thick trees, and no other human in sight.

There was no danger in carrying on here. With my footprints in the snow it was impossible for me to get lost. I kept on for another hour or so and saw a plume of smoke. Even when I was near it I could not make out what it was. It seemed to be an underground fire. When I was on top of it I saw that it came from a deep hole in the ground. In the bottom of the hole three Chinese girls were warming themselves over a fire. I said hallo and they looked up at a long-nosed barbarian in a silly hat and mittens and a coat bulging with layers of sweaters. They looked truly startled, as though I might be a Siberian who had wandered over the border, which was indeed only about eighty miles away. They emitted the characteristic Chinese gasp, *Ai-yaaaah*.

'What are you doing?'

'It is our lunch break!'

They climbed out of the hole to look at me. They were wearing padded jackets and felt boots and scarves over their heads and faces.

They said they were working here, and showed me where they were planting seedlings behind windbreaks. The loggers had come and gone, and whole hillsides had been cut down. The idea was that in another 300 years or so the forest would be replaced and ready for re-cutting. With China's record for acid rain this prospect seemed unlikely. But the windbreaks were elaborate, like many rows of hedges lying parallel on the hillside; the overall impression was one of lines on a contour map.

Before I headed back I jumped into the hole and warmed myself before the fire, as the three Chinese girls knelt at the edge of the hole, looking in at me. When I got out, they got in.

I found Mr Tian tramping towards me. He said, 'So you like it here, eh?'

'This is wonderful.'

'Primeval forest,' he said. 'Original forest.'

'Wouldn't you like to build a house here and live alone with your wife?'

'Yes,' he said. 'Have a family and write something – poems and stories.'

'Maybe have four children.'

'It is not permitted,' he said. Then he smiled. 'But this is so far they wouldn't know. It wouldn't matter. Yes. I would like that.'

We walked to where the lumberjacks were working. Few of them wore gloves or hats. They wore rather thin jackets and glorified sneakers. It amazed me that they could endure this cold so skimpily dressed. They were dragging bundles of freshly cut logs into stacks to be loaded on to trucks. Some of the younger ones stopped to stare at me – perhaps because I was so warmly dressed; but the foreman barked at them and all these ragged tree-cutters went back to work. The human voices and the chugging tractors sounded bizarre and unpleasant in this dense forest, perhaps among the last forested wilderness in China.

Mrs Jin had wandered back to the road. When we caught up with her it was already growing dark. Walking to the car we talked about capital punishment. Mr Tian agreed with it – kill them all, he said. It was the only way. Mrs Jin disagreed. Forget the death penalty for embezzlers and pimps, she said; just execute murderers.

This led to a discussion about the true numbers that had been executed.

'Most Chinese people don't believe the news they hear on the radio,' Mr Tian said, when I asked whether the government broadcast such figures.

Mrs Jin frowned, probably wondering whether it was wise for Mr Tian to be telling me this. But Mr Tian pressed on, clawing his hair and gabbling.

'The government sometimes tells lies,' he said.

'Then how do people know what's going on in the country?'

'Foreign broadcasts. The students listen to the BBC and Voice of America. That's how I found out about the demonstrations in Peking. It was not until two or three days later that the government said what was happening.'

I was very touched by his talking to me in this candid way, although, sensing Mrs Jin's disapproval, I decided not to ask too many questions. In spite of the cold, I was in a good mood. I felt I had reached a part of China that was hard to get to, but worth the trouble. It was not a sense of achievement, but rather a hopeful feeling, because it was a place I would gladly return to: that was something to look forward to.

I ate at 5.00 and then got into bed and listened to my radio under the blankets: that was Langxiang by night. And the next day at dawn Mr Tian and I left the town by train. It was so cold I felt parts of me would break off if I bumped into anything. And this was another morning of razor-slashing wind. The sky was grey. It had never been anything but cloudy here. Some of the clouds glowed slightly. That was the sun, that blur – just a crude suggestion of what a sun might be, if there were such a thing.

I read, I slept, I gritted my teeth in the cold. This was an open train, each coach crammed with wooden seats. It stopped at all the stations on the line, and at each station all the doors opened, and for a few minutes the wind blew through it, freezing it. Then the doors closed, and just as the coach began to be almost bearable, the train stopped again, the doors opened, and the wind picked up.

The meal on the train only cost twelve pence, but it was one dish with rice. It was a northern Heilongjiang vegetable, called 'yellow flower', like a chopped heap of lily stalks.

Thinking of the driver, and how I had bawled him out for shooting birds, I asked Mr Tian about losing face. The phrase in Chinese means exactly that: lose face (*diu lian*).

I quoted my friend Wang in Shanghai and said, 'Foreigners have no face.'

'But we have face,' Mr Tian said. 'It is the Chinese way.'

'What if you don't lose face?'

'There is an expression. *Lianpi hou* – a face with thick skin. But that is a bad thing. It means you're insensitive. A shy person loses face.'

That was good, or at least desirable, because it was human.

Mr Tian said, 'If someone criticizes you and you don't lose face you're not a good person.'

'During the Cultural Revolution a lot of people were criticized. Did they all lose face?'

'The Cultural Revolution was a total mistake,' he said.

'What was the worst thing that happened?'

'That people died.'

Later, the dining-car attendant came by and sat with us. He said I should wear two pairs of long underwear, not one, and that it should be the thick Chinese kind (I was wearing skier's long johns). He was from Jiamusi. It was a good day in Jiamusi, only minus thirty-four. Usually it was minus thirty-eight. He laughed and slapped me on the back and went back to work.

Mr Tian had not said anything. He was thinking. He was nodding.

'That was a good idea,' he said. 'Build a house in the forest. Have some children. Write something.' He sat there in the cold in his threadbare coat, twisting his wool cap. He was still nodding, his hair spiky, his sleeves in the soy sauce. 'That's what I'd like to do.'

16

The Boat Train to Dalian: Number 92

It was monotonously cold – always, everywhere – inside and out in Harbin, and so the only way to get warm was to leave the city and the province and head south. Seven hundred miles away in Dalian, a port on the Bohai Gulf, the weather was pleasant, judging by the reports in *China Daily*. Mr Tian told me again that warm weather made him feel sick.

We were having an animated conversation, Mr Tian and I. He was describing how the various Red Guard factions had battled against each other on the streets of Harbin – school against school, factory against factory, each group claiming that they were the purest Maoists. At the station, Mr Tian told me how the walls had been daubed with slogans and Mao portraits. 'It was a total waste,' he said. Chinese candour always touched me and made me grateful. When the whistle of my approaching train blew I took off my sheepskin mittens, my scarf, and the winter hat I had bought for this cold place. I handed them to Mr Tian.

'I won't need them in Dalian,' I said.

Mr Tian shrugged, shook my hand, and without another word walked off. It was the Chinese farewell: there was no lingering, no swapping of addresses, no reminiscence, nothing sentimental. At the moment of parting they turned their back, because you ceased to matter and because they had so much else to worry about. It was like the departure after a Chinese meal, the curtain falling abruptly with a thud and everyone vanishing. I did not mind that such rituals were perfunctory – it certainly kept them from being hypocritical. Mr Tian was soon a little blue figure in a mob of blue figures.

But I should never have given him my gloves and scarf. This was another unheated train. Did they ever heat anything? It was in the low forties Fahrenheit in the compartment and even colder in the dining-car. There was ice on all the floors and frost on the windows. It was too cold to sit still, so I walked back and forth, from one end of the train to the other.

But what was I complaining about? Outside, people were digging and repairing fences and walking to work and hanging laundry outside their small huts in the snowfields. And the strong wind that battered the windows of the train was yanking at these people, too. They looked plump in their winter clothes, like stuffed dolls, and their faces were crimson – visible from a long way off. Knowing what their lives must be like I resolved not to grumble about my lunch of dried fish and gristly meat.

Changchun, which we reached in the early afternoon, was full of vaporous locomotives. The freezing weather made them immensely steamy, and great gusts billowed from the fourteen engines shunting at the station. Icicles hung from the black wheels, and smoke came out of their chimneys, and shrieks of steam from their pistons. It was impressive for being a study of fire and ice, and also for its tones of black and white, the engines bowling along the snowy tracks.

One of China's major film studios is in Changchun, and at that moment a co-production about the life of China's last emperor was being made. If the film had concerned his time as emperor it could have been a very short film. He was only three years old when he took the throne and he abdicated three years later, in 1912. His name was Pu Yi, but he took the name Henry when he was older. And later when the Japanese formed the puppet state of Manchukuo and needed a puppet to run it, they chose Henry and worked his strings in Changchun until the silly state collapsed and Henry was arrested as a war criminal by the Russians. His life ended in the same violent confusion as it began, when he died of cancer as Red Guards howled outside at the beginning of the Cultural Revolution. Henry Pu Yi represented everything that Mao set his face against: the decadent Manchus, the ruling class, wealth, privilege, Japanese collaboration and the humiliations of Chinese history. No wonder when the time came they seized Henry Pu Yi and had his guts for garters.

I debated whether to stay in Changchun; but it was an easy decision. Changchun was very cold, so I moved on. The ice thickened on the walls of the train. Time passed slowly. I put on all my clothes, bit by bit, until by the middle of the afternoon I was sitting with my hands up my sleeves, reading the *Analects* of Confucius and turning the pages with my nose.

Beyond the glittering rime on the window small padded moon-people went slowly across the snow. And so did cyclists and ox carts and schoolkids carrying knapsacks. I saw horses hopelessly foraging for food among blunt spikes of stubble. Sometimes there was a great whiteness and its only identifiable feature a row of telephone poles – the Chinese variety, mile upon mile of tragic-looking crosses. We were in the province of Jilin now, and a cloud of frozen vapour hovered close to the snowy ground.

Few people in the train looked out of the window. They were eating noodles out of tin cups, guzzling tea, shouting and sleeping. Many were taking advantage of the recent relaxation of the rules governing card games. They were actually gambling in Hard Class and some groups were playing mah-jong.

As I walked along from coach to coach I said hallo and after a few exchanges, 'It's cold.'

They just smiled, or shrugged. They were indifferent to the icicles in the toilet, the ice on the floor, the wind whipping through the dining-car, the igloo that had formed between the coaches. I admired them for not caring. I had seen plenty of wimps in China, but the predominating characteristic of the Chinese was stoicism.

Everyone winced when a man waved his arms at me in a kind of aimlessly dangerous way. And he began screaming, 'America! Kissinger! Nixon!'

He went on chanting this and following me.

Someone said, 'He's drunk.'

'He's been drinking wine,' someone else said.

But he wasn't drunk – he was crazy. A Chinese person who was solitary and aggressive had to be unbalanced.

He kept following me, so I shouted back. 'I hear you, comrade, but I don't understand.'

People laughed at that, because it was a stock phrase for stonewalling someone and pretending to be dim. He got off the train at Siping on the border of the province of Liaoning. He was still raving.

In the early winter sunset all the villages were smoking, because it was mealtime – all the stoves alight. The tiny huts lay like simple blocks on the hillsides, toy towns in the snow, and rising from them were symmetrical cones of smoke.

In my rambles through the train I met a Frenchman, Nicolas, who was on his way back to Peking. He was a carpenter from Nice. He had no idea where he was. He did not speak Chinese, and he was trying to teach himself English. He said he was not enjoying China at all. The food was disgusting, he said. The hotels were filthy. Had I been to Harbin?

'I am in Harbin. I am very cold. I go into a cinema to get warm. It is not a cinema! It is a big room. With shares. Chinese people in the shares. And they are all watching a small television. I sat there all day. It was not warm but it was better than the street.'

We swapped stories of low temperatures in Manchuria.

He was reading a textbook titled *Easy Steps to English*, but he was only on chapter three.

'How can you say this word?' he asked, putting his mitten on the vocabulary list.

'Believe.'

'Booleeve,' he said.

'Want an English lesson?' I said, because I saw a way of asking him a number of personal questions in this way. He gladly agreed.

I explained the verb 'believe' and then said we were going to practise a number of drills.

'Nicolas, do you believe in God?'

'Non. I do not booleeve een Gott.'

'Do you believe that Klaus Barbie is guilty of Nazi war crimes?'

'Maybe.'

'You have to repeat the whole sentence.'

'Maybe I booleeve –'

I asked him about the Chinese, the French, the Americans; about his travels, his ambitions, his family. But his answers weren't interesting, and eventually I abandoned the effort and suggested that he should try to learn Chinese.

The lights in the train were dim. The snow on the floor had not melted. I was stiff from the cold. Nicolas said he wished he were back in Nice. I tried to think where I wanted to be. I considered the possibilities and reached the conclusion that I wanted to be right here, doing what I was doing – heading south towards Dalian on the China coast. Perhaps it was a simple choice – of being home or being elsewhere. Surely this was elsewhere?

By the time the train reached Shenyang, after thirteen hours of travel from Harbin, I decided that I had had enough. I could get another train tomorrow and continue on my way. In the mean time I could look at Shenyang.

It was a Chinese city, and therefore a nightmare, and tonight it was minus thirty in Shenyang – tiny needles and etchings of ice on every surface. The streets were practically deserted, and on this dark night Shenyang had the look of a city depicted in an old black and white photograph. It was perfectly still, and in the glare of its few lights it was black and white. My problem was that when I exhaled my glasses became opaque with frost.

It is an official Chinese government statistic that one-third of all Chinese travellers on trains are going to meetings in distant cities. It is one of the bonuses of any job. The pay is lousy but the meetings are held in tourist spots, and so what is supposed to be business is actually a sort of holiday. The same system operates when American companies hold sales conferences in places like Acapulco or the Bahamas.

Because so many Chinese people travel, even in sub-zero winter weather like this, one is never sure of getting a hotel. But in Shenyang I had no problem. The 500-room Phoenix Hotel had just six other guests. It was only 7.30 at night but already the dining-room was closed. I begged them to open it, and they said I could eat providing I did not require anything very fancy. The specialities of the Phoenix were bear's paw (350 *yuan*) and moose nose, and 'fillet of pork in the shape of a club'. I had crunchy chicken and cabbage. It was no good but that didn't matter. What mattered was that for the first time in weeks I was warm. This hotel was heated. My room was full of light-fixtures. There was imitation fur on the walls. The toilet didn't work, but the room had a television.

I needed help getting a ticket to Dalian, because (but how was I to know this?) the trains to Dalian were always full and tickets were almost unobtainable at short notice. That was how I met Mr Sun.

Mr Sun was self-educated. He had spent what should have been his schooldays on a farm, another casualty of the Cultural Revolution. But he still believed in self-reliance and serving the people, and in order and obedience. In the course of his getting me a train ticket we had several illuminating conversations, and I was glad he was a frank hardliner, because I sometimes had the feeling that everyone I met resented the past and felt that Mao had created a society of jackasses.

'I think the students have no right to criticize the government,' Mr Sun said, and then launched into a harangue. 'I had to teach myself English. I had no chance to go to any university. The government has given these students the right to go to university. It is paying for their education. And what do the students do? They demonstrate against the government! I don't agree with them at all. If they demonstrate they should be removed.'

Mr Sun showed me the gigantic epoxy-resin statue of Mao in Shenyang. It is the apotheosis of Mao the founding father, surrounded by fifty-eight figures which represent all phases of the Chinese revolution. I did not have to be told that it was erected during the Cultural Revolution. Like the Mao statue in Chengdu it showed the old man beaming his benediction down upon the proletariat. Such statues were expensive. The money for the Chengdu statue had been earmarked for a sports stadium, and the Shenyang one had been built with civic funds.

I asked Mr Sun whether he thought it was all a waste of public money.

'No,' he said.

'Do you think the statue should be pulled down and destroyed like the other Mao statues?'

'There is no need to pull down the statue just because it was put up during the Cultural Revolution,' Mr Sun said. 'Mao was a great man and we must not forget his achievement.'

There was no question that Mao had been a remarkable man. He had said that he had pondered for years a means by which he might shock the Chinese people, and then he had hit upon the idea of the Cultural Revolution as the perfect shock. But he had overdone it: no one had known when to stop.

Mr Sun was an interpretor. He was not a very good one – we spoke a mixture of Chinese and English in order to carry on an intelligible conversation. But he surprised me by saying that he would soon be going to Kuwait in the Persian Gulf to be an interpreter for a Chinese work-gang.

One of China's newest money-making schemes was the export of skilled labourers on construction projects. They were putting up buildings in Saudi Arabia, and indeed all over the Middle East. It seems very odd that the Chinese are hired as architects and builders, since their own buildings are so undistinguished, not to say monstrosities. It was rather as though Poland were exporting chefs, and Australia sending elocution teachers to England, and Americans running classes in humility or the Japanese in relaxation techniques. Post-1949 Chinese buildings were among the very worst and shakiest and ugliest I had ever seen in my life.

'Won't you have to speak Arabic in Kuwait?'

'No. The other workers are Germans and Koreans and Pakistanis and Americans. Everyone speaks English. That's why I am needed.'

I asked him whether he was apprehensive about the new job.

'My friend just came back and he told me the weather is bad.'

'It's not much like Shenyang' – minus twenty-eight today, by the way. 'What are the people like?'

'Not friendly.'

'And the housing?'

'Everyone sleeps in the same room.'

'What about the food?'

'He just ate tins.'

'Cans of Ma Ling cows' tendon and White Lotus pigs' trotters in gelatin and Sunflower pork luncheon meat and China National

Foodstuffs boneless chicken pieces in spicy broth – that kind of thing?'

'Yes. And noodles. I think so.'

I imagined crates and cartons stacked to the ceiling of the dormitory where this team of workers lived.

'Is there any advantage to living that way and eating out of cans in the sandstorms of Kuwait?'

'You can buy some things.'

'What did your friend buy?'

'One refrigerator. Three television sets – one had remote control. A radio. A video recorder. An oven for the kitchen – microwave. Cassette recorder. And a Honda motor cycle. All Japanese.'

It was as if the fellow had won the jackpot on a game show.

'It must have cost him a lot of money,' I said.

'He earned 107 US dollars every month.'

And lived on cans of Ma Ling loquats in syrup and Double Happiness dried noodles for two years – pass the Lucky Eagle can-opener, Abdul.

'What will he do with all those televisions?'

'One for his mother, one for his brother, and one for himself.'

'What are you planning to buy in Kuwait?'

'A Japanese refrigerator.'

'What will you do with it?' I asked, because Mr Sun had already told me that he lived with his parents.

'I will need it, because after two years in Kuwait I will be of marriageable age.'

He told me that the legal age for marriage in the north of China is twenty-six for a man and twenty-four for a woman; and that in the south it is a year lower. But I bought a pamphlet of the Chinese marriage laws a few weeks later and it seemed to dispute what Mr Sun had said.

'Is that all you want – a refrigerator?'

'I also want a video camera. I want to take pictures of Kuwait and of different places in China. Then I can show these pictures to my mother. She has never been anywhere except Shenyang.'

It was smoggy in Shenyang that day – a brown sky and icy streets; and it was as cold as Harbin.

Mr Sun said, 'You should stay longer here.'

'It's too cold,' I said. 'I want to go south.'

'Where do you come from in the United States?'

'Not very far from Portsmouth, New Hampshire.'

He looked puzzled. He didn't have a clue. Why did so many Chinese have an intimate knowledge of ancient history, the Yellow Emperor and the Tang Dynasty, and have no information at all about more recent Chinese history?

I said, 'Does the Treaty of Portsmouth mean anything to you?'

It was the treaty that ended the Russo-Japanese War and that gave Shenyang – then called Mukden – to the Japanese. It was only eighty years ago, probably in the lifetime of Mr Sun's grandmother. This treaty was suggested by Teddy Roosevelt and signed in that little town – actually in the Portsmouth Naval Yard which happens to be just over the state line, in Kittery, Maine, but I felt that would only confuse Mr Sun.

He didn't know anything about it. He wanted me to see what Shenyang was famous for now – not only its 'three great treasures' (ginseng, sable pelts and furry antlers), but its factories and its automobile assembly plant. Just as the Chinese make steam engines and spittoons and quill pens, so they also make brand-new old cars – the Red Flag is a slightly bloated and swollen version of a 1948 Packard. I declined a visit to Fushun, China's largest open-pit mine – more than four miles across and 1,000 feet deep. In this smog and frosty air it was impossible to see the bottom, much less get a glimpse of the other side of the mine. I wanted to leave this great dark city.

Mr Sun persisted. Did I know that the Liaoning Tourist Board offered specialist tours? There were cycling tours. There were 'local dishes tasting tours'. There were 'convalescence tours' and 'recuperation tours' – 'traditional Chinese physical therapies are applied for better treatment and recuperation results'. Far from being a place you visited to get well, Shenyang seemed to me a place where even the healthiest person would end up with bronchitis.

These tours were a consequence of the brisk competition among the various provincial tourist boards. Mr Sun also mentioned one called a 'lawyers' tour'.

'Any foreign friend who is interested in Chinese laws and our legal system can come on this tour, attend courts in session and visit prisons,' he said. 'This provides them a chance to understand another aspect of China.'

That was one I would have taken, but I could not do it at short notice. We talked about the legal system for a while, and I asked him – as I had other Chinese – about capital punishment. He was an enthusiast. But he claimed that the condemned prisoner was shot in the head, while I maintained the bullet was aimed at the back of the neck.

I asked him to reflect on capital punishment in China, the 10,000 corpses that had accumulated in the past three years (and they had just added prostitution to the list of capital crimes, so there would be many more).

'Capital punishment in China,' he said, and paused, 'is swift.'

I was overcome by the cold weather; by the sight of people cycling through the snow with frost on their faces; by the bitter air; by temperatures that made me feel bruised.

Mr Sun got me a ticket out of town, but when we took the car to the station, he twisted his face and said, 'That driver is ominous. The last time I was with him he crashed his taxi.'

It was 7.30 on a frosty morning in sooty old Mukden. We had half an hour to get to the station. We immediately confronted a traffic jam (trolley-bus with its poles off the wires blocking the road) and were held up for fifteen minutes. Then we started again, and a rumble and thump from the rear wheel slewed the car: a flat tyre.

'I told you. This driver is ominous.'

'How will I get to the station?'

'You can walk,' he said. 'But first you must pay the driver.'

'Why should I pay him? He didn't get me to the station. I might miss the train!'

'In this case you pay ten *yuan*, not fifteen. Cheaper! You save money!'

I threw the money at the ominous driver and hurried to the station, slipping on the ice. I caught the train with a minute to spare – another refrigerated train, but at least it was going south.

On this train I met Richard Woo, who worked for Union

Carbide, and had been in and around Shenyang for almost two years. I asked him what his qualifications were for this assignment.

'I was in Saskatchewan.'

Ah, that explained everything. He also knew all the lingo. 'We sell them the design package . . . We provide input on the plant.' But Union Carbide did not get involved in the construction of the plants. He had views on Chinese workers.

'The work mentality is quite different from that in Europe or America. They are slow, the pay is little. The Chinese are not bad workers, but the system is bad. If they have incentives they perform better.'

I was not planning to ask him what Union Carbide was making in Shenyang, because I did not think I would understand it; but I was bored, so I asked.

'Antifreeze,' Mr Woo said.

The train continued through the flat snowy fields, all of them showing plough-marks and furrows and stubble beneath the ice crust. There were factories – and they looked beautiful, blurred and softened and silvered by frost and the vapour from their chimneys.

There might have been berths on this train, but if so I didn't see them. I was afraid that if I got up someone would snatch my seat – I had seen it happen. I did not want to stand for six hours – it was almost 300 miles more to Dalian. As it was we were jammed in, shoulder to shoulder – the smokers, the noodle-eaters, the spitters, the bronchial victims, the orange-peelers.

There was no dining-car on this train. A woman wearing a nightcap came around with a pushcart selling dried fish and heavy blobs of sponge cake – the favourite snacks of the Chinese traveller. I chose the fish. It was tough and tasted (and looked) like an old inner sole of a shoe – a Chinese inner sole, and a minority one at that. On the wrapper it was described as 'Dried Fish With Minority Flavour'.

I was still cold. The cold was mystifying. I hated it like boredom or bad air. It was like aches and pains – perhaps a fear of death informed my feeling and made the cold frightening, because degree zero is death. I found it dehumanizing and my heart went out to the people who had to live and work in Mongolia,

Heilongjiang, Jilian and Liaoning. And yet it is well known that the spirit among the people in these provinces is especially bright – the hinterland of China is famous for having high morale, the people regarding themselves as pioneers.

But the cold affected me. It is a blessing that cold is hard to describe and impossible to remember clearly. I certainly have no memory for low temperatures. And so afterwards I had no memorable sensations of the month-long freeze I had been through – only the visual effects: frosty faces, scarves with frozen spit on them, big bound feet, and mittens, and crimson faces, flecks of ice on that crow-black Chinese hair, the packed snow, the vapour that hung over the larger cities and made even the grimmest city magical, and the glittering frost – the special diamond-like shimmer that you get when it's thirty below.

After a few hundred miles the snow grew thinner and finally, with an odd abruptness, at the town of Wafangdian there was none. The landscape had the shabby and depressed look that places have when you are used to seeing them covered with snow. There was something drastic about there being no more snow.

The symmetry and twiggy patterns of bare brown orchards below the Qian Shan, and the stone cottages not far from Dalian, gave these hills the look of Scotland and its ruined crofts.

A young Chinese woman smiled at me as I stepped on to the platform at Dalian. She was very modern, I could see. Her hair had been waved into a mass of springy curls. She wore sun-glasses. Her green coat had a fur collar – rabbit. She said she had been sent to meet me. Her name was Miss Tan.

'But please call me Cherry.'

'OK, Cherry.'

'Or Cherry Blossom.'

It was hard to include those two words in an ordinary sentence. 'What is the fare to Yantai, Cherry Blossom?' But I managed, and she always had a prompt reply, usually something like, 'It will cost you one arm and one leg.' She had a fondness for picturesque language.

She led me outdoors and as we stood on the steps of Dalian Station, she said, 'So what do you think of Dalian so far?'

'I have only been here seven minutes,' I said.

'Time flies when you're having fun!' Cherry Blossom said.

'But since you asked,' I went on, 'I am very impressed with what I see in Dalian. The people are happy and industrious, the economy is buoyant, the quality of life is superb. I can tell that morale is very high. I am sure it is the fresh air and prosperity. The port is bustling, and I'm sure the markets are filled with merchandise. What I have seen so far only makes me want to see more.'

'That is good,' Cherry Blossom said.

'And another thing,' I said. 'Dalian looks like South Boston, in Massachusetts.'

It did, too. It was a decaying port, made out of bricks, with wide streets, cobblestones and trolley-tracks, and all the paraphernalia of a harbour – the warehouses, dry docks and cranes. I had the impression that if I kept walking I would eventually come to the Shamrock Bar and Grill. It was also Boston weather – cold and partly sunny under blowing clouds – and Boston architecture. Dalian was full of big brick churches that had probably once been called St Pat's, St Joe's and St Ray's – they were now kindergartens and nurseries, and one was the Dalian Municipal Library. But reform had come to Dalian and with it such businesses as the Hot Bread Bakery and the Hong Xing (Red Star) Cut and Perma.

'And also men hurry to Hong Xing to get a perma,' Cherry Blossom said. 'They go licketty split.'

The streets looked like Boston's streets. Never mind that the main thoroughfare in Dalian was called Stalin Road (Sidalin Lu). It looked like Atlantic Avenue.

At the turn of the century the Russians had schemed to make Dalny (as they called it; it means 'far away' in Russian) a great port for the tsar's ships. It was valuable for fighting the Japanese, because unlike Vladivostok it would not freeze in the winter. After the Russo-Japanese war, when the Japanese flew kites in Dairen (as they called it) – each kite saying THE RUSSIANS HAVE SURRENDERED! – this port city was handed to the Japanese. They simply completed the Russian plan for turning what had been a fishing village into a great port. It prospered until the Second World War, and when the Japanese were defeated the Russians were given the city under the Yalta terms. The Russians remained until well after the Chinese Liberation, when the Chinese renamed it Dalian ('Great Link'). I liked it for its salt air and sea-gulls.

'What desires do you entertain in Dalian?' Cherry Blossom said.

I told her that I had come here to get warm after the freeze in Dongbei, the north-east. And I needed a ticket on the ship that travelled from Dalian across the Bohai Gulf to Yantai. Could she get that for me?

'Keep your fingers crossed,' she said.

She vanished after that. I found an old hotel – Japanese pre-war baronial; but I was turned away. I was accepted at the dreary new Chinese hotel, a sort of Ramada Inn with a stagnant fishpond in the lobby. I spent the day looking for an antique shop, and the only one I found was disappointing. A man tried to sell me a trophy awarded to the winner of a schoolboys' javelin competition in 1933 at a Japanese high school. 'Genuine silver,' he whispered. 'Qing Dynasty.'

The next day I saw Cherry Blossom. She had no news about my ticket.

'You will just have to keep your hopes up!'

We agreed to meet later, and when we did she was smiling.

'Any luck?' I asked.

'No!' She was smiling. And with this bad news I noticed that she had a plump and slightly pimply face. She was wearing an arsenic green wool scarf to match the wool cap she herself had knitted in the dormitory (she had four room-mates) at the Working Women's Unit.

'I have failed completely!'

Then why was she smiling? God, I hated her silly hat.

'But,' she said, wiggling her fingers, 'wait!'

She had a sharp way of speaking that made every sentence an exclamation. She reached into her plastic handbag.

'Here is the ticket! It has been a total success!'

Now she wagged her head at me and made her tight curls vibrate like springs.

I said, 'Were you trying to fool me, Cherry Blossom?'

'Yes!'

I wanted to hit her.

'Is that a Chinese practical joke?'

'Oh yes,' she said, with a giggle.

But then aren't all practical jokes exercises in sadism?

I went to the Free Market – open since 1979. Every sort of fish, shellfish and seaweed was on display – a pound of big plump prawns was £3, but that was the most expensive item. They also sold squid, abalone, oysters, conch, sea-slugs and great stacks of clams and flat-fish. The fishermen did not look Chinese; they had a flat-headed Mongolian appearance and might have been Manchus, of whom there are 5 or 6 million in this peninsula and in the north. The market gave me an appetite and that night I had abalone stir-fried in garlic sauce: delicious.

Cherry Blossom said that foreign cruise ships stopped in Dalian in the summer. The tourists stayed for half a day.

'What can you see in Dalian in half a day?'

She said they all got on a bus and visited the shell-carving factory, the glassware factory, a model children's school (the kids sang songs from *The Sound of Music*) and then it was back to the ship and on to Yantai or Qingdao.

'I'd like to see Stalin Square,' I said.

We went there. In the centre of it was a statue to the Russian army which had occupied the city after the war.

'There are no Stalin Squares in the Soviet Union, Cherry Blossom. Did you know that?'

She said no, she was surprised to hear it. She asked why.

'Because some people think he made a few mistakes,' I said, though I did not mention the pogroms, the secret police, purges, or the moustached brute's ability to plan large-scale famines in order to punish dissenting regions.

'Is there a Mao Zedong Square in Dalian, Cherry Blossom?'

'No,' she said, 'because he made a few mistakes. But don't cry over spilled milk!'*

I told her that I had read somewhere that the evil genius Lin Biao had lived in Dalian. She said no, this was not so. She had lived

---

* She was wrong. Mao was the mover of a resolution to forbid the naming of provinces, cities, towns or squares for himself or other living leaders (*Selected Works of Mao Zedong*, Vol. IV, p. 380).

her whole life in Dalian and no one had ever mentioned Lin's connection.

But the driver was older. He said yes, Lin Biao had lived there in Dalian. Lin Biao, a great military tactician, was now maligned because he had done so much to build up Mao – it was Lin who devised the *Little Red Book* and chose all the quotations; and in the end (so it was said) he had plotted to assassinate Mao, when Mao was weak and at his heffalump stage; and Lin in trying to flee the country ('seeking protection from his Moscow masters . . . as a defector to the Soviet revisionists in betrayal of the party and the country') had crashed in dear old Undur Khan, in the People's Republic of Mongolia. Foul play was never mentioned. It was regarded as natural justice that this heliophobe should meet an untimely death.

It was his heliophobia that made me want to see his house. This weedy little man had a horror of the sun. I thought his house might not have any windows, or perhaps special shutters; or maybe he lived in a bomb shelter in the basement.

Cherry Blossom was saying in Chinese to the driver, 'I did not know that Lin Biao lived in Dalian,' and then to me in English, 'It's too dark to find his house. Let's go to the beach instead.'

We headed for the south part of Dalian, to a place called Fu's Village Beach. Because of the cliffs and the winding road, the driver went very slowly.

Cherry Blossom said, 'This car is as slow as cold molasses in January.'

'You certainly know a lot of colourful expressions, Cherry.'

'Yes. I am queer as a fish.' And she giggled behind her hand.

'You should be as happy as a clam,' I said.

'I like that one so much! I feel like a million dollars when I hear that.'

These colloquial high jinks could have been tiresome, but it was such a novelty for a Chinese person to be playful I enjoyed it. And I liked her for not taking herself too seriously. She knew she was mildly excruciating.

Meanwhile we were descending to Fu's Village – great rocky cliffs and an empty beach of yellow sand with the January wind off the sea beating the waves against it. Offshore there were five blob-like islands floating blackly on the gulf. A couple was canoodling on the beach – the Chinese do it standing up, out of the wind, usually behind a rock or a building, and they hug each other very tightly. It is all smooching. These two ran away when they saw me. A drunken fisherman staggered across the beach, towards his big wooden rowboat that was straight off an ancient scroll: a sharply rockered bottom, very clumsy, the shape of a wooden shoe, probably very seaworthy.

I asked Cherry Blossom whether she took her tourists here. She said there wasn't time.

'Some of the people have funny faces,' she said.

'What is the funniest face you have ever seen, Cherry?'

She shrieked, 'Yours!' and clapped her hands over her eyes and laughed.

'Another of your saucy jokes, Cherry Blossom!'

She became rather grave and said, 'But truly the Tibetans have the funniest faces. They are so funny I get frightened.'

'What about American faces?'

'Americans are wonderful.'

We had tea at a vast empty restaurant. We were the only customers. It was at the top of one of Fu's cliffs, with a panoramic view.

'Do you want to see the Dragon Cave?'

I said yes, and was taken upstairs to see a restaurant decorated to resemble a cave. It had fibreglass walls, bulging brown plastic rocks, lights shining through plastic stalactites and each table was fixed in a greeny-black cleft, with fake moss and boulders around it. The idea was perhaps not a bad one, but this was a vivid example of the Chinese not knowing when to stop. It was shapeless, artless, grotesquely beyond kitsch; it was a complicated disfigurement, wrinkled and stinking, like a huge plastic toy that had begun to melt and smell. You sat on those wrinkled rocks and bumped your head on the stalactites and ate fish cheeks with fresh ginger.

Cherry Blossom said, 'Do you think it's romantic?'

'Some people might find it romantic,' I said. And I pointed out the window. 'That's what I find romantic.'

The tangerine sun had settled into the Gulf of Bohai, colouring the little islands and the cliffs of Dalian, and the long stretch of empty beach.

Cherry Blossom said, 'Let your imagination fly!'

We left the Dragon Cave (and I thought: It must have a counterpart in California). I said, 'I understand there are recuperation tours. People come to this province to try out Chinese medicine.'

'Yes. It is like a fat farm.'

'Where did you learn that, Cherry Blossom?'

'My teachers at the institute were Americans. They taught me so many things!'

She had loved her years at the Dalian Foreign Languages Institute. She was now only twenty-two, but she intended to go on studying and working. She had no intention of getting married, and in explaining why, she lost her joky manner and became distressed.

Her decision not to marry was the result of a trip to Peking. She had taken a group of visiting doctors to see a Chinese hospital – how it worked, how the patients were treated, the progress of surgical operations, and so forth. The doctors expressed an interest in seeing a delivery. Cherry Blossom witnessed this and, so she said, almost went into shock at the sight of the baby issuing forth with its squashed head and its bloody face and streaming water. The mother had howled and so had the baby.

In all respects it was a completely normal birth.

'It was a mess,' she said, and touched her plump cheeks in disgust. 'I was afraid. I hated it. I would never do it – never. I will never get married.'

I said, 'You don't have to have babies just because you get married.'

She was shaking her head. The thought was absurd – she couldn't take it in. The whole point of marriage these days was to produce one child. Even though the party was now stressing that the best marriages were work-related, the husband and wife joint members of a work-unit, a busy little team, Cherry Blossom could not overcome the horror of what she had seen in the delivery room of Capital Hospital in Peking. She said she intended to remain in the dormitory of the Working Women's Unit and go on knitting.

It was late at night when we crossed Dalian to get to the harbour, where I intended to take the ship to Yantai. We passed through the old bourgeois suburbs that had been built by the Japanese and the Russians. On the sloping streets of these neighbourhoods there were seedy semi-detached villas and stucco bungalows under the bare trees. I had not seen anything quite like them in China. They were appropriate to the suburban streets, the picket fences and the brick walls; and then I saw the laundry in the front yards and the Chinese at the windows.

I often passed down streets like this, seeing big gloomy villas with gables and jutting eaves and mullioned windows; but always in nightmares. They were the sort of houses which first looked familiar in the dream, and then I saw evil faces at the windows, and I realized that I was no longer safe. How often in nightmares I had been chased down streets like these.

'I am sorry to see you go,' Cherry Blossom said, when we arrived at the boat.

She was the only person in China who ever said that to me. In her old-fashioned way, with her old-fashioned clichés, she was very nice. I wished her well and we shook hands. I wanted to tell her that I was grateful to her for looking after me. I started to say it but she cut me off.

'Keep the wind at your back, Paul,' she said, and giggled again, delighted with her own audacity.

17

On the 'Lake of Heaven' to Yantai

This ship, the *Tian Hu*, made a nightly journey across the Bohai Gulf to Yantai, on the coast of Shandong Province. It carried over 1,000 passengers, mostly in steerage, and some in six-berth cabins. From this ship Dalian was merely black hills and a black harbour, and Yantai was under the moon somewhere, a hundred-odd nautical miles away.

The *Tian Hu* was full of spitters – something to do with the sea air, perhaps, and the wish to have a good hoick. I had resolved that I was going to ignore them, but it was on this ship that I realized what had been bothering me about Chinese spitting. It was, simply, that they were not very good at it.

They spat all the time.* They cleared their throats so loudly they

---

* One of the Boxer chants in 1900 was:

> 'Surely government banner men are many;
> Certainly foreign soldiers a horde;
> But if each of our people spits once,
> They will drown banner men and invaders together.'
> (*Poems of Revolt*, Peking, 1962)

could drown conversation – they could sound like a Roto-Rooter or someone clearing a storm drain, or the last gallon of water leaving a jacuzzi. With their cheeks alone they made the suctioning: *hhggaarrkh!* And then they grinned and positioned their teeth, and they leaned. You expected them to propel it about five yards like a Laramie stockman spitting over a fence. But no, they never gave it any force. They seldom spat more than a few inches from where they stood. They did not spit out, they spat down: that was the essential cultural difference that it took me almost a year in China to determine. It was not one clean shot with a ping into the spittoon, but a series of dribbles that often ran down the outside of the revolting thing. They bent low when they spat, there was a certain bending of the knees and crooking of the back that was a preliminary to Chinese spitting. It was not aggressive propulsion. It was almost noiseless. They just dropped it and moved on. Well, it was a crowded country – you couldn't just turn aside and hoick a louie without hitting someone. But after the snarkings, the mucus streaking through their passages with a smack, Chinese spitting was always something of an aimless anticlimax.

I had just about settled into my bunk for the voyage, and had begun to dream, when a bell clanged and a foghorn sounded. We had arrived in Yantai. It was 4.30 in the morning. The pier was shrouded in freezing fog, there was ice on the gantries, and I could hear the sea lapping the docking posts, but I could not make it out – fog and ocean were mingled. The lack of visibility did not deter or slow the passengers. All 1,000 of them plunged into the sea-fog and shuffled across the quay to – where? There were no buses or taxis at this hour of the morning, and few of these people lived in this small town. They had to wait for morning, when the big broken buses would come and take them away.

It is a melancholy fact that Chinese transportation is always full – seldom a spare seat, never a spare coach. Every train, every bus, every ship – no matter what the day, the time, the season. It was interesting to me that on a weekday night in a month when people normally did not travel, the 'Lake of Heaven' was full. The train to Dalian had been full, and so had the train to Shenyang. It was never possible to be sure of a seat, and in these conditions even if you got the seat you were crammed in. Transportation in China is always crowded; it is nearly always uncomfortable; it is often a struggle. The pleasures are rare, but they are intense and memorable. Travel in China, I suspected, would give me a lasting desire for solitude.

I had been travelling steadily south for a number of days, and so I took a day off in Yantai. It was unseasonably cold, with a sleety wind blowing off the sea and icy snow spread thinly on the town. It was a bleak and battered place, of low rubble-strewn hills and bouldery beaches. It was full of abandoned brick huts on which Maoist slogans had been defaced. After a day of sitting listening to the wind and drinking tea and writing and mooching in the town I had dinner (scallops in egg white with rancid spinach: vegetables in winter could be dire). And I conceived a plan.

For months I had wanted to see a commune. I had wondered what had happened to the commune outside Canton that I had seen in 1980. This province of Shandong was famous for its agricultural communes – or at least it had been. And the Chinese had always boasted about them before; so, now that they had been reformed, what did they look like?

Mr Hu, my guide in Yantai, tried to dissuade me from seeing a commune. He said wouldn't I be happier seeing the padlock factory, the embroidery and needlepoint factory, or the place where they made grandfather clocks. I wanted to say, 'And you make steam engines and hat-racks and chamber-pots and quill pens and doilies. Who does your market research?'

'A commune is what I would really like to see,' I said.

'They were cancelled in 1979. There are none. So you see it is impossible.'

'Then what about a village or a co-operative that used to be a commune? I'm sure they didn't just burn them down, Mr Hu.'

'I will find one for you.'

He kept his word and the next day we drove to what had once been the Xi Guan (Western Pass) Commune. It was now called the Bright Pearl Co-operative. Its new name had come from a newspaper article that had been written praising it as 'The Pearl of Shandong'. It had 500 households – about 1,500 people. It looked like a small township about twenty miles outside Yantai, and it seemed an unprepossessing place. But as soon as I arrived the party secretary told me that it was now an extremely wealthy co-operative. In 1971 the per capita income had been 100 *yuan* a year; in 1986 this figure was now 9,000 *yuan*. People had more money than they needed, and so each person was given 1,000 a year and the rest was invested in the village.

How had they managed this extraordinary increase in their fortunes? The party secretary Ma Weihong gave me a long explanation, but in effect he was saying that everything changed after the government got off their backs.

'During the Cultural Revolution this co-operative was a commune with a one-crop economy – wheat. That's all. We were capable of doing more, but then we couldn't because the party would not permit it. After 1979 we began to diversify – new crops, a nursery, various industries, transport, commerce and a hotel. These projects were all profitable.'

'You have more money, but do you have more purchasing power?' I explained the term to him.

Mr Ma said, 'It's true that prices are higher. But we have more than compensated for the rise.'

'Couldn't you have achieved that high income with one crop if you had worked hard?'

'We worked hard,' he said. 'But the policy of one crop was incorrect.'

'At the time, did you know that you were working to carry out an incorrect policy?'

'Yes, but it was the Cultural Revolution. We could not do anything about it,' Mr Ma said. 'But now we have changed all that. We have more relationships with the free market. We are rich now.'

It was so strange to hear a Chinese person utter this dangerous word.

I said, 'Is it good to be rich?'

'Yes. Very good.' He hadn't blinked. He was sitting with his arms folded. His expression said: *Next question*.

'But isn't that a capitalistic attitude?'

'No. You and I are on different roads, but we are going to the same place.'

'Which place?'

'To more richness and wealth,' Mr Ma said, uttering more heresies. 'Listen, we used to have a slogan, *We should be rich together or we should be poor together*.'

'Do you still believe that?'

'Not exactly. I think if you can be rich your own way you should do it.'

'Then you'll be bourgeois.'

'There is absolutely no danger of that.'

He spoke with such conviction that I could not think of any more questions. He was an older man. He had been in this place twenty years ago when it had been a poor commune. Who could blame him for gloating a little about the success of the place today? And I liked him for never saying *I*. He nearly always replied saying *we*; but it was a socialist *we*, not a royal *we*.

'What would you do if things continued to improve and you ended up with an enormous amount of money?'

'We would donate it to a poor village, or we would give it to the government in taxes.'

I had met him in the big draughty meeting-room, and he had offered me some apples to eat; they had been grown on the co-operative – one of the newer projects. They were firm and juicy. Mr Ma said they were sent all over China. We walked outside – Mr Hu bringing up the rear – and he showed me the other money-making projects. This commune grew and sold mushrooms. It seemed a modest business, but I later learned that mushroom sales to the United States are phenomenal: most Pizza Hut mushrooms are from China.

I said, 'During the Cultural Revolution, were intellectuals sent to work here on this commune?'

He shook his head. 'No. Even this place was considered too good for them. Most intellectuals were sent into the countryside – to farms and into the mountains. They went to the most backward provinces, like Qinghai, Ningxia and Gansu. And Mongolia – lots of intellectuals ended up in Mongolia. They had to suffer. That's what we said.'

'Do you think the suffering did them any good?'

Mr Ma said, 'The policy was incorrect.'

And yet it was so natural. I thought of all the upstarts, know-it-alls, teachers, critics and book reviewers that I would love to have seen herded on to a train to Mongolia to shovel pig-shit and live in barns. But of course I would be among them. In China, an intellectual is usually just someone who does not do manual labour. And there we would all be, digging holes, as a punishment for being so boring. It was an awful fate, but it was easy to imagine how the policy had come about. Everyone in his life has wished at one time or another for someone he disliked to be trundled off to shovel shit – especially an uppity person who had never got his hands dirty. Mao carried this satisfying little fantasy to its nasty limit.

Mr Ma showed me his hotel. Two years ago this building was put up, on the theory that it couldn't fail, because there were only two hotels in Yantai. The Bright Pearl Co-operative Hotel had forty rooms, it was painted green and yellow, and by Chinese standards it was a bargain. It was draughty but clean. It was not expensive. I said I would not mind moving in but Mr Ma said that they could not take foreigners yet.

There was a slimy pool in the lobby, and over the waterfall (which worked in spurts) a mural of the Great Wall and a stuffed tortoise. These were standard items of interior decoration in the newer Chinese hotels. The only variables were the size of the pool, the dimensions of the tortoise, the depth of the algae, and was the Great Wall painted or embroidered? This one was painted, and a wall fixture – a light socket – had been included in the mural.

'Hu Yaobang visited us last year,' Mr Ma said, referring to the high-spirited party secretary who had been regarded as Deng Xiaoping's successor. 'He held a briefing in here.'

We entered the conference room. There was no commemorative photo of Hu Yaobang, but there were other knick-knacks: an ivory sculpture of a small dragon, a statue of a Chinese poet, sixteen tiny Buddhas, lots of ashtrays, a palm tree and a stuffed penguin in a glass case with a plaque saying: PRESENTED BY THE CHINESE ANTARCTIC EXPEDITION.

'Does everyone in the co-operative get an equal amount of money?' I asked.

'No. Our income is determined by the number of people in our household, and our productivity.'

'How do you keep track of productivity?'

'It would take too long to explain.'

We went to the mayor's house. He was a sort of figurehead, appointed by the committee. He was not home but I was allowed to wander around his house. Two things interested me in his house. He had a number of books – novels, stories, poems, all sorts; not political tracts. And he had old-style Chinese furniture – black-wood chairs and rosewood tables, a carved settee and several elegant cabinets. They were antiques, but they were being used as ordinary household furniture.

Mr Ma said that the co-operative was especially proud of their hospital. They had built it themselves. It was the only co-operative in China that had raised the money and then built and staffed its own hospital. It had cost 400,000 *yuan* – less than £65,000 – and it was not just an acupuncture parlour. It had modern equipment and qualified doctors. It had electrocardiographs, an x-ray unit, an operating theatre and a family planning consulting room (the abortion clinic: probably the busiest department in any Chinese hospital). There was an acupuncturist on the staff, and also a full-time herbalist (who ran the department, dispensing from his stock of 300 herbs). It was a clean hospital. It did not smell. Its charges were low. In fact it had been built because the people at the co-operative hated going into Yantai to the county hospital and paying what they regarded as excessive amounts. It had cost twenty *yuan* to have a baby at the county hospital, it cost half that here – less than £2.

'Our motto is *Serve the people*,' Mr Ma said.

It was a Maoist phrase but he made it sound as friendly and eager as a supermarket slogan.

Yantai was a sorrowful-looking town, like a grey windswept place on the coast of Ulster. It had had a large foreign community, so it was more than the wind and weather – it was the architecture, the oversized detached houses, the rather forbidding hospital, the villas made of granite blocks and red bricks, and the low stone cottages. These were all from the turn of the century, but they had lasted well. The ones built for a single family were hives – a family in each of the twelve rooms. The black and stony sea-shore was

Irish, and so was the tangle of tidewrack, the overturned rowboats, the coils of nets and the people carrying baskets of mussels. The only un-Irish feature was a pictorial sign showing two Chinese saying LATE MARRIAGE AND LATE CHILDBIRTH ARE WORTHY. To make the point the woman (a new mother) was shown with swatches of grey hair. Since the Chinese don't normally get grey hair until they are in their sixties, this was a remarkable birth.

I liked the people of Yantai for complaining about the weather. It had turned from wet and windy to stormy – it was pelting with freezing snow that hardened the mud in the streets, and plastered the sides of buildings with ice. There was none of the bewildering indifference to cold that characterized the people in Shenyang and Harbin. Here people bitched and groaned and squinted at the sleet and said, 'What's this supposed to be?' They kicked it in the streets and developed an angry way of walking, a sort of exasperated shuffle, so that they wouldn't fall down. They hardly stopped commenting on it and they apologized for it to me. All these reactions made me feel warm.

But the truth was that a little snow improved Yantai. It was not a pretty place. It looked stricken, random, exploited, Irish. The snow gave gentle contours to the big dry hills. The hills of Shandong lost their topsoil years ago. Nothing grows on them. They are heaps of mud and loose stones, like rubble-piles and slag-heaps. It is not an ugly landscape but an exhausted one.

To the manufacture of quill pens and chamber-pots and grandfather clocks, Yantai had added the making of tapestries. The Chinese made eighteenth-century products in nineteenth-century factories, and so it was not odd that they should reach even further back in time and revive a medieval art form that was made by hand. It is obvious to anyone who travels even a little in China that the Chinese can be painstaking in their production of kitsch. The Yantai Woollen Needlepoint Tapestry Factory was an extreme example of this effort, which had its counterpart in the hobbyist who makes a model of the Spanish Armada with glue and toothpicks, or (as I saw once in New Hampshire) the front of a large building faced with old bottle caps.

I asked the manager whether they would do me a copy of the

Bayeux Tapestry, and even after I had described it he unhesitatingly said yes. There were women picking out copies of the *Mona Lisa*, Vermeer's lute-player and at least one Rembrandt. They were also doing generic birds and flowers, and the creature that is the unmistakable emblem of Chinese kitsch, the fluffy white kitten playing with a ball of yarn or worrying a goldfish. It is nearly impossible to travel in China at all without seeing this white kitten, and if you are especially valued as a foreign friend or compatriot you will be given one, under glass in needlepoint, as a present. Orville Schell, in one of his later and less enthusiastic books about the Chinese, mentions this white kitten and implies that its tastelessness signals the decline of Chinese culture. But surely it is merely a bit of harmless fun and misplaced artistry; nothing looks more like kitsch to the Chinese than our crazed production of chinoiserie – little fake pagodas and portraits of yellow-faced mandarins with silly pigtails. I did not mind the cat (made in huge quantities by the Yantai needlepointers) but I was unspeakably grateful no one gave me one.

These days the call was for needlepointing snapshots of favourite aunts and uncles, or fat children. At their needlepoint frames the women at the tapestry factory were doing large portraits of Roger and Betty Landrum in front of their piano in a suburb of Sydney, Australia; Mr and Mrs Chew Lim Hock, wincing at a bowl of flowers; two spoiled-looking Japanese kids on a seesaw, and the mayor of Timaru, New Zealand, Yantai's sister-city. The likenesses and colours are surprisingly exact, and for about £250 they will do a needlepoint of that picture you took last summer of Uncle Dick waving from the porch. But why anyone wants to pay that money for a small and slightly blurry snapshot made into a gigantic tapestry or a wall-hanging I cannot imagine.

In the end I was less interested in the fishing and manufacturing side of Yantai than I was in the recent history of Mr Hu. After a few days he disclosed to me that he had been married for just two weeks. That information was like catnip to me; I asked him ceaseless questions. But he did not mind. He was a jaunty, thin man, with two distinct sides to his head. He was also very pleased with himself, and happily talkative; with an air of a man of the world. He was proud of the fact that he had travelled out of Yantai

– he had been as far as Qingdao and Qufu (the birthplace of Confuscius). And, in his telling, his wedding had been quite an event.

Two years before, in one of the pebbly and decrepit Yantai parks, he had met a girl who was out walking with her friends. Mr Hu was captivated by her. Her name was Mu. After a year of taking her for walks and buying her noodles and watching TV with her at her parents' flat, Mr Hu decided to get to the point.

He said, 'What do you say, Mu – shall we register?'

Mu was excited. She could hardly speak. *Shall we register?* was an unambiguous proposal of marriage. Registering leads in only one direction. Article 7 of the Marriage Law of the People's Republic of China (1986) specifies, 'Both the man and the woman desiring to contract a marriage shall register in person with the marriage registration office.'

Mr Hu was twenty-six, and Mu was twenty-five. Article 5 states: 'No marriage shall be contracted before the man has reached twenty-two years of age and the woman twenty years of age.'

When their ages, status, jobs and addresses were verified a marriage certificate was issued. Other clauses in the marriage law explain that cousins cannot marry, nor can lepers. Mr Hu had expected that his work-unit would give him a place to live – a room in Yantai. He put in several requests, but was bypassed.

Mu told him to forget it. If they waited for a place to live they might never get married. She urged him to consider going through with the marriage. Could they live with his parents? Mr Hu said OK – let's do it. But there was another problem. January was deemed an unlucky month, according to an old tradition, for the way it falls just before Spring Festival. Both sets of parents implored the couple not to get married in an inauspicious month.

I said, 'Did you agree that the month was unlucky?'

'Not really,' Mr Hu said, but he seemed uncertain. 'But for their sakes, we changed the date.'

'Are you superstitious?'

His face became very thin with the chattering laugh that meant: *You have just asked me a tactless question but I will nevertheless answer it.* He said, 'I don't think so.'

'Do you believe in God?' I asked.

'Sometimes,' he said. He did not laugh.

By pretending to satisfy the old folks he could calm himself. He chose to get married just after Christmas. Chinese who study English tend to make a thing of Christmas – the eating, drinking, card-sending and gift-giving part: all its heathen elements.

Mr Hu bought basins of food and cartons of wine and beer. His schoolfriend Hua did the cooking. On the big day he rented a taxi – something he had never before done on his own – and he was driven to Mu's house. He wore a western suit and necktie. He picked up Mu and proceeded to his parents' house, and on his arrival there strings of firecrackers were unleashed. That was 11.00 in the morning. The guests arrived at noon and everyone ate and drank until 10.00 that night.

At that point Mr Hu and Mu went upstairs. They did not go to work for two days, nor did they stir out of the house. Their romantic tryst was sporadic, and this was not exactly a love-nest because seven people lived in the three-roomed house, and the TV set was in the room occupied by Mr Hu and Mu. Occasionally members of the household wanted to watch their favourite programmes.

Article 9 of the Marriage Law states, 'Husband and wife enjoy equal status in the home.' This was a bit tricky in the house owned by Mr Hu's parents, because his mother did all the cooking – Mu could not cook – and 'home' was really just a euphemism for the TV room with its convertible bed.

A unique feature of the Chinese Marriage Law is its unambiguous treatment of birth control. That is Article 12: 'Husband and wife are in duty bound to practise family planning.'

I did not ask Mr Hu how they managed this aspect, though I was deeply curious. I simply asked him how he was enjoying marriage.

'So far, very nice,' he said.

He said it did not bother him that his wife kept her own name. The law allowed children in China to adopt the name of either parent. The law insists that parents be kind and that they act responsibly. This is spelled out in specific detail: 'Infanticide by drowning and any other acts causing serious harm to infants are prohibited.'

If Mr Hu's marriage did not work out, and Mu was of the same mind, a divorce could be very speedy. There were restrictions, of which the most interesting was Article 27: 'The husband is not allowed to apply for a divorce when his wife is pregnant or within one year after the birth of a child.' However, Mu could apply and could be granted a divorce, even though she happened to be pregnant. That seemed an enlightened and considerate way of looking at divorce. In general, the Marriage Law was as straightforward as a driver's manual.

The snow did not let up. The sleet accumulated in Yantai. It was a grim place, with the wind blowing from Siberia.

One snowy day a large group of pilgrims appeared in the hotel, wearing the smile that one instantly associates with people in possession of the Christian message. These were Americans, from Texas. They had come in search of a missionary who had been in this part of Shandong 100 years ago. Her name was Lottie Moon. The group had discovered the ruins of Miss Moon's house about forty miles away at the coastal hamlet of Penglai. I was told that they regarded this woman as a saint and that they had volunteered to reconstruct the house and the church with their own money. The Chinese government was on the point of agreeing to this. In Mao's China that would have been unthinkable.

Only six years before, I had copied down an inscription under the photograph of a Catholic church in Nanjing. Its tone was very fierce. It read in part:

> American imperialism took preaching as its cover. All over China they erected churches like this and carried out destructive activities . . . The American missionaries joined up with the Qing Dynasty troops and attacked the Small Sword Society troops, and the church acted as a stronghold.

I asked Mr Hu what he thought of this difference in official attitudes.

'If people know about Lottie Moon and other missionaries in Yantai, they will visit here and enjoy themselves.'

By 'people' he meant foreign tourists. His attitude was characteristic of the Chinese in general: if it brought in tourists and it was not immoral it was to be encouraged, whether it was missionaries, rebuilt churches, or city tours of the bourgeois suburbs of old Shandong. But there were obvious dangers in tourism. After the complete eradication of venereal disease (the fifty-year personal struggle of an idealistic doctor from Buffalo, NY, who became Chinese, George Hatem transmogrifying himself into Ma Hai-teh), the VD clinics were reopened in 1987, to cope with a new outbreak of the disease. But antibiotics were not the only remedy. The Chinese also recently decreed that the punishment for engaging in prostitution would be a bullet in the neck.

18

The Slow Train to Qingdao: Number 508

On these one-day railway trips, the Chinese could practically overwhelm a train with their garbage. Nearly everyone on board was befouling the available space. While I sat and read I noticed that the people opposite, after only a few hours, had amassed on their table (I scribbled the details on my flyleaf): duck bones, fish bones, peanut shells, cookie wrappers, sunflower seed husks, three teacups, two tumblers, a thermos, a wine bottle, two food tins, spittings, leavings, orange rinds, prawn shells, and two used nappies.

They could be very tidy, but there was also something sluttishly comfortable about an accumulation of garbage, as though it were a symbol of prosperity. The coaches were smoky, and so crowded it was an effort to make my way down the aisle. It was full of shrieks and stinks. The loudspeaker played a Chinese version of 'Flower Of Malaya' ('*Rose, Rose, I love you, with an aching heart . . .*'). Some big card games were in progress. Passengers read the *Yantai Workers' Daily*, and romantic novels (People's Liberation Army soldier and his gal back home in Wuhan), and a Chinese magazine I had not seen before, called *World Screen*, with a portrait of Roger Moore (as James Bond) on the cover.

It was not an old railway line. At a time when steam trains were being phased out in the United States, and lines closed, this line from Yantai to Qingdao was being built. It was 1950, and a few years later a brand-new, old-fashioned steam engine went gasping down the track with red flags flying from its boiler. It should have happened sooner, but it was not in the interests of the Germans or the Japanese (who had occupied this province) to build the line. In any case, the vision and altruism that are espoused by colonialists are not readily apparent in China. Unlike in Africa and India, the imperialists in China set themselves up in competition against the Chinese, which was another reason Mao execrated them. They were not all racketeers but they all thrived on China's disunity.

This train still had a fifties feel – a little grim. Most of the passengers had boarded at Yantai and begun eating. They ate noodles, buckets of rice, and seaweed – and nuts, fruit, and everything else. They did not stop until we arrived at Qingdao in the evening. Unusually for a Chinese train, there were plenty of drinkers – and drunks: spitting, wheezing, puffy-faced.

Only half a dozen of the passengers used the dining-car for lunch. They were picking at Chinese spinach and another sinister-looking vegetable.

'What will you have?' the supervisor asked.

'How about some of that?' I said, pointing to the other people's dishes.

'You don't want that stuff,' he said. 'We have many dishes. Different prices. Do you want the two, the four, the five, the eight or the ten?'

'Which is the best one?'

'The ten,' he said. 'You won't be sorry.'

He meant the ten *yuan* lunch. It was a worker's week's pay. The dishes kept coming, the food was good, and there was so much food I made a tally of it. It was the largest meal I had on any Chinese train and might have been the best one. How odd that it should be served on this slow train in this out-of-the-way place. There was first a cold dish, sliced meat and white seaweed; and then shredded pork with carrot and bamboo slivers; shrimp and Chinese cabbage; diced chicken and celery; reconstituted dried fish; deep-fried eggs; Chinese spinach; egg-drop tomato soup, and a big basin of rice. I ate some of it and I marvelled at the remainder of the £1.70 meal.

My ticket had cost me a little over £1. This was all a bargain. But there were other prices to pay. It took seven hours to go the 150 miles, so our average speed was about twenty miles an hour. We stopped every five minutes, literally that. Steam trains have a sort of jerky clanking way of stopping and starting – an indecisive motion – and all day, to this slow conga, clouds of smoke from the stack tumbled past the windows, as we crossed the flatness of Shandong in a reddening winter sun. We travelled through all the daylight hours, slowly, like a branch-line train moving through a backward shire in rural England, the train full of bumpkins, everyone talking and eating and enjoying themselves, and we stopped everywhere.

We had crossed the peninsula – it had the shape of a turtle's head and Qingdao lay on the south coast, the bottom of the beak. They said it was the coldest night of the year. There were frost crystals glittering in the air under the glaring lights. And in the swirling steam of the engine the German station and its tower and its stopped clock produced that nightmare feeling I got in China when I was among European buildings in dramatic weather. After all, a nightmare is the world turned upside-down, and thousands of Chinese mobbing a German railway station on a frosty night is a good example of that. It was a tangle of the familiar and the absurd, to produce fear. And all around it was very dark.

At the edge of the darkness, braving the cold, young men and women with flags and loud-hailers and megaphones called out, 'Come to our hotel!', 'You are welcome at our guesthouse!', 'We have good food and hot water!' They tried to out-shout each other, in the spirit of competition and free enterprise, as they touted for business among the arriving passengers.

The irrational dream-like quality of Qingdao did not vanish when the sun came out the next day. It looked almost as odd in the daylight as at night, though less menacing. I don't feel at home in foreign cities that have been heavily influenced by European buildings. When homesick imperialists put up granite mansions and Baptist churches and Catholic cathedrals with spires, and semi-detached houses with prim front gardens, I find it all a bit scary. It is out of place, it disorients me; anyway, what are all these Chinese doing here? I think. Or what is that stately Lutheran church doing near those noodle stalls? I am fascinated by such architectural capriccios (the Gothic spires among the pagodas, the Chinese faces at the windows of the English-style bungalows), but it is no more relaxing than the bad dream it strongly seems to mimic.

It is intensely reassuring to imperialists to build versions of their fat and monumental buildings, whether they fit the place or not. The Germans used a feeble pretext in the eighteen-nineties to threaten the Chinese and finally to force them to hand over various valuable concessions. In 1898 the Germans stuck a German town on to a small fishing village. One of the strangest buildings in China is in Qingdao, the former residence of the German governor, modelled on the kaiser's palace. I went inside and looked around until the caretakers chased me away. It is palatial; it has ramparts, granite and stucco balconies, Tudor-style beams, glazed tiles, circular staircases, porticoes and galleries (on the inside, under the high vaulted ceiling) and a conservatory. It was built in 1906. It is in perfect condition. It looks as though it will last for ever. Chairman Mao stayed in it when he visited Qingdao in 1958. For that reason, the Red Guards – who had a field-day smashing up the diabolical foreign influences in Qingdao – left the governor's palace alone. It remains unoccupied. It serves no useful purpose.

The Chinese in 1898 were browbeaten into granting the Germans a ninety-nine year lease, but less than twenty years later – just after the outbreak of the First World War, in 1914 – the Japanese occupied Qingdao. It is amazing that the Germans managed to accomplish so much in such a short time. Virtually all their buildings still stand, the railway still runs to Jinan, and the brewery produces the best beer in China – and sticks to the old spelling, Tsingtao beer.

The Chinese guidebook to Qingdao begins: 'Qingdao is a relatively young city with only eighty years of history. It used to be a small village. Since 1949, rapid developments have been made.' So much for the imperial designs, the foreign occupation, and two world wars. Even the US Marines and the American Seventh Fleet had a spell in Qingdao. None of these humiliations is forgotten;

they are simply not mentioned. The city is actually overrun with Japanese businessmen. I met Germans in my hotel (I asked them what they thought of the German buildings; they said, 'Too old, too hard to heat'), and the Seventh Fleet was invited back in 1986, forty years after they had backed the wrong side (they had helped Chiang Kai-shek), and were given a warm welcome.

The Chinese history of Qingdao was available, but the German history was obscure. I asked Mr Ling, a university student, what he knew about it – how big was the German settlement, what was the population, how did they put up all these large buildings and suburbs?

'There are no figures,' said Mr Ling.

'There must be,' I said.

'Yes. But the authorities do not release these figures. It might seem too humiliating if we knew how few Germans there were occupying the town. It is bad history – that's what we think.'

'Do you really think it is bad history?'

'No,' he said. 'I am interested in knowing the truth, but we have no books.'

That was a Chinese phenomenon. There was the distant past – the glorious anecdotal history; and there was the recent past – mostly Mao. In between, 1,000 years of Chinese history, everything was obscure. Perhaps it was politically questionable, or humiliating, or contradictory, or – like the years that had been expunged from the Mao Museum in Shaoshan – a hideous embarrassment.

In its way, Qingdao was as weird in its monuments and structures as the lost city of Gaocheng, in the boondocks of Xinjiang. Instead of a mud monastery or a crumbling mosque in the desert, Qingdao's counterparts were churches. The largest of them was the Catholic cathedral, built in a sort of twilight period in the early nineteen-thirties when the city was under the control of the Nanking government and the city abounded with missionaries.

It was a big bare church, made of grey stucco, with two spires. It had been completely renovated – freshly painted, regilded statues and crosses, the Stations of the Cross newly touched up, the ornamented nave picked out in gold; everything was bright and pious-looking, with baskets of fresh flowers on the altar. There was room for 600 people here – and it was said to be full on Sundays – but there were only three people praying on the day I went. It was mid afternoon on a weekday, the kneeling people whispering their prayers were elderly. Over the high altar was a scroll painted on the wall: VENITE ADOREMUS DOMINUM. The mass in Qingdao is said in Latin.

'I remember when they tore the crosses off the steeples of this church, during the Cultural Revolution,' Mr Bing said. He was a young man who had recently graduated from Shandong University. He had only been nine years old in 1967, but he had a very clear memory of the Cultural Revolution, because it had been fierce in Qingdao: this city was full of poisonous foreign influences, and such malignant and feudalistic harbingers of the right-deviationist wind (so to speak) had to be smashed by the vanguard of Mao Zedong's shining thought. It was well known that they had kicked the shit out of foreign-looking Qingdao.

But the steeples on the cathedral were very high.

'How did they get up there?' I could not understand how they had scaled these steeples. The crosses towered eight feet above the steeples, so getting to them was another problem.

Mr Bing said, 'The Red Guards held a meeting, and then they passed a motion to destroy the crosses. They marched to the church and climbed up to the roof. They pulled up bamboos and tied them into a scaffold. It took a few days – naturally they worked at night, and they sang the Mao songs. When the crowd gathered they put up ladders and they climbed and threw a rope around the Christian crosses – and they pulled them down. It was very exciting!'

After that, they did the same thing to two other churches, a sort of Venetian-looking one and a vast solid Lutheran one with a witch's hat for a steeple. They stacked the crosses at the Red Guard headquarters, but pious people stole them and took them away, burying them in the hills east of the city. These crosses were only disinterred a few years ago, when the reforms came into force. But the change is dramatic. For example, I bought a locally made crucifix – they were mass-producing them now in Qingdao – for fifty pence.

Mr Bing said he had vivid memories of the Cultural Revolution, because he had not had to go to school. He chased after the Red Guards, watching them destroy houses and persecute people; he had found it all thrilling, and he had always been part of the crowd when some spectacular piece of vandalism was unleashed.

He had even watched persecutions nearer home.

'There was a man in our compound whom we called "The Capitalist". He lived on the far side of the courtyard. We had a label or a name for everyone there. One we called "The Carpenter", and another "The Scholar". We paid rent to "The Capitalist" – he owned the houses.'

I said, 'If you were only nine years old how did you know what was going on?'

'There was nothing else for me to do except watch. And it was like a fever. All day, for years, I watched and listened.' He smiled, remembering. 'One day in 1967, the Red Guards held a meeting –'

I saw Mr Bing, a little raggedy-assed urchin peering through the window at the screaming youths with their red armbands.

'They decided to criticize "The Capitalist". There were about eight or nine of us following them – we were just little kids. We made a paper dunce cap for "The Capitalist". His name was Zhang. We went into his house – pushed the door open without knocking. He was in bed. He was very sick – he had stomach cancer. We shouted at him and denounced him. We made him confess to his crimes. We forced him to lower his head so that we could put on the dunce cap – lowering the head was a sort of submission to the will of the people, you see.'

'Did you parade him through the streets?'

'He had cancer. He could not walk. We mocked him in his bed. Then the neighbours came in. They also accused him – but not of being a capitalist. I remember one woman shouted, "You borrowed cooking pots and materials and never gave them back!" She was very angry about something he had done many years ago. Others said, "You tried to squeeze people" and "You took money".'

'What did the man say?'

'Nothing. He was afraid. And we found a great thing. On one of his old chairs there was a tiny emblem of the Guomindang. That proved he was a capitalist, and a spy. Everyone was glad about that. We screamed at him, "Enemy! Enemy!" He died soon after.'

This had almost taken my breath away. I said, 'That's a really terrible story.'

'Sure,' Mr Bing said, but without much force. 'It is terrible.'

But it was by the book. Mao said:

> To right a wrong it is necessary to exceed proper limits, and the wrong cannot be righted without the proper limits being exceeded.

That was turning a compassionate Chinese proverb on its head, one about the evil of going beyond proper limits to right a wrong. But Mao said that it was necessary to parade landlords down the street in dunce caps, and sleep in their beds, and take their grain, and humiliate them, 'to establish the absolute authority of the peasants'.

This little treatise 'On Going Too Far' was written in 1927. It was part of the script for the Cultural Revolution. The old man was greatly in favour of going too far ('going too far' has 'a revolutionary significance'). He went on:

> To put it bluntly, it was necessary to bring about a brief reign of terror . . .

But this German imperial outpost on the Chinese shore, which had been besieged at various times, and occupied by successive waves of Japanese, Americans and Nationalist Chinese, as well as the fiercest Red Guards (maddened by the city's look of European feudalism and all these Christian nests of superstition), had in the end turned out to be that quaintest of settlements, the seaside retirement town. The houses would not have disgraced the streets of Bexhill on Sea, on England's geriatric coast. Qingdao even had a breezy promenade, and slowly strolling oldies. It had a pier. It had ice-cream sellers. But it wasn't raffish and blowsy, a place for day-trippers. It was like its English counterpart – it was just as bungaloid.

High party officials – secretaries, directors and deputies (known universally in China as cadres) – longed to get a room or an apartment in Qingdao and spend the rest of their days in the sea air with its snap and tang. It was perhaps a bourgeois dream, but who could blame them? It was more a town than a city. It was not heavily industrialized. The weather was lovely most of the year – pleasant in the summer, bracing in the winter. There was only the occasional typhoon, but it was obvious that Qingdao was able to withstand such storms. It was not a congested place. It was almost unique among Chinese towns for having a unity of architectural style – it just so happened that it was German and not Chinese unity, but so what? That was the luck of its youth and the fact that it had been planned and built in such a short time. It wasn't the centuries-old accretion of monuments, pagodas, ruins, factories, blocks of flats, political boondoggling and bad ideas that made up the average Chinese city. It was not only a pretty place – the familiar and absurd its strongest features – but it was manifestly prosperous. Yantai was not a patch on it. It looked well-to-do. Its food was excellent – fresh seafood, Shandong vegetables. Its beaches were clean. There were plovers strutting on them. And those old folks you took to be members of the clean-up brigade, grubbing around the rocks and poking in the sand, stuffing sea-urchins and black kelp into their bags, were actually market traders who were selling this stuff to eat; but the result of their gathering left the beaches of Qingdao bright and tidy. No wonder the Chinese wanted to retire here.

I walked around, wishing I could stay longer. Generally speaking, it was not an ambition I had very often in China. I would visit a place, and get hold of it, and after three or four days I would want to let go and move on. The Chinese themselves were always telling me that I should go here or there – see this garden or that pavilion. In Qingdao they said, 'You should go to Mount Tai' – the holy mountain on the east of the peninsula. But I was happy in beautiful breezy Qingdao, and it was a bonus that after dark it looked slightly nightmarish.

It had been perfectly placed on the shore, taking full advantage of the cliffs. With the sea in front, and the apple orchards behind it, and the heavy industry well hidden, it seemed well planned. It also had a number of colleges and universities; it had several technical schools and an oceanographic institute. So, in addition to the vacationers and retired people, it also had a great number of students.

Qingdao was one of the pleasantest Chinese cities for walking in – I guessed that that had been part of the scheme to make it habitable. I met students on my walks. I asked them everything and I justified my interrogations by the observation about Confucius in the *Analects*: 'When the Master entered the Grand Temple he asked questions about everything.'*

There had been no demonstrations here. One girl said, 'A few years ago I would have demonstrated, but now I have too much to lose. The government would destroy me.'

She was twenty-one and was about to become a student teacher. She shrugged when she told me that, as though it was not quite what she had wanted.

'Is there anything wrong with being a teacher?' I asked.

'No. It's good work. But, you know, factory workers earn more than teachers, because they have bigger bonuses.'

Another girl said, 'I feel old' – she was twenty-two. And she explained, 'It is as if my life is all decided and mapped out. Nothing unexpected will happen. I will graduate. I will get an MA. The government will say that I must become a teacher. I will spend my life that way.'

'What would you do if you had your choice?'

'I would travel – not necessarily to foreign countries,' she said. 'I would wander, just wander, in China. Have you noticed that no one wanders here? No one is open-minded and aimless. Everyone has a purpose. But I would go here and there, talking to people, and I would choose out-of-the-way places, like Gansu and Xinjiang.'

The male students I talked to were much less adventurous than the women; much more conventional. The women seemed a little giggly, but that was only shyness. They could be very direct.

'When did you first feel old?' one asked me.

I answered truthfully. 'When I was six or seven, in the first grade. And then when I graduated from high school. And when I turned

---

* Confucius said, 'The asking of questions is in itself the correct rite' (III, 15).

thirty. Since then I have felt fairly young – that is, until you asked me the question.'

Most of them had been born in the first years of the Cultural Revolution, so they had no memory of it. They regarded it the way I had regarded the Great Depression in America, or the Second World War. They seemed episodes from the past – not very remote, but what mattered was that they were over. The Depression had had an end, and so had the war. 'People with college degrees sold apples on the street' went one of my father's depression stories. 'The neighbourhood air-raid warden yelled "Put that light out!"': that was the war. The young Chinese had the same sort of exemplary stories of the Cultural Revolution. Unlike Mr Bing, they had not even tagged along after the Red Guards. Theirs were always stories of disappearances, of neighbours and relatives sent into the countryside.

Their sharpest memories were of Mao's death, the Gang of Four, and Deng and his reforms, but even so they were more impatient than hopeful.

'If you live through these changes they seem very slow,' one said. 'It is only because you are a foreigner, on the outside, that the changes seem dramatic. For us they are very ponderous.'

When I considered that it was still illegal for a foreigner to talk at random with any Chinese citizen – the old rule was seldom enforced, but it was a well-known rule none the less – I was grateful for this frankness. The healthiest sign in China was this straight talk.

Because they were not of the Maoist years they were ambivalent about the old man. Indeed, I sometimes found talking to the young that I was more enthusiastic about Mao than they were. I admired his military brilliance, his subtle mind, his wit and charisma, his ingenuity and toughness. Who could not admire the Long March, or his tenacity against the Japanese, his voluminous writing, his ability to unify this enormous country? Of course, Confucianism also kept these people unified and family-minded, but Mao – who loved contradiction (and even wrote a long essay on the subject) – remained for me the most fascinating and ambiguous figure in Chinese history.

For these students he was an uninteresting riddle. He had cast a long shadow, yes; but they were still living in that shadow, and they didn't like it very much.

'He was a strange man,' a student in Qingdao told me.

I asked whom he resembled, because Chinese life is full of models, like the heroic soldier Lei Feng, the inspired worker Iron Man Wang (Wang Jinxi), and The Foolish Old Man Who Removed the Mountains.

'He was unlike any other Chinese man,' the student said. 'I think he read too many books, and began to make a place for himself in Chinese history. He was an arrogant and self-important man. He behaved like an emperor.'

My reaction was *Yes, but* – yet why bother to sell them on Mao? They had to live the rest of their lives here. I could leave any time I liked. In the end, it was for them to deal with his memory, not me.

'When Mao died I knew I had to cry,' another student said. 'We had been required to love him. I was just a little kid at school. I didn't feel anything, but the teachers were watching. I had to force myself to cry.'

Ice was packed into the bays and inlets. It was January, after all. But it was sunny and during the day it was almost warm. The rocks on the promontories of Qingdao were fluted with ice, too, and some were ringed by glassy skirts of ice crust. I wondered whether it was because it was out of season that the place was so pleasant. There was a swimmer on Beach Number Two one day. He strolled down and plunged in, as people were said to do in freezing Harbin in the winter – breaking ice in the river to go for a dip. But it wasn't swimming. It was a rather pointless act of willpower, like holding a lighted match under your finger (a loony pastime advocated by the convicted Watergate flunkey, Gordon Liddy, by the way). Would people do such things if no one were watching, or if they couldn't tell someone about it later on?

I had arrived on a freezing night, feeling I had stepped into a nightmare made up of old German movies and winter storms – steam locomotives, and fog, and the black station with the hands missing from its clock-face. I left on a dazzling spring-like day, and now in the sunshine I could see that the station was a relic, with the red star of China planted on its conical roof. The loud whistle blew, and a moment later the train was tracking past the islands, and lighthouse, and breezy streets, into the open country of Shandong that was so flat it had the look of a flood-plain.

19

The Shandong Express to Shanghai: Train Number 234

This featureless brown farmland with its ditches and its telephone poles and its tile-roofed houses looked as dreary as Belgium. From the farmers' point of view it was the worst time of year. The muddy lanes, the ruts, the puddles, the cold, the January drizzle. There was nothing to eat yet. The people laboured along on bikes, they thrashed their oxen, they pushed carts that rolled uncertainly on big wobbly wheels.

There was a Belgian man in my compartment. After we got acquainted I nerved myself and asked him the question I had been rehearsing.

'Does this part of Shandong look like Belgium?'

We looked at the ditches, the ploughed fields, the puddles, the poles.

'Yes. Is similar.'

So I had not been imagining it. These winter journeys in China were tiring, and I sometimes suspected that my weariness blurred my perceptions – or else made me giddy and fanciful. And these long stretches of brown, ploughed China could be depressing. The whole of this overpopulated region was like that. Like Belgium, it tired my eyes.

Alain was from Antwerp. He was travelling with his Chinese counterpart Li. They were going to Hefei, but they did not know that Hefei was the new centre of student protest. They had no interest in politics. They were telephone engineers in a Belgian-Chinese joint-venture to upgrade the telephone system. Alain said, 'I think we arrive here just in time.'

It was well known that Chinese phones were hopeless. It was impossible to direct-dial any Chinese city, and it was very hard to make even a local call. And when you got through you often heard five other voices – or more – holding simultaneous conversations. A Chinese phone was like Chinese life: it was full of other people, close together, doing exactly what you were trying to do. Often the phone went dead. You could wait eight hours to be connected. Occasionally a whole city would be cut off. For several days it might be impossible to make a call outside Shanghai. In Taiyuan, the provincial capital of Shanxi, any calls, other than local ones, were out of the question: the city was isolated, though it could be reached by morse code on the telegraph. The old Chinese phones were heavy black bakelite that shattered or chipped if they were struck; the new phones were lightweight plastic, like toys, and were usually a colour that did not inspire confidence, such as flamingo pink or powder blue. It was possible to imagine how the Chinese felt about them from the way they shrieked into them. It was always shrieks. No one ever chatted on a telephone in China.

I told Alain these things. He knew them, he said. He was aware that his task was monumental. Fortunately he had a sense of humour, or at least a sense of silliness, that made life bearable. His English was shaky. He said things like 'Will you traduce her for me?' and 'I feel happy as a roy' and 'The Chinese has good formation but bad motivation.'

He was the complete Foreign Expert. He did not speak Chinese. He had no interest in politics. Chinese art to him was the enamelled ashtrays and bamboo back-scratchers they sold at the Friendship Stores. Apart from Qingdao and Hefei and Shanghai, he had not travelled anywhere. He said he knew Belgium intimately, though. He was fluent in both Flemish and French. He tried to teach me the almost unpronounceable Flemish word *schild* (shield), but I could do no more than approximate it and sounded as though I were swallowing a quahog.

We played capitals, to kill the time. Mr Li knew little more than Alain, who failed on Hungary, India and Peru (Mr Li knew Hungary). Alain did not read. He amused himself with his video camera, for which he had paid £750 in a duty-free shop. He sent tapes home – tapes of Shandong looking horribly like Belgium.

Mr Li was somewhat similar.

'Think of a country,' I said.

He was baffled. 'I cannot think of one.'

'Any country,' I said. 'Like Brazil, or Zambia, or Sweden.'

He made a face: nothing. He did not know any geography at all. He was not just geocentric; he was ignorant.

Their field was telephones – wiring, systems, satellites, exchanges, link-ups, computers. They had this very narrow but very deep area of expertise, and it was all they cared about. They could talk animatedly about computer telephone systems, but about nothing else. Mention the rain in Guangdong or the snow in Harbin and they looked blank. Don't mention books.

They were the new people in the world, the up-and-comers, the only employable folks: they had technical skills, they were problem-solvers, and they were willing to travel. In every other respect they were stupid, but their stupidity did not matter. I found them very friendly, because they were enthusiastic about their work.

'My boss is not happy with me today,' Alain said. 'But the fault is the workers. Chinese workers like to sleep.'

Mr Li agreed with this.

We looked at Alain's snapshots – a great stack of cosy Belgian interiors. Fat people in bright clothes. People eating or sitting in small parlours.

'This is my grandmother. This is my sister. My mother. My father. . .'

We went through the stack twice. I got to recognize the porcelain figures on the mantelpiece at Alain's grandmother's, and a particular cushion, and his father's blue sweater. He loved looking at them. He said he missed home.

'What do you miss most?'

'Beef,' he said. That was what the man had told me in Harbin. What was it about beef? Alain said, 'But I have this.'

He brought out a bulging knapsack. It contained a stock of canned goods. Alain called it his emergency kit. He had brought it from Antwerp. He had canned carrots, canned mackerel, cans of sardines, and a brand of cocktail sausages called TV Meat. They were for nibbling in front of a television. Alain also had one of those, a twelve-inch set, for playing his tapes. He had more luggage than anyone I had ever seen on a train. 'My landlord in Antwerp told me I could not leave my things in my apartment, so I took it all to China.' He also had many cans of beef chunks in gravy, packages of a pemmican-looking substance called Bifi, a can of chocolate paste called Choco that he spread on bread, and a dozen chocolate bars.

It had been my intention to get off this train at Xuzhou, in a remote corner of Jiangsi Province, and to make my way somehow about 100 miles south-east to the little town of Huai'an, which was on the Grand Canal. In that town, in 1898, Zhou Enlai was born. I wanted to see his house. Had it been made into a shrine, like Mao's in Shaoshan? And if so, was it now as deserted as Mao's birthplace, or was it teeming with well-wishers? It was whispered by many people that Zhou was the secret hero of the Chinese revolution. Of course he had written very little, and he was no theorist; but he was urbane and compassionate. He was a gentleman – the sort described and praised by Confucius: temperate, kind, magnanimous, and so forth.

The trouble with the stop in Xuzhou was that it occurred at 3.00 in the morning. At that hour the whole of China is asleep. I would be emerging from the train at this ridiculous hour on a winter night, and have six hours to kill before knowing whether it was possible to find a bus or a car to Zhou Enlai's homestead.

I decided to stay in bed.

Alain and Li got off at Bengbu at 5.00 in the morning to transfer to a Hefei train. Before we turned in they piled their boxes and suitcases outside in the corridor. The Head of the Train complained about Alain's trunk, but Mr Li explained that it contained the Foreign Expert's worldly goods from Belgium.

'Regulations, regulations,' the Head said. 'You must register it.'

They didn't bother. More people knocked on the door in the night to complain about it, but I was asleep at 5.00 when they got up. I woke up when one of them sat on my foot, but then they were gone. That was the way with trains – something dream-like in the way people came and went. By 8.00 there was someone else in Alain's berth, reading a comic book. It was a young woman, with a veil drawn tight over her face, because of the dust.

'The Great River,' she said, using the Chinese name for the Yangtze.

I decided to piss into it. I went to the toilet. On the door was a long Chinese word, TINGCHESHIQINGWUSHIYONG, which was seven characters run together, meaning 'While the train is stopped please don't use this room.' But it hadn't stopped; it was crossing the long railway bridge over the Yangtze. I entered the room, peered into the open hole and let fly.

Having seen Xinjiang and the north-east and the open spaces of Inner Mongolia, I now knew that this eastern part of classical China was the least interesting to look at. It was brown factories, and black canals separated by flat cabbage fields. It was no miracle that anything at all grew here, since it had been ploughed and fertilized and planted for thousands of years. The secret is revealed every morning, as men with long-handled dippers scoop human shit out of dark barrels and fertilize the fields. It was the flattest, ugliest and most populous part of China; but its shitters kept it in business. Shanghai residents produced 7,500 tons of human shit a day.* It was all used. Farm yields were high, but the place epitomized drudgery. Everyone's energy was expended in simply existing there, and every inch of it had been put to use. Why grow flowers when you can grow spinach? Why plant a tree when you can use the sunshine on your crop? And the untillable soil was perfect for a factory. People praised Wuxi's lake, but the lake was dead, and Wuxi was simply awful-looking, part of the sprawl of Shanghai, although it was seventy-five miles from the Bund.

In any kind of travel there is a good argument for going back and verifying your impressions. Perhaps you were a little hasty in

* *China Daily*, 7 July 1987.

judging the place? Perhaps you saw it in a good month? Something in the weather might have sweetened your disposition? In any case, travel is frequently a matter of seizing a moment. It is personal. Even if I were travelling with you, your trip would not be mine. Our accounts of the journeys would be different. You would notice how I provoked people with questions, and how I loitered in the market, and my fear of Chinese water that amounted almost to hydrophobia. I might mention your impatience, or your liking for dumplings, or the way you wilted in the heat. You would write about the kinds of Chinese food, and I about the way they wolfed it. If you spoke about Mao I would contradict you.

On a second visit to Shanghai I was startled by its crowds and traffic – people and cars vying for the right of way; and by its contrasts of horror and beauty; and by its neurotic energy, a sort of frenzy that was unique to Shanghai. The Shanghainese have a sense of belonging to the city that resembles the New Yorker's strong identification with New York. It is not chauvinism or civic pride. It is a sense of shared experience, the same headaches and complaints, a sort of it's-awful-but-I-love-it attitude. It is also a sense of being possessed by the place, locked in its embrace and embattled at the same time. Speaking as someone from out of town, I find both Shanghai and New York pretty dreadful. The noise alone is cause enough to regard them as uninhabitable. I grew up in the big-enough city of Boston, and when people talk about New York's (or Shanghai's) vitality I simply see a lot of frantic pedestrians. And writers who celebrate cities always seem laughable to me, because every city-dweller, in order to keep sane and survive, invents his own city. Your New York is not my New York. On the other hand, my Shanghai would probably be yours. It is simple but dense; it is horizontal; and it has remarkably few landmarks. New York is vertical, a city of interiors – and secrets; but Shanghai is its streets. There is not enough room for so many people indoors, and so people work, talk, cook, play and carry on their businesses on the pavements. There is no other way for the city to cope with its overpopulation. It is the most visible and obvious of cities – perhaps therein lies its charm for those who praise it: that its modes of life and work are so apparent to even the casual stroller. There is also a strong sense of old China in the street life, and such sights seem to give it 'atmosphere'. But I would rather live in a place where I could walk without incessantly bumping into people, or dodging traffic, or where I could hear myself think.

But the sense of urban solidarity that characterizes Shanghai had a marked effect on the student demonstrations. It was the only city where factory-workers linked arms with students. And the numbers were so great (they varied from 100,000 to 200,000) that the city came to a halt – no buses, no taxis, and no one was able to work.

I went out to Fudan University on the outskirts – and very wretched-looking outskirts at that – where I talked with students about the demonstrations.

One student told me, 'We held meetings, but we wanted to disassociate ourself from the party, so we insisted that student cadres had to leave the hall. These cadres are appointed by the party – we didn't want them.'

'Did the cadres join the march?'

'No,' the student said. 'We put their names on our posters, but we printed their names upside-down or in slanted characters.'

'What was the point of that?'

'It is disrespectful to print someone's name upside-down.'

True, a Chinese person's name is everything to him. It represents himself, his parents, his extended family and even his village. The worst, most insulting curse anyone can utter in China against a Chinese person is *Cao ni de xing!*, 'Fuck your name!'

The student said that the term 'running dogs' was used in the demonstrations, for the first time since the Cultural Revolution. And big-character posters were another artefact from that time that had been pressed into service, but they now read MORE FREEDOM and WE WANT DEMOCRACY. Rising prices, low salaries, poor public transportation, byzantine election procedures, and difficult rules governing studying abroad were other grievances.

I carefully noted these down, and then a young man named Mr Hong said, 'You know about the Jan and Dean Concert?'

Jan and Dean? 'Baby Talk', 'Surf City', and 'Ride The Wild Surf'? The early sixties, southern California, totally tubular surfer-duo? *That* Jan and Dean? I had been under the impression that after Jan wrapped his car around a tree in 1966, suffering paralysis and brain damage, this group was no longer operational.

But I was wrong. This American group, a spin-off from the music of the Beach Boys (who were their sometime collaborators), had undergone a recrudescence and were yapping to beat the band, actually singing 'Surf City' in Shanghai, twenty-nine years after they had released their first record. Perhaps I should not have been surprised. After all, Mr Tian had sung me a Neil Sedaka song in the Langxiang wilderness only a month before.

Mr Hong said, 'We liked Jan and Dean very much. The students were excited. Jan and Dean invited some students on to the stage to dance. They were dancing and enjoying themselves. But afterwards those students were accused by the police of being disruptive.'

'What happened to them?'

'They were taken into custody. They were beaten.'

This also fuelled the students' enthusiasm for a demonstration. But there was a feeling that the students had been led into a trap, since the conservatives used the demonstrations as an excuse to call for a limiting of the reforms.

Everyone agreed that what was happening in China indicated a power struggle in the inner party, between the reformers, led by Deng Xiaoping, and the eight or ten so-called leftists, who were anti-reformers, led by Peng Zhen (chairman of the National People's Congress). In spite of his dogmatic Maoist views, Peng had never been purged. These puritanical old troopers, many of whom had shared the privations of the Long March, were outraged by students who were making demands. Their American counterparts might be the Veterans of Foreign Wars, who also hated student protests. The problem was that there were also people in the inner party who were pushing harder for reform.

I paid a call on Mr Brooks, the American consul-general, who had impressed me so much a few months before by telling me that he didn't have the slightest idea of what would happen next in China.

'The Chinese will go on doing business,' he said. 'Foreign investors aren't concerned with student demonstrations. What would worry them is a return to Stalinism.'

We then talked about Deng's successor. Would it be Hu Yaobang, Deng's bridge partner? Deng himself had indicated this.

Mr Brooks said that Deng had hoped to step down, but that he wanted to make sure his policies would continue. When Deng went he wanted to take all the doubtful people with him.

'The trouble is,' Mr Brooks said, 'Mr Hu has disappeared from view. A foreign minister told a visiting Japanese delegation, "He's tired." In Chinese terms that means he can't do the work.'

I listened to the radio that night and heard a news report that Hu Yaobang had been forced to resign after a session of self-criticism in which he said he had 'made many mistakes'.

So, just like that, Mr Hu was gone, and Deng didn't have a successor.

Dr Xie Xide, the president of Fudan University, was a member of the Central Committee. I saw her the following day and asked her how she had found out about Mr Hu's resignation.

'I heard it on the Voice of America,' she said. 'But I was not surprised. He tended to make decisions without consulting anyone. For example, once he was on an official visit to Japan. He was very enthusiastic. He invited 3,000 Japanese students to visit China.'

'For studying?'

'No. Just for a visit,' Dr Xie said. 'But we are a poor country. We can't afford that sort of thing.'

Mr Hu had often had his foot in his mouth. He had begun to wear western suits, and although he had been designated a sort of official greeter of Eastern Bloc delegations (the nine Poles in pork-pie hats, the Rumanian wrestlers, the Hungarian joint-venture in making paprika), Mr Hu's sympathies were with the western capitalists. He became very excited at one stage about contagious diseases and he advocated the abandonment of chopsticks in favour of knives and forks. And why not have individual portions, he exclaimed, instead of the Chinese dish in the middle of the table, and everyone shoving their chopsticks in? He had recently gone to Tibet and suggested that the Han people should leave the region forthwith and let the Tibetans run it themselves. (In itself it was a bold thought, but it would have set a disastrous example to other autonomous regions, like Xinjiang and Inner Mongolia.) He had also said, rather tactlessly (considering his post as party secretary), 'Marxism cannot solve China's problems.'

The official version of Mr Hu's departure was that at 'an enlarged meeting of the Political Bureau of the Communist Party of China's Central Committee, Hu Yaobang made a self-criticism of his mistakes on major issues of political principles in violation of the party's principle of collective leadership'. This was reported by China's official mouthpiece, the Xinhua News Agency. Mr Hu was further accused of having caused 'a slackening of ideological control'.

In a word, Mr Hu was being blamed for the student protests. He was spineless, weepy, ideologically unsound. In the pantheon of modern Chinese goblins and enemies, which included a running dog, a paper tiger, a snake spirit and a cow demon, Mr Hu had become one of the slimiest and least trustworthy, a bourgeois liberal. The Maoist view still stood: a liberal was a dangerous hypocrite.

He was not the only one. A day or so later, the writer Wang Ruowang was expelled from the Communist Party. Was this interesting, and did anyone care about such boring political ambushes? My feeling was that I would much rather have been bird-watching in Heilongjiang, yet that these political events were not without their amusing ironies. For example, this man Wang had had his problems before. In 1957 he had been labelled 'a rightist' in Mao's Anti-Rightist Campaign – a witch-hunt that had followed the Hundred Flowers Campaign (when the rightists had been suckered into making public criticisms of the party). And then, in 1966, Mr Wang had fallen again. He was 'struggled' with and finally charged with being 'a cow demon'. This he had to live with for ten years. He was then rehabilitated and made a council member of the Chinese Writers' Association and of the Shanghai Writers' Association. His crime (so Xinhua said) was that he 'advocated bourgeois liberalization' and criticized the party saying, 'You [the party] have nothing left to do now that the people have the freedom to write and to pick whatever theatrical performances they like.'

Shanghai had just seen a Chinese run of the torrid O'Neill play, *Desire under the Elms*, so there was a grain of truth in that (it had been banned until recently). In a sense, the only heresy that Mr Wang committed was that he said what everyone knew to be true.

It was very obvious that many people behaved like capitalists and petit-bourgeois traders. They had family businesses. They owned shops. Just the day before Wang fell I had a ride in a privately owned taxi. 'I own this car,' the man said. It was a jalopy, but it was all his. People were changing jobs, making dresses, peddling their own wares, and selling their vegetables off their own pushcarts. But it was a great mistake for anyone to call this capitalism. You had to call it The Chinese Way. And it was an error for anyone to draw attention to the new freedoms. Hypocrisy was necessary. The government did not want to appear soft; and the party preferred to live with the illusion that it was more repressive than it actually was.

It was another instance of the Chinese hating idle talk. It was a puritanical dislike for loose behaviour and foolery. The Chinese attitude was: *Get on with the job, don't talk so much, don't ask questions.* It did not matter very much if someone was making a fat profit out of his cabbages, or if he was putting on a western play, or if he believed in the hygiene of the knife and fork. The error was in talking about such things, because that created conflict. I remember my Chinese friend in Peking, when I was protesting about Mr Fang being my nanny. This knowledgeable Chinese fellow looked at me, closed his eyes, and shook his head, a gesture that meant: *Don't say another word.*

In the mean time, as long as you didn't gloat about it, you could do pretty much as you liked. These days no one breathed down my neck. They had forgotten that I was wandering through China. And one day in Shanghai I saw some students from Nankai University in Tianjin – about twenty of them – who were about to leave for a tour of the United States. They were a theatrical troupe, who were on their way to Minneapolis and St Louis and a dozen other cities to perform a play adapted from the novel, *Rickshaw Boy*.

They were friendly, eager students, very excited about their overseas tour. I took one aside and asked him about the production. The novel, by Lao She, is the story of a rickshaw-puller in Peking in the nineteen-thirties.

I said, 'Wasn't Lao She hounded to death by Red Guards?'
'Ha! Ha!' the student said, and the laugh meant emphatically: *Don't bring that up*.

I stayed in Shanghai a while longer. I bought an old goldfish bowl at the antique shop. I saw a truly terrible Chinese film: it was violent and thoroughly philistine. It rained. People talked about the power struggle in the inner party. They were not cynical or indifferent to such big changes – the expulsions and resignations – but since they could do nothing about them they had to accept them. The rain began to leak into my soul. I walked through the rat's maze of back-lanes near the cathedral, and got glimpses of ancient China in the drizzle. I was happiest those nights, trudging alone in the rain, glancing into windows, seeing people ironing and making noodles and pasting up the red banners for the Chinese New Year, watching people roistering in cheap steamy restaurants and strangling chickens. It was wonderful to be anonymous those dark nights in Shanghai, when no one could see my face, and I heard a mother scolding a child with 'Where have you been?'

20

The Night Train to Xiamen: Number 375

It was the familiar exit from Shanghai, the main line through the cabbagey province of Zhejiang and tarted-up Hangzhou, the haunt of tourists and nifty little Japanese; and as soon as the hills appeared the sun slid behind them and night fell. There were three Chinese in my compartment when I pulled the blanket over my head, but by morning only one remained. This was Mr Ni. He explained that the others had got off at Yingtan, when the train turned left on to the spur line through Fujian, the coastal province that faces Taiwan. Mr Ni was also going to Xiamen, and even referred to it (for my benefit) by its old name, Amoy.

He was beginning work on an offshore dredging operation. He explained that he was a surveyor and that he disliked south China. It was his sorry fate to have been posted here for two years. He was Shanghai born and bred and had all of that city's characteristic bumptiousness – he was blunt, offhand, presumptuous and fluent. He regarded himself as cultured. Southerners were yokels, in his view. They were greedy. That was why so many of them had left China. (It was true the world was full of spirited and hard-working Fujianese.) We were at Zhangzhou, where tangerines grow.

'In Shanghai we are sick for knowledge,' Mr Ni said. 'But these

Amoy people are only interested in making money. That is their main characteristic. They don't like reading or education. Just business.'

A moment later, Mr Ni asked me if I wanted to change money – my Foreign Exchange Certificates for his *Renminbi*. Or did I want an interpreter in Xiamen? Or he could accompany me on my way. He had taught himself English and wanted to practise it. Also – he repeated – what about changing money?

Mr Ni was invaluable to me that day in unravelling the news of the political confusion in the *People's Daily*. Such subtle news did not get into the English-language *China Daily*. The first interesting item quoted a high Politburo member, Li Peng, as saying, 'The party has full confidence in intellectuals.'

An intellectual in China is someone with a high-school education, doing a white-collar job. It is not a bespectacled nerd who sits around sipping tea and quoting Mencius. In the way that Chinese society is more easily defined by negatives, an intellectual is not a factory worker nor a peasant farmer. It is a person who can read and write, who does not get his hands dirty.

The main report in the paper was of Zhao Ziyang: a strong implication that he had taken Hu Yaobang's place. He had been elevated by Deng. That was incontestable. He had met a Hungarian delegation – meeting such delegations had been Mr Hu's old job. But the clearest sign that he had displaced Mr Hu completely was his unambiguous criticism of Mr Hu.

He said that Mr Hu had been 'incapable of fighting against westernization'; that he had sought 'to push political reforms too far', and – in an unusual burst of frankness from a Chinese leader – that Mr Hu 'had been warned several times over the years'.

It was obvious that Mr Zhao was in the ascendant and that Mr Hu was on his way to becoming a non-person. Mr Zhao was a natty dresser – he nearly always wore a western suit and tie. He jogged. But he was careful to distance himself from westernization, which was almost synonymous with bourgeois liberalization. It had already taken hold, and seemed at the moment to be irreversible. And because its adherents – so-called intellectuals – were nervous, displeased and demoralized, Mr Zhao had to be especially enigmatic.

Mr Ni and I puzzled over the paper, and then I asked him what he thought would happen? Would Mr Zhao ultimately replace Deng Xiaoping?

'I do not know,' he said, and raised his hands in surrender: it was the Chinese funk when considering the future. After the shocks and reverses that had surprised the Chinese, only an ignoramus would risk making a fool of himself in speculating on what was to come.

But what about the Chinese liking for gambling? Wasn't that a sort of forecasting and speculation? I felt it was, but gambling in Chinese terms is not rational. It isn't a judicious indication of a possible outcome. It is a fling, something reckless, with a hint of hysteria in it. You might bet on the result of two fighting crickets (it is a popular pastime in China) or on a throw of the dice, because triumph depends entirely on luck or good fortune – spiritual qualities. But politics wasn't moral and it certainly wasn't a lottery. It had to do with ambition, power-seeking and greed, and it was not only unreadable but regarded as unsuitable as an occasion for a gamble. The Chinese would have a flutter on a cricket but never on a commissar.

Mr Ni was cautious, but Mrs Deng, who joined us, was talkative. She was also headed for the coast. She was thirty, she had one child, her husband was studying engineering. She worked in a government office. She wore her hair fashionably curled, and her bright yellow sweater had poppies embroidered on it. She also wore a skirt. 'But it's cold!' she cried, smacking her knees. 'I should put on my trousers.'

I asked her whether she had been surprised when Mr Hu had been forced to resign.

'Not surprised at all!' she said. She blinked fiercely. She had small teeth. She silenced Mr Ni. 'What a man! Did you hear about the way he invited all those Japanese people to visit China? The Japanese pay for thirty Chinese, but we pay for 3,000 of them. It makes no sense!'

'Maybe he was being generous,' I said.

She batted me on the arm.

'Ha! Generous! He doesn't know what he's saying! He once read a speech at a general's funeral. "We are so sad," he said. But he was smiling! He just talks and talks. We say, "He's so happy he doesn't know his name." You understand? Ask him his name and he says, "Ha! Ha! I forget!"'

'Do you think it is bad that he talks a lot?' I asked, knowing full well that blabbing is seen in China as dangerous and stupid.

'It is just big talk,' Mrs Deng said. 'You know the saying about the skinny face?'

'Sorry, I don't.'

'If you have a skinny face you beat your cheeks' – she smacked her face with her stiff fingers – 'to make your cheeks swell up.'

'What's the point?'

'Your cheeks get fat because you beat them, and you try to make people think you're rich.'

'I see. A pretence to make yourself look good.'

'Hu Yaobang is like that. Can such a man be head of this big country of China? Never.'

This made more sense than the *People's Daily* which linked Mr Hu with bourgeois liberalization and student protest. He simply talked too goddamned much.

Another fellow I met on the trip to Xiamen had a familiar request. Would I please give him an English name? His Chinese name was Li Guoqing – or 'National Day' Li, because he had been born on an auspicious day in October. I was a little sceptical about the Chinese who called themselves Ronny and Julian, but Guoqing insisted, so I said, 'How about George?'

He smiled and muttered it.

I asked him how much he was paying for his ticket from Shanghai to Xiamen. He said 40 *yuan* (£7). Mine had cost me 148 *yuan* (£26). If we had flown, his plane ticket would have cost him 83 *yuan* (£14.50) and mine 173 *yuan* (£30). Foreigners in China always pay more. It is the policy. They also get better treatment, on the whole – though not in railway trains. I had heard of Chinese being bumped from Soft Class in favour of a foreigner, but I never saw it happen.

'Foreigners have more money,' Guoqing said. 'Why shouldn't they pay more?'

'If you come to America do you think you should pay less because you're Chinese?' I asked.

But he wasn't listening. 'Please call me George,' he said.

Xiamen, on the hilly coast, had the reputation for being the richest city in China, for having the best houses and the happiest people. It also had the largest proportion of families with relatives living abroad. Stop anyone on the street in Xiamen, it was said, and they would tell you that they had an uncle in Manila, or a cousin in Singapore, or that a whole branch of the family was settled in California. They stayed in touch. In general, when people left China for fresh pastures they left the poverty-stricken province of Fujian (Fukien) – this was in the nineteenth century – and most of them set sail from Xiamen (Amoy). They were seafaring people from one of the greatest Chinese ports: millions of them slipped away.

But they did not forget their homeland. They came back to marry. They sent money home. In many cases they returned and built large houses and retired here. Without question, Xiamen has the noblest houses, the grandest villas, the most elaborate walls and gardens, and the most magnanimous charitable and philanthropic enterprises. These are all the result of successful emigrants, who became rich overseas and for sentimental reasons remitted their funds.

The ships that were involved in the Boston Tea Party had come from here. The English word 'tea' is Xiamen-dialect Chinese. Xiamen's style of building is found in Canton and also in old Singapore and rural Malaysia – the tall shop-house with an overhang, and the pavement running underneath that second storey. It is associated with Straits Chinese – the shopkeepers of South-East Asia. It is not found elsewhere in China. It is practical and pretty, and I cannot think of it without seeing men in flapping pyjamas, and women measuring out rice from sacks, and young Chinese girls with soulful faces gazing out of shuttered windows upstairs.

The villas – big stout houses with high ceilings and wrap-around verandahs – also resembled the old houses of Singapore and Malaysia that were torn down to make room for the banks and hotels. Until recently they were kept in Xiamen because no one had the money to tear them down or to replace them; but then they were valued for aesthetic and historical reasons, and a preservation order was placed upon them. The new buildings of Xiamen are in a suburb beyond the Causeway, where they belong.

I found it almost impossible to find fault with Xiamen. Because it is in the south the fruit is wonderful and cheap – all kinds: haws, oranges, tangerines, apples, pears, persimmons, grapes. And because it is on the sea the fish is plentiful and various – all sorts of eels, and big garupas, and prawns. The best and most expensive were the lobster-sized crayfish. They were kept in tanks in the restaurants – the southern Chinese habit (because of a lack of refrigeration) of keeping food alive until the last moment. In other tanks were eels, fish, frogs and ducks – and even ducklings. You were invited to point out your proposed entrée, and they cut its throat.

On a back-street in Xiamen, at a grubby little restaurant, I saw two cages, one containing a baby owl and the other holding a scowling hawk. There was hardly enough meat on either of them to fill a dumpling. They perched unsteadily, confined by the small cages, and they trembled with anxiety. When I stopped to look at them, a crowd gathered. I asked the owner how much he wanted to make them into a meal. He said 20 *yuan* for the owl and 15 *yuan* for the hawk.

'Why not let them go?'

'Because I paid for them,' he said.

'But they're unhappy.'

His laugh meant *You are a fool.*

He said, 'They taste very nice.'

'They are small,' I said. 'One mouthful and that's it.'

'The meat of this bird is very good for your eyes,' he said.

'That is not true,' I said. 'Only savages believe that.'

He was offended and angry. His mouth went strange and he said nothing.

'It's a superstition,' I said. 'It is old thinking. Like eating rhino horn for your dick. Listen' – he was now turning away – 'this bird eats mice. It is helpful. You should let it go.'

The man began to hiss at me, a sort of preliminary to blowing up in my face. I had no money. I went back to the hotel and got 35 *yuan* out of my room, but by the time I walked back to the restaurant the cages were empty. I had imagined holding a little revival of the Liberation of Living Creatures, in which I would release the birds from their cages. But I was too late today. The owl and the hawk had been eaten.

As a consolation I went to Xiamen market, bought two mourning doves for about £1.25 the pair, and let them go. They flapped over the harbour, past the hooting boats, to the nearby island of Gulanyu. Believing it might be a sign, I followed them the next day.

Gulanyu was a small island containing a lovely settlement in which no wheeled vehicles were allowed – no cars, no bicycles, no pushcarts. It was a five-minute free ferry ride across the harbour, and from its highest point – Sunlight Rock – it looked like Florence, or a Spanish city, a tumbled expanse of tiled roofs, all terracotta and green trees, and church steeples. There were three Christian churches at the centre of the settlement: this island had once held only foreigners – Dutch, Portuguese, English, Germans. It was Japanese until the end of the war, and then there were a number of tough battles, against the Nationalists, who ultimately took Quemoy – which is quite visible to the north-east.

'Enemy territory?' I asked.

'We are all Chinese brothers,' Mr Wei said.

'Then why the trenches and foxholes?'

The east coast of Xiamen was all military earthworks and gun emplacements.

'Because sometimes they shoot at us,' Mr Wei said.

But I liked old coastal China. It had been influenced by its traders and occupiers, and because of its sea-going communities it was outward-looking. The dutiful and pious tycoons who had made millions overseas had obeyed the Confucian precepts and become philanthropic. The houses and schools they built blended with the church with its sign ECCLESIA CATHOLICA, which was Romanesque, and the old German consulate, which might have been designed by Joseph Conrad. The philanthropoids had built villas in a section of Gulanyu called Sea View Gardens, and there they lived among foreign compradors and tea merchants and petty consular officials, each on his own colonnaded verandah, under the palm trees.

The building regulations on Gulanyu are unique in China for

their fastidiousness. No building may be higher than three storeys, all have to be made of red brick and carved stone, and all designs have to be approved by the Architectural Commission. They were good old-world designs, and even the newest buildings – the vegetable market and the museum – were being put up with great care. Restoration work was being carried out on the villas in order to turn them into hotels and guesthouses without losing their character. It was odd for the Chinese, so practical and penny-pinching, to spend extra time and money to make a thing look right. The magnificent city wall around Peking, with its forty-four bastions and sixteen gates had simply been bulldozed by Mao's goonish philistines chanting, 'Down with the Four Olds! Up with the Four News! New Thinking! New Customs! New Habits! New –!' In this same spirit, two miles of the Great Wall were pulled down between 1970 and 1974 by an army unit at Gubeikou, and the ancient stone blocks of the wall were used to build army barracks.

But this vandalism of China's recent past did not extend to Gulanyu except in the form of big-character graffiti (LONG LIVE THE THOUGHTS OF MAO ZEDONG! was still legible in two-foot characters on the walls of a villa) and in selective desecration. The Catholic church was turned into a factory, hate meetings were held in the Protestant ('Three-In-One') church, and the Buddha statues were smashed in the temples – a quarter of Xiamen is Buddhist.

I asked Mr Wei the reason for the meticulous restoration of Gulanyu.

'Because the government wants to turn this into a tourist island,' he said. He also said that he was relieved that the government had not decided to tear the place down, as they had so much else.

We were walking towards Sunlight Rock and ran into a junkman on a back-street. He was a fat boy with a pole across his shoulders, carrying loads of waste paper. I stopped him and because his dialect was incomprehensible to me, Mr Wei helped me quiz him.

The boy said that if the waste paper was good quality, like old, neatly stacked newspapers, he would pay 50 *fen* for one kilo – about four pence a pound. That seemed to me pretty fair. But for other paper he paid less than a penny a pound.

How was business?

'No good,' he said. 'This is hard work for very little money.'

Off he went, his pole bouncing from the weight of the waste-paper bundles.

'Why are you so interested in the Cultural Revolution?' Mr Wei asked me.

'Because it influenced me at the time – twenty years ago when I was in Africa,' I said. 'I thought of myself as a revolutionary.'

Mr Wei smiled. He was twenty-one. His father was my age.

I said, 'What did your father do during the Cultural Revolution?'

'He just stayed in the house.'

'For how long?'

'Six or seven years.'

We climbed to the top of Sunlight Rock. In 1982, at the age of seventy-eight, the chain-smoking Mr Deng Xiaoping climbed to this summit. He was followed by a flunkey with an oxygen bottle, but he didn't need it.

Looking across the harbour to Xiamen city I could see how the areas of light industry and banking had expanded westward. This was said to be one of the busiest boom towns in China. Once upon a time they made paper umbrellas and firecrackers and chopsticks for export. These days they manufactured bicycles, toys, Camel cigarettes, and microchips. And the Kodak Company was installing a film-making plant at great expense.

The harbour was full of freighters and fishing-boats. Beyond it, in the lanes and streets, there were stalls – people selling fried noodles, fruit, sweets, vegetables, fish soup. One of the happiest pastimes of people in south China is eating out – at greasy little restaurants or at stalls, by lantern light. I could not forgive them for stuffing rare birds into their mouths, but very few had the money for such delicacies. They were great noodle-eaters, and because of the pleasant climate they liked milling around the town and eating when the mood took them, a habit they had exported to Malaysia and Singapore and Indonesia.

Xiamen was the only place in China where I was repeatedly accosted by pretty girls. They sneaked behind me and snatched my arm. 'Shansh marnie?' they said, and pinched me delightfully and held on. Was that all they wanted?

They were good-tempered people, but always in a flap. Inevitably there are squabbles among the Chinese, who live on top of each other. It is surprising that fighting is not more frequent. Fist-fights are rare. Often children are beaten, and hit very hard. But the most common mode of conflict is the screaming out-of-hand row – two people screeching at each other, face to face. These rows are long and loud, and they attract large crowds of spectators. For face-saving reasons such disputes can only be resolved by a third party, and until that person enters the fray the two squabblers go on shrieking.

I witnessed a barracking like this in Xiamen one day. All tourist sites have so-called Viewing Places, where the Chinese visitor is obliged to go – otherwise the trip is futile. The ritual element in tourism is carefully observed. In Xiamen there were the Eight Major Views, the Eight Minor Views and the Views outside Views. It is customary to have your picture taken on the spot, and since few Chinese can afford to buy cameras, professional photographers stand around these Viewing Places and offer their services for one *yuan* a shot. The shouting match I saw was between one of these photographers and his dissatisfied customers.

Mr Wei translated the screams. At first they were all about money – a man and wife claiming that the photographer had put the price up after they had agreed on a lower one. But for face-saving reasons, the screaming became more general and hysterical. It wasn't an argument. It was a random howling – everyone at once, the couple, the photographer, and then the onlookers joined in. It started at the Viewing Place, moved down the path, flowed behind a rock, and then continued in a shed. It was extremely loud and went on without a break, a remarkable torrent of abuse and exclamation.

'First we're told it's one *kwai*, and then the thief changes it to two!'

'I'm not speaking to anyone until the unit leader comes. But I've never been so insulted –'

'Someone get the unit leader!'

'This is ridiculous! All these people are liars!'

'We're being cheated!'

'Thieves –!'

They were almost certainly tourists, Mr Wei said. He could tell from their northern accent. Shanxi, he thought. He was whispering, 'The woman says that they are thieves. The man is saying liars. There is a child in the shed. The photographer is banging the table with his fist –'

Then there was a greater commotion and the child began to scream. Someone was howling at the child. Then everyone was howling at once.

'What happened, Mr Wei?'

'The child cursed the worker.'

'What did he say?'

'He called him a *wang ba* – a tortoise,' Mr Wei said, with some reluctance.

'Is that bad?'

'Yes. Very. If a wife sleeps with other men her husband is called a tortoise.'

'Is that expression used all over China?'

'No. Mainly in the north. Northerners are very tough. North of the Chang Jiang they are loud and muscular. They use violent language. That's why the demonstrations in the north were large and noisy. But we are thin and small and very gentle. We don't use such language, calling someone a "tortoise" because he over-charges you.'

The screaming match was still in full cry fifteen minutes after it had started. I got bored and went away. Mr Wei said he found it distasteful having to translate this abuse for me, but I told him I had to know these things in order to understand China. And I explained that our version of a tortoise is a cuckold, which (coming from cuckoo) is a more logical word. Female tortoises, I told him, are not great copulators. They only need one screw and they are able to lay fertile eggs for years!

'You are interested in arguments and also interested in biology.'

'I'm interested in everything, Mr Wei.'

'In China we specialize in knowledge. One person studies agriculture, and another does engineering.'

He went on in this vein until, soon after, we saw a child being beaten by its mother in a yard. I was riveted by it. The child was smacked so thoroughly that he became hysterical and could not be calmed. He went around hitting his mother and wetting himself and howling. He was about seven years old. The usual Chinese reaction to someone in distress is laughter, and soon Mr Wei and the others watching began to find the tormented child an object of amusement.

Xiamen gave me vivid dreams, but the dreams were not of Xiamen or its ghosts – Marco Polo, foreign traders, Manichaeans, missionaries, pirates, or the compradors of old Amoy. I dreamed of home in one, and of Tadjiks in another (was it a coincidence that the Tadjiks were the only Indo-Europeans among China's minorities?), and of Ronald Reagan again (a lulu); and a few nights later I dreamed of walking through the ravines that I had seen earlier that week in the hills of Fujian. I was captured by some Mongolian-looking men who were led by a small and very fierce woman. They all had curved knives that they kept jabbing into me, as if impatient to kill me.

'Empty your bag!' the woman shrieked.

Only then did I realize that I had a bag and that I was carrying some little antique statues that I had bought in a Chinese market.

'Show your certificate!'

'Here,' I said, finding a piece of paper in my bag. It was the wrong certificate, but I thought: The Gurkhas will save me.

The woman read my mind and replied, 'We are the Gurkhas!'

That was probably more a nightmare of buying trinkets illegally than a nightmare of travelling on the open road in China and encountering strangers – nothing was safer than that, judging from my experience of traipsing up and down in China.

The wonderful market in Xiamen, and the drapery stores under the shop-houses, reminded me that the best buys in China are not in the souvenir shops and the Friendship Stores – not jade carvings, cork sculpture, ivory letter-openers, stuffed pandas, turquoise jewellery, cloisonné, brassware, plastic chopsticks, lacquerware, bone bracelets, or the really dull and derivative paintings on scrolls. If I were to recommend anything special in China that was a bargain – good quality, one of a kind, worth bringing home – I would say: socket wrenches, screwdrivers, water-colour paints and brushes, pencils, calligraphy, sturdy brown envelopes, padlocks, plumber's tools, wicker baskets, espadrilles, T-shirts, cashmere sweaters, bonsai trees, silk carpets and silk cushion covers, tablecloths, terracotta pots, thermos jugs, illustrated art books, herbs, spices, and tea by the pound. Bamboo bird-cages are also lovely, though the thought of keeping a bird in them is depressing. China may also be the only country in the world where you can buy a cricket-cage – made either of split bamboo or of porcelain.

A number of these items are made in Xiamen, in the Huli Industrial Area. In more revolutionary times this area was part of a land reclamation scheme. The Red Guards and work-gangs decided to build a causeway linking Xiamen to the west side of the harbour, and then to fill in the land behind the causeway and plant rice. But the land was poor and salty. Rice would not grow. And time passed. Now it is a stronghold of money-making ventures – banks, light industry, factories, as well as the city's new municipal buildings.

There had once been a commune here. There had been agricultural communes all over Xiamen. I had been interested by the ones I had seen elsewhere, by the way they had developed into co-operatives and family farms, so I visited what had been the Cai Tang commune in the countryside north-west of Xiamen to see what had happened.

Walking through the fields at Cai Tang I came across an ancient grave. Two eight-foot guardian figures, a man and a woman, had been placed at the entrance of the grave site. This was behind a hill, at the margin of a field of carrots. A bird – perhaps a flycatcher – was flitting back and forth. And buried to their necks were stone animals – a horse, a ram, lions and other broken beasts. There was an altar, too, with carved tablets. It was all unnoticed and it had not been seriously vandalized. In an earlier period a traveller would have taken it and crated it and shipped it to the Fogg Museum at Harvard. The tablets said (according to Mr Wei) that it was a Qing Dynasty grave of the Hu family, and it was so far off the beaten track that no one had disturbed it.

A farmer and his wife were working nearby, hurrying back and forth in the carrot field, each one of them wearing a yoke with a balanced pair of watering cans. A loudspeaker at the far side of the field played a Chinese opera.

'This was once part of the Cai Tang Commune,' the man said. 'We planted rice, because they wouldn't let us plant anything else. And we listened to the thoughts of Mao Zedong on that loudspeaker all day.'

I had to follow him through the carrot field. He would not stop watering in order to chat. But he said he didn't mind my questions.

'This is my family's land. I never liked the commune idea. I would rather work in my own fields.'

'Do you think about freedom to do as you want?'

'Yes. I have more freedom now,' he said. 'I can plant what I like. They used to say "Plant rice" whether it was a good idea or not. Know what the trouble was before? Too many officials.'

He squelched through the mud to the standpipe, filled his buckets, filled his wife's buckets, and off they went again through the plume-like carrot tops.

'You have a healthy crop of carrots,' I said.

'These are for pigs,' he said. 'The price of carrots is low in the market at the moment, so instead of accepting a few *fen* I'll feed them to my pigs. It makes more sense. I can fatten ten pigs, get them up to a hundred kilos and sell each one for about a hundred *yuan*. When the price of carrots goes up I'll sell the carrots at the market.'

He was still splashing water and gasping up and down the field.

'This is much better business!' he called back.

From there I went to the eastern part of Xiamen, called 'The Front Line' (Qian Xian) because Quemoy (Jin Men) is just offshore and belongs to Taiwan. The east coast road had been closed for thirty-five years, because of the periodic hostilities, but just recently it was opened. There were trenches, pillboxes and fortifications everywhere, but there was also a lovely beach of palm trees and white sand and dumping surf – and not a soul on it.

I broad-jumped a foxhole and made my way through the palms.

'Don't, Mr Paul! You might get shot!'

Mr Wei trembled at the edge of the road, calling me back.

'Who would shoot me?'

'The army!'

'Which army?'

'Maybe ours – maybe theirs.'

He tried to console me – perhaps one day there would be peace between China and its easternmost province of Taiwan, and then I would be able to swim here. Because it had been dangerous and off-limits (Quemoy had been bombarded from these gun-emplacements in 1958, provoking an international incident), and because of the fear it aroused in the local Chinese, the beach was unspoiled and lovely.

One of the largest buildings in Xiamen was the Workers' Palace. Other Chinese cities had Soviet-inspired community centres like this – they had all been built in the nineteen-fifties – but I had never been inside one. Mr Wei was bewildered by my interest, and he said it might be difficult to get permission to enter. I now knew enough about Chinese bureaucracy to realize that the quickest way to see the Workers' Palace would be to walk in and not bother with permission. It was such a dithering and buck-passing civil service that special requests were almost invariably turned down, while blatant trespassing was seldom challenged.

Once this Workers' Palace had been all hate films and sessions of political indoctrination. Now the film theatre was showing a documentary about the Dunhuang Caves, and the reading-room was full of people perusing newspapers and magazines (among them, movie magazines and body-building monthlies); and in the drill hall there was an aerobics class. A dancing class had just ended.

I asked one of the women doing aerobics why she had decided to sign up.

'I do this for health and beauty,' she said. 'Also I have headaches.'

It was in the library of this building that I found a copy of Dong Luoshan's translation of Orwell's *1984*. It had been published in Canton in 1985. He had told me it was regarded as *neican* – circulated to safe and unexcitable intellectuals. But obviously that was wrong. Anyone in Xiamen could come here and borrow it from the library – I specifically asked the librarian.

'Is it any good?' she asked.

'Excellent. You'll love it.'

'I'll take it home with me tonight!'

Another room was lined with electronic games. I wondered whether anyone used them. Mr Wei said they did, but that no one had spare cash to squander on them. I saw about eight children lurking near the machines and asked them whether they knew how these things worked. They said they did. Would they teach me? I asked. Oh, yes. So I pushed a few coins into these space-invader machines and the children sprang into action, their fingers flying. They were as expert as any person in America, misspending his youth at the controls of an electronic game.

A young woman had just finished her dancing class and was on her way home when I accosted her. She was Wan Li, a cadre at the economics ministry. She had gone to the Dalian Foreign Languages Institute (she hadn't met Cherry Blossom there, unfortunately) but she had been raised in the central Fujian town of San Ming. That town had the reputation in China of being somewhat utopian. It had been developed by people from all over China, before the Cultural Revolution. Miss Wan claimed that everything that had been said about San Ming was true – no problems, no pollution, perfect integration, a model city.

'Any Tibetans in San Ming?'

'No,' Miss Wan said. 'They have to stay in Tibet and solve their own problems. But people in San Ming are very civilized. They are from all places. Like the United States!'

She was about twenty-five and seemed very frank beneath her nervous giggle. She came to the Workers' Palace every day, she said, because she liked meeting people here – she enjoyed talking to strangers.

Mr Wei merely looked on, but I could see he was quite taken by this young woman's boldness.

I said, 'Are you a member of the Chinese Communist Party?'

'You are the second American in Xiamen to ask me that!' she said. 'There are 300 people in my unit at the ministry. Only twenty are members of the party.'

'Why so few?'

'Because it is hard to be a member. You don't volunteer. You have to be asked to join the party. You must first act very well and leave a good impression. Do your work diligently – work overtime, study, be obedient.'

'Like Lei Feng the Model Soldier,' I said. Lei Feng had scrubbed floors all night because of his love for Mao. In China he was a joke or else a paragon, according to whom you were talking to. Most Chinese I had spoken to had found Lei Feng a bit of a pain, if not an outright fake.

Miss Wan gave me a Chinese reply. 'Not like Lei Feng. You have to be noticed.'

Lei Feng had only been noticed after he was crushed to death by a truck in 1962, when his diaries were found with such exclamations as 'I have scrubbed another floor and washed more dishes! My love for Mao is shining in my heart!'

Miss Wan said, 'You have to be selected for the party. The party needs the best people – not just anyone who wants to join. If the party works well the country will work. The party needs high-quality people.'

'I'm sure you're a high-quality person.'

'I don't know.'

'Do you have healthy Marxist-Leninist thoughts?'

'I am trying,' she said, and laughed. 'I also like dancing!'

After she left Mr Wei said, 'She gave me her card. Did you see?'

'Are you glad?'

'Oh yes. I hope I see her again. It is so hard to meet girls in China.'

He said he probably would not get married for another five years. Twenty-six was a good age for marriage.

With the greatest tact I could muster I asked him whether he had ever slept with a woman. I put it obliquely. He proudly said no.

'It seems to be a problem in China. No sex for young people.' It had been one of the issues in the student demonstrations.

'It's a problem. Even if you meet a girl there is no place to take her. But I don't mind.'

'You mean you don't believe in sex before marriage?'

He looked slightly disgusted. 'It is unlawful and against our traditions.'

With that, 2,000 years of sensuality went straight out the window. Mr Wei seemed blind to the fact that Chinese culture was rooted in sexual allusions. The Yellow Emperor had made himself immortal by sleeping with a thousand women; and even a common object like a piece of jade had sexual associations – it was said to be the petrified semen of the celestial dragon. The dragon was phallic, the lotus was a sort of ikon for the vulva, and so forth.

'Would you be arrested if you were caught with a woman?'

'You might be. You would be criticized. You could be reported.'

'But surely you could be very careful if you had a lover.'

'Someone would know,' Mr Wei said. 'And even if you didn't get caught, people would look down on you.'

That seemed to settle it, but Mr Wei equivocated when I asked him about Miss Wan.

'I will keep her card,' he said, breathing hard.

That was the last I saw of Mr Wei. But I had no trouble fending for myself in Xiamen. For one thing, Spring Festival was about to begin, and this the happiest of Chinese holidays put everyone in a good mood, as they bought greeting cards and calligraphy and red paper banners with New Year greetings inked on them.

Just before I left Xiamen I met an American, Jim Koch, a Kodak employee who had been hired to supervise the installation of a coating machine. This sounded a fairly modest contraption but it had cost the Chinese $70 million and the entire project was costing $300 million. The object was for the Chinese to make their own film for cameras and not be dependent upon the Japanese for photographic supplies.

Jim Koch had recently been married to Jill and had been looking forward to this post. But after three months in Xiamen he admitted to being rather doubtful. He was not pessimistic, but he was certainly cautious. What had surprised him most was Chinese ineptness.

'They're used to working with their hands,' he said. 'that's the problem. They can rig up something with a piece of wire and a stick. But they have never relied on sophisticated machinery or hi-tech. I have to show them every detail about a hundred times.'

'But the young Chinese must be teachable.'

'They're the worst. The laziest, the slowest, the most arrogant. The older workers are the best – the over-fifties. The ones from thirty to forty seem to have a chip on their shoulder, as if they were cut out for better things.'

'They were in the Cultural Revolution, so perhaps they're feeling cheated.'

'Maybe. But I thought this was going to be pretty straightforward. Maybe eight months. The Chinese said twelve. But it will take longer.'

'What the biggest problem?' I asked.

'Cleanliness,' Jim said. 'If a floor looks clean they think it's clean. They use these bunches of twigs and straw to sweep. But that's not good enough. For this kind of equipment you need an absolutely dust-free environment, otherwise particles get into the film and wreck it. So now we have to seal the plant and install an air-conditioning system.'

'Are you sorry you came to China?'

'No. But I thought it was going to be different. You know, the Chinese are supposed to be so clever. But a lot of these projects in Xiamen have had problems. That's why there are so many empty factories here.' His voice dropped and he added, 'It's going to be a long haul.'

But it did not strike me as a tragedy if Xiamen's factories were working at half strength. There would always be money flowing into the city from her native sons and daughters who had prospered overseas. And Xiamen was a pretty place precisely because it had not developed heavy industry, and because – pressured by the romantics and the retirees – it had not vandalized its old buildings and elaborate gardens.

The Lunar New Year came. The whole country was on the move, and people threw firecrackers into the streets. It was impossible to travel in the crush of passengers enacting the yearly ritual of going home. I could not buy train tickets. So I did nothing but wait until the festival ended, and then I resumed my travels, heading westward.

21

The Qinghai Local to Xining: Number 275

On my way to Xian to catch the Qinghai local I ran into the mountaineer, Chris Bonington. He said he was in China to climb Menlungtse, a mountain near Everest and almost as high.

'We're also looking for a yeti,' he said.

His good health and his courage and his tigerish way of turning his head made him seem very youthful. He had a look of smiling innocence and strength, a happy man whose life was devoted to adventuring up mountains.

He was serious about the Abominable Snowman. A previous Everest expedition had photographed a yeti footprint on the Menlung Glacier.

'Are you going to bring one back in a cage?'

He smiled. Was that a twinkle in his eye? He said, 'No, all we want is a picture.'

Presumably that was worth money. There was no profit in climbing a 23,000-foot mountain and risking your neck; but if you managed to get a picture of the great hairy monster of the Himalayas you were newsworthy and bankable. Money was always a problem in mountaineering. Bonington's small team of four or five climbers had forty cases of supplies among them, which entailed numerous sherpas and yaks.

Along with bear-hunting in Xinjiang, and sport-fishing in Liaoning, equipping mountain-climbing expeditions was another enterprise of the Chinese.

Bonington said that 90 per cent of China's mountains had not been climbed and that many of them were over 20,000 feet. But it was expensive to climb in China, he said.

'For example, a yak costs thirty *yuan* a day to rent,' he said. 'I wonder how much of that goes to the owner?'

I said that I would ask someone in Qinghai, where many of the yakherds were found.

That was the first of March. In Xian I read in a *China Daily* that Deng Xiaoping told the visiting American secretary of state that the recent trouble in China had been caused by 'a leadership crisis'. It was a euphemism for a power struggle. 'It is now over,' he said, and added cryptically, 'but it may continue for a while in the minds of the Chinese people.'

Xian lay under winter mist, denuded and dusty. In sunlight it was stark, a flat city of plain buildings inside a city wall that was powerful and elegant, with great roofed gates. Xian's city wall actually looks as though it could repel an invading army. I visited the terracotta warriors a second time. They had the same eerie artistry and a bizarre, half-human and buried alive look, like an army that has been petrified by time. The curio sellers were frenzied, because this was the off season, a winter month in which few foreign tourists visited. The Chinese are more like threadbare pilgrims than tourists. They are not spenders. They have no money. Their work-units rent beat-up buses and pack them with employees and off they go, hundreds of miles to look at a pagoda or the warriors. They also regard the hotels for foreign visitors as worth gaping at. They stood at the gates of Xian's Golden Flower Hotel (£60 a day) watching foreigners come and go. The Chinese in their innocence still regard their looking at foreigners as a form of sightseeing.

Like many other Chinese cities, Xian was not clean but it was very bare. The Chinese are not scrubbers, but they are inexhaustible sweepers. Sweeping doesn't freshen a city. It gives it a disconcerting baldness. The effect is of a place that has been trampled.

I walked in the back-lanes of the city, among the little tumbled compounds and the stinks of dampness and dust, and the fragrant smells of cooking. I lingered near the windows of lighted rooms, where children were doing homework, and women were working at kitchen tables. I saw a restaurant – tiny; filthy; people with steamers and pots on the table. I longed to go in, but every seat was taken. On my morning walks I bought the Chinese pedestrian's winter breakfast, 'fried sticks' (*you tiao*) – deep-fried dough, which resembled elongated pieces of Yorkshire pudding. They were fried outdoors in a wok. People on their way to the factory bought little bundles of them and ate them on the way.

On this second visit to Xian I saw that the city prospered without tourists. It had a life of its own, and its economy was that of an inland capital, dealing in industrial and agricultural products. The discovery of the terracotta army had given a boost to the tourist trade, but the tourist economy was parallel to the existing economy. The Chinese government had a policy of being brisk with tourists – shipping them in, squiring them around and shipping them out. They hated people who lingered and found cheap rooms and simply strolled around looking through people's windows. They really didn't want me there at all. But what could they do? I didn't have a nanny any more. They could not keep track of travellers. It was possible to arrive in China and more or less vanish. I had now managed this, and I saw people like me all the time. Their reference point was always the local post office. I saw tall, dusty, long-nosed foreigners. We exchanged glances, and there was little more that; but I recognized them as kindred souls. Were they writing books about China? Probably. Everyone seemed to be doing that. The only justification was that any travel book revealed more about the traveller than it did about the country.

Even late on a Thursday night in clammy March the main railway station was crowded – and more than crowded. It was almost impossible for me to make my way from one side to another. I could not understand the density – the people sleeping on benches, making noodles in the corner, milling around, sitting on their luggage, nursing babies. It was a huge station and yet there was nowhere for me to sit – no spare room. There were about eight trains departing within a few hours, and they were long trains; but that still did not explain the mobs. It was amazing to see so many people on the move, and it was useful to me, because I could lose myself in the crowd.

In the sleeping-compartment lottery I was assigned with three soldiers. Even wearing thick long underwear they were much too small for their uniforms. They were young, about twenty or so, and had sweet faces. They began making tea, and remarking politely on what luck it was for them to be travelling with an American friend, and so forth.

I said, 'I'd like to know whether you call yourselves "soldiers" [*bing*] or "fighters" [*zhanshi*].'

It was a Maoist distinction that had been introduced to the People's Liberation Army – I had been told that 'fighters' was the accepted word. They agreed with this and said that 'fighters' was the usual word, but that no one worried about the difference any more. And by the way, the word 'comrade' (*tongzhi*) was not very commonly used.

The soldiers snuggled into their berths and pulled out romantic novels; they read and dozed.

'This is very good tea,' one of the soldiers said later on, lifting my can of Dragon Well tea.

'I like green tea,' I said.

'We are red tea people,' he said. 'I lived on a commune that grew tea. I was too young to pick it, but my parents did.'

'Were they sent there during the Cultural Revolution?'

'It was during the Cultural Revolution, but they went willingly,' he said.

Farther down the sleeping-car a man was smoking a Churchillian-sized cigar. The man himself was very small, and I saw this cigar-smoking as a form of aggression. The whole coach was filled with this smoke, and although the cigar was truly noxious no one told him to lay off.

'I hate that smoke,' I told the soldier. 'I want to tell that man to stop smoking his cigar.'

The soldier became twitchy when I said this.

'Better not,' he said, and laughed – his laugh signifying: *Let's pretend that cigar-smoker doesn't exist.*

The next time I walked past the cigar-smoker I saw he had an army uniform on a hook over his berth. Officers were said not to exist in the PLA, but it was obvious that he was one – superior to the three fighters in my compartment.

I was reading *Chinese Profiles*, which had been put together as a series of interviews by Sang Ye and Zhang Xinxin. I had met Sang in Peking just after I started my China trip. The book was a pleasure, and it was ingeniously simple and revealing. It also confirmed my feeling that the Chinese, who are supposed to be so enigmatic, can be blunt and plain-spoken and candid to the point of utter tactlessness. That was why the book was so fresh.

All night the compartment door opened and closed, as people came and went. One sleeper snored for hours. Someone in an upper berth kept his light on. The door banged. There was always chatter in the passageway. The lights of stations made yellow stripes in the compartment, and then we were in the darkness again. In the morning, a man sat on the lower berth, sipping tea.

'Where are you going?' he asked.

'Xining. And then Tibet.' I used the Chinese name, Xizang.

'You'll be gasping in Tibet. It is very hard to breathe there because of the altitude.'

'I'll do my best.'

We were in the yellow rubbly gorges of Gansu, one of the roughest-looking landscapes in the whole of China – I knew that now. There were no trees, there was very little water except for the muddy Yellow River which the train followed for part of the way into Lanzhou. The soil was crumbly, the colour and texture of very old Cheddar cheese – the sort that has remained untouched in a mousetrap all winter.

I woke hungry and decided to 'register' for breakfast. For about twelve pence I bought a breakfast coupon. I was told to report at 7.30. I did as I was told. On the dot of 7.30 the dining-car filled with people sitting rather impatiently. A girl in a nightcap and apron went through the car with a tray, plonking bowls down. There was a sudden hush; a silence; and then a tremendous slurping. The chopsticks clicked like knitting-needles for a minute or so, and then the people stood and shoved their chairs back and went away. That was breakfast.

Towards mid morning, the Yellow River widened in the cheesy gorge and we arrived at Lanzhou. I had been here before; I had no desire to stop. I bought some peanuts to eat and walked along the platform while the locomotive's boilers were filled with fresh water. I noticed that most of the people got out at Lanzhou, and very few boarded. It had rained slightly in Lanzhou. Chinese rain often made a city look filthier and sometimes much dustier. It had had that effect on Lanzhou, which looked very dismal and rather parched after the sprinkle. The steam engine was reconnected and we set off again, slowly, with many stops on the way.

After about fifty miles we entered the province of Qinghai. 'There is nothing in Qinghai,' the Chinese had told me, which gave me an appetite for the place. We were soon among big smooth mountains of mud – great heaps and stacks of hard-packed dirt. It had the look of an endless dump. It was the most infertile place I had seen in China – less fertile than Inner Mongolia, more arid even than the Turfan Depression and the ravines of Gansu. The river, which seemed to have the name 'the Yellow Water', looked poisonous, so the water was not a source of life; it was another way of ridding the landscape of vegetation.

But people had figured a way of living here. They had made bamboo frames and stretched plastic sheeting over them. Inside these crude greenhouses they grew vegetables. The only produce in Qinghai is grown in these things. At night the people cover them with straw mats, because it is below freezing. The daytime sun warms them through the plastic. In ditches I could see ice, even though it was noon.

They were so poor here that they could not afford to feed donkeys or buffaloes. They ploughed, using two people to pull the plough and one to guide it. There they were in the middle of the whirling dust, dragging the thing. It was the first time in my life I had seen human beings pulling a plough. They also pulled carts and wagons in Qinghai and had totally replaced animals with their own labour. I had the impression that after the field was ploughed a system of plastic greenhouses was erected over the furrows.

The mountains and heaps of mud reddened, grew brown and then grey, and became clawed with eroded gullies; and then rocky, and stonier. But they never looked less barren. It was odd, then, to see people preparing the ground for crops – digging, ploughing, raking; and to see lives being lived – schoolkids frolicking in the playground under the red flag; other kids carrying water in buckets and picking coal out of the rubble. And in the middle of nowhere I saw a man strolling along and smiling, with a monkey skittering on a leash.

The settlements were clusters of square squat houses with mud-walled courtyards. Walls were the rule here. And there was some irrigation, some vegetable gardens exposed to the wind and weather. But the clearest impression I had, early on in Qinghai, was of every village looking like a prison farm. Indeed, that is how many of them started out – the villagers sent to Qinghai as punishment. They were to be reformed through labour, as the saying went, and turned from prisoners into pioneers.

The station signs were written in three scripts – Chinese, Mongolian and Tibetan. I had no idea how far we had come. We were travelling very slowly still. The province was bigger than the whole of Europe, but it was empty. The trees were stark and dead, like symbols of trees, the six lines that a child might draw with a crayon. The ground was bare, the houses and mountains were brown, the river was grey and the ice at its edges filthy. The valley was twenty miles wide. Having seen Xinjiang I suspected that these fields might be green in the summer and that it might not be the dreary place it seemed. But it was odd to be in this brown and lifeless world, where there is nothing visible that can be eaten. It looked like a dead planet. This is the sort of landscape that frightens visitors to China – frightens the Chinese too. To the Chinese this was not part of the world: it was the edge of it, so it was nothing.

By talking to the other passengers I established that the mountains to the north were the Dabanshan. Gansu was on the other side. Cave-dwellers inhabited some of those mountainsides, and in some cases the caves were elaborate, with windows and doors and crude plumbing. I could see on some of them a sort of superstructure protruding, a balcony which made a façade.

The train was creaking along, gaining altitude. We were now at about 7,000 feet – it was chilly, the air was thin, the wind was strong. In the cliffs above the track there were caves, an opening on every cliff-face, with its own shelf and precarious stairs cut into the rock. Some cave-dwellers were sitting in sunshine, others hanging laundry, hacking at trough-like gardens that seemed magnetized to the mountainside. They were cooking, too. Why think of this as a mountain when you could just as easily think of it as a tenement? This wasn't a cliff – it was the west wing, and that summit was a penthouse. There was a whole world of troglodytes here in Qinghai.

Only its altitude made Xining breathtaking. In other respects it looked like what it was, a frontier town: square brown buildings on straight streets, surrounded by big brown hills. All the water in the creeks and streams had turned to ice. It was an ugly friendly place, and its bantering people had chafed red cheeks like bruised peaches. Its terrible weather gave it drama. Its rain was black and very cold. But it did not rain long. Most of the time it was notoriously dry – too arid for growing vegetables outside the plastic greenhouses. Snow also fell, in big, wet, plopping flakes. And its wind had torn off all its topsoil. Inside of a week I experienced all those conditions – rain, dust storms, blinding sunlight and snow. If I climbed stairs too quickly I had to stop and get my breath. I developed a plodding way of walking that enabled me to keep going. There were Muslims all over town, wearing a sort of chef's cap and side-whiskers, and also spitting Hans, and Tibetans who favoured cowboy hats and frock-coats.

'What's that music?' I asked the driver as we travelled to the hotel from the station.

The driver said nothing, but his pal said, 'Beethoven.'

'Beethoven,' the driver said. 'I like Beethoven.'

The driver's name was Mr Fu. He said he could drive me to Tibet. It would be about five days to Lhasa, through the Qinghai desert and then into the mountains. Sleep in army camps on the way. How about it?

I said I was very interested.

Mr Li, his pal, said, 'I think it's Symphony Number Two.'

'Isn't it Six – the Pastoral?'

Mr Li laughed. He had yellow teeth. His laugh simply meant: *Wrong!* It was a bark-like noise. He said, 'The Pastoral goes dum-dum-dee-dee-dum. No, this isn't Number Two. I know Two, Five, Six, Seven and Nine. This isn't a symphony. It is an overture.'

Mr Fu went fossicking in his glove compartment. He brought out the cassette holder and showed us. It was the Coriolan Overture. Mr Fu said it was a Beethoven work he particularly liked.

'This is the best hotel in Xining,' Mr Fu said.

Mr Li laughed in a stern correcting way. 'This is the only hotel in Xining.'

This hotel reminded me of something I could not quite place – a building I had known in the distant past. It had been built by the Russians, and it retained its fiftyish look. It was very fusty, it was mildewed. Why did all Chinese carpets stink with decay? I hated the hotel hours. Dinner at 6.00, no hot water until 8.00 at night. The room girl kept the keys. The toilet didn't flush until you emptied two buckets of water into it – and that bucket was the waste basket.

And then I remembered the old Northampton Hospital, where I had worked as a student, and thought: *Of course!* The Xining Guest Hotel was exactly like a madhouse. The tiny rooms, the smells of food and disinfectant and sewage, the sudden squawks from locked rooms, the TV no one watched, the scarred walls suggesting violence, the bars on the windows, the eternal figure down the shadowy corridor slowly toiling with a mop, the silent inmate squatting on a chair-seat, roosting like a chicken. It was all a re-enactment of life inside the old-fashioned hospital I had known. Even the room-girls were more like fearless untalkative madhouse orderlies than they were compliant Chinese *fuwuyuan*. And in this loony-bin-like hotel I could not decide whether I was a patient or a visitor; but I sometimes suspected that I would be like one of those poor creatures who is taken in for observation and somehow forgotten, and twenty years later discovered behind a bolted door, driven totally insane by the place.

These anxieties impelled me to make plans for Tibet. I told Mr Fu I wished to discuss this matter.

'My father went to Tibet,' Mr Li said.

But I asked him more questions and realized that the man

had gone there twenty years ago, on horseback, as a volunteer teacher.

'There was no road then,' Mr Li said.

'There's a good road now,' Mr Fu said. 'I've driven to Lhasa a few times.'

But my questions elicited only vague answers from Mr Fu, and I could not tell whether he really had driven there or not.

'And it's a lovely drive from here to Golmud,' Mr Fu said.

'I can take the train to Golmud.'

I had wanted to do that. The train to Golmud was the ultimate Chinese train. The line had been constructed as far as this town, and then because of the impossibility of penetrating the Tibetan Plateau, it had been abandoned, in the middle of nowhere. I would not have missed that ride for anything.

'It's a horrible train,' Mr Fu said. 'It's a steam locomotive. It goes through the desert. It is very slow.'

That was music to my ears.

'You drive to Golmud,' I said. 'I'll meet you there and we'll both go to Tibet. We'll stop on the way. I'll bring some food. We'll listen to Beethoven.'

Mr Fu did some figuring and presented me with a bill for the Chinese equivalent of £375. That included his little Japanese car and his labour as driver and all the petrol. I would pay for meals.

'It's a deal,' I said, and we shook on it.

The car seemed rather fragile for such a difficult trip of 1,200 miles across the bleakest part of Tibet. It was called a 'Galant'. I hated the name. It was a car you saw on scrap-heaps. When the wind blew through Xining Mr Fu's Galant swayed. It was not a vehicle for Tibet. 'Mitsubishi' said another plate. It looked like a 'dodgem' car.

'You think it'll make it?'

'This is a good car,' Mr Fu said.

'Remember to bring two spare tyres,' I said.

He swore that he would. There was something in the heartiness of his assurance that made me think he was lying to me.

After that I decided to spend my time in Xining making preparations for the journey. I bought dry noodles, and canned goods, and fruit and soup. I bought storage containers and canteens and thermos jugs. I bought another hat. I found a place that sold jars of quails' eggs and bought a case. The food was so cheap I did not bother keeping track of the cost – it was a few dollars, no more. In my wandering around town I discovered that a special sort of dumpling was made in Xining. It was a stuffed pancake, fried in a wok – a doughbun crammed with scallions, and they served them fresh out of the pan, hot and dripping, just the thing for a snowy day in Qinghai.

Xining was the sort of simple ramshackle place I had come to like in China. It was not pretty, but that didn't matter. The food was delicious in an unremarkable way: not fancy but good to eat. The weather was full of surprises. The people said hallo to me and were pleasant to each other. I liked Xining as I had liked Langxiang in Heilongjiang – and for the same reason: it was a country town. By degrees I realized that I was the only barbarian in the place. It was off-season, the middle of March in the back of beyond. That was also the reason people talked to me. It was a novelty to see a barbarian so far from his home.

Xining had department stores – of a kind. It had movie theatres – at least two. It had an enormous mosque. But Mr Fu's was one of only about twenty cars in the place, and as the main streets were four lanes wide one had the impression of almost no traffic at all. The buses were the broken rusted kind found in all parts of rural China.

It was alarming to be told by people in Xining that Golmud was horrible and primitive. Bring warm clothes, they said. Bring food. Bring water. Tea, too. Bring everything you need. Nothing is stranger than being in a fairly bad place and being told that another place – your destination – is a great deal worse. But such warnings also made me deeply curious.

They grew potatoes here. They ate french fries – thin, crunchy, greasy and unappetizing, like the ones sold at McDonald's: exactly like those.

I met a young recent convert to Buddhism, Mr Xun, who was studying English. I told him how much I liked the stuffed pancakes. He somewhat dismissed this, as Chinese do when you mention your liking for peasant food like dumplings, or lotus roots, or fried noodles, or steamed buns. Meat was the thing.

Mr Xun said, 'Sheep vein. Yak vein. Mongolian hot-pot. Caterpillar fungus. And stir-fried camel's foot. That's what I like.'

There was also a variety of black moss from the mountains called 'hair grass' that was tasty. They made it into soup. It was indistinguishable from seaweed. But the fact was that west of Xining, and through the whole of Qinghai and the whole of Tibet, there is only one vegetable (barley) and only one kind of meat (yak). As might be supposed, faced with only two ingredients the people of these regions have learned to cook them a number of different ways. But that is no more than a gesture. The taste is unvarying. It is the taste of yak.

Mr Xun the Buddhist convert went with me to the Taer'si, a monastery about fifteen miles south-west of Xining. The founder of the Virtuous Order (Gelukpa), a pure form of Buddhism, was born here about 500 years ago. This man, Zong Kapa, went to Lhasa and preached at the Ganden Monastery there. He was the founder of the Yellow Sect. After he had been away for some years his mother wrote, imploring him to return. He said no, but added: 'If you want to do something useful build a temple in my honour.' Before the old woman could act, a *pipal* tree sprang up on the spot where Zong Kapa was born – the same sort of *bhodi* tree under which the Buddha received enlightenment. The mother built a pagoda over the tree, and then built a temple. Later the monastery was built – in 1588. Dalai Lamas and Panchen Lamas have visited here. The present Dalai Lama was born nearby, in the hills. The white horse of the Ninth Panchen Lama dropped dead soon after bearing his master here in 1903. This animal was stuffed and is venerated in one of the temples. So Mr Xun said.

What Mr Xun did not say was that this monastery, recently reopened by the Chinese, had the stuffing kicked out of it, and not only in the predictable battering of the Cultural Revolution. In 1958, Mao issued the edict of Religious Reform. It began as a political programme; it became religious persecution. But now, thirty years later, the Kumbum Jampa Ling – the Tibetan name of the Taer'si – is growing again. There had been 3,600 monks. This was reduced to none at all. In the past few years 500 monks have established themselves, and there are sanyasis – novice monks:

grinning little red-cheeked boys who trot around combining high spirits and mischief with their chores.

'In three months these people will believe in communism,' Mao had said thirty years ago, as he defrocked the monks. But the monastery has reformed, and it is vigorously Buddhist. It seemed to me that it was so far off the beaten track that it had not received the pestering attentions of the bureaucrats. The complex of temples, stupas, courtyards, the print works, hospital, medical college (for teaching herbal remedies), and dwellings (housing thirteen Living Buddhas and their mothers), is scattered on the brown lower slopes of the valley. A small town has grown to one side of it, down the road.

Having Mr Xun with me was a help, and being at Taer'si on a cold winter day meant that I was seeing the place with its prayer wheels turning. We followed a procession of Tu people, who wore black hats with upturned brims and padded jackets and high boots.

The pilgrims prostrated themselves and then entered the Lesser Temple of the Golden Roof. In its courtyard they hung little swatches of sheep's wool. For a good harvest, Mr Xun said; but this was contradicted by my guidebook which claimed that about-to-be-slaughtered animals received grace in this way ('similarly, sheep and cows may be led clockwise around a monastery, as their final act on earth'). In this temple, children with runny noses and wild hair were snatching at the barrel-like prayer wheels. A man with a shrieking voice was chanting and beating a drum inside a locked room; the incense burners were crammed with cypress leaves and smoking fiercely, and pilgrims had glued Chinese coins to the burner's side (there was a pot of fish-glue next to it). On the balconies to the right and left were two large stuffed yaks draped with gauze offerings, two stuffed goats and a stuffed brown bear – they were propped up on the rails to look like judges surveying the pilgrims below, and they had wild grinning faces from their stretched skin and glass eyes. It was the sort of holy place which could look only bizarre to an unbeliever, and there hung about it the stink of rancid yak butter.

That is the smell of monasteries from Mongolia to Tibet, the sour cruddy hum of yak butter. It resembles the smell of an American family's refrigerator after a long midsummer power cut.

It is the reek of old milk. But yak butter is not just a ceremonial fuel. It is used for cooking, for lamps, for sculpting, and it is good for greasing axles. Yak butter is Tibetan lubricant in a spiritual and also in an industrial sense. The pilgrim who has just finished lubricating his wagon wheels brings a can of it and deposits fat yellow lumps of it in a vat near the temple altar.

Mr Xun said there had been lots of miracles here – not just the *bhodi* tree that sprouted on Zong Kapa's birthplace, but clusters of trees that appeared at the Flower Temple. They were miraculous, Mr Xun insisted. Messages had appeared on them.

'I must see them,' I said.

Mr Xun was delighted by my fervour. He introduced me to the monk at the Flower Temple.

The monk said, 'Look at the trunks of these trees. Look closely.'

I looked closely. There were small scratchings, like worm tracks on the flaky bark.

'Tibetan characters,' the monk said.

'Read them, please,' I said.

'I cannot.'

'Do they say anything?'

'We do not know. But I will tell you this. They are not man-made.'

He did not mean worms. He meant something supernatural.

He saw some Chinese tourists smoking.

'Do not smoke!' he said in his Tibetan-accented Mandarin. 'It's all wood, and if this catches fire who's responsible? This temple is 700 years old' – it wasn't, actually, but I felt he wanted to make them feel bad – 'and you don't care! All this yak butter would go right up in smoke!'

After the Chinese tourists left, the monk said, 'They don't care. They smoke all the time. They throw cigarettes everywhere – even under these holy trees.'

It was fairly obvious that the Tibetan monks disliked the Chinese, but they shrugged and grumbled rather than revolted. At the monastery printing works several monks told me that during the Cultural Revolution they had been sent to work at a power station.

'How did you like that?'

'It was a waste of time,' one said.

This printing works was medieval in its way of working. The monk inked a slab of script and then pressed a rectangle of rough paper over it. He peeled this off and hung it to dry, a finished page of text.

One page was a ribbon of writing.

'Stick that over your door and thieves will never come in.'

'What does it say?'

'It is Indian writing. Sanskrit. We don't know.'

He inked another slab and printed a new piece of paper.

'If you put that on your house your guests will always be happy.'

But as with the first one, the message was incomprehensible to him.

I went to the Meditation Hall and was almost overcome from the smell of yak butter. I went to the kitchen. It had the look of a tannery – full of deep vats, each one about seven feet across.

'This kitchen was last used in 1958,' Mr Xun said. 'Those cauldrons could cook thirteen yaks at a time. The whole monastery could be fed in this kitchen.'

The remains of the third Dalai Lama are at this monastery, in a temple called the Nine-Roomed Hall. This man, Bsod-nams-rgya-mtsho, was the first to be called 'Dalai'. The Mongol chief, Altan Khan, conferred this title on him when he visited the khan's court in the sixteenth century. 'Dalai' means ocean in Mongol and it implies boundless wisdom. But the special features of the Nine-Roomed Hall are not the bones of this holy man. Interest in the place is usually centred on two tall demons.

'Notice the curtains?' Mr Xun said.

Dusty drapes covered the bases of the statues.

'They have put them there so that you cannot see the figures beneath them.'

'Why would they cover those figures?' I asked.

'One is an ox having sexual intercourse with a lady,' Mr Xun said.

'What sort of lady would have intercourse with an ox?'

'I don't know,' Mr Xun said, 'because it is covered up.'

The buildings were not beautiful, nor even pretty, but they had a rough mountain charm and some of the carved pillars looked both godly and weird. The attractiveness of the place was in its life, its pilgrims and monks, the novice monks fetching water and eating popsicles, and penitents draping the white and yellow gauze on the statues, and burning butter, and whirling prayer wheels, and prostrating themselves in a sort of religious athleticism that was very impressive – they are required to flatten themselves against the ground 100,000 times a year. It is not a fastidious kowtowing but a calisthenic so vigorous that they wear mitts and knee-pads to prevent bruising.

Mr Xun and I walked down the road, past the souvenir stalls and the little shops, and had lunch in a restaurant that was otherwise empty. We had grilled yak meat, melon, squash, pig-fat, buns, seaweed soup and french fries. The yak meat stuffed into the buns was my dish of the day, and I entered it into my notebook under dumplings and smoked duck and all the rest of the dishes I had favoured.

We were sitting near a Franklin stove with a ten-foot tin chimney. Mr Xun said that he had visited the United States the previous year. He had been an interpreter for a trade delegation. In order to secure this job he had had to pass a competitive exam in English. He said he had travelled all over.

'I went to San Francisco,' he said, and, smiling, he told me how much he had hated Chinatown. He regarded the very word as insulting, but also he had found it all hackneyed, ridiculous and embarrassing. 'And the food was bad,' he said.

'What did you think the first time you saw New York?'

'Not as nice as Vancouver.'

I then asked him what he had bought in the United States to take back to China.

'A pen. A book of stories. A photograph album.'

He had no money. But what things he would have bought if he had the cash! A refrigerator, a motor cycle, a television, an electric noodle-maker!

We talked about Tibetans.

'They have black and red faces,' Mr Xun said. 'The Hans are white and red. You can tell the Hans by their red cheeks. And the Tibetans are very dirty.'

'There isn't much water around here,' I said.

'On the grasslands in the west of Qinghai there is no water at all. The people wash their hands in yak's milk. And they never take a bath in their whole life.'

'How about the Hans?'

'We wash once a week.'

Mr Xun said he usually went to a public bath-house in Xining for a bath – on Fridays. He lived in a three-room flat on the outskirts of the town, with his family.

Without warning, Mr Xun said, '"It is a truth universally acknowledged that a single man in possession of a fortune must be in want of a wife –"'

'You read Jane Austen, Mr Xun?'

'My favourite book is *Pride and Prejudice.*'

A very Chinese title, when you come to think of it. He also liked Dickens and Thackeray. There was apparently plenty of time out here on the high plains of central Asia for the plump and populous English novel. He said that he also read religious texts. After middle school he had decided to become a Buddhist. 'I wanted good fortune in my life,' he said. He was now a firm believer.

'Want one of these?'

'Oh, yes,' he said, gratefully accepting a portrait of the exiled Dalai Lama.

I had brought fifty pictures of the Dalai Lama with me. I had been told that they were impossible to obtain in China and that I was likely to win friends with people in this region if I handed them over. It was a simple expedient; I had no personal objection to presenting pictures of this solemn bespectacled incarnation of Buddha; and it seemed to work.

On the way back to the monastery we ran into a pilgrim who said he was a yakherd – he had about thirty of them. They sold for about £60 each (but Chris Bonington was paying £5 a day just to rent them), and he had had to sell two of his yaks to pay for this pilgrimage to Taer with his wife and two small children. The Chinese word for yak was 'hairy cow' (*mao niu*). The yak is a lovely long-haired animal, like a cow on its way to the opera.

Taer Monastery is known for its butter sculptures, and as yak butter is the medium they are pungent works of art. A hall about forty yards long held statues and friezes of multi-coloured flowers, cherubs, trees, temples, little animals and gods and goddesses. One of the largest statues was of Guan Yin, the goddess of mercy. But the Yellow Sect interprets this deity as having thirty-six forms, and in this yak butter statue she was a moustached man.

The monk watching over the butter sculpture took the portrait of the Dalai Lama I offered him and folded it into his robes. Then he gave me a surreptitious blessing.

'You have made him happy,' Mr Xun said.

This present Dalai Lama, number fourteen, was born not far away from here at Hong Nei Village in Pingan County, in 1935. He came to Taer Monastery at the age of two, borne on a sacred white yak and guided by three lamas from Lhasa who had gone in search of him.

It happened in this way. After the death of the thirteenth Dalai Lama, the corpse was found to be facing east. The head was repositioned, but soon after it moved again, to face north-east. The state oracle put on his mask and went into a trance and he too faced north-east. The three lamas set out for the north-east to find the new Dalai Lama. They interviewed the parents of three or four children. One child was Lhamo Dhondrub. His family was very poor. But there had been portents at his birth, in particular the strange visitations of crows, in a place where there had never been any crows. Still, the lamas were not convinced. It takes a while for a Dalai Lama to be proven. But this child passed all the crucial tests, chose the correct beads when they were offered, answered all the questions, and was physically the Holy One: he had oversize ears, sorrowful eyes, 'tiger stripes' on his legs, and the rest of the eight bodily marks. He was brought to Taer and then to Lhasa. He was named: Jetsun Jamphel Ngawang Lobsang Yeshi Tenzin Gyatso – Holy Lord, Gentle Glory, Eloquent, Compassionate, Learned Defender of the Faith, Ocean of Wisdom.

'When he was here in Taer'si he stayed over there, in a house.'

The monk was pointing at nothing.

'I don't see anything.'

'His house was wrecked by the Red Guards.'

This monk was one of the few people I met in China who refused to talk to me about the Cultural Revolution. He was not afraid; he was simply furious and disgusted. He lived in the stables of Taer, in a small cell, with another monk. On the walls of his cell were pictures of Buddha. He had a teapot, a little brazier, a pallet, and a faded quilt. It was not severe, but it was very simple. Over his tiny bed was a poster of a tiger. He too had a large can of yak butter.

In the market outside Taer business was slow. There were no foreign tourists because it was winter, and there were very few Chinese tourists. The shops sold beads, brassware, wolf pelts, Tibetan cloaks and hats and horns, walking sticks, Buddhas, and trinkets. Also this – a shop selling cans of cooking fat. The label on the can said:

Norwegian EDIBLE FAT Sandarit Brand – 5 lbs
Supplied by the World Food Programme
Gift of Norway
Produced by Jahres Fabrikker A/S Sandefjord Norway

'How much?' I asked.

'Fifteen *yuan* a can.'

'How many cans do you have?'

'Plenty.'

The cases were stacked in his shop. How had the stuff arrived here? Perhaps through India or Afghanistan. In any event, this free gift, courtesy of the Norwegian people, was generating income for a prosperous little shop in remote Qinghai.

In that same market, Tibetan men were haggling over grey otter pelts, and buying beads, and swapping silver for chunks of amber. There was a brisk trade in pretty ornaments, and some were trying on the Chinese-made cowboy hats that are so popular among Tibetans.

Remembering the cassette-player in Mr Fu's little car, and our impending trip to Lhasa by road, I went into a music shop and bought some tapes. When I went back to Xining I did the same, but the music shops and department stores were so well stocked I emboldened myself and asked for tapes with political songs on them.

'What kind of songs?' the salesgirl asked. 'Do you know the names?'

'"The East is Red",' I said. 'And one that starts, "I Love

Peking's Tian An Men Square." "The Liu River Song." "The White-Haired Girl".'

They were the Maoist revolutionary songs that had been sung for the past two or three decades.

'We don't have those.'

Mr Xun said, 'We are sick of those songs.'

But they had pop songs, they had Hong Kong rock, and they had tapes of *Oklahoma*. They also had Strauss, Mendelssohn, Bach, and the complete Beethoven symphonies, which I bought for the trip to Tibet.

A few days later I was walking through Xining in the middle of the day and the sky darkened. It began to snow, at first softly, and then blizzarding down. No one seemed to mind. There was hardly any traffic, anyway. And the place looked better under a few inches of snow. A blind boy was caught in it, and tapping his stick he squawked when there was no sound or echo – in just a few minutes he had lost his way, because he could not hear his stick in the snow. But he turned his face up and as the snow hit it he licked the flakes from his lips. Then a troop of black-cloaked Muslims came by and rescued the blind boy. The Muslims were either old bearded patriarchs with severe eyes, or else bratty boys fooling with each other. I followed them to their mosque, which was the biggest one I had seen in China, but like every other religious building I had seen it had a vandalized-and-renovated look.

I stayed in Xining longer than I had planned, because I liked its stuffed pancakes and snowy skies, its red-cheeked Hans and the ragged Tibetans in their greasy cloaks who went smiling down the street. I climbed all the nearby hills – to the Tao monastery with its cave-dwelling monks and its temples balanced on cliffs, the whole thing looking like a wooden fire-escape; and on the tops of these hills I could see that Xining was larger than I had imagined – but the rest was merely brown shoebox-shaped buildings which had no visible function. After the snow melted, the harsh wind from the mountains whirled dust into the air. It was a terrible-looking place, but it was friendly; and I liked being the only barbarous foreign devil (*yang guedze*) in town.

22

The Train to Tibet

In the more remote regions of China, where people are not trusted to be orderly, the authorities devise specific drills for boarding the trains. Xining had one of the cruellest I had seen. The Hard Class passengers were lined up in front of the station – perhaps 1,000 cold, impatient people in a long shuffling line. But it was a directionless line. It led nowhere. It was formed in the windy plaza in front of the station, behind an ugly statue depicting a dozen contending minorities. That was appropriate, because the railway line was composed of the same minorities, contending for seats.

Ten minutes before the train left, a railway guard blew a whistle, and these people snatched up their bales and bundles and ran. They went flapping 200 yards across the plaza, panted another 100 around the station, and wheezed down the platform to where the train sat steaming. That race sorted them out, and so there was a gasping free-for-all for the seats, women and children last.

It was a horrible train. But that was not a bad thing. It is almost axiomatic that the worst trains take you through magical places. I had a strong feeling – and I was proved right – that I would be travelling through one of the most beautiful landscapes in China. This train was dirty, scruffy and extremely crowded. Before it set off there was a fight among the passengers, as five heavily laden Tibetans tried to get into the wrong coach. No punches were thrown. It was all push and pull, and some snarling. The Tibetans smilingly resisted. The most explicit sign that it was a bad train was that it ran out of water an hour after it started. No water – for tea more than for washing – is a catastrophe rather than a simple hardship in China. But no one got angry. No one even complained. They enquired in froggy voices, and then took it without muttering further. I was impressed but annoyed. Without hot water this long trip – thirty hours or so – would be unbearable. We were headed for Golmud, in the Qinghai desert, and there the train stopped. I planned to make my own way to Lhasa, with Mr Fu.

There was no food either. I made noodles in a cup with the last few inches of hot water. People congregated in the dining-car, but nothing was served. There was a certain amount of shouting and lots of abuse, but these sounds were drowned by the rattling and clanking steam engine. There were no lights on the train either. I was exasperated, then uncomfortable, and finally bored stiff. I couldn't eat, I couldn't read. I hated the friendly honks of passengers, the yells, the squawking kids. I dug out some of my food and ate it, and wished I had more. The floor was covered with spat-out sunflower seeds.

I was in a compartment with a young man and an old man. The young one smoked, the old one spat. But they were otherwise very courteous. They were also going to Golmud. As we went along in the trembling train it struck me that we were a great distance from what most people would regard as fruitful and bounteous China. We were over the edge, way past the old Chinese frontier, four days at least from civilization and its vast stinking cities.

The scenery was lovely. The train had risen and snaked through the mountain passes west of Xining, and then had travelled down to the cold valleys. The frozen river was a startling chalky white, and it showed up clearly even in twilight, like a road covered with snow winding through the brown valleys.

'Going to Xizang?' the old man asked, meaning Tibet.

He assumed that no one would go to Golmud to stay, and of course he was right. That was why this was the train to Tibet.

The other passengers were Salars in embroidered jackets, and small brown people wearing stiff little felt bowls on their heads, and Kazakhs in boots and goatskin cloaks, Huis in skullcaps, and enormous Tibetans with ragged rucksacks and shaven heads and greasy robes. They were mostly country folk – shepherds and yakherds and tent-dwellers – heading home after their pilgrimage in Taer'si or else their foray at Xining market. There were many soldiers, there were rowdies and spitters and shitters and oddballs in long underwear who pitched up in the train's corridors and blew their noses on the curtains.

The mountains nearby had bright sharp peaks and warm slopes, but beneath them in the shadows the valleys were frozen and the square mud-walled villages looked like habitations left over from the Neolithic age. They had been built by Mao's pioneers in the nineteen-fifties, the Hans who left settled homes and headed west to bring order – as if it needed more order than Buddhism – to Tibet. Night came quickly, a sky of black and blue which was all cloud, and beneath it the brilliant whiteness of the ice on the river.

I lay in bed, cursing the lack of hot tea on this cold train and reading *The Hole in the Wall*, by Arthur Morrison. It was an old novel about the East End of London in its days of banditry. Leaving Xining, I had asked the young man what those quarries were. He said, 'Lime pits.' In the novel, lime figures in a hideous way. Blind George, having been assaulted by the bully Dan Ogle, takes his revenge by sneaking into Ogle's room and pressing lime into his eyes to blind him ('The thumbs still drove at the eyes the mess of smoking lime that clung and dripped about Ogle's head . . . Blind George gasped, "Hit me now you's as blind as me!"').

That gave me a nightmare, and its terror arose from my confusing snow and lime – they looked the same – and disfiguring myself as I slipped in it. But it was fitful sleep. The cold in the train increased and woke me a number of times. In the morning there were mountains in the north, and sandy waste all around. It was the roughest land I had seen in China, wild and stony, and later on, towards noon on this overcast day, there was snow thinly covering the desert – it had an uneven, spilled look – and swatches of snow lay in the ridges of the far-off mountains. The wind blew hard on the ground, and though it was flat all its boulders were exposed.

There was no vegetation at all, no one lived here, and even the railway stations seemed pointlessly positioned, because no one got on or off the train; the station-master stood at attention with his green flag – no one else.

There was still no water. It amazed me that no one complained. I witnessed a man in the kitchen who was actually pouring water into a pot. He did not speak. He came over to me, smiled briefly, then slammed the door in my face.

A boy in a smock was selling tickets in the dining-car. I asked what the tickets were for. Noodles, he said. So I bought some tickets and lined up at a window leading on to the kitchen. I waited ten minutes and when nothing happened I said, 'What about the noodles?'

'No more left!' the ticket-seller said. He was smiling, but it was an ambiguous smile.

I complained: 'I just gave you some money –'

'Come back in an hour.'

'I want my noodles or else my money back.'

'Later.'

It was like prison, or the army, or an old-fashioned nut-house.

I said, 'You are not being very friendly. There is no food, no heat, no water on this train. This is very bad.'

The ticket-seller was still smiling. I wondered what would happen to me if I hit him. They would probably regard this as a very serious breach of discipline and send me to a far-off place for re-education; indeed, they would probably send me here, to Qinghai, where they had sent so many other rebels. So I had nothing to fear: I was already in exile.

'Yes. It's bad,' the ticket-seller said, when he realized I was angry.

'At least get me some water for tea.'

'There is no water.'

'There is water in the kitchen. I saw it.'

You win, he seemed to say, and he brought me a thermos of hot water, much to the delight of the men in my compartment as we shared it.

The landscape became even wilder, though I had not thought that to be possible. It was colder, windier, more rubbly; the mountains blacker. This made bleak Xinjiang seem lush by comparison. A cold wind howled across stony ground. It was hellish and memorable. I thought how the corners of China were so strange and inhospitable and unearthly that the Chinese had come to believe that they represented the edges of the flat world they knew as the Middle Kingdom.

The younger man in the upper berth was Mr Zhao. He came from Liaoning and said he had never seen a place as bad as this. He was a factory supervisor, something to do with magnesium, and was going to be in Golmud for several weeks.

'I'd rather be somewhere else,' he said.

But I was pleased to be here, in such a wilderness. I sat in the safety of the train and looked upon the desolation of the land with a sense of mounting excitement. In the Lop Nor desert of Xinjiang and in Hami and Turfan they say, 'Marco Polo came through here' or 'This was the Silk Road.' But here in Qinghai no claim at all could be made. There was never anyone here. It was death to attempt a crossing. No one passed through. And it was always like this – just as empty.

Mr Zhao was travelling with his father, who visited him from another part of the train. This old man sat and stared at me. I tried to speak with him, but he was deaf. He had a deaf man's bright smile. Whenever I wrote in my notebook the old man put his teacup down and pressed his nose against my notebook page, marvelling at my handwriting.

At last, the mountains and hills utterly vanished and in their place there was a light brown desert. I looked closer and saw that it was all low snowdrifts covered with fine sand. Later in the day it was stony. Still later, it was dark and rubbly – but still a desert – and the brown twisted symmetry of the rubble made it seem like an immensity of dog turds.

There was a station every twenty miles, but a station here was three small square buildings, the same brown as the turdy desert, standing in the wind, with emptiness on every side, and clouds madly blowing over them.

'It is not good,' Mr Zhao said. Obviously he missed the traffic and drizzle of urban Liaoning.

'I like this place,' I said.

He erupted in the short spitting laugh that in China means: *You must be out of your mind.*

'I just wish we had some water,' I said.

I asked the Head of the Train, who seemed very young, why there was no water.

'Because this is the desert.'

He spoke English with a slight American accent.

'But you have boilers,' I said.

'The water in the boilers is for the engine.'

'Are people complaining about the lack of water?'

'You are complaining,' he said, in a friendly way, 'and other people are complaining too. But I tell everyone it is a problem, and they understand.'

'I don't understand.'

'Because you are a foreign friend,' he said, which was a polite Chinese way of saying that I was a Martian.

He said he was twenty-two. I asked him his name.

'My name is Gold Country,' he said in English.

'Jinguo?' I asked.

'Yes. My father named me that because he wanted China to be prosperous.'

He seemed rather ineffectual for such an important job – he was in complete charge of the train. But he was pleasant. He said he had not had much formal education and in fact had learned his English on the Voice of America.

Towards the end of the afternoon the rubbly desert gave way to rockier ground, and mountains appeared to the south-west. Two mountains were distinct and beautiful, and the snow was a luminous bluish colour, covering the entirety of these slopes, because they faced north and received no sun. They were the mountains (I could see from my map) Yagradagze and Har Sai, each of them just under 20,000 feet. They rose out of great flat snowfields, while in the foreground was rough desert and the chugging train.

'It has recently snowed,' Jinguo said. 'That is not unusual. It often snows heavily in March here. And in the passes it snows all year. Foreign friends like snow!'

As if in welcome a flock of eight grey cranes gathered themselves together and made off, just ahead of the train, rising and still folding as they flew, like large mechanical bumbershoots blown sideways by the stiff wind.

Golmud was hardly a town. It was a dozen widely scattered low buildings, some radio antennas, a water-tower. One of the few cars in town was Mr Fu's ridiculous Galant. There were some buses, but they were the most punished-looking vehicles I had seen in China – and no wonder, for they toiled up and down the Tibetan Plateau.

'Snow,' Mr Fu said – his first word.

I had not expected this snow, and it was clear from his gloomy tone that neither had he. The snow lay thinly in the town, but behind the town it was deep and dramatic – blazing in the shadows of the mountain range.

We were still at Golmud Station. Mr Fu had driven from Xining, and had met me. But he was very subdued in the car.

When I asked him how he was he did not reply directly. He said, 'We cannot go to Lhasa tomorrow. Maybe the day after, or the day after that, or –'

I asked him why.

'The snow. It is everywhere – very deep,' he said. He did not even glance at me. He was driving fast through the rutted Golmud streets – too fast, but I had seen him drive in Xining and I knew this to be normal. At the best of times he was a rather frantic driver. 'The snow is blocking the road.'

'You are sure?'

'Yes.'

'Did you see it?'

He laughed: *Ha-ha! You idiot!* 'Look at it!'

He pointed out the window. But I was not looking at the snow. I noticed that he was wearing a pair of elegant driving-gloves. He never took the wheel without donning them. They seemed as old-fashioned as spats or gaiters.

'Did anyone tell you that the road was blocked with snow?'

He did not reply, so that meant no. We continued this sparring. The snow was bad news – it glittered, looking as though it was there for ever. But surely someone had a road report?

'Is there a bus station in Golmud?'

He nodded. He hated my questions. He wanted to be in charge, and how could he be if I was asking all the questions? And he had so few answers.

'People say the road is bad. Look at the snow!'

'We will ask at the bus station. The bus drivers will know.'

'First we go to the hotel,' he said, trying to take command.

The hotel was another prison-like place with cold corridors and squawks and odd hours. I had three cactuses in my room, and a calendar, and two armchairs. But there were no curtains on the windows, and there was no hot water. '*Later*,' they said. The lobby was wet and dirty from the mud that had been tracked in. An ornamental pond behind the hotel was filled with green ice, and the snow was a foot deep on the path to the restaurant. I asked about food. '*Later*,' they said. Some of the rooms had six or eight bunk beds. Everyone inside wore a heavy coat and fur hat, against the cold. Why hadn't my cactus plants died? The hotel cost £5.50 for a double room, and £1.25 for food.

'Now we go to the bus station,' I said.

Mr Fu said nothing.

'We will ask someone about the snow.'

I had been told that buses regularly plied between Golmud and Lhasa, especially now that there were no flights – the air service to Tibet had been suspended. Surely one of these bus drivers would put us in the picture.

We drove to the bus station. On the way, I could see that Golmud was the ultimate Chinese frontier town, basically a military camp, with a few shops, a market, and wide streets. There were very few buildings, but since they were not tall they seemed less of a disfigurement. It was a place of pioneers – of volunteers who had come out in the nineteen-fifties, as they had in Xining. They had been encouraged by Mao to develop the poor and empty parts of China; and of course, Tibet had to be invaded and subdued, and that was impossible without reliable supply lines – settlements, roads, telegraph wires, barracks. First the surveyors and engineers came, then the railway people and the soldiers, and then the teachers and traders.

'What do you think of Golmud, Mr Fu?'

'Too small,' he said, and laughed, meaning the place was insignificant.

At the bus station we were told that the snow wasn't bad on the road. A Tibetan bus had arrived just that morning – it was late, of course, but it was explained that all the buses were late, even when there was no snow.

Mr Fu was not placated. He pointed south and said, 'Snow!'

He was clearly apprehensive, although I was convinced that we should set off.

I said, 'We will go tomorrow, but we will leave early. We will drive until noon. If the snow is bad we will turn back and try again another day. If it looks OK we will go on.'

There was no way that he could disagree with this, and it had the additional merit of being a face-saving plan.

We had a celebratory dinner that night – wood-ear fungus, noodles, yak slices and the steamed buns called *mantou* that Mr Fu said he could not live without (he had a supply for the trip to Tibet). There was a young woman at the table, sharing our meal. She said nothing until Mr Fu introduced her.

'This is Miss Sun.'

'Is she coming with us?'

'Yes. She speaks English.'

Mr Fu, who spoke no English at all, was convinced that Miss Sun was fluent in English. But at no point over the next four or five days was I able to elicit any English at all from Miss Sun. Occasionally she would say a Chinese word and ask me its English equivalent.

'How do you say *luxing* in English?'

'Travel.'

Then her lips would tremble and she made a choking sound, '*Trow*'.

And, just as quickly, she forgot even that inaccurate little squawk.

Over the dinner I said, 'What time are we leaving tomorrow?'

'After breakfast,' Mr Fu said.

The maddening Chinese insistence on mealtimes.

'We should get an early start, because the snow will slow us down.'

'We can leave at 9.00.'

'The sun comes up at 6.30 or 7.00. Let's leave then.'

'Breakfast,' Mr Fu said, and smiled.

We both knew that breakfast was at 8.00. Mr Fu was demanding his full hour, too. I wanted to quote a Selected Thought of Mao about being flexible, meeting all obstacles and overcoming them by strength of will. But I couldn't think of one. Anyway, a Mao Thought would have cut no ice with young, skinny, frantic Mr Fu, who played Beethoven and wore driving-gloves and had a freeloading girlfriend. He was one of the new Chinese. He even had a pair of sun-glasses.

'We can buy some food and eat it on the way,' I said, as a last desperate plea for an early start.

'I must eat *mantou* when it is hot,' Mr Fu said.

That annoyed me, and I was more annoyed the next morning when at half past nine I was still waiting for Mr Fu, who was himself waiting for a receipt for his room-payment. At last, near 10.00, we left, and I sat in the back seat wishing I were on a train, and feeling sour at the prospect of spending the whole trip staring at the back of Miss Sun's head.

Lhasa was 1,000 miles away.

Looking towards Tibet I had a glimpse of a black and vaporous steam locomotive ploughing through a dazzling snowfield under the blue summits and buttresses of the Tanggula Shan. It was one of the loveliest things I saw in China – the chugging train in the snowy desert, the crystal mountains behind it, and the clear sky above. Everything visible was jewel-like, smoke and sparkle in a diamond as big as Tibet.

About twenty miles farther on the line ended, at the first high pass in the mountain range. That was the end of the line in China – though only soldiers were allowed to go that far by rail – and after that there was only the narrow road, on which Mr Fu was now skidding in his Galant.

Mr Fu, I could see, was terrified of the snow. He did not know its effect first-hand. He had only heard scare-stories. That was why he had wanted to stay in Golmud for another week, until the snow melted. He believed that there was no way through it. But the snow was not bad. The road was fairly clear – anyway, two distinct ruts had been mashed into it by passing trucks. But they had created a ridge in the centre of the road and this hard hump of snow and ice kept bumping and tossing the little car with its low clearance.

In the first passes, so narrow they were nearly always in shadow, there was ice. Mr Fu took his time. He was a poor driver – that had been obvious in the first five minutes of driving with him – but the snow and ice slowed him and made him careful. The icy stretches looked dangerous, but by creeping along (and trying to ignore the precipitous drop in the ravine by the roadside) we managed. For miles there was slippery snow, but this too Mr Fu negotiated. Two hours passed in this way. It was a lovely sunny day, and where the sun had struck the snow some of it had melted. But we were climbing into the wind, and even this sun could not mask the fact that it was growing colder as we gained altitude.

In his terror, Mr Fu did not speak a word for those hours, but his breathing – and his snorts and gasps – were like a monologue.

We passed the first range of mountains, and behind them – though it was cold – there was less snow than on the Golmud side. Mr Fu began to increase his speed. Whenever he saw a dry patch of road he floored it and sped onward, slowing only when more snow or ice appeared. Twice he hit sudden frost-heaves, and I was thrown out of my seat and bumped my head.

'Sorry!' Mr Fu said, still speeding.

Most of the curves were so tight that Mr Fu had no choice but to go slowly. And then I sipped tea from my thermos and passed cassettes to Miss Sun who fed them into the machine. After a hundred miles we had finished with Brahms. I debated whether to hand her the Beethoven symphonies, as I listened to Mendelssohn. I drank green tea and looked at the sunny road and snowy peaks and listened to the music, and I congratulated myself on contriving this excellent way of going to Lhasa.

There was another frost-heave.

'Sorry!'

He did not slow down. The road straightened and he went even faster – about eighty, which seemed ridiculous for such a small car on such a narrow road. The only other traffic was trucks – big rusted ones, loaded, with flapping tarpaulins and Tibetan drivers. Mr Fu always leaned on his horn and passed them carelessly, not seeming to notice whether there was a curve ahead.

He was an awful driver. He could not have been driving long. He had probably gone to a state driving school and earned a certificate, and had been assigned to a Xining work-unit. The driving-gloves were merely an affectation. He ground the gears when he set off, he gave the thing too much accelerator, he steered jerkily, he went too fast; and he had what is undoubtedly the worst habit a driver can have – but one that is common in China: going downhill he always switched off the engine and put the gears into neutral, believing that he was saving petrol.

I am not a retiring sort of person, and yet I said nothing. A person who is driving a car is in charge, and if you are a passenger you generally keep your mouth shut. I had an urge to say something, and yet I thought: It's going to be a long trip – no sense spoiling it at the outset with an argument. And I wanted to see just how bad a driver Mr Fu was.

I soon found out.

He was rounding bends at such speed that I found myself clutching the door-handle in order to prevent myself being thrown across the seat. I could not drink my tea without spilling it. He was going ninety – I could not tell whether the dial said kilometres or miles per hour, but did it matter? And yet if I said, '*Slow down*', he would lose face, his pride would be hurt, and wasn't it true that he had got us through the snow? It was now about noon, with a dry road ahead. At this rate we would get to our first destination, the town of Amdo, before nightfall.

'Play this one, Miss Sun.'

Miss Sun took the Chinese cassette of Beethoven's Ninth Symphony. She rammed it into the machine and the first few bars played. The sun was streaming through the windows. The sky was clear and blue, and the ground was gravelly beneath the grey hills. There were snowy peaks to the left and right of us, just peeping over the hills. We were approaching a curve. I was a little anxious but otherwise very happy on the highest road in the world, the way to Lhasa. It was a beautiful day.

I remembered all of this clearly, because it was about two seconds later that we crashed.

There was a culvert on the curve, and a high bump in the road that was very obvious. But Mr Fu was doing ninety, and when he hit the bump we took off – the car leaped, I felt weightless, and when we came twisting down we were heading into an upright stone marker on the right. Mr Fu was snatching at the steering wheel. The car skidded and changed direction, plunging to the left-hand side of the road. All this time I was aware of wind rushing against the car, a noise like a jet-stream. That increased and so did the shaking of the car as it became airborne again and ploughed into a powerful wind composed of dust and gravel. We had left the road and were careering sideways into the desert. Mr Fu was battling with the wheel, as the car was tossed. My clearest memory was of the terrific wind pressing against the twisted car, the windows darkened by flying dust, and a kind of suspense. In a moment, I thought, we are going to smash and die.

I was hanging on to the door-handle. My head was jammed against the front seat. I was afraid that if I let go I would be thrown out the opposite door. I thought I heard Miss Sun screaming, but the car noise and the wind were much louder.

This went on for perhaps seven seconds. That is an achingly long time in a skidding car; terror has everything to do with time passing. I had never felt so helpless or so doomed.

So I was surprised when the car finally stopped. It was on its side. Only the deep gravelly sand had prevented it from turning over completely. I had to push the door with my shoulder to open it. The dust was still settling. The rear tyre on my side of the car had been torn off and I could hear it hissing.

I staggered away to be as far as possible from the car and saw Mr Fu and Miss Sun gasping and coughing. Miss Sun was twitching. Mr Fu looked stunned and sorrowful, because he saw the damage to the car: all its chrome had been torn off, the grille was smashed, the wheel rim twisted, the doors smashed; and we were fifty yards from the road, sunk in desert gravel. It seemed incredible that the sun was still shining.

Mr Fu laughed. It was a cough of blind fear that meant: *God, what now!*

No one spoke. We were wordlessly hysterical that we had survived. Mr Fu tramped over to me and smiled and touched my cheek. There was blood on his finger. I had got out of the car not knowing whether I was hurt – I suspected I might have been. But I checked myself. My glasses had smashed and dug into my cheek, but the wound was not bad – anyway, not deep. I had a bump on my forehead. My neck ached. My wrist hurt. But I was all right.

It infuriated me that this had happened on a dry road, under sunny skies, so early in the trip. Now we were stuck, and it was all because of the incompetence of Mr Fu. He had been driving too fast. But it was also my own fault for having said nothing.

Mr Fu had unpacked a shovel and was digging around the car. What good was that? We could not go anywhere on three wheels. It seemed hopeless. I debated whether to grab my bag and start hitch-hiking; but in which direction? Mr Fu had got himself into this mess; he could get himself out of it. I could not imagine how this car could ever be dragged on to the road. I looked around and thought: This is one of the emptiest places in the world.

We took turns digging for a while, but this merely seemed a cosmetic endeavour, unearthing the car. And the more we saw of the car the more wrecked it seemed.

After twenty minutes or so, we were exhausted. Miss Sun was making little piles of broken bits of plastic that had been torn from the grille and scattered. These she intended to save, as if collecting them showed her deep concern.

Some brown trucks were labouring slowly down the road. We had passed them hours ago.

'Let's stop them,' I said.

'No,' Mr Fu said.

Chinese pride. He shook his head and waved me away. He knew they were Tibetans. What a loss of face for him if these savages witnessed this piece of stupid driving. He had no excuses.

'Come back,' Mr Fu said. 'Help me dig.'

But I did not turn. I was waving to the approaching trucks, and I was delighted to see them slowing down. It was a three-truck convoy, and when they parked the Tibetans came flapping slowly through the desert, laughing with pleasure at the tipped-over car and Mr Fu on his knees digging, and Miss Sun squatting like a lunatic with her piles of broken plastic. There were seven Tibetans. They looked very greasy in their old clothes, but I was reassured by their laughter and their squashed hats and their broken shoes: their ordinariness gave them the look of rescuers.

I dug out my *List of Useful Tibetan Phrases* and consulted it. I said, *'Tashi deleg!'* ('Hallo – good luck!')

They returned the greeting and laughed some more.

I pointed to the car. *'Yappo mindoo.'* ('That is not good.')

They nodded and replied. 'True,' they were saying. 'That's not good at all.'

'Nga Amayriga nay ray,' I said. ('I'm an American.')

They said, *'Amayriga, Amayriga!'*

I looked at my list again and put my finger on a phrase. I said, *'Nga Lhasa la drogi yin.'* ('I am going to Lhasa.')

By now one of them had taken the shovel from Mr Fu, and another was digging with his hands. One was unloading the boot – pulling boxes out, unbolting the spare tyre. Several of them were touching the wound on my face and going *tsk*, *tsk*.

'Want a picture of the Dalai Lama?' I said.

They nodded. Yes, yes!

The others heard. They said, 'Dalai Lama, Dalai Lama!'

They dropped what they were doing and surrounded me as I pulled out the roll of portraits I had brought for just such an emergency. They were tough men, but they took the pictures with great gentleness and reverence, each one touching the paper to his head and bowing to me. They marvelled at the pictures, while Mr Fu and Miss Sun stood to the side, sulking.

'Everyone gets a picture,' I said. 'Now you have a nice portrait of the Dalai Lama. You are very happy, right?' – they laughed, hearing me jabber in English – 'And you want to help us. Now let's straighten that axle, and get the wheel on, and push this god-damned car back on to the road. Get some ropes – hitch it up' – they were laughing and nodding – 'and push us over there, because *Nga Lhasa la drogi yin*, and if I don't I am going to be very annoyed. What do you say?'

They all said *'Ya, ya!'* and set to work.

It took less than half an hour for them to fix the wheel and dig out the car, and then with eight of us pushing and Mr Fu gunning the engine we flopped and struggled until the car was back on the road. As the wheels spun and everyone became covered with dust, I thought: I love these people.

Afterwards they showed me little pictures of the Dalai Lama

and the Panchen Lama on the sun-visors in the cabs of their trucks.

'Dalai Lama, Dalai Lama,' they chanted.

Mr Fu thanked them in Chinese. It meant that he had to swallow his pride to do that. They didn't care. They laughed at him and waved him away.

It was now early afternoon. It had all been a shock, and yet I was encouraged, because we had survived it. It seemed miraculous that we were still alive. But Mr Fu said nothing. When we set off again, he seemed both dazed and frenzied. His glasses had broken in the crash, and I could see that he was wild-eyed. He was also very dirty. Miss Sun was sniffing, whimpering softly.

The car was in miserable shape. It looked the way I felt. I was surprised that it had restarted; I was amazed that its four wheels were turning. That is another way of saying that it seemed logical to me, a few minutes after we set off again, that a great screeching came from the back axle. It was the sort of sound that made me think that the car was about to burst apart.

We stopped. We jacked up the car. We took a back wheel off to have a closer look. The brakes were twisted, and pieces of metal were protruding into the rim. At low speeds this made a clacketty-clack, and faster it rose to a shriek. There was no way to fix it. We put the wheel back on, and while Mr Fu tightened the nuts I looked around. I had never in my life seen such light – the sky was like a radiant sea; and at every edge of this blasted desert with its leathery plants were strange grey hills and snowy peaks. We were on the plateau. It was a world I had never seen before – of emptiness and wind-scoured rocks and dense light. I thought: If I have be stranded anywhere, this is the place I want it to be. I was filled with joy at the thought of being abandoned there, at the edge of the Tibetan Plateau.

'I think it is heating up,' Mr Fu said, after he had driven a hundred yards down the road.

He was breathing hard and noisily through his nose. He slammed on the brakes, ran around to the back wheel and spat on the rim. It wasn't frustration. It was his way of determining how hot the hub was.

He remained kneeling by the back wheel, his head bowed.

'Are you all right, Mr Fu?'

He stood up and staggered, and then he grinned horribly at me. He seemed manic. He yelled that he was fine and it was obvious from the way he said it that he wasn't.

'It is very high here!' he cried. There was dust on his face. His hair was bristly. His colour had changed, too. He looked ashen.

After that, we kept stopping. The wheel noise was dreadful. But that was not the worst of it. Mr Fu's driving changed. Usually he went fast – and then I told him clearly to slow down. (No one will ever make me sit in a speeding car again, I thought: I will always protest.) Mr Fu's over-careful slow driving unnerved me almost as much as his reckless driving.

This did not last long. We came to a pass that linked the Tanggula Shan with the Kun Lun mountains. It was a Chinese belief that in a valley nearby there was a trickle that rose and became the great brown torrent that ended in Shanghai, the Great River that only foreigners know as the Yangtze. The river is one of the few geographical features that the Chinese are genuinely mystical about. But they are not unusual in that. Most people are bewitched by big rivers.

This pass was just under 17,000 feet. Mr Fu stopped the car and I got out and looked at a stone tablet, which gave the altitude and mentioned the mountains. The air was thin, I was a bit breathless, but the landscape was dazzling – the soft contours of the plateau, and the long folded stretches of snow, like beautiful gowns laid out all over the countryside, a gigantic version of the way Indians set out their laundry to dry. I was so captivated by the magnificence of the place that I didn't mind the discomfort of the altitude.

'Look at the mountains, Mr Fu.'

'I don't feel well,' he said, not looking up. 'It's the height.'

He rubbed his eyes. Miss Sun was still whimpering. Would she scream in a minute?

I got in and Mr Fu drove fifty yards. His driving had worsened. He was in the wrong gear, the gearbox was hiccupping; and still the rear wheel made its hideous ratcheting.

Without warning, he stopped in the middle of the road and gasped, 'I cannot drive any more!'

He wasn't kidding. He looked ill. He kept rubbing his eyes.

'I can't see! I can't breathe!'

Miss Sun burst into tears.

I thought: Oh, shit.

'What do you want to do?' I asked.

He shook his head. He was too ill to contemplate the question.

I did not want to hurt his pride, especially here at a high altitude, so I said carefully, 'I know how to drive a car.'

'You do?' He blinked. He was very thin. He looked like a starving hamster.

'Yes, yes,' I said.

He gladly got into the back. Miss Sun hardly acknowledged the fact that I was now sitting beside her. I took the wheel and off we went. In the past few hours the ridiculous little Nipponese car had been reduced to a jalopy. It was dented; it made a racket; it smoked; and the most telling of its jalopy features was that it sagged to one side – whether it was a broken spring or a cracked axle I didn't know. It had received a mortal blow, but it was still limping along. I had to hold tight to the steering wheel. The sick car kept trying to steer itself into the ditch on the right-hand side of the road.

Mr Fu was asleep. This cycle of frenzy and fatigue was something I had seen before in China. It seemed a Chinese way of living: working very hard, with tremendous concentration or else flailing arms, and then stopping suddenly and going to sleep. Often in trains, two chattering and gesticulating people would crap out and begin to snore like bullfrogs.

I could see in the rear-view mirror that Mr Fu's colour had changed; the sallowness had replaced his papery look of fear and illness. In sleep he looked calmer, and he had a bold snore. Miss Sun, too, was asleep. I pushed in Beethoven's Symphony Number 6 and continued towards Lhasa. I liked this. I liked listening to music. I liked the fact that the other passengers were asleep. I loved the look of Tibet. I might have died back there on the road; but I was alive. It was wonderful to be alive and doing the driving.

The road was oddly straight – few curves, no mountainside stretches, none of the alpine circling and hairpin bends I had expected. I had to force myself to keep my eyes on the road, because I kept wanting to look at the surrounding landscape. I was driving in a dry snow-flecked desert that was quite flat, and the snowy peaks at the edge were like the heads and shoulders of giant Druids showing around an immense table. In the distance the mountains were vast and black, rather frightening, with sharp cliffs and flinty-looking slopes. But the road was even. It was innocent-looking. No other vehicles appeared on it. It occurred to me that a person could easily travel down this Tibetan road on a bicycle, and I began to plan a trip that involved riding a bike around Tibet.

There were no people here that I could see. But there were yaks grazing on some of the hillsides – presumably the herds of the nomadic tent-dwelling Tibetans who were said to roam this part of the province. The yaks were black and brown, and some had white patches. They were ornamented with ribbons on their long hair, and they all had lovely tails, as thick as any horse's. In some places, herds of Tibetan gazelles grazed near the road.

Mr Fu slept on, but Miss Sun woke up, and before I could change the cassette she slipped in one of her own. It was the soundtrack of an Indian movie, in Hindi; but the title song was in English.

I am a disco dancer!
I am a disco dancer!

This imbecilic chant was repeated interminably with twanging from an electric guitar.

'That is Indian music,' I said. 'Do you like it?'

'I love it,' Miss Sun said.

'Do you understand the words?'

'No,' she said. 'But it sounds nice.'

It sounded awful. I kept driving. I had no idea where we were, but it hardly mattered. There was only one road. The accident had made me cautious. I was averaging about fifty miles an hour. And the car was making such ominous noises that I thought if I went any faster it would fly apart. Mr Fu woke up, but he showed no inclination to drive. I was glad of that, because it was glorious to be bouncing down this Tibetan road in full sunshine, past the yaks and the gazelles, with mountains all around.

At about 4.00 we were almost out of petrol. Mr Fu said he had spare petrol in the back, in big cans, but just as I noticed the petrol gauge we approached a small settlement.

'Stop here,' Mr Fu said.

He directed me to a shack, which turned out to be a petrol station – old-fashioned nozzles on long hoses. It was, like all petrol stations in Tibet, run by the People's Liberation Army.

'We should get the tyre fixed, too.'

Mr Fu said, 'No. They don't fix tyres.'

In Xining I had asked Mr Fu to bring two spares. He had brought one, and it was being used. So we were travelling without a spare.

'Where will we get the tyre fixed?'

He pointed vaguely down the road, towards Lhasa. It meant he didn't have the slightest idea.

I walked over to the soldier filling the tank.

'Where are we?'

'This is Wudaoliang.'

Names look so grand on a map. But this place hardly justified being on a map. How could a petrol station, some barracks and a barbed wire fence even deserve a name? And the name was bad news, because Wudaoliang was not even half-way to our destination, which was Amdo.

As if to make the moment operatic, the weather suddenly changed. A wind sprang up, clouds tumbled across the sun, and the day grew very dark and cold. My map was flapping against the car roof. It would be night soon.

'When will we get to Amdo, Mr Fu?'

'About six o'clock.'

Wrong, of course. Mr Fu's calculations were wildly inaccurate. I had stopped believing that he had ever been on this road before. It was possible that my map was misleading – it had shown roads that didn't exist, and settlements that were no more than ruins and blowing sand.

Mr Fu had no map. He had a scrap of paper with seven towns scribbled on it, the stops between Golmud and Lhasa. The scrap of paper had become filthy from his repeatedly consulting it. He consulted it again.

'The next town is Yanshiping.'

We set off. I drove; Mr Fu dozed.

Miss Sun played 'I am a disco dancer'.

After an hour we passed a hut, some yaks and a ferocious dog.

'Yanshiping?'

'No.'

In the fading light and freezing air this plateau no longer seemed romantic. 'This country makes the Gobi seem fertile in comparison,' a French traveller once wrote. It was true. Moonscape is the word most often applied to such a place; but this was beyond a moonscape – it was another planet entirely.

There were more settlements ahead. They were all small, and all the same: huts of stained whitewash, square walls, flat roofs, and red, blue and green pennants and flags with mantras written on them, flying from propped-up bush-branches. As these prayer-flags flapped, so the mantras reverberated in the air, and grace abounded around them. There were more yaks, more fierce dogs.

'Yanshiping?'

'No.'

It was nearly dark when we came to it. Yanshiping was twenty houses standing in mud on a curve in the road. There were children and dogs, yaks and goats. Several of the dogs were the biggest and fiercest I had ever seen in my life. They were Tibetan mastiffs – their Tibetan name means simply 'watch-dog'. They lollopped and slavered and barked horribly.

'There is nowhere to stay here,' Mr Fu said, before I could ask – I was slowing down.

'What's the next town?'

He produced his filthy scrap of paper.

'Amdo. There is a hotel at Amdo.'

'How far is Amdo?'

He was silent. He didn't know. After a moment, he said, 'A few hours.'

'Hotel' is a nice word, but China had taught me to distrust it. The more usual Chinese expression was 'guesthouse'. It was the sort of place I could never identify properly. It was a hospital, a madhouse, a house, a school, a prison. It was seldom a hotel. But, whatever, I longed to be there. It was now 7.30. We had been on the road for ten hours.

We continued in the dark. It was snowier here, higher and

colder, on a winding road that was icy in places. There was another pass – choked with ice which never melts at any time in the year because of the altitude, another 17,000-footer.

Mr Fu woke and saw the snow.

'Road! Watch the road!' he yelled. *Lu! Lu! Looooooo!*

The altitude put him to sleep, but each time he woke he became a terrible nag. I began to think that perhaps many Chinese in authority were nags and bores. He kept telling me to watch the road, because he was frightened. I wanted to say, '*You almost got us killed, Jack*' but to save his face I didn't.

I often mistook the lights of distant trucks on the far side of this defile for the lights of Amdo. There was no vegetation at this altitude, and the freezing air was clear. In the darkness I saw these pinpricks of light.

'Is that Amdo?'

'Watch the road!' Mr Fu's voice from the back seat set my teeth on edge. *Lu! Loooo!*

His nervousness made him nag. He was the passenger. I was the chauffeur. They were both in the back seat now – she was whimpering still, he was chattering. 'Keep your eyes on the road,' he was saying; 'watch the road. *That's not Amdo – it's a truck!*'

Now and then he would tap me on the shoulder and cry, 'Toilet!'

That was the greatest euphemism of all. It was usually Miss Sun who needed to have a slash. I watched her totter to the roadside and creep into a ditch, and there just out of the wind – and it was too dark even for the yaks to see her – she found relief.

Three more hours passed in this way. I wondered whether we might not be better off just pulling off the road and sleeping in the car. Midnight on the Tibetan Plateau, in the darkness and ice and wind, was not a good time to be driving. But the problem was the narrowness of the road. There was nowhere to pull off. There was a ditch on each side of the road. If we stopped we would be rammed by one of the big army trucks that used the road.

I was glad we were still going. Why didn't the back wheel fall off? Why was the axle still screaming? Why didn't we get a flat tyre? After all, we were travelling without a spare. Nothing bad happened. The moon came out from behind a cloud and showed me a snowy mountainside and the black pit of a valley beside the road.

I glanced at it and almost immediately Mr Fu yelled at me.

Towards midnight I saw the sign saying Amdo. In the darkness it seemed a bleak and dangerous place. I did not know then that it would look much worse in daylight.

'We are staying at the army camp,' Mr Fu said.

To save face, Mr Fu changed places with me and drove the last twenty feet to the sentry post. Then he got out and argued with the sentry.

He returned to the car trembling.

'They are full,' he said.

'What now?'

'The guesthouse.'

Miss Sun was quietly sobbing.

We drove across a rocky field. There was no road. We came to a boarded-up house, but before we could get out a mastiff bounded into the car lights. It had a big square head and a meaty tongue, and it was slavering and barking. It was as big as a pony, something like the Hound of the Baskervilles, but vastly more sinister.

'Are you getting out?'

'No,' Mr Fu said, hoarse with fear.

Beyond the crazed and leaping dog there were yaks sleeping, standing up.

Mr Fu kept driving across this rocky hillside, pretending he was on a road. Was he trying to prove something, after a full day of yelling in the back seat?

There were more dogs. I could take the yak-meat diet; I could understand why the Tibetans didn't wash; I found the cold and the high altitude just about bearable; I could negotiate the roads. But I could not stand those fierce dogs. I was not angry or impatient. I was scared shitless.

'There is a guesthouse,' Mr Fu said, grinning at some dim lights ahead.

It was a dirty two-storey building with bars on the windows. I guessed it was a prison, but that was all right. We checked for dogs, and while Miss Sun threw up next to the car, we went inside. A Tibetan sat on a ragged quilt on the floor gnawing raw flesh off a yak bone. He was black with dirt, his hair was matted, he was barefoot in spite of the cold. He looked exactly like a cannibal, tearing shreds of red meat off a shank.

'We need a room,' Mr Fu asked in Chinese.

The Tibetan laughed and said there was no room. He chewed with his mouth open, showing his teeth, and then with aggressive hospitality he pushed the bone into my face and demanded I take a bite.

I took out my *List of Useful Tibetan Phrases*.

'Hallo. I am not hungry,' I said in Tibetan. 'My name is Paul. What is your name? I am from America. Where are you from?'

'*Bod*,' the cannibal said, giving me the Tibetan name for Tibet. He was grinning at my gloves. I was cold – it was way below freezing in this room. He gestured for me to sit with him on his quilt, and in the same motion he waved Mr Fu away.

It is a Tibetan belief that all Tibetans are descended from a sexually insatiable ogress who had six children after copulating with a submissive monkey. It is just a pretty tale, of course; but looking at this man it was easy to see how the myth might have originated.

He batted away Mr Fu's identity card, but he took a great interest in my passport. Then he put his juicy bone down and fingered the pages, leaving bloodstains on them. He laughed at my passport picture. He compared the picture with my grey frozen face and the wound under my eye. He laughed again.

'I agree. It's not a very good likeness.'

He became very attentive, hearing English spoken, like a dog listening to footsteps in the driveway.

'Do you have rooms?' I asked. I held out a picture of the Dalai Lama.

He mumbled a reply. His shaven head and big jaw made him look ape-like. I switched to Chinese, because I couldn't understand what he was saying. He took the picture gently.

'One person – six *yuan*,' he said, clutching the portrait.

'Oh, thank you, thank you,' Mr Fu said, abasing himself.

'Tea, tea,' the cannibal said, offering me a tin kettle.

I drank some salty buttery tea and as I did so a truck pulled up outside. Twelve Tibetans, women and children, entered the room, went into the corridor, threw quilts on the floor and fell on them.

I paid my money, got my bag from the car and found an empty room on the upper floor. The light on the stairwell had shown me what sort of a place it was. Someone had vomited on the landing. The vomit was frozen. There was worse farther on, against the wall. It was all icy, and so the smell wasn't bad. It was very dirty, a bare cement interior that was grimmer than any prison I had ever seen. But the real prison touch was that all the lights were on – not many of them, but all bare bulbs. There were no light-switches. There were howls and murmurs from the other rooms. There was no water, and no bathroom. No toilet except the stairwell.

Not far away I heard Miss Sun berating Mr Fu in a exasperated and whining sick-person's voice. I closed the door. There was no lock. I jammed an iron bed against it. There were three iron bedsteads in the room, and some reeking quilts.

I realized that I was shivering. I was cold, but I was also hungry. I ate half a jar of Ma Ling orange segments, and a banana, and I made tea from the hot water in the jug I had brought. I was light-headed and somewhat breathless from the altitude, and also nauseated from the frosty vomit in the corridors. Just as I finished eating all the lights went out: midnight.

I put on my gloves, my hat, my extra sweater, my coat, my third pair of socks and thermal-lined shoes; and went to bed. I had been cold in my life, but I had never worn a hat with earmuffs to bed before. I had a quilt over me and a quilt under me. Even so, I could not get warm. I could not understand why. My heart palpitated. My toes were numb. I tried to imagine what it must be like to be Chris Bonington. After a while I could see moonlight behind the thick frost on the window.

In the middle of the night I got up to piss. I used an enamel basin that I guessed was a chamber-pot. In the morning it was frozen solid. So were the rest of my orange segments. So were my quail eggs. Everything that I had that could freeze had frozen.

I had hardly slept, but I was gladdened by the sunlight. I found some peanuts and ate them. I ate my frozen banana. I visited the cannibal (he looked even dirtier in daylight) and drank some of my own tea with him. He did not want Chinese tea. He made a face as if to say, 'Disgusting stuff! How can you drink it?'

The frail warmth of the morning sun only made the place worse by wakening the stinks on the stairs and corridors. There were dark clumps and little twists of human shit throughout the building. In this heavenly country, that toilet.

Mr Fu was up and fussing. He said Miss Sun was not at all well. And he felt sick, too.

'Then let's go,' I said.

'Breakfast first.'

'Oh, God!'

But he insisted.

There was a dead dog lying at the entrance to the smoky hut where Mr Fu and Miss Sun had their breakfast: eggs stir-fried in yak fat. Other dogs cowered and barked. An old dead sheep was flattened on the road, as stiff and worn as a hearth-rug. Across a frozen pond was the army camp. A few scattered buildings stood in the rubble of the settlement. Tibetans with crimson head-dresses watched me walk down the path. I kept walking until the dogs started barking, and then I headed back to the main road. The place was full of dead animals that had been turned into flat, stiff corpses – gruesome little mats in the road.

It was another late start. But this time I did calculations on my map, estimated the distances between towns, figured an average speed, and felt much better until I remembered the tyre.

'Did you get the spare tyre fixed, Mr Fu?'

He had said that he would do it this morning, before breakfast. Although Amdo was a dump, there were garages here; and it was the only place of any size for miles.

'No. Better to get the tyre fixed in Nagqu.'

That was over 100 miles away.

Mr Fu took the wheel. A few miles down the road he stopped the car and clawed at his face.

'I cannot do it!' he shrieked. In Chinese it sounded like a pitiful surrender.

It was another attack of the wobblies. I welcomed it, I soothed Mr Fu as he crept into the back seat. I slotted Brahms into the cassette player and drove south, under sunny skies.

I was feeling wonky myself. I had a bump on my head, a neckache, and a deep cut on my face from the car crash. My right wrist hurt, probably a sprain, from my holding on during our careering. And the altitude affected me, too – I felt lightheaded and nauseous, and my short walk in Amdo had given me heart palpitations. But this was nothing compared to Mr Fu's agony. The colour had drained from his face, his mouth gaped, and after a while he simply swooned. Miss Sun also went to sleep. Crumpled together on the seat they looked like poisoned lovers in a suicide pact.

There were no more settlements until Nagqu, nothing except the windswept tableland, and it was so cold that even the *drongs*, the wild yaks, were squinting and the herds of wild asses did nothing but raise their heads and stare at the badly damaged Mitsubishi Galant. After a few hours the road ran out and was no more than loose rocks and boulders, and more wild asses. The boulders clunked against the chassis and hammered the tyres. We had no spare tyre. We were ridiculously unprepared for Tibet, but I did not mind very much. I felt, having survived that crash, that we had come through the worst of it. There is something about the very fact of survival that produces a greater vitality. And I knew I was much safer as long as I was driving. Mr Fu was not really very good at all, and as a nervous new driver he had no business to be in Tibet.

On some hillsides there were huts flying coloured prayer flags. I was cheered by them, by the whiteness of whitewashed huts, by the smoke coming out of the chimneys, and by the clothes that people wore – fox-fur hats, silver buckles, sheepskin coats, big warm boots. Miles from anywhere I saw a mother and daughter in bright blowing skirts and bonnets climbing a cliffside path, and a handsome herdsman sitting among his yaks wearing a wonderful red hat with huge earflaps.

Mr Fu was very annoyed that there was nowhere to eat at Nagqu. He was stiff and cranky from the altitude, and reluctant to stay, but I pestered him into finding someone to fix the spare. This was done in a shed, with fires and chisels; and while this primitive vulcanizing went on I walked around the town. John Avedon's *In Exile from the Land of Snows* (1984), which is mainly an anti-Chinese account of the recent turmoil in Tibet, and pleasantly passionate on the subject of the Dalai Lama, claims that Nagqu is the centre of the Chinese nuclear industry. The gaseous diffusion plants, the warhead assembly plants and the research labs have been moved here from the Lop Nor Desert. Somewhere in this vicinity – though you'd never know it from looking at it – there was a large repository of medium-range and intermediate-range nuclear missiles. But all I saw were yaks.

Snow came down like soapflakes, big damp things. It was only minus ten Centigrade, but in the high wind and blowing snow it felt colder. I took shelter in a Chinese store and ate my jar of Golden Star pickled quails' eggs. I noted that a Tibetan woman was buying an orange plastic bag and a middle-aged Tibetan man was trying out a blonde doll. A metal key stuck out from between her buttocks like an enema; he wound her up and her legs and arms moved. The man laughed and bought the thing.

On a back street of Nagqu I was accosted by some Tibetans who wanted to change money. They also had artefacts – copper tobacco tins and silver coins and Tibetan seals, for stamping messages or names on to documents. I bought a silver seal with a Tibetan motto that said: *Worship the sky for enlightenment.*

I wanted to hand out pictures of the Dalai Lama in this remote place, but to avoid attracting a crowd I followed individuals down the little icy lanes and when there was no one else around I whispered in phrase-book Tibetan, 'Dalai Lama picture, Dalai Lama picture.'

They hissed with pleasure as I handed over the pictures, and they always touched them to their foreheads before folding them into their quilted coats. They reacted to these pictures in a way that I found deeply moving. It was not their profuse thanks – though Tibetan gratitude was hardly ritualized: they were able to communicate great warmth in the simplest gestures. There was no question about their devotion to their god-king, the Fourteenth Dalai Lama, Tenzin Gyatso.

They were like early Christians, and I was among them, encouraging them with little ikons, spreading sedition. Virtually every Tibetan is a Buddhist and it is impossible to overestimate their love and respect for the Dalai Lama. The Panchen Lama, a political cleric, was in Peking where he was reputed to be a member of the Central Committee. But this Dalai Lama had never capitulated to the Chinese. When he was attacked on St Patrick's Day in 1959 he hurried away disguised as a herdsman on a horse, fleeing his Summer Palace, the Norbulingka, with thousands of his followers, while monks and warriors fought a rearguard action against the confused Chinese attackers. He has been in exile in India ever since, swearing that he will not return to Tibet until the Chinese have left.

Relations between Tibet and China had been uneasy from the seventh century (the Tang Dynasty) onward, and for the next 1,300 years it is a history of patchy diplomacy, marriages of convenience and invasions (by the Chinese) using flimsy pretexts. Tibet was a sovereign country when the Chinese invaded in 1950. Tibet was also extremely isolated in every sense. There were no motor vehicles at all in Tibet. There were no schools (although monasteries provided education of a religious kind for novice monks and nuns). There were no banks. Money was not used much. There were no wages, for example – payments were usually made in kind, with barley, tea, yak butter and cloth. It was a medieval system, and the Dalai Lama had a Divine Right to govern. The class-structure ranged from the nobility and a handful of rich aristocratic families to the lowest class of outcasts, whose single function in Tibetan society was to dispose of corpses.

The Chinese were eager to snatch Tibet and turn it upside-down. 'A good comrade is one who is more eager to go where the difficulties are greater,' Mao had said. The exhortation had got Chinese settlers into Qinghai. Now the armies began to march into eastern Tibet. What good were swords and pikes against modern Chinese armaments? And when the Tibetans were overwhelmed, and they appealed to the UN, and tried to publicize their case against the Chinese, the world turned its back while a Tibetan delegation signed a treaty that had been dictated by the victorious Chinese. No one had gone to Tibet's aid; and a few years later in the maniacal Maoist spasm known as Religious Reform, ancient monasteries were dynamited, monks were sent to work in factories, and all Buddhist rituals were banned, including all prayers and insignia. The Chinese believed that the liberation of Tibet was complete, especially when the humiliated Tibetans fought back in various uprisings in 1956 and were flattened.

Anti-religious feeling in Tibet was a perfect frenzy during the Cultural Revolution. The few monasteries that remained were either pulled down or else used for secular functions. Pigs were kept in the most sacred chapels of the Drepung Monastery in Lhasa, and the Jokhang Palace, the holiest of holies, was renamed Guesthouse Number Five. Soldiers bivouacked in its chapels and cloisters. The Buddha statues were beheaded. The gold filigree altar relics were melted down. The Red Guards yanked down the ancient medical college, Mendzekhang on Chakpori Hill in Lhasa, and a television antenna was erected in its place. Except for the Potala, Lhasa was destroyed.

'It was a mistake,' a Chinese official told me. He was not belittling the damage. This after all was a man who had lived through the Cultural Revolution in China. Part of the Great Wall had been pulled down and plenty of temples and monuments had been wrecked. The whole of China had been vandalized. So what were a few dusty shrines and painted statues to that?

What happened in Tibet was an excess. It was not an outrage in Chinese eyes. Many Chinese I spoke to could not understand why anyone would prefer an old Buddhist medical college to a tall new TV antenna bolted to a ferro-concrete block.

And official Chinese vandalism is unlike any other vandalism on earth. You imagine gangs of crazy chanting youths smashing their way into a monastery and kicking the slats out of it. But it wasn't that way. It was Chinese wrecking. When the order went out, *Smash the feudalistic nests of monks!*, the soldiers, Red Guards and assorted vandals made chalk marks all over the monasteries – save these timbers, stack these beams, pile these bricks, and so forth. Brick by brick, timber by timber, the monasteries were taken down. The frugal, string-saving, clothes-patching, shoe-mending Chinese saved each reusable brick. In this way the monasteries were made into barns and barracks.

The Dalai Lama has stayed in exile, but some rebuilding has been carried out by Chinese who admit that wholesale destruction was a mistake. A little bit of old Tibet was given back. But schools were built, factories were put up, and army camps and gun emplacements sprang up everywhere in Tibet (in this way it greatly resembles Soviet-dominated Mongolia). And portraits of the Dalai Lama were banned. I was aware that in handing these pictures out I was breaking the law. But what the hell. They had nuisance value. They made the Tibetans happy. And they allowed me to feel like John the Baptist.

Nagqu has the only hotel worth the name, north of Lhasa, but even so I thought: Next time I'll bring a tent and a sleeping-bag. Mr Fu drove us out of Nagqu – perhaps a face-saving gesture, because a mile outside town he stopped the car and clutched his eyes.

'I cannot do it!'

And he slumped in the back seat.

I was happier than I had been since starting this trip on the Iron Rooster. I was driving, I was in charge, I was taking my time; and Tibet was empty. The weather was dramatic – snow on the hills, a high wind, and black clouds piled up on the mountains ahead. I also thought: I didn't die the other day.

Today, below the snowy and majestic Nyenchen Tanglha Range, nomads rode among their herds of yak, and the road was straight through the yellow plain. That tame road contributed to my feeling of well-being – it was wonderful to be in such a remote place and yet to feel so secure. Mr Fu and Miss Sun were asleep in the back seat. There were no other cars on the road. I drove at a sensible speed towards Lhasa, and watched the birds – hawks and plovers and crows. There were more gazelles, and once a pale yellow fox bounded across the road.

There was a sudden snowstorm. I went from a dry sunny valley, around a corner, into a black slushy one, the large cottony flakes whipping sideways. Mr Fu, who was terrified of snow, mercifully did not wake. The snow eased; it became a dry flurry in a valley farther ahead, and then the sun came out again. Tibetans call their country 'the Land of Snows', but in fact it doesn't snow much and it never rains. The gales pass quickly. The Tibetans are not bothered by any of this. I saw children playing in this sudden storm.

I had wanted at the outset to reach Lhasa quickly. But now I didn't mind a delay. I would gladly have spent more nights on the road, provided it was not in a place like the dump at Amdo.

Damxung looked promising. It was at a bend in the road, there was an army camp nearby, and half a dozen one-roomed restaurants. We stopped and had four dishes, which included wood-ear fungus and yak meat, and Mr Fu revived enough to accuse the serving-girl of overcharging him – or rather me, since I paid the bill.

There were six soldiers in the kitchen, warming themselves, but they fluttered away when I tried to talk with them. Travellers in China had sometimes told me that they were harassed by soldiers or officials. This was never my experience. When I approached them they always backed away.

I found Mr Fu spitting on the wheel to see whether it had overheated. He was kneeling, spitting, smearing, examining.

'I think we should stay here,' I said.

We were watched by a small boy who had a playing-card sized picture of the Dalai Lama tucked into the front of his fur hat. When I peered at him he ran away and returned without the picture.

'We cannot stay here. Miss Sun is sick. Lhasa is only 105 miles.'

'Do you feel well enough to drive?'

'I am fine!'

But he looked terrible. His face was grey. He had not eaten much. He had told me he had a pain in his heart. He also said that his eyes hurt.

'This wheel is not hot,' he said. 'That is good.'

He gasped and gave up at a place called Baicang, saying he could not do it. I took over and in a pretty place called Yangbajain on a riverbank we entered a narrow rocky valley. It was the sort of valley I had been expecting ever since Golmud. I had not realized that this part of Tibet was open country, with flat straight roads, and distant snowy peaks. But this valley was steep and cold, and half in darkness it was so deep. A river ran swiftly through it with birds darting from one wet boulder to another. I saw from my bird book that they were thrushes, and the commonest was the white-winged redstart.

When we emerged from this valley we were higher, and among steep mountainsides and bluer, snowier peaks. We travelled along this riverside in a burst of evening sunshine. Farther south, this little river became the mighty Brahmaputra. The valley opened wider, became sunnier and very dry; and beyond the beautiful bare hills of twinkling scree there were mountains covered with frothy snow.

Ahead was a small town. I took it to be another garrison town, but it was Lhasa, for sure. In the distance was a red and white building, with sloping sides – the Potala, so lovely, somewhat like a mountain and somewhat like a music-box with a hammered gold lid.

I had never felt happier, rolling into a town. I decided to pay off Mr Fu. I gave him my thermos bottle and the remainder of my provisions. He seemed embarrassed. He lingered a little. Then he reached out and put his fingers on my cheek, where there was a wound from the crash. It was scabby, the blood had dried, it looked awful; but it didn't hurt.

'I am sorry,' Mr Fu said. He laughed. It was an abject apology. His laughter said: *Forgive me!*

It is immediately obvious that Lhasa is not a city. It is a small friendly-looking town on a high plain surrounded by even higher mountains. There is very little traffic. There are no pavements. Everyone walks in the street. No one runs. These streets are at 12,000 feet. You can hear children yelling and dogs barking and bells being rung, and so it seems a quiet place. It is rather dirty and very sunny. Just a few years ago the Chinese bulldozed the Chorten, a stupa which formed the entrance to the city. It was their way of violating Lhasa, which had always been forbidden to foreigners. Even so, it is not crowded. The Chinese badly damaged Lhasa and hoped to yank the whole thing down and build a city of fine ugly factories. But they did not succeed in destroying it. Much of it, and some of its finest shrines, were made out of mud-bricks – easily broken but cheap to replace, like the Buddhist statues that were made anew every few years, or the yak butter sculptures that were expected to go rancid or melt in order for new ones to be fashioned. The whole of Buddhism prepared the Tibetans for cycles of destruction and rebirth: it is a religion that brilliantly teaches continuity. You can easily see the violence of the Chinese intention in Lhasa; but it was a failure, because the Tibetans are indestructible.

Lhasa is a holy place, so it is populated by pilgrims. They give it colour and because they are strangers themselves to Lhasa they don't object to foreign travellers – in fact, they welcome them and try to sell them beads and trinkets. Chinese cities are notorious for their noise and crowds. Lhasa has a small population and because it is flat it is full of cyclists. To me that was a complete surprise. I had expected a dark craggy city of steepnesses and fortifications overrun by Chinese and hung with slogans. I found a bright little war-torn town full of jolly monks and friendly pilgrims and dominated by the Potala, which is an ingenious and distracting shape.

Half the population of Lhasa is Chinese, but those who are not soldiers tend to stay indoors, and even the soldiers of the People's Liberation Army keep a low profile. They know that Tibet is essentially a gigantic army camp – the roads, the airports and all the communications were a military effort – and they know that the Tibetans resent it. The Chinese feel insecure in Tibet, and so they retreat into a sort of officiousness; they look like commissars and imperialists but their swagger is mostly bravado. They know they are in a foreign country. They don't speak the language and they have not managed to teach Chinese to the Tibetans. For over thirty years they maintained the fiction that the official language of Tibet was Chinese, but then in 1987 they caved in and changed it to Tibetan.

The Chinese imply that they have a moral right to run the Tibetans' lives, but since the late seventies, when they began to despair of political solutions to Chinese problems, they have felt more uneasy about being in Tibet. They have no right to be there at all. The Tibetans themselves would probably have found a way to tax the rich families, get rid of exploiters and raise up the Ragyaba – the scavenging class and corpse-handlers – and free the slaves (slavery persisted into the nineteen-fifties). But the bossy ideology of the Chinese compelled them to invade and so thoroughly meddle with the country that they alienated the majority of the population. They did not stop there. They annexed Tibet and made it part of China, and however much the Chinese talk about liberalizing their policies it is clear that they have no intention of ever allowing Tibet to become a sovereign state again.

'It feels like a foreign country,' Chinese friends of mine confided to me. They were bewildered by the old-fashioned habits and clothes, and by the incomprehensible rituals of Tibetan Buddhism, celebrating the sexual mysticism of the tantric rites, and the hugging and fornicating statues illustrating the mother-father principle of *yabyum*, and the big, toothy, goggling demons that Tibetans see as protectors. Even with the Chinese watching closely and issuing decrees and building schools and initiating public works, Lhasa is a medieval-seeming place, just like Europe in the Middle Ages, complete with grinning monks and grubby peasants and open-air festivals and jugglers and tumblers. Lhasa is holy, but it is also a market town, with pushcarts and stacked-up vegetables and dirty, air-dried cuts of yak which will keep for a year (grain keeps for fifty years in the dry Tibetan climate). The most medieval touch of all is that Tibet has almost no plumbing.

The pilgrims hunker and prostrate themselves all over Lhasa, and they shuffle clockwise around every shrine. They flatten themselves on stair-landings, outside the Jokhang and all around the Potala. They do it on the road, the riverbank, the hillsides. Being Tibetan Buddhists they are good-humoured and because they are from all over Tibet, Lhasa is their meeting-place – they enrich the life of the town and fill its markets. They come out of a devotion to the Dalai Lama, the incarnation of the Bodhisattva Avalokitesvara. They pray, they throw themselves to the ground, and they strew tiny one-*miao* notes and barley grains at the shrines, and they empty blobs of yak butter into the lamps. The very pious ones blow horns made from human thigh bones – a femur like an oboe – or carry water in bowls made from the lopped-off top of a human skull. They venerate the various thrones and couches of the Dalai Lama in the Potala, and even his narrow Art Deco bed, his bathtub and toilet, his tape recorder (a gift from Nehru) and his radio. The Dalai Lama is worshipped as the Living God, but the pilgrims also pay homage to the images of Zong Kapa – founder of the Yellow Sect, and of the Lord Buddha, and other Dalai Lamas, notably the Fifth whose great buildings dignify Lhasa. Pilgrims have made Lhasa a town of visitors who are not exactly strangers, and so even a real foreigner feels a sense of belonging there. Its chaos and dirt and its jangling bells make it seem hospitable.

Lhasa was the one place in China I eagerly entered, and enjoyed being in, and was reluctant to leave. I liked its smallness, its friendliness, the absence of traffic, the flat streets – and every street had a vista of tremendous Tibetan mountains. I liked the clear air and sunshine, the markets, the brisk trade in scarce antiques. It fascinated me to see a place for which the Chinese had no solution. They admitted that they had made grave mistakes in Tibet; but they also admitted that they did not know what to do next. They had not counted on the tenacious faith of the Tibetans, and perhaps they found it hard to believe that such dark grinning people, who never washed, could be so passionate. The visiting party officials strolled around looking smug and hard-to-please. They are mostly on junkets. Tibet is a junketer's paradise: a subject people, two fairly good hotels, plenty of ceremonial functions, and so far from Peking that anything goes. The Chinese reward each other with junkets and official trips – they often take the place of bonuses – and Tibet is the ultimate junket. But it is for sightseeing. Tibet has made no economic gains at all. It is entirely dependent on Chinese financial aid. These Chinese nearly always look physically uncomfortable in Lhasa – it is the altitude, the strange food, and the climate, but it is also the boisterous Tibetans who seem to the Chinese a bit savage and unpredictable – superstitious primitives if not outright subhuman.

The other aspect of Lhasa – and Tibet, too – is that like Yunnan it has become the refuge of hippies. They are not the dropouts I met years ago in Afghanistan and India, but mostly middle-class, well-heeled hippies whose parents gave them the air-fare to China. Some of them come by bus from Nepal. They seemed harmless to me and they were a great deal more desirable than the rich tourists for whom Lhasa was building expensive hotels and importing ridiculous delicacies – and providing brand-new Japanese buses so that groups of tourists could set out at dawn and photograph such rituals as the Sky Burial (Tibetans deal with their dead by placing them outside for vultures to eat). As Lynn Pan remarks in her analysis of recent Chinese history, *The New Chinese Revolution*, 'it is difficult to avoid the conclusion that Tibetan culture, which has survived the worst that Maoism and force could do to stamp it out, has been left to be killed by tourism'. But I had my doubts. Tibet seemed too vast and inaccessible and strange for anyone to possess it. It looked wonderful to me, like the last place on earth; like a polar ice-cap, but emptier.

*

It took me a while to recover from the drive. My head still hurt from the crash. My neck had been wrenched. I still had an interesting wound under my left eye. The altitude gave me insomnia. I lay in bed in the cold hotel room, with my heart pounding, my pulse racing. Outside I would sometimes forget where I was and begin running and have to gasp for breath.

I found a young Tibetan fellow who had an encyclopaedic knowledge of the monasteries. He did not speak Chinese at all. He had left Tibet as a child with his parents – when the Dalai Lama escaped in the exodus of 1959, with his 70,000 followers. After his education in Kashmir and Ladakh and in various Tibetan refugee schools in Simla (he had been in India for twenty-five years), he returned home. I asked him what it was like being back in Chinese Tibet.

'It is all right. But my heart is not here. My heart is in Dharamsala – you know what I mean?'

'The Dalai Lama is in Dharamsala.'

'That is correct. He is not here.'

His name was Ralpa. It was very funny to see him addressed in Chinese. He smiled at the Chinese speaker and said, 'No, no, no, no.' He could not even utter that useful Chinese sentence that means, 'I hear you but I don't understand you.' Since the Chinese did not speak Tibetan, and rarely spoke English, Ralpa in a year of being back in Tibet had never had a conversation with a Chinese. I asked him whether it bothered him. He said no. He said, 'This isn't China.'

We went to the Drepung Monastery. Before Mao's Religious Reform of 1955, Drepung had 12,000 monks. It was said to be the largest monastery in the world. It was a sprawling place of whitewashed buildings piled up high in a ravine on a hillside just outside Lhasa. Its nickname was 'The Rice Mound'. Its population had been much reduced. It now had 500 monks, but they had returned to monastic life only recently. One I spoke to had spent the twenty years between 1959 and 1979 on a farm in eastern Tibet, digging vegetables. He was wearing thick brown robes.

'Did you wear these robes on the farm?'

'No. I had farm clothes. A blue suit. I hated it.'

'Did you do any praying?'

'No. It was forbidden.'

'How did you get back here to Drepung?'

'I heard that things were improving politically, so I made a request. I asked whether I could return to my monastery and they said yes.'

Another monk at Drepung was a muscular, broad-shouldered man with a deep laugh.

'I was in prison for twenty-one years,' he said.

'What was your crime?'

'No crime!' His laugh attracted attention, and pilgrims stared at him, but he didn't lower his voice. 'I protected the Dalai Lama at the Norbulingka when he escaped. I was fighting, you see, so that he could get away.' He looked very pleased as he said this. 'The Chinese caught me and put me in prison.'

'Where was the prison?'

'Not one, but many prisons. They kept moving me from place to place.'

'What do you think of the Chinese?'

'I don't hate them. I just want them to leave,' he said. 'But most of all I want the Dalai Lama to come back. Then I can die happy. I will be very unhappy until then, and I don't want to die until the Dalai Lama returns.'

'Do you think he will?'

He said nothing, but his gesture was eloquent. He pressed his big hands together and shut his eyes and made a prayerful sign.

I gave him and other monks pictures of the Dalai Lama. Some monks approached me and asked in halting English, 'Dalai Lama picture?' I was not the first traveller to pass through, handing out portraits.

Ralpa pointed to a cluster of white buildings on the hillside.

'That is the Nechung Monastery, where the Oracle lives. But he is with the Dalai Lama now, in India.'

'What does the Oracle do?'

'He meditates near the Oracle statue in the chapel, and he speaks for it.'

He showed me the Oracle statue. It was a small doll on a shelf, robed, with staring eyes, outstretched arms and its mouth open as if in a shriek. It gave me the creeps. I wondered whether I was alone in finding most dolls of this kind rather distressing things.

The pilgrims at Drepung had come hundreds of miles – and in some cases more than 1,000 miles – three or four days jouncing in the back of a beat-up truck. They brought what little money they had, they brought all their children, and quilts, and food; they brought meat and vegetables to sell at the market in Lhasa. I was impressed by the way these extremely poor people shared their food, and gave money at the shrines, and money to beggars. They even fed the dogs which hung around the monasteries in yelping mangy packs.

We walked around, Ralpa identifying the various pilgrims from their headgear or their robes or their earrings, or the way they braided their hair.

At one chapel he said, 'Do you see that Tara figure on the wall? It appeared all by itself. It was not carved by a human hand. One morning the monks looked at the stone wall and it was there.'

I peered at it.

'You don't believe it,' Ralpa said.

'I don't know,' I said. It didn't seem any more absurd than the Mormon belief in the Golden Tablets and the Angel Moroni, and it was a good deal more tangible than the apparition of the Lady of Fatima or those Italian priests who began bleeding with the stigmata every Good Friday.

There were more miraculous murals – and some spontaneous statues – at the Jokhang, Tibet's holiest place: Manjushri's head popped out of one wall, a Tara had sketched itself on a shelf, and a small stone buffalo had materialized in a corner of a chapel.

I had arrived near the end of the Tibetan New Year, which is a fifteen-day festival known both for its piety and its rambunctiousness. That was why there were so many pilgrims in Lhasa. The monks – about 1,000 or more – had gathered at the Jokhang to chant mantras. They were led by an elderly bald figure called the Ganden Tipa, the holiest monk in Tibet and the spiritual leader of all these monasteries. He sat cross-legged and robed in gold, facing away from the monks. The monks fidgeted and laughed. Some chanted, others fooled and giggled. They were all ages – some were no more than teenagers, and some were women; but they had shaven heads and were robed like the men, and so they were almost indistinguishable. I watched it all from an upper balcony, where Tibetans tossed scraps of paper with mantras written on them to the monks below, who made piles of them.

Through Ralpa I asked a monk whether it was true that the Tibetan tradition of Buddhism was characterized by debating subtle points of theology.

The monk nodded vigorously and said, 'Yes, yes!'

'Could you give me an example?'

'Yes. The abbot asks, "Does a rabbit have a horn?" And a monk may stand up and say, "No. A rabbit does not have a horn." Then the abbot hits the monk with a stick and the other monks laugh. Another monk may say, "Yes. A rabbit *does* have a horn. He digs a hole in the ground, and what does he use? Not his paw, but the nail on his paw. That is his horn."'

'Does that settle the matter?'

'Maybe they argue a bit more, about whether it is a horn or not.'

All this time, everywhere in Lhasa, the prayer wheels were spinning. Most pilgrims had the hand-held variety, a sort of upright pencil sharpener. The pilgrims plodded clockwise and spun the wheel – often very quickly, because the prayers uttered by the wheel (there is a scribbled mantra inside) are weaker than spoken prayers. These prayer wheels were usually copper or brass, but occasionally they were embossed with silver or else gilded. Prayer wheels were fastened in the temple enclosures – some were the size of oil drums and very hard to turn, others were no larger than nail kegs, and you could hear the flutter of the mantras in their innards as they spun. They had handles, they were greased with yak butter, and they were all inscribed in Tibetan and Sanskrit with the efficacious mantra *om mani padmi hum* – the *om* is the most powerful and mystical element in the mantra, a combination of three Sanskrit sounds that sum up the three-in-one nature of the universe. These prayers are so sacred that just writing them or carving them in stone (the sacred *om* is frequently seen hacked into cliff-faces) is regarded as much more pious than putting up statues.

Tibetan pilgrims thronged the Jokhang Palace, muttering prayers, prostrating themselves, and gawking at the monks. They were from distant places and they were dazzled by this Vatican of

Tibetan Buddhism to such an extent that their pilgrim piety seemed to vanish among the gold statues and lurid murals (of hell and heaven) and incense (sandalwood, cypress leaves) and dull clopping drums. The pilgrims' eyes glittered in the half-dark of the cloisters and these people took on the odd curiosity of tourists with their squints and stares, as if, so startled were they by the droning monks and the aromas and the drooping tankas, they had forgotten to pray.

Here, very recently, in the inner sanctum of the Jokhang, under the serene gaze of the holiest figure, Jowo Shakyamuni, the Precious Lord, the Chinese army had kept pigs, and the rest of the Jokhang had been commandeered as a barracks. They had been following the Mao dictum set out in the well-known essay 'On Going Too Far':

> To right a wrong it is necessary to exceed proper limits, and the wrong cannot be righted without the proper limits being exceeded.

That was the Chinese epitaph for Tibet. You did not close the temples – you kept pigs in them. You did not simply shut the monasteries – you defrocked the monks, put them into factories and forbade them to pray; and you used monastery timbers for chicken-coops. The Mao policy of systematic humiliation of traditional belief reached its apotheosis in Tibet. Now the Chinese admit to 'mistakes . . . excessiveness and errors during the ten chaotic years of the Cultural Revolution', as the Chinese diplomat, Zheng Wanzhen, put it in his defence of Chinese policies in Tibet which he wrote for the *Washington Post* in 1987. The Chinese reiterate the sums spent on restoration work, but it goes without saying that the Tibetans will never forgive the desecration of their holy places and the impertinence of the Chinese occupation. Buddhism teaches restraint and moderation and propriety. The worst, most anti-Buddhist, aspect of Chinese policy was that it stipulated that liberators and revolutionaries must go too far.

Rebuilt and restored buildings in Tibet have the Disneylandish simplicity of fresh paint and characterless frippery – and it is true all over China: the style is pervasive. Only the Potala was spared the philistine fury of the Cultural Revolution, and that was because Zhou Enlai intervened. But it was in the Potala that a monk showed me a series of monasteries depicted on an old mural.

He pointed to one monastery.

'China destroy,' he said.

He pointed to another.

'China destroy.'

He indicated six more and said the same thing. For this information I rewarded him with a portrait of the Dalai Lama. He clasped his hands and hissed at me.

'Dalai Lama come! China go!'

The Chinese have invited the Dalai Lama back, but he has so far refused to return until his conditions are met. It is unlikely that the Chinese will agree to the conditions, the central one of which is independence. Feeling is so strong in Tibet, and his devotees are so passionate and numerous, that he would not have any difficulty leading a rebellion. He is a peaceful soul, so that is unlikely. But even if any Tibetans attempted an uprising it would fail. The Chinese would crush it without mercy – and not out of revenge, but (as they would explain) for the good of Tibet. Party officials are happy to admit their mistakes in Tibet, but the thing they find hardest to understand is why the Tibetans are not more grateful for roads and buses and schools that were brought at great expense to this plateau. They say: 'It's modern! It's progress! It's civilization!'

It seems like proof to the Chinese that they are dealing with sentimental savages when Tibetans say the roads and schools are just another Chinese outrage. But that does not weaken the Chinese resolve – quite the opposite. It just means there is much more work to do in this benighted place, they say, echoing missionaries and colonizers and imperialists and encyclopaedia salesmen the world over.

The Chinese have a fatal tendency to take themselves and their projects too seriously. In this they resemble some other evangelizing races, spreading the word and travelling the world to build churches, factories, or fast-food outlets – the intention may be different in each case but they are all an imposition. What the evangelizer in his naive seriousness does not understand is that there are some people on earth who do not wish to be saved.

The Tibetans were too isolated to understand what a very great favour it was for them to be admitted to the Chinese world: that is the Chinese view. But it is plain that the Chinese are themselves isolated and do not understand how deeply their version of progress and modernity is hated by many sensible people. Partly this is due to Chinese insensitivity and the clumsiness brought about by their isolation. But their seriousness doesn't help – nor does it mean they are particularly watchful or wise, since seriousness can often indicate that someone is vacant and stupid.

Not much opprobrium was ever attached to the Chinese invasion of Tibet. In one respect the rest of the world did not care much. But the prevailing view was that the Chinese were possessed of a kind of wisdom. How could such people fail the Tibetans? But that view accepts the Chinese as inscrutable, and working out their solutions in mysterious ways.

I do not accept Chinese inscrutability. I think like many people on earth they are knowable, and they are a great deal more scrutable and obvious than most. Now the Tibetans know them much better and would probably agree (as I do) with Doctor Johnson who wrote two hundred years ago:

> The boundless panegyricks which have been lavished upon the Chinese learning, policy, and the arts, show with what power novelty attracts regard, and how naturally esteem swells into admiration. I am far from desiring to be numbered among the exaggerators of Chinese excellence.

Tibet is so underpopulated that the Chinese have relaxed their One-Child Policy for Tibetans – it is also practically unenforceable in such a wild place. And the emptiness of the country means that any crowd of people is a novelty. That is why the Lhasa market is so busy: many of the people are merely spectators who have come to Lhasa on a New Year's pilgrimage and can't get over the sight of fresh oranges and bananas or the hundreds of highly ornamented Kham men swapping beads and necklaces.

The Lhasa market was the most interesting one I saw in China, because the Chinese have found it impossible to regulate it. As a consequence, the traders sell everything they can lay their hands on, at whatever price they can get. There is a lively trade in antiques – silver, pewter, semi-precious stones, knives, swords, saddles, horse-brasses and harnesses, whips, rugs, carpets, and more Buddhist paraphernalia than you can shake a stick at. Some of the objects are copies. Many are fakes. Some are genuine. I was offered a silver charm box – a sort of sporran studded with jewels. Tibetan jewellery is heavy and often handsome. Enough tourists have come to Tibet for even these country-folk to demand hundreds of dollars for their strings of coral and turquoise. After I bought a silver bowl from a young man he saw me as a serious customer and lifted up his robe, giving me a glimpse of an antique gold statue of Tara. Everyone had rare antiques stuffed up their cloaks and sleeves.

I walked from one end of Lhasa to the other. The distance was not great – just a few miles – but the altitude made it slow going. I went to the carpet factory, the tannery, the boot and shoe factory. The bazaar atmosphere of the Free Market made it seem much busier than any of these industries. The factories operated at half speed, with abundant tea-breaks and giggling employees and work-in stoppage – a far cry from the sweatshops of Canton and Shanghai.

There are no suburbs to Lhasa. Walk for fifteen minutes and you come either to the mountains or the river. A yak-skin boat, a sort of unstable coracle, takes people across the river. On the other side there is a sandbank, a gravelly plain and more mountains.

An early European explorer to Tibet burst into tears when he saw one lovely mountain covered with snow. When I saw the landscape of Tibet that did not seem to me an odd reaction. The setting is more than touching – it is a bewitchment: the light, the air, the emptiness, the plains and peaks. Dusty crags and steep slopes surround Lhasa, and on some of the mornings I was there they were covered with snow from flurries in the night. Tibet has none of the winding roads and black cliffs of the Alps, nor the impenetrable and dangerous look of the Rockies. It is a safe and reassuring remoteness, with the prettiest meadows and moors buttressed by mountains. It was, somehow, a mountain landscape with few valleys – a blue and white plateau of tinkling yak bells, and bright glaciers and tiny wild flowers. Who wouldn't burst into tears?

I got used to the smell of yak butter. It did not bother me that the Tibetans didn't wash.

'The water is too cold,' Ralpa said.

'Of course,' I said.

It was much harder for me to understand the fresh-air fiends in Harbin who chopped holes in the ice on the Songhua river and jumped in.

'They will get sick if they take baths,' Ralpa said.

'Of course.'

They were very dirty, but the cold pinched the smell and it was so windy the stinks were academic. And Tibetans wore such gorgeous jewellery, and furs, and coiffures, they did not look dirty. In the end, the only thing I objected to were the fierce and rabid dogs, and in particular those mastiffs they called *dhoki*, watch-dogs. I kept imagining myself riding a bike down these lovely roads on a long peregrination of Tibet, and the vision was interrupted by a mastiff lunging from behind a rock and messily dismembering me.

While I was in Tibet I read in a two-week-old *China Daily* that the Politburo had met in Peking and decided that Lei Feng was still relevant as an example to Chinese youth. The Politburo issued a statement saying that Lei Feng ought to be emulated. This made strange reading in Tibet.

Lei Feng was 'the rustless screw', a model soldier and fervent Maoist. No one had really known him; but his diary, found after his death, showed him to be exemplary. He wrote how he reread and adored Mao's writings. He worked night and day, so he said. One night he went without sleep in order to wash a ton of cabbages. He did not stop there, but spent the early morning mopping floors.

In the diary (which some sceptical Chinese have called a forgery), Lei Feng wrote, 'A man's usefulness to the revolutionary cause is like a screw in a machine. Though a screw is small, its use is beyond measure. I am willing to be a screw.'

Twenty-five years later, Yu Qiuli, an important Politburo member, said that what was needed in China today was more of 'the Screw Spirit'.

It was very hard to imagine a laughing Tibetan in his home-made, fleece-lined coat with four-foot sleeves, his fantastic hat and boots, and red silk plaited into his hair, and his silver charm box and dagger, with jewelled earrings and ivory buttons, hollering at his dogs and gnawing bones and tying ribbons to his yaks – this freebooting man of the mountains – saying piously, 'I am willing to be a screw.'

It was even less likely that a Tibetan woman would be so submissive. No women in Asia were tougher or freer. Polyandry was still practised in Tibet – some women had three or four husbands (the men were nearly always brothers). I could not imagine such a woman in a blue boiler suit, washing cabbage and losing sleep for the revolutionary cause.

It was not in the Tibetan's nature to be a robot. As nomads and the descendants of nomads, as hut-dwellers in the emptiest region of the world, they were independent, and they were a great deal more self-reliant than the Lei Fengs. They were nearly always smiling, probably because they were either heading somewhere to pray or had just returned – prayers seemed to put Tibetans in a good mood. They seldom looked tired. They were brisk but they never hurried. They never ran. Unlike the Chinese they never nagged. They had made Lhasa a town of jolly pedestrians. They walked in the clean air through spindly winter-bare willows. They often stopped to admire the mountains. The mountains around Lhasa in new snow looked to me as though they had been made out of starched and crushed bedsheets, a mountain range of frozen laundry. Farther off the mountains were higher, bluer, and softened by the deeper snow. The snow represents holiness and purity to the Tibetans, whose glissading spirits need this symbol of innocence to prove they are still free: such snowy mountains are proof of God's existence.

You have to see Tibet to understand the Chinese. And anyone apologetic or sentimental about Chinese reform had to reckon with Tibet as a reminder of how harsh, how tenacious and materialistic, how insensitive China could be. They actually believe this is progress.

And yet, even with the policy of going too far, and the

turbulence and damage in Tibet's recent history – the bombings, massacres, executions 'for economic sabotage', oppressive nagging, crucifixions, tortures, desecrations, idiotic slogans, political songs, humiliations, edicts, insults, racism, baggy pants, army uniforms, brass bands, bad food, forced labour, compulsory blood donation, struggle sessions and pink socks – the scars hardly showed. Tibet had a way of looking inviolate. The mountains helped, but the people's attitude mattered most. They had found a way of distancing themselves from the Chinese, and they had done so in the most effective way, by laughing at them.

The most serious development in recent years is the Chinese discovery that Tibet is a tourist attraction. Tourists want monasteries. Tourists want temples and gong-ringing. Tourists adore monks. So the Chinese allowed Tibet to return, at least superficially, to its spiritual slumber. The Chinese doubled all the prices in Tibet. They welcomed the Holiday Inn to run their best hotel, and they promised to rebuild the dynamited Ganden Monastery. There is a trickle of tourists; China has said it would like to have 100,000 a year. In that event, the destruction of Lhasa might be assured.

But it is a hard place to get to – six days overland from Xian, or else a long and frightening flight from Chengdu to Lhasa's small and dangerous airfield – so far from Lhasa that people must go there the night before if they have to catch a morning flight. These difficult journeys are part of the reason that Tibet has remained untouched. And the altitude can make even a strong person feel unwell – your head is two or three miles in the air most of the time. But the main reason Tibet is so undeveloped and un-Chinese – and so thoroughly old-fangled and pleasant – is that it is the one great place in China that the railway has not reached. The Kun Lun Range is a guarantee that the railway will never get to Lhasa. That is probably a good thing. I thought I liked railways until I saw Tibet, and then realized that I liked wilderness much more.

Quite by chance I saw Mr Fu before I left Lhasa. He was anxious to show me that he had overcome his horror of snow and his altitude sickness. He was being an exemplary Lei Feng for a change.

Was there anything I wanted to see?

'Let's go for a drive,' I said.

He slipped on his driving-gloves. We set off alone. Miss Sun was in her room, playing cassettes, wagging her head to 'I am a disco dancer'.

'It is a lovely day,' I said. It was clear and cold.

But I had a destination in mind – a gateway that was said to have been destroyed by Red Guards. I had read a clear description of it but it was not on any of the maps. Mr Fu drove. We went past the carpet factory, and easterly past a ruined monastery; past barracks, past ugly Chinese houses, past barbed wire fences. Dead dogs were flattened against the road – the wheels of Chinese army trucks had reduced the corpses to hairy stains. The red flags that flew were not prayer flags which repeated mantras as the wind made them flap; they were army pennants.

Mr Fu lost his way. In his confusion he became reckless. He drove too fast. There were more recently ruined cloisters with slogans on them. Mr Fu began to gasp in impatience.

'I think we have gone too far,' he said. *Women qu le tai yuan le.*

'You sure have,' I said.

Surprised by hearing English, he gave me a wild look, as if I had made an unpleasant noise. He had already forgotten what he had said. He saw me frowning, and in fear he started to laugh.

This Chinese trip was so long and it had claimed so much of me that it stopped being a trip. It was another part of my life; and ending the travel was not a return but a kind of departure, which I regretted.

When I left Tibet some days later I lifted up my eyes to the mountains and clasped my hands and invented a clumsy prayer that went: Please let me come back.

Index